LIFE IN A JEWISH ORPHANAGE:
One Child's Story

AHUVA GOLDENTHAL

MIRKOV PUBLICATIONS, INC.
Pittsburgh, Pennsylvania

MIRKOV PUBLICATIONS, INC.
P.O. Box 81971
Pittsburgh, Pennsylvania 15217
1-(800)-851-8303
WWW.MIRKOV.COM

Library of Congress Control Number 2001096237

10 9 8 7 6 5 4 3 2 1

ISBN 0-9648508-8-5

Manufactured in the United States of America

Table Of Contents

בס"ד

ק"ק נוא העמפסטעד
ע"ש הרה"ג אהרן יפה זצ"ל

12/7/00

Mrs. Shuva Feldman's book "Life is an Orchestra, One Child's Story" is a very poignant and emotional depiction of the myriad trials and tribulations faced by an unusual child in a series of unfortunate circumstances. The book presents the philosophical message of the ability of one's inner strength and fundamental optimistic beliefs to triumph over trying events.

Readers can readily find the book both fascinating and philosophically and religiously rewarding.

Sincerely,
Rabbi Mordechai Tendler

KEHILLAT NEW HEMPSTEAD
RAV ARON JOFEN z"l
COMMUNITY SYNAGOGUE
720 Union Road • New Hempstead, NY 10977 • (914) 362-2425

Letter from Rabbi Mordecai Tendler

B"H

December 7, 2000

Mrs. Ahuva Goldenthal's book, "Life in a Jewish Orphanage: One Child's Story" is a very poignant and emotional depiction of the myriad trials and tribulations found by an unusual child in a series of unfortunate circumstances. The book presents the philosophical message of the ability of one's inner strength and fundamental or benevolent belief to triumph over trying events. Readers can readily find this book both fulfilling and philosophically and religiously rewarding.

Sincerely,

Rabbi Mordecai Tendler

ב"ה

אני גאה ומוקסמת מאחותי אהובה, היקרה, והחשובה שהיתה לה את התבונה, הכוח, והסבלנות לשבת לילות שלמים ולכתוב את הספר על מנת לתאר את הייסורים שעברו עלינו בילדותינו בבית היתומים.

אני מודה להקב"ה שנתן לה את הכוח להיאבק במחלה קשה וארורה. אני מאמינה שהקב"ה חנן אותה בסגולה ונתן לה את הדעת להבין שהמנהלת, המדריכות, והבנות שהשפילו ודכאו אותה סבלו יותר ממחלות נפשיות מאשר

המחלה ממנה אחותי סבלה; לכן, היא שחקה איתן ועזרה להן במקום לנקום.

אחותי אהובה, תמיד הצלחת בלימודיך, הגשמת את כל שאיפותיך ולא נתת לאף מכשול לעמוד בדרכך. התנדבת לטפל ביתומות ובילדות חולות ששכבו בחדר החולות במוסד ובבתי חולים, בקרת ועזרת לזקנים בבתי חולים ואפילו דאגת לבקרם בבתיהם לאחר שחרורם. למרות שהיית צעירה ממני בשנים, באת לקראתי כשהייתי במצוקה. תמיד עזרת לאמא בעבודות הבית ובבישולים. את דאגת לאחינו הצעיר בשעורי הבית, לקחת אותו לישיבה, לימדת אותו נגינה ושירה ושחקת אתו משחקים כדי להעסיק אותו בזמן שאמא עבדה.

אחותי היקרה, את שטפלת באמנו ז"ל במשך שמונה עשרה וחצי שנים האחרונות של חייה, בתקופה שבה סבלה ממחלות קשות. את טיפלת בה בנאמנות, למרות שהיתה לך משפחה עם ילדים קטנים שנזקקו לטיפול רב ולחינוך. הצלחת להגשים את חלומותיך ולהצליח בלימודים תוך כדי קיום חובותייך הרבים. את כמלאך שנשלח מהשמים לטפל ביתומים ולעשות חסדים עם זקנים ועניים. מה שנותר לי זה, לברך אותך, אחותי היקרה, בהצלחה עם הוצאת ספר זה, הרבה בריאות, אושר ועושר, והרבה נחת. אני מקווה שהקוראים ילמדו מהספר הזה להתמודד עם החיים למרות שהם קשים, בתקווה שהעתיד יביא אור חדש לעולם.

באהבה מאחותך האוהבת
טובה מארק

Letter from Tova Mark

I am very proud of my dear sister Ahuva who was brave enough to spend her sleepless nights in writing our dramatic autobiographies as children in an orphanage. What amazed me was that nothing stood in her way to prevent her from accomplishing her goals. Her grades in school were always outstanding and she was always busy playing and running even with the same girls who harassed her. My righteous sister prevented harm to come to younger children also. She was always there for them. When I fainted, she screamed until I got help and she saved my life too.

She occupied herself by helping others while she was abused. Other children would have lost their minds. Even though, at times, she had a chance to leave her faith, she fought the urge and became stronger and more dignified.

I love my sister very much now, just as I loved her then. She was the only one who helped my mother during her bitter ordeal, she took care of our youngest brother Motty , and whenever our parents criticized her, she took the criticism constructively.

My sister Ahuva has many talents. She is a dreamer, a creator, a good person, and one who has already contributed to humanity through her kindness. I congratulate my sister Ahuva for publishing her books, and I know it will be very helpful to the parents and children who are going through the nightmare we went through. I still don't understand why my sister did not fight back when she was being abused. How could she love those who hurt her most?

How did she survive such an illness after she was told by doctors that she would die? My sister had such deep love for humanity that she even understood why her abusers attacked her .

Even though my sister and I went through such traumatic experiences, it did not compare to the horror that her abusers lived through during the Holocaust. If you want to know where to find an angel, my sister Ahuva is one sent by Hashem (G-d).

Tova Mark

בס"ד

יום ב׳ ג׳ בשבט תשנ״ג

לאמא היקרה והחשובה.

מאמעשי, איך מוז זיך פארענטפערן פאר
דיר אז איך שרייב דיר דעם בריוו אבער
איך האב נישט צו ווארטן ביז ווען און
זיך אויסוויינען מיין הארץ.

היינט האט מיר די מנהלת צופאטשט ווייל
איך האב געהאט שטארקע קאפ שמערצן
און איך האב נישט געקענט אויסגיין פון
בעט. איך האב א תור צו דר׳ סקאן
די אונטערזוך וואך אבער איך וויל נישט גיין
צום דאקטאר מיט די מנהלת.

אמא טייערע, איך ווייס גאנץ גוט אז דיין
לעבן איז פארביטערט אבער די ביסט די
איינציגע וואס וועט מיר פארשטיין. איך
האב נישט כח מער צו ליידן אבער איך
מוז זיך שטארקן פאר דיר און פאר מיין
שוועסטער ווייל אפילו איך וועל שטארבן וועט
איך צולייגן עפעס צרות פאר מיינע לייבע
נשמהס וואס זיינען מיר לובשואבט. איך האב
שוין נישט קיין כח צו וויינען און די שמערצן
וואס איך האב געהאט מיר נעמען לעבן.

העלף מיר מאמעשי וועל איך דיר
קענען העלפן.

דיין טאכטער וואס האט דיר ליב
אהובה

Ahuva’s letter to her mother

B"H

ABOUT THE AUTHOR

Ahuva Goldenthal was born in 1952, in Haifa, Israel, to Samuel Eliyahu and Chava (Eva) Schlag. Both of her parents were Holocaust survivors. She has three siblings (these names and those of other relatives have been changed) - Meyer, Tova, and Motty. When Ahuva was five years old, her parents decided to place her and her older sister Tova in an orphanage, so that they could focus their attention on work and recapturing the lives they lost during World War II. Her parents were still reliving the Holocaust, which would haunt them for the rest of their lives. Because of their emotional and physical instability, they believed they had to put their children in a safe place where they could have all their needs met.

The Schlags were very devoted to their children. They went to visit them at the orphanage and provided them with everything they needed every week. The two girls went home for every holiday, vacations, and for special family events.

Ahuva was a child with many talents. At the age of eight, she excelled in sewing, knitting, crocheting and weaving. She was also involved with many recreational activities and participated in sports and plays. She enjoyed helping other children, but spent even more time taking care of Tova, who suffered from severe asthma. The two sisters were very close to each other and always stayed together.

At the age of ten, Ahuva was severely abused by a new principal at the orphanage. This woman believed that the author resembled her daughter, who had been killed by the Nazis. Ahuva believes that her brain swelled as a result of this abuse, and she suffered temporary blindness. The abuse did not stop, and Ahuva was often admitted to the hospital in critical condition. The administration knew about this abuse, but officials ignored her cry for help.

At the age of fourteen, Ahuva made many attempts to run away from the home, but no other school wanted to take her in. Her parents were afraid that their daughters would be taken away by social service authorities, who threatened the family several times that the girls would be placed in a non-Orthodox kibbutz. The Schlags believed they needed to keep the girls in the orphanage until they could find a better solution for them.

Around this time, Ahuva decided to turn her life around by getting a job working with autistic children. She was highly praised for her outstanding work. She eventually dropped out of high school, and got a job as an assistant kindergarten teacher. During weekends and holy days, she also took care of autistic children who lived in her community. On days when she was off from school, or was not too busy with the children, she worked in the orphanage's infirmary. Ahuva also took music lessons, and when she had enough money, she bought a melodica (wind instrument played like a small keyboard), which she used to entertain the children in the orphanage and her friends.

During the Six Day War, Ahuva volunteered to help the orphanage's housemother prepare meals for the children, as well as for the homeless who stayed in the orphanage during the war. She also provided emotional support for children who needed to be hugged and loved during these frightening times. Ahuva always found enough time to volunteer in hospitals, and at the age of fifteen, she had the honor to attend a surgery that was performed on one of the girls from the orphanage. The doctors and the nurses knew her very well, and she often attended seminars with the nurses. She had the opportunity to attend nursing school, but was afraid to take it up because she knew that she would be punished for studying with non-Orthodox students.

At the age of sixteen and a half, Ahuva left the orphanage and went to her mother's home, with whom she was very close. Her mother helped her get a job in an architect's office, where she was assigned to issue the pay stubs; a few months later, she found a job in a bank's foreign department, which she liked very much. Her father, however, started putting pressure on her and forced her to marry at the age of seventeen. By the time she was eighteen, she was the mother of a beautiful little girl.

Three years after her wedding, Ahuva and her family immigrated to the United States, where she attended nursing school. She worked as a nursing assistant for one year, and then went to the university to learn English and recreational therapy. While going to school, she worked in schools, community centers, hospitals, and nursing homes until she completed all required classes towards her Master's degree.

With her husband's support, the author devoted herself to taking care of her sickly mother and volunteered in nursing homes and in hospitals, where her mother was a patient for many years. She would feed the elderly, sing and tell stories to hospital patients, and make many helpless people laugh. She also helped many orphans and children from broken homes by taking them into her own home, helping to marry them off and providing them with a great deal of emotional support.

Married to her husband Avraham for thirty one years, Ahuva also has three children and three granddaughters.

The author now spends her time writing books and giving lectures in orphanages. By having this book published, her goal is to give children in similar situations the will to overcome difficulties in life. She believes that by helping those in need, one can overcome one's own pain. There are more good people in this world than bad, and one cannot blame the whole world for one's pain despite the actions of a few individuals.

ACKNOWLEDGMENTS

To my dear sister Tova:

I am dedicating this book to my righteous sister. She gave up her childhood to look after me, protected me from harm, and acted like a mother. As difficult as our childhood was and despite the suffering we went through, I felt honored and blessed by Hashem for giving me a sister like you.

When I was beaten up, you caressed me; when I was dirty, you washed me and changed my clothes; when I needed clean clothes, you boiled water and washed my clothes; when I was sick, you healed me; when I cried, you wiped my tears away; when I fractured my arm, you helped me with your little hands; and when I was unable to eat on my own, you fed me. You combed my hair and rid my head of lice when I was infested. You hid me under your desk when I was afraid to go to kindergarten, and sat with me in kindergarten for two months until I got used to it. When I was afraid to sleep at night, you took me into your bed; and when you were beaten up for allowing me into your bed, you hid me underneath. When I needed the love of a mother, you gave it to me. You accompanied me every step I took in my young life. When someone made fun of me, you stuck up for me and you gave me strength. Tova, you held me by my hand when we were taken to the orphanage, and you held my hand when you led me to my *chuppa* (wedding canopy). And when my first child was born, you came running and helped me.

Tova, what amazes me is that forty years later, you are still helping me. I have no words that can describe my thanks to you. I can only ask *Hashem* to help you and your children, and I want him to bless you so that you should see only joy from your children and grandchildren, and that you should never have to depend on others. I love you now just as I loved you then, and I hope that by writing this book, I will be able to teach other children how to love a sibling and help one another when needed.

Additionally, it is never too late to dedicate a few words to some very special people who provided love to orphans and children. I would like to praise our housemother, Hass- Neiny Z"L (meaning Aunt Hass in Hungarian; her real name was Rosie Hass), for being such a good mother to me and to my friends. Without you, many children would not have made it in this world. You are gone, my dear substitute mother, but your daughter Shifra and her children are here and they deserve to know their roots.

Shifra, your mother's role in the orphanage was to take care of all our needs just as a true mother would do. Despite her sick, painful legs, she was never too lazy to run and take care of the children. She loved us, kissed us, and gave us the will to continue to live. We, just like you, are very proud of your mother and I hope that your children will carry on her good qualities.

I must not forget the three wonderful and good-hearted cooks: Laufer-Neiny, Z"L, Glick-Neiny, and Steinmets-Neiny, who made sure we were all nourished. In our spare time they taught us how to cook and bake, and it was a fun experience for us. Because of their lessons, today my family and friends think that I am an outstanding cook. I must never forget Schlezinger-Neiny Z"L, and her daughter Rachel Z"L, the assistant cook. Schlezinger-Neiny's medicine for our emotional problems was food. She was one of the finest, caring people I have ever known. Her maternal love to us was unending. When I got married she and her daughter constantly visited me. Even through her personal problems, mainly, that her daughter was blind and dependent on her, she still had a happy, healthy outlook on life.

I owe special gratitude to Rabbi Shlomo Poppenheim and his wonderful family. *Hashem* always sends us an angel to protect us. Rabbi Poppenheim and his family were our angels. I remember the beautiful *shabbatot* and *yomim tovim* when you came to our home to make the most moving *Kiddush* for us. We felt as though it came directly from your holy *neshama* (soul), and now I can tell you that your *Kiddush* kept me alive from Shabbos to Shabbos; you were my emotional strength. I remember the times when you invited my family and me to your home for various occasions and the way you and your *eishes chayil* (woman of valor, referring to the revered role of the wife in Jewish tradition) practiced *hachnosos orchim* (hospitality); you made us feel so wanted. I also remember when you wiped my tears off my face and you were like a father to me. If it wasn't for you saving all the *Yiddishe neshamas* (Jewish souls) and seeing to it that we all received an Orthodox education, who knows how many Jewish *kinderlach* (children) would be lost to the missionaries? When you and your *rebbetzin* (rabbi's wife) came to my *chasuna* (wedding) you made my *simcha* (joyous occasion). I would also like to thank your *rebbetzin* for all the emotional support she gave me.

FORWARD

As a child of Holocaust survivors, I spent eleven years in a Jerusalem orphanage. Although the institution provided everything for the children who lived there, I was physically and emotionally abused by one of the principals and counselors. Mrs. Cahana, the principal, who was also a Holocaust survivor, believed that I resembled her child who was killed by the Nazis; she wanted me to admit to her that I was indeed her child. I believe this abuse caused my brain to swell, resulting in temporary blindness and the need for continuous medical care.

A variety of children lived in this institution. Many came from fine families and wanted to receive a good Jewish education. Some children were orphans; some came from dysfunctional families; others were saved from the hands of the missionaries or from secular kibbutzim by Rabbi Shlomo Poppenheim. There were also children with physical and emotional disabilities who needed special attention and care. The children in the orphanage were very much involved with the care of other children, and we grew up like one big family. As bad as my situation was, there were many positive things about the orphanage. It provided the children with three daily cooked meals, clean beds to sleep on, a good education, and medical care. We learned valuable skills that would later help us become good housewives. We sang and played, took hikes and walks and went on trips; and we had many other special events to keep our morale high.

The orphanage was built by Rabbi Poppenheim, a fund raiser who provided a father-like image to the children; and Rabbi Naftali Rosenfeld. Both of them were very special individuals. Rabbi Rosenfeld was not involved with the care of the girls. These two men wanted to better the children's lives by making sure they were fed, clothed, and bathed. They provided the children with medical treatment, education, and the chance to develop their own talents and skills. The home, which I believe served thousands of children, would not be in existence, though, without the many sponsors who donated money to build it. This institution was a home away from home for many children from all over the globe. Even though the children came from different countries, spoke many different languages, and brought their own personality, values, and backgrounds to the orphanage, we learned to become one big family, and we remained life-long friends.

I am writing this book for other children and their parents who may be in similar situations. I want people to understand that I am not writing this book to criticize anybody, or even to justify the wrongdoing that happened to me. My goal is to teach young people that regardless of how difficult life is, we can find a way to better ourselves. We don't have to escape into the streets, or to drugs, prostitution, or to people who tell you they love you and then belittle you and hurt you for life. We must learn to love ourselves and not wait for people to love us. The most important message that I want to impress on other children is to preserve your dignity and live by the law of the *Torah* (Bible) from where we get our strength. *Hashem* (G-d) is not the one that makes our lives miserable, it is human beings who think that they have the right to control innocent children and other people. At times, we must cross several small bridges before we can cross the main bridge that leads us from our birth to the time we die. My mother brought me to one small bridge when she took me to the *mosad*, and my husband waited for me on the other side to lead me to my new home.

Committing suicide is also not an option. Remember that death is the end for the dying, but the living must go on. I often became very depressed and I too wanted to end my pain, but instead of killing myself I escaped from my miserable situation by helping other people who needed more help than I did. I hope this book helps others to review their lives, and to think rationally before making rash decisions. Be strong – *Hazak v'amatz libecha.*

MY PARENTS AND SIBLINGS

My family can be described as the most lovable people anyone can imagine. There was always so much love between our parents and among our siblings. How can I convince anybody that my siblings and I never fought and that we were never jealous of each other? When one of us was happy, we were all happy.

If that was the case, what could have gone so wrong that we ended up in an orphanage? I know that people might ask, "How can you love your child when you put that child into an orphanage; is this called love?" The answer is yes, and it is true love. My parents were very outgoing people who loved life. But they had to deal with difficulties in a new country after living for six years in concentration camps, and they faced the constant threat by social service authorities that their children would be taken away from them and possibly end up in the hands of missionaries. Far from neglecting us, my mother sacrificed herself to save her children.

The Torah teaches us that when a person is poor he is like a dead person. As much as Israel was a promised land with milk and honey, the milk and honey does not automatically come with the land. My parents had to work two and three shifts in order to buy some milk for their hungry children. My parents became depressed, and suffered from diseases that they brought with them from Poland to the Holy Land. They also had to learn a new language, compete for jobs, and try to give their children the best education. My parents were striving to raise G-d-fearing children in Israel, and with G-d's help they were successful.

There was a lot of tension between my parents because of

their emotional instability, they had flashbacks from the war that often made them cry, scream and shiver, and it made them so physically ill that they were no longer able to cope with their emotions. Eventually, they divorced.

Their separation, though, was done out of love. They wanted their children to be placed in homes where they could visit them whenever they desired and without having to fight in court for custody. It gave them time to learn to cope with their new problems, and they needed to rebuild their lives, work and earn enough money to support their children. My parents paid our tuition and provided us with medical insurance, clothing and any supplies we needed; other children at the orphanage got everything for free. My mother in particular was an angel who relived the war until she died. She was known as a *ba'alat chesed* (charitable person) and helped many women after childbirth, never asking a penny for her services. She worked hard for many years until her body gave out and she became crippled for the remainder of her life.

My father had a heart of gold, but his emotions fluctuated because of the memories he had from a war that haunted him until the day he died. My father was loved by all of his friends, relatives, and neighbors for his sense of humor, and he made people laugh.

MEMORIES FROM SAFARIA

It is the first day of the month of Shevat 1960. The night is too long, and I am afraid to sleep, as I have many nightmares. Instead, I am standing near a window and thinking about the three years that I have been in the *mosad* (orphanage). I am eight years old, and my third-grade teacher is the best I have ever known. I have many friends and a sister who always takes good care of me. I am an excellent student and I score one hundred percent on all of my tests. But as I stare at the clouds I recall the time I said goodbye to my old home in Safaria, a farm that is about a ten minute ride from Tel Aviv. I loved it so much. I always dream that I am there, but when I wake up and I realize where I am, it makes me sad.

It was one day after Rosh Hashana, *Tzom Gedalia* (fast of Gedalia) 1956, when Tova, my brother Motty and I were playing on our one dunam of land on the beautiful farm. A short, bearded man dressed in a long black coat and black hat approached and asked to speak to our mother. Tova went inside the house to call her. Our mother, whom we called Ima, and the man sat outside under the fig tree talking.

Suddenly fear radiated through my little body. I held on to Tova, asking her not to talk to this stranger. I had a feeling that he was the man who was helping Ima find a home for us. Ima spoke to us about hert plan for some time. Sh e wanted us to be prepared emotionally so that, when the day would come, we would not be shocked. Tova was only seven years old and I was five and already we felt the threat of being taken away from home. Anxiety started building up in our little hearts, and we looked into each other's eyes, hoping that it was only our imagination.

Tova, the eldest of the three (our oldest brother Meyer was

in yeshiva), pulled Motty and me toward Ima because she wanted to hear what they were talking about. The man asked us not to be afraid and gave us a friendly smile to reassure us that he was not a dangerous person. He took out four little plastic dolls and gave them to us. Two dolls were black and two were pink. Tova reached out her hand and took the dolls from him because she was afraid that Ima would be angry if she did otherwise.

I was about to burst into tears, but instead I pulled Tova and Motty away and we took a long walk to the train station. There were many children playing there, but Tova and I were not in the mood to join in, so we just watched the others have fun. It was a gorgeous, spring-like day. We looked into the woods and at the many flowers that grew all over the farm. The wind moved the wheat and the trees and the breeze went through my hair, which made me feel wonderful.

As we walked near the shul where we used to go every Sabbath and holiday with Ima, we felt compelled to stop there and pray that nobody would take us away, but it was locked. The shoemaker's wife Huma stopped us when we passed her house, but we said nothing about our visitor. We passed by the post office where Motty and I used to visit daily, and on the way home we took a walk in the orchard behind our house. There were many farmers picking oranges and tangerines. When one of the farmers saw us watching them he gave one orange to Tova, one to me, and one to Motty. We walked in the forest and ate those sweet, delicious fruits. When we got home, the man was gone. Tova and I decided not to ask any questions because Ima was in tears and we did not want to cause her more pain. Tova was the kind of child who never asked questions – she did everything she was asked to do without an argument.

An aroma wafted from the kitchen from the meal Ima had prepared, but I had no appetite. Frightened by the thought that we might be taken away, we held on to each other for support, believing this terrible day was approaching. Our father, Aba, came home from work late at night and when he saw how we were sitting, he asked us to lie down. We told him that we were waiting for him to come home. He had no idea about my mother's plan. If he had known that we were moving into an orphanage, he would have lost his mind. He did not find out, I believe, until after we had already moved in.

I remember the times when Ima had to run away and hide us because social services wanted to place us in a home where we would never see our families again nor learn about our Jewish heritage. She took us to beaches in Tel Aviv and Bat Yam, where she fed and bathed us and then spread out a blanket under a tree. We would sleep there. When we were frightened, she would hold us in her arms and sing to us until we fell asleep. Finally, my father's uncle advised her to place us in a home where we would be safe and nobody would touch us. Out of her good heart, Ima started to look for a home until this fine, short man, a friend of my father's uncle Moshe Yosel, volunteered to help her.

Two weeks before Hanukkah 1957, the man returned to tell Ima that he found a home for us in Jerusalem. Fear suddenly surged through us, but we did not dare say a word. Tova and I held hands, crying. Ima looked at us and she too burst into tears.
Tova and I took a walk. We reminded ourselves of the many good times we had in Safaria. Our father had joined the Israel Defense Forces near our home, and we used to stand near the window watching the soldiers singing and marching with a gun on their shoulders. Many times they used to crawl on the ground like snakes and hide under the trees, logs, in the bushes, or in the forest that was behind our home.

One time I wanted to find out what a good soldier my father was, so I hid under my bed and waited for him to find me. My parents thought that I was lost and called my name, but I did not answer. My plan was for Aba to find me. It would not have been any fun if I had told him where I was. I was proud of myself because nobody knew where to find me. They ran to the forest and the farm, but they still did not find me. All of the farmers came to our home, but nobody thought about looking under my bed. I was only four years old, but when I saw that my parents were crying and were so upset, I climbed out from under the bed. My father asked me to stay home and went to call my mother to tell her where I was. They were so happy to see me, and I just told my parents that Aba was supposed to find me because he was a soldier and knew how to find people who were hiding.

We also recalled playing with Aba's feet, he was so ticklish that we couldn't touch him. We used to chase him and he would run away; I would pull his nose and ears and he would crack up. He pretended that he was going to eat my nose! We remembered when Ima used to take us to the matza bakery where she worked and let us bake our own little matzos. Ima was always making us foods like fresh, homemade bread, cheese, and delicious soups. She used to let us help her feed the geese every morning. And when my brother Motty was born, Ima prepared a nice party in our house after the *bris* (circumcision); she even did all the cooking.

Ima was a woman full of life. Ima used to feed us either outside in the yard under a tree, or high up on the table or the kitchen counter. As she fed us she sang Yiddish songs that she learned at home and in the Warsaw Ghetto, and then she would tell us about her parents, siblings, and about the war. As frightening as her stories were, we always listened to them because we knew that Ima had to tell someone about her experiences and what our people lived through. She always found comfort in her children and we loved her very much.

I cried when I thought about leaving our beloved neighbors. Our home sat on one dunam of land filled with the best fruits and vegetables. There was a feeling of holiness in this farm. There were always parties, songs and laughter. The Lubavitch hasidim used to dance and sing in the street every Saturday night. One could hear their songs from a distance, which made the evening very pleasant.

And our Yemenite neighbors used to make their weddings out on the streets. They would have their dinner at home, and afterwards would come out on the street and gather near the bride's or groom's family's house, where we would dance all night. The Yemenite women would drum on big pickle cans, and then put their fingers to their mouths and scream "ulululululu." They would all dress in their beautiful, native clothes.

Our Yemenite neighbors were very kind to us and it was a blessing to have them so close by. Rumia, our next door neighbor, would often invite us into her home and have us sit on the floor next to the rest of her family and guests. She gave us fresh peanuts, sunflower seeds, chickpeas, and popcorn. The men sat on the floor of their porch smoking a *nargila* (huka pipe) and drinking fresh coffee from grounds that Rumia had freshly crushed. I used to enjoy playing with their goats and donkey.

I also remember when Meyer, Tova and I built a carriage for our baby brother Motty from a box of oranges that we picked up in the orchard. We put the box on top of wheels and tightened a rope to the box so that we could pull the carriage. I used to take him to the post office in this beautiful buggy to show him how the mailmen stamped the envelopes. We also went on horse and donkey rides, visited our neighbors to help them milk their cows and goats, and watched the Bedouins herd their cattle and sheep. We constantly felt G-d's spirit while living on the farm with his beautiful creatures. There was so much to do there. Ima let us take the chickens or geese to the slaughterhouse and when we came home, she would hang them up on a tree. Together we would pluck the feathers, which she used to make pillows and blankets. Nothing went to waste. She would stuff and sew the necks from the chickens or the geese and put it into a roast or a *cholent* (Sabbath stew). This was absolutely delicious. Ima was very famous in our community for making the best *p'tzah* (gale). Our neighbors and friends would often come to our home after shul to eat some of it. We also used to visit the delicatessen owned by a man named Mr. Tabak. My father used to spend a lot of time socializing with him and other friends. At times we would visit him there, and Mr. Tabak would give us a delicious ice cream stick.

My memories from Safaria are endless. Every morning before sunrise while the farmers were still asleep, the roosters called out "kukuriku," the cows went "mee," the goats "eeee," the sheep "baba," and even the horses sounded musical. The dogs were barking; the black snakes slithering up and down the trees and walls were hissing. Otherwise, there was complete silence on the farm. Every day at about five A.M., our next door neighbor Zecharia would call another neighbor to go to work. From complete silence we could hear him call "Seadia, *kum la'avoda*" (Seadia, get up to work). He was our alarm clock. My father used to get up early to go to the market to buy produce for his store, and my mother went to the chicken coop to feed the geese. A man named Mr. Salminowitch would then come to buy the geese and their eggs. Interestingly, I met his daughter in the same orphanage where I ended up and we remained lifelong friends.

One day, my brother Meyer, accompanied by our dog, went out to play with some friends. Somebody poisoned our dog and he died, and later, we were not able to find Meyer. My mother was crying and we were all upset. We looked everywhere for him in vain. Finally, one boy, Peretz, felt sorry for us and told my mother that the others had buried him in a ditch. They had covered him with a metal sheet. I remember my mother's tears and her pain when she was told that Meyer was buried; she did not know whether he was still alive. Peretz led us to the ditch and helped Ima pull off the cover; thank G-d Meyer was alive and unharmed, only having some minor bruises.

While we loved living on the farm, there were still difficulties. My parents had to work hard to meet their financial needs, and they were still suffering physically and emotionally from the six years they spent in concentration camps. Tova had a severe case of asthma, which only seemed to get worse as she grew older. My parents missed a lot of work because they were so busy taking her to the hospital. Every Saturday she would have a major attack, and our family was falling apart from the stress.

I was three years old on the eve of Rosh Hashana 1955. Only a few hours after my sister came home from the hospital, I took a little red button and pushed it into my nose. When I tried to take it out, I pushed it in deeper until I could not breathe. My mother ran to my aunt Blime to ask her to watch the three other children; again, my father borrowed a horse and rushed me to Sarafent Hospital. There, my mother stayed with me for the holiday while the button had to be removed surgically.

My parents received a lot of help from my father's uncle Moshe Yosel and his wife, who never had children of their own. This uncle, the eldest of the family, served as its unofficial judge. All of my father's cousins used to gather in our uncle's house every Saturday night and tell him their problems. He used to make peace in the family and all the final decisions. The men and the women spoke to Moshe Yosel while Aunt Blime would occupy the children. She gave us home-baked cakes and told us many stories. We all loved her very much. Uncle Moshe Yosel and Aunt Blime were just like our grandparents. We all respected them, and they were special people that none of us would ever forget.

One day, my mother came home from the matza bakery exhausted, her hands bleeding from hard labor. She was about to drop into bed and get a good night's sleep until we told her that we could not find our two year old baby brother. She immediately washed her bleeding hands and ran to look for Motty. We ran to our neighbors and asked them to help us find him. All of the farmers gathered in a span of a few minutes and mapped out a plan to find this little boy. People went into the orchard, to the woods, near the shul, and to the train station.

One man, who became tired from searching, decided to rest

under a tree near the station. Suddenly, he heard the siren of the train as it approached. Seeing the bright lights and hearing a noise from the tree, the man looked up and found my brother asleep on a branch like a bird. Motty was happy to see our mother and started to cry, telling her that he was waiting for her to come home.

This was not the last time he went to sleep like that. He made the trees his home. He would sit in the forest or on any tree for hours. Unfortunately, we never knew which forest he was communing in nor on which tree he would sit. Hunger was never a problem, since he used to eat the trees' fruits. This is how Motty lived until he was thirteen or fourteen years old. He used to meditate while sitting in the tree, and would often invite a friend to stay with him there, where they would play games, hide and seek, or swing on the twigs like little monkeys.

Tova also liked the trees, but preferred to climb the ones we had in our garden. Whenever she was hungry, she would climb up a tree and eat the fresh fruits. The fruits that my father had in his store or that my mother had in the house were not good enough for her. She needed to pluck them from their branches. She never ate alone and would always share the fruits with her sister and brothers. Tova looked like a monkey because she used to swing on and off the trees, holding on to the branches.

One time Tova wanted to eat a banana, but the ones we had in our garden were not ripe. So, she climbed into my father's store from the window to take four bananas, one for her, and the other three for her siblings. While we had a lot of fun, it was not easy for my mother having to work with so many interruptions. We were very good children, but our parents had a hard time looking for their little birds and monkeys.

As sick as Ima was from the war, she was the best housekeeper in the world. She took care of four children, worked outside the home, fed the geese, took care of our garden, and our house was always sparkling clean. She cooked, baked, washed the laundry by hand and hung the clothes outside to dry. She even found time to mend our clothes. My father did not help her much in the house, but she still got so much done. She was the kind of woman who made gold out of garbage. Regardless of the difficult life she had and how hard she worked, she was always dressed nicely. She did not have a variety of clothes, but knew how to mix and match the two or three outfits she had. She washed her clothes at night and in the morning she had clean ones to wear. She put on lipstick and powder and wore perfume, and she looked and smelled like a million dollars. She never wanted people to know how poor or how sick she was.

If everything looked so wonderful, then why did we have to go to an orphanage? It was the post-war syndrome that haunted my parents, and they always feared that something might happen to their family. At this time, many kidnappings of children were taking place in Israel by groups such as missionaries. By placing us in a home, she knew that we would be safe and free from harm. Also, an Orthodox education was very important to her and she wanted to raise her children according to the Torah.

In May 1956 the Sinai War broke out. My parents feared that this war might be similar to the one they lived through in Europe. The army drafted my father, and my mother had to work. In the beginning, she took us along because she wanted to make sure that we had enough food and she could watch us. Whenever we thanked her for feeding us or giving us a piece of matza she would hug and kiss us with tears in her eyes. Her children meant everything to her. We knew about Ima's plan to send us to a home; yet, we were not mad at her because she loved us so much and would only do something like that out of love. Ima promised us that she would never forsake us and she kept that promise.

Two weeks before Chanukah 1957, Ima was washing laundry outside, and we were helping her hang up the wet clothes. As I bent down to take more laundry from the basket, I noticed the short man again. I pulled Motale close to me, and the man told Ima that we were accepted to the *mosad* (orphanage). We would leave that same evening. He told us that we were going to a school in Jerusalem where we would get the best care, education, and medicine, and he promised us that our parents would be able to visit us whenever they wanted to and without restrictions.

Ima smiled with her mouth but cried with her eyes and heart. She was happy that we had a place to go to, but sad that she had to send her two daughters away. (Meyer was eleven years old and was already settled into a boarding yeshiva, while Motale was still too young to be sent to school). Ima then took us to a lady named Devorah, who owned a little clothing store in her home. She bought white ribbons for our hair, white blouses, navy blue pleated skirts, and knee-high white stockings with pompoms on the sides. She then took us to the shoemaker and bought black and white glossy shoes for Tova and me.

On the way home, Ima stopped by the photographer and ordered him to come to our home to take some pictures. Ima boiled water and gave each of us a bath. She then gave us delicious food that she had cooked earlier and asked us to rest until the photographer came. In the meantime, she packed our stuff and prepared all the papers that she needed to take to the orphanage, such as medical insurance, medical records, social security numbers, and our birth certificates. Neither Tova nor I were able to rest, so Ima dressed us in our new clothes, and we went outside to take in the fresh air and see our garden one last time.The photographer arrived at about 4:30 P.M., pulled over a little table that stood in our garden, put a cover on top of it, and then put us on top of the table so that he could take pictures. Ima cried the entire time.

Ima was not going to give us up; she just wanted to make sure that we would be safe and have everything we needed. It was hard for us to understand why she had to send us away, but with time we learned that what she did was for *Kiddush Hashem* (G-d's sake) as well as for our own. She had a tremendous amount of faith in G-d, and her love for her children was written all in her eyes. If she was able to withstand this horrible test and send her children away from her, then she was surely a *tzadeikes* (saint).

At about 5:15P.M., a jeep pulled into our driveway, and the driver told Ima that he came to take us to the bus stop. Ima got dressed quickly, took Motale to our Aunt Blime, and then grabbed our bags. Off we went on the bus to Jerusalem. I started to cry hysterically and held on tightly to Tova. I could see that Tova was crying on the inside, but she was the older sister and had to be strong for me.

Before we reached the main road, we saw our father walking home from work. Tova and I started to scream, "Aba!" He looked into the jeep, and when he saw us he started to run and cry, "Children, where are you going?" We cried, "Aba, come!" He reached out his hands to us and we reached ours to him. As he was running after us, his body seemed smaller and smaller until we could not see him anymore. It looked to me as if he had melted away. Ima was choking on her tears, and she was speechless. She took us into her arms and hugged us. She told us that she was not giving us away and promised to visit us every single week and whenever we needed her. We knew that Aba and Ima loved and cared about us; this is something that is very important for children to know. Ima explained to us that she had to send us away because they had to take care of themselves; when things got better, she would take us home.

OUR NEW LIFE BEGINS

The bus to Jerusalem arrived at 5:30 P.M. On the way there we did not talk much. Ima took us into her arms and she and Tova fell asleep. I was thinking about my father, and I wanted to know why he did not know that we were leaving. I wanted to know if he knew where to find us and if we were going to see him and our brothers again.

We arrived in Jerusalem at 7:30 P.M; from there Ima took a cab to the orphanage. In front of an old building was a big sign that said, "*Bayit Lepletot v'Yetomim*" (a home for refugees, immigrants and orphans). Ima opened the metal gate, and we walked into the front yard and then up a few steps that led to a big terrace. The building looked deserted from the outside, it was night and the weather was freezing. The ground and the trees were covered with a thin layer of snow, the first time we had ever seen any.

Petrified by this scenario, I threw myself down on the floor kicking and crying, not wanting Ima to leave us there. I pulled Tova to me, asking her to take me away from there. Tova sat on the floor, kissed and hugged me, and promised to take good care of me. The door to the dining room opened, and a girl named Hana Mikler came out. She gave me napkins that she had collected as a hobby and promised to be my best friend.

I got up from the floor and went in with Hana. Ima and Tova followed us into the dining room, where we were welcomed by Mrs. Hass, the housemother. The dining room was empty and dark. There were only a few older girls sitting in one corner talking. Hass-Neiny (Aunt Hass in Hungarian) took us upstairs and showed us our room. There were four children sleeping in one bed, but I was glad that I did not have to sleep alone in such a strange place.

Ima put our bags down and sat next to us for a little while. She reminded us that she was not giving us away and promised never to forsake us. She also reassured us that she loved us now and would always love us.

Ima got up and was ready to leave because she had to catch the last bus from Jerusalem to Tel Aviv, and from there she would catch the last bus to Safaria. Tova hugged me and we both cried. Ima hugged and kissed us, and her tears were dripping all over us. Ima walked out, stopped, and looked back several times. Seven-year-old Tova and I, only five years old, stood near the window crying and looking after Ima, hoping that she would change her mind and take us back home. Ima heard our crying and her heart was broken, but she called out to us to go to sleep. She promised to come see us. She then burst into tears and walked away. We were too young to understand why she did this when she loved us so much, but she knew that she did it for our sake.

The first night in the orphanage was very frightening. The trees were shaking, the wind was blowing, and the shade from the trees appeared inside our room. I got out of bed and saw that the sky had a reddish tint; the ground, trees, and the roofs were covered with snow; and homeless people were gathered under the roof. I was scared, so I woke up Hana and she told me who these people were. Hana gave me a smile and introduced me to them. The skinny man with the hat was Uri Kadury; the lady with the layers of clothing was Sarah latke Schmates (Sarah in the rags); the unshaven man with the hat was Tzemach; the tall fat man was Lopka; the lady that scratched her head was Susanah Kinim (Susanah with the lice); the fat lady was Rosa'le; and sitting next to her was her husband Feval'le. This couple had a home but they preferred to live on the streets with their friends. There was even a lady hiding under a table named Hana Banana. Now that I knew who these people were, I was no longer afraid of them and I went back to bed. There was no way that I was going to sleep, though, because there was not much room in a bed with four children; besides, the bed was always wet.

It was only two weeks after coming to the orphanage that

Tova and I found lice in our hair, and sores from bed bugs covered our bodies. Lice infested every single child, causing an outbreak whenever a new child came in. They were in our hair, eyebrows and on our foreheads, and it was impossible to sleep because we were itching and bleeding from scratching our skin. The lice in our heads, the sores on our bodies, and the smell of urine changed our identity; we now had to live just like all the other orphans.

Contagious diseases were another feature of life in the orphanage. As soon as one child got the mumps we all had swollen faces; and when we had chicken pox, measles, or roseola, we looked like dominos. When we had strep throat, upper respiratory infections, or other infectious diseases, we were all burning from fever, a very unpleasant time to share a bed with other children.

In order to be an official *mosad* resident, I had a picture taken by a photographer to put into my file, and I was examined by Dr. Tzitron, the house doctor. Once everything checked out, and I was found to be in good health, I was sent to school with the other children. As much as I wanted to go to school, I did not want to be separated from Tova for even one minute. I managed to hide in my sister's class for two months under her bench, until one day I sneezed and the children started to laugh. Tova's teacher called Greita, the kindergarten principal and she came to the class to take me back to my class in another building. I fought her and screamed, so she grabbed me by my feet and dragged me down a whole flight of steps. I managed to run away but she finally caught me. I sat in my kindergarten class in one corner and cried the whole time, so my teacher called my sister and she sat with me in class for eight weeks until I got used to my new surroundings.

Benot Yerushalayim was an outstanding school, but it had its faults. The school was split into many buildings; each building had its own environment and a story behind it. I was unhappy that Tova was in a different building; she was too far away from me and I was unable to see her during recess. Many teachers in school and especially the administration spoke German, and the rest spoke Yiddish. (In the *mosad*, the staff spoke German and Hungarian, and the counselors and children spoke Yiddish, Hebrew, and many other languages). Many girls in school were dressed in dark long dresses, braided hair, and black heavy stockings, which is the uniform of Hasidic girls in Jerusalem as a reminder of the destruction of the holy Temple. Others had shorter hair and wore lighter colored dresses and brown heavy stockings. Yet, there was love and harmony among all the children, and I cannot remember ever fighting with anybody from school. The only problems I had with other children were with those from the *mosad*.

My kindergarten classroom was large, with little tables on the sides of the room and four chairs next to each table. The walls were decorated with beautiful paintings that the children had made, and there was a Sabbath corner, a play kitchen with real miniature dishes, and shelves filled with toys. There was also a big yard where we used to play with our friends and teachers.

Praying was the first thing we did when we got to class, followed by the reading of *Tehillim* (Psalms) for the sick. If the children brought notes with names of the sick, we would first pray for these people; otherwise, we would pray for all the sick and poor people in the world. The school did not teach too many secular subjects, but our extensive religious studies helped us cope with our daily lives. We learned the commandments as well as principles of respect, modesty and honoring our parents and older siblings or friends. We learned to do good deeds for the elderly, the sick, and those who were pregnant by helping them with their groceries or their children and by standing up on the bus or in a clinic for those unable to. We also learned to walk in public in a quiet and modest manner.

I believe that there is no educational system today that provides the benefits that our school did for the students. We were not worried about our self-esteem, because we were happy with the way we looked and whatever we had. Whenever an older girl, another teacher, a parent, or any visitor came into our class, we would stand up and wait for our teacher to give us permission to sit down. During class hours we had to sit straight up with our hands behind our backs and not play during class. Nobody was permitted to talk when the teacher was talking unless we were asked to.

Recess time was always fun. The teachers would play with us and they came up with a song for each game. Every day, another teacher was assigned to serve tea for the girls during recess. It did not take more than two minutes for the little girls to line up for a delicious cup. It was not the cup of tea that made it so special, it was the way the teachers would call and speak to us.

The lunches were also exceptionally delicious. I can still taste the fish that became part of my weekly menu, the couscous we had as a side dish, the soups, and other dishes they prepared. Every spoonful of food was given to us with love and with pleasure. Before our meals, we had to line up, wash our hands, and stay silent until our teacher made the blessings. The room was very quiet and the only thing we could hear was the sound of the children chewing their food. I remember how the cook, a short, middle-aged woman dressed in black, would look into our mouths and call us little lambs. Once in a while she would gently wipe off our mouths and ask us if we liked the food. After reciting the *benching* (grace after meals), each child cleaned off her plate and the garbage from the floor, and when the room was nice and clean, the teacher would turn off the light and ask us to put our heads down on the table and rest.

My teachers were my best friends, and I trusted them because they were kind and spoke gently to me. They listened to me and always had a smile on their faces. They would find a song to match my personality, with each song addressing something special about me. I always managed to find peace and love in school. I loved to learn, and I liked my teachers and all of my classmates. They were warm and good-hearted children. Going to school also gave me a few hours a day away from the *mosad*.

My friends were very talented and we were always singing, dancing, and putting on festivals, plays, comedy shows, and the like. I was shy and would often blush when my teacher talked to me or asked me to perform in a show. I would hide my face and my teacher or my friends would pretend they were looking for it. During holiday seasons, our teachers would invite mothers, aunts, and grandmothers to come to our plays, but my mother worked very hard and had difficulty coming to see them. If she could not come to the play itself, she would arrive later in the evening, ask me to tell her all about it and sing along with me the songs from the play.

To me, it was ironic that the girls in school never bullied the girls from the *mosad*. They were kind to us and always invited us to play with them. If we were sick they would visit us and even bring a little gift to cheer us up, and they would often invite us to their homes on a Sabbath or holiday and give us some nosh.

It was very hard for me to adjust to a strange, new place because my heart was, understandably, with my family and my own home. I would compare the food I ate in the *mosad* to that cooked by my mother. The building itself was too big for me, and I missed the little house where my parents and my siblings lived. I compared the playgrounds in the orphanage to the dunam of land we had and the vegetables and fruits that grew on it. I compared the animals who lived on the farm with us to the human animals who possessed so much evil and were emotionally disturbed. Whenever I cried in the orphanage, I only had my sister to wipe my tears; at home I had my parents, siblings, wonderful neighbors, and loving animals to comfort me. During the first few years, we lived with lice in our hair and bed bugs, and had to get used to dealing with many emotionally disturbed people and children. Everybody came from different backgrounds and cultures. I had to change my appearance and dress to match the new environment I lived in - unlike at home, where my mother dressed us with class and style.

There were many challenges I had to deal with in the *mosad,* but I learned to take care of myself by becoming independent early in life and overcoming many obstacles that were in my way. I learned to go to the doctor by myself when I did not feel well and I took my medication without supervision. I also learned to keep silent and suffer quietly instead of turning the world upside down. The first five years in the *mosad*, I liked everybody and I felt loved in return. Despite my attachment to my sister, who was the only one I trusted, I had friends. The home offered us a good education, and we had plenty of time to play and enjoy ourselves. I had many friends both in the *mosad* and in school, and I was never bored. I learned to sew, knit, crochet, weave, and acquire many other skills. We danced and sang, and I participated in every activity I wanted to. The people in the community were very involved with our well being and would often invite us to their homes to play with their children. We were always respected in school and on the street, and people treated us nicely because they felt sorry for us for living in an orphanage. The food in the *mosad* was always fresh and delicious, and we ate with the tables set on time and with counselors close by. We always had help with our homework; those who did not do well in school had tutors. We met in groups in the *moadon* (club) to do our homework and the students always helped one another, with assistance from the counselors as well.

The little girls were learning the alphabet in groups, and I loved listening to them. After they finished, I would read stories and sing to a few of them, and I especially liked when they used to play with my braids. Their tiny little hands would give me the chills when they undid my braids and argued over who would brush and put pins into my hair. Whenever I felt depressed I would go to the little ones and hold and kiss them and talk to them. They understood me and gave me so much love. I felt great when they hugged me and put their little heads on my shoulder. Each one of them was more gorgeous than the other; they came in all colors, shapes, and variations of beauty; I never found a child who did not look beautiful. I used to love to feed them. I was so glad to hold them and give them the love they needed.

The *mosad* may not have been my home, but it was a home away from home. We had up to two hundred and fifty children living there from the ages of two until the time they were married. With thousands of children waiting for a home, I was very lucky to live in the orphanage. These other children wandered the streets hungry and filthy; others had mentally disturbed parents or relatives and were taken in temporarily by good samaritans until a permanent home was made available.

Things were not perfect in our first few years living in such an old building; yet, the place was cleaned daily and we were taken care of. The building was heated in the winter, and in the summer we kept the windows open for fresh air. In the early sixties when the new building was completed, the older girls moved into it, and *Bayit Lepletot* became one of the nicest facilities in the country. Most children were orphans or children from dysfunctional families, but we had many immigrants who came from all over the world. We also had children who came from the best families who wanted to get a good education, or they were bored at home and wanted to be with other children. I came from a good, loving home, but my parents were Holocaust survivors traumatized by their memories, and they were not well enough to take care of us. The main reason I was here was for the fine education my parents wanted me to have. We were able to leave the orphanage to shop and go home to our families, and we were free to do whatever we wanted as long as our counselors approved and it did not harm ourselves or other children.

Each child had a sponsor who used to come visit her and give money to the home. We called them "*menschen.*" Some sponsors would bring nice things for their child; others would just give money to the orphanage. One day, I stood near the dining room window daydreaming and adoring the snow that had covered the grounds.

Suddenly, I felt a light tap on my shoulder. I turned around and saw Rabbi Poppenheim standing next to me with a big smile on his face, and he told me that I was going to have visitors from South Africa. He asked me to put on festive clothes and come down to the office. I ran down to the kitchen where Tova worked, and told her that my "*menschen*" were coming. She told Hass-Neiny that she had to prepare me for my meeting, and Hass-Neiny gave her permission to leave. Tova had me take a shower, and gave me a clean towel, shampoo, and soap. She laid out a dress that she had made for me along with my Sabbath shoes, hair ribbons, a brush, and a toothbrush, and helped me get ready. She combed my hair, and when I was dressed and ready, she went back to the kitchen to finish her work. I sat next to the office where I was told to wait for my adoptive parents. I had to wait forty five minutes until they came, but I did not mind. I was glad that there were people in this world who cared about me. It was nice of them to come from Africa to visit me, and it was worth the wait.

My visitors finally arrived. The couple went into the office, and half an hour later came out together with Rabbi Poppenheim. The man was of medium stature. Somewhat balding, he had some gray hair on the sides, and his wife appeared to be a little taller and on the obese side. But they both looked lovely and very nice. The man stretched his hand out to me, and I looked at the rabbi for his approval because it was improper for a religious girl to shake hands with a man. He gave me a smile and nodded his approval. The lady hugged me tightly, pulling me gently toward her chest and bursting into tears. She called out, "G-d, you are so beautiful." She gave me a kiss, and wanted me to kiss her too. I looked at the rabbi and again he nodded his head, so I gave her a juicy kiss, fell on her shoulder, hugged her and started to cry.

The man held my right hand and the lady my left, and together we left the building. Outside, a black taxi took us to Jerusalem's Jaffa Street. First, we stopped in an ice cream parlor. I was too shy to eat the ice cream and was afraid that my mouth and my hands would get dirty, but the lady took out a new handkerchief and wiped my mouth. The man looked at me and told me that he would like to take me to his home in Africa. They were able to understand my Yiddish, but I had great difficulty understanding their broken Yiddish, let alone English. We went window shopping and in the evening, they took me to a restaurant on Geulah Street. While we were eating our dinner we tried to communicate but it was hard for me. I wanted to ask them to take me home with them, but they did not understand what I was telling them. After dinner, they took me back to the *mosad.* Before they left, the man gave me a pack of Kit Kat chocolates and the lady gave me a six-pack of handkerchiefs and a white and blue blouse they had bought for me. They both kissed me, and promised to return very soon.

I went up to Tova's room and as soon as I showed her my beautiful presents, I had a visitor from the office. Mr. Spitzer, the secretary, asked me to give him my presents and told me that they belonged to the orphanage. I felt as if he stuck a knife into my heart and I started to cry. I gave them to him but in an angry voice I reminded him about all the new clothes that my Ima had bought for Tova and me that was taken from us by Korn-Neily, the *Mahsanit* (the lady in charge of the clothing room). She had also told us that all our clothes belonged to the *mosad.* Tova reminded him about the two flutes that Ima had bought for us and our counselors had asked Ima for them and said they would give them to us whenever we wanted them, but the counselors took them and never gave them back to us. We also reminded him about the money our Aba sent us every month for pocket money. Mr. Spitzer would give us the open envelopes but the money would be gone. My Aba finally complained and we were then able to get the money that he sent us. Tova and I were crying and thinking: "Everything belongs to the *mosad*, what belongs to us?" I wished these sponsors would have given me their name and address, and then I would have reported this behavior to them so that they never sponsored anything again. I was not very concerned, though, because they promised that they would come every year to visit and write letters.

Very often, the secretary would call me into her office and ask me to sign a thank you letter for my "*menschen*," but I never knew why. Not only did I never receive a letter from them, but I never saw them again. One day I told the secretary that I would no longer sign any letters until I received one from them, and she did not answer me. I was told many times to dress up and get ready for them when they came to visit, but I would wait for hours and never see them. I had the feeling that they were assigned to other children and that they might have thought that I was the child because we all looked alike. Another time when I was asked to write a thank you letter, I shouted at the secretary to sign it herself, and called her a thief.

The truth is that I did not need adoptive parents, because I had my own, and I was not an orphan, thank G-d. My sister was very good to me, and my two brothers were also very special and we were very close to one another. Every child in the *mosad* had a sponsor and most children kept their presents, but mine were taken away from me. I did not want to feel like an orphan nor a beggar, but I was still a child and wanted to keep something that was given to me.

When I look back, I realize that as bad as the *mosad* was, we had many good things too. I was taught to be a good housewife, and learned everything a woman needs to know. I developed my own personality, and learned to take care of myself and the younger children. I learned right from wrong and that I must be responsible for my own life. Many children who grew up in the *mosad* became wonderful role models for society.

The children who helped in the kitchen were always rewarded with a sour pickle, cake, or other treats. We were never hungry, and we could have as many fruits of the season that we wanted. I used to take the fruit that I got for breakfast and supper and sell them to my classmates; from the money I made, I would buy a drink or an ice pop during the hot summer days. I did not like to take any assigned jobs, but I always cleaned my room and helped my sister with hers. I helped Hass-Neiny in the kitchen, and took care of the little ones and the sick children. A woman named Telezele cleaned the bathrooms and the decks in the new building, and another lady named Fee Fee cleaned the old building. They were both very nice ladies, and they kept the building very clean. These ladies were also our friends. They loved to sing, and while cleaning they would dance and have a lot of fun.

Everybody who worked in the *mosad* appeared to like their jobs, and we liked these people too. In the mornings, Telezele would show me how to brush my teeth properly. The home did not have washing machines, so Hass-Neiny hired two women who used to sit on the roof of the building and wash laundry. They would boil the laundry and wash the clothes later by hand. The laundry was always clean, and we never got back stained clothing. I used to spend a lot of time helping the women hang up the clothes on the lines.

I also liked to spend time on the roof because I was able to see the whole city of Jerusalem. I could hear the church bells ringing, and hear the Arabs' prayers from their loudspeakers. When I looked down from the roof I was able to see Jews and Arabs walking the streets, but each stayed within their own borders.

In a diary that I began to keep at the age of nine, I wrote the following: "Today is the first day of the month of Elul, 1961. The sky is bright and the world looks very beautiful. While standing on the roof, and looking up to the heavens, and down to the land, I can only praise *Hashem* (G-d) for creating such a beautiful world. I also know that in this beautiful world there are also many bad things happening. I feel alone and scared because if I am not able to tolerate the pain, I will have to run away. Where can I run to? And where will I end up? Today I learned in school that *Hashem* (G-d) weighs all our sins and all the good deeds we do the whole year. I too decided to weigh the good I had done since I was born, and the bad that I have seen, felt, and lived through... But when I took a piece of paper and I wrote in a line all the trouble I have, and another line with all the good I have, I learned that I had more good than bad.. the good is pleasurable and very rewarding. But the little bit of bad that I have, is so painful..."

I tried to work out a plan to balance the good and bad, but it was very hard. I thought to myself that if I had a lot of money, and did not have to work for it, I would probably be very happy. But I know that when I have a bad toothache for even one day, I see how unimportant money is. Money is only good when we can enjoy it. The same is true with life. After working on this plan, I turned around and saw Keizer, a man who came to fix the *mosad*'s plumbing. He was a very short man, with *payes* (sideburns). We always tried to figure out how his *payes (*sideburns*)* could stand out so straight without falling. We used to laugh whenever we saw him, and he would laugh with us too. As bad as it was in the *mosad*, G-d always found someone or something that would make us laugh.

Fridays in the *mosad* was always a very special day. The girls were busy cleaning their rooms and polishing their shoes. The older girls washed their clothes, changed their linens, and helped the younger girls prepare themselves for the Sabbath. On Friday, we were off from school, so we had enough time to prepare ourselves for this holy day. Breakfast was a regular meal; we ate Israeli salads, eggs, bread, cheese, fruit and coffee, but for lunch we had only spaghetti with cocoa and sugar on top. By Friday afternoon, when the fresh hot *challah* (special bread for the Sabbath) arrived on a truck, all the girls ran down to the kitchen, broke off pieces of *challah*, spread butter and jelly on top, and ate it. Hass-Neiny and the cook used to order plenty of *challot* (plural of *challah*) because they knew that we were hungry and that we loved to eat it.

We certainly had plenty to eat and snack on at the orphanage.

After we finished eating the *challah*, the girls used to go out to the *shuk* (market) and buy sunflower seeds, peanuts, and chickpeas sold by Mordechai. We then went to Tzipy's kiosk (candy store) where we had a piece of cake and soda as a pre-Shabbat nosh. We shared our snacks with the girls who did not have their own money to buy them; we never let a child down. At four P.M. every Friday afternoon two girls were in charge of handing out four tea biscuits to each child, and if one of our friends was in charge, she would give us extras.

It is hard for me to describe what it was like observing the Sabbath at the *mosad*. We felt such an aura of holiness once we were all groomed and dressed in our Sabbath clothes and shoes. After Hass-Neiny lit the Shabbat candles, the children formed little groups around the building, and we all prayed *kabbalat Shabbat* (welcoming of the Sabbath). From each corner of the *mosad* we could hear the sounds of songs like "*Lecha Dodi*". When we reached the section in the prayer where one turns around to welcome in the Sabbath queen, those girls wearing hoop skirts or dresses used to turn a little bit harder so that they could show off their beautiful outfits. We would put down our *siddurim (*prayerbooks*)* before heading down to the dining room together with friends. The lights in the dining room were off, but the candles and the Sabbath lamps gave off a dim light, and the smell from the candles added to the Shabbat spirit. The fish, the chicken soup, and the chicken smelled so good, and we anxiously waited for Rabbi Poppenheim to make *Kiddush (*prayer for the wine*)* for us so that we could eat our dinner.

While we waited for Rabbi Poppenheim, we would chat with Hass-Neiny about anything we wanted. She could hardly wait to sit down and talk to us. When she smiled, she lit up the entire room with her large blue eyes and red cheeks. She was not a pretty woman, but she had such beautiful eyes, and her facial expressions gave her all the attractiveness she needed. Her daughter Shifra also used to sit with us, but did not interact with the girls much; she had her own friends from the school she attended.

When Rabbi Poppenheim came back from *shul* (the synagogue), he would bring his wife and children with him to make *Kiddush* for us and offer us all a "*Gut Shabbos*." He preceded the *Kiddush* with "*Shalom Aleichem*," "Ki Malachav Yetzave *Loch*," and "*Eishes Chayil*." Everybody stood still, and no one made a sound until the rabbi was finished. He and his family blessed us and then went home to eat their Shabbat dinner. His beautiful voice will linger in my heart forever. No matter how many times I heard his voice, he made me cry. He was such a good father to his own children, and he made those in the *mosad* feel like a part of his family. I believe that Rabbi Poppenheim was the greatest father a child could wish for.

I remember one Shabbat when a group of thirty girls from another school came for a *shabbaton*. One guest named Tziporah, a girl from Haifa, sat next to me at the table. We immediately became friendly, and she and three other girls slept in my room. When Rabbi Poppenheim made *Kiddush*, she burst into tears. I held her hand, and after *Kiddush* I told her that I felt the same way every single week. That entire Shabbat she kept on telling me what an angel he was, that normal human beings do not have such a moving voice. I have heard many people make *Kiddush*, but I yearn to hear Rabbi Poppenheim's voice again. I am as proud of him as if he were my real father.

We had three cooks during the eleven years that I spent in the *mosad*, Laufer-Neiny z"l, Glick-Neiny, and Steinmetz-Neiny. All three were outstanding cooks as well as good people. Their food was always fresh and tasted great. But when the Sabbath came, the food was even better. Although the preschool children ate in their own dining room during the week, on the Sabbath we ate together like one family, and sang Shabbat *zemirot* (songs) throughout the meal. After we recited the *Birkat Hamazon* (grace after meals), each child cleaned her area, and the girls in charge would take the dirty dishes into the kitchen. Once everything was cleaned off, we would form a circle and dance until after midnight. The girls were full of life, with their feet tapping to the songs and their voices filling the air with music – we had no need for a live band. I was too shy to push through the circle unless a girl invited me to, so I would either stand on one side or pull over a chair to sit on and watch the girls dance. Tova never danced because she suffered from asthma and would easily become short of breath, but she enjoyed watching everybody else have a great time.

Shabbat morning always started out pleasant. We were permitted to sleep as long as we wanted to. During the week we had to wake up at six A.M., so on Shabbat we were able to catch up on some sleep. We also had the choice to spend the day as we wanted. Some girls went to shul by choice. I went to the Gerer Yeshiva because my family belonged to the Gerer Hasidic sect; other girls preferred to *daven* (pray) in the *mosad*. Some girls read books, while others took walks in the *shuk* (market) or in various neighborhoods in Jerusalem, where many people on Shabbat and holy days anxiously waited to give us a little goody bag. I was too shy to go with these girls and ask for anything; besides, I did not feel it was right for me to take nosh from people when I had plenty to eat already. My mother was a giver and not a taker; she taught us to act in the same manner. I preferred to go on Fridays to Mr. Shushan's store. He used to sell a little bag of nosh for one *grush* (penny); sometimes, Tova would ask me to buy a sour tomato or pickle and we ate it with our main course.

I did go for walks with my friends to the Mea Shearim *shuk*, which used to smell of *cholent* (stew), potato kugel, noodle puddings, cakes and cookies. Young children and old people used to carry hot pots from the bakery, and we felt the aura of holiness in the streets. In those days, most Jerusalem residents did not use electricity or gas on the Sabbath in their houses, so they used to prepare everything at home on Friday and then take their food to the bakery to keep it warm for Shabbat. The streets of Jerusalem were always filled with many Hasidic Jews coming and going to *shul* (synagogue), to their relatives' homes, and especially to visit their parents to wish them a "*Gut Shabbos.*" We saw children, their parents, siblings, neighbors, and friends all walking the streets quietly and peacefully.

But what amazed me even more was seeing very old men and women holding their great-grandchildren with one hand and a cane in the other. It was a dream that we can only hope to see again in the time of Messiah. In the Tanach there is a *pasuk* (phrase): "*Od yeshvu zkenim v'zkenot, berechovot Yerushalayim. V'ish misanto b'yado berov yomim.*" ("There will come a day when grandmothers and grandfathers will sit on the streets of Jerusalem with a cane in their hands and all they will see is joy from their young grandchildren").

Everybody greeted one another with a "*Gut Shabbos,*" and when Shabbat fell on a *Rosh Chodesh* (new month), they would wish each other a "*Gut Shabbos* and a *Gut Chodesh.*" Even when *Rosh Chodesh* fell on a weekday, we had to get dressed in Sabbath clothes, were not permitted to do any work, and greeted each other with "*A Gut Chodesh.*" The spirit of *Hashem* (G-d) and his angels always permeated our environment.

During Shabbat lunch, Hass-Neiny stood ready with wine, and as soon as we all gathered around her she would make *Kiddush.* Hass-Neiny had an Hungarian accent, and sounded so funny when she recited the *Kiddush* that everybody burst into laughter. Hass-Neiny got used to it. The children in the *mosad* always found a reason to laugh. When Laufer-Neiny, the cook, used to make *Kiddush*, we would also laugh because she too said it as if she was reading a story to us in Hungarian. The children who had *toranut* (kitchen duty) brought out the hot dishes and once again, we ate, sang, laughed, and had a great time. In the afternoon, whoever wanted to go to Shabbat school went for one hour; those who wanted to relax did as they pleased. Some girls read books; others, like myself, played games and sang. There were many girls who liked to read *Tehillim (*Psalms*)*. I too read them daily.

Toward the evening we would go out onto the streets, where many Jews were demonstrating. We called it *machoye* (war). Men and boys formed barriers to prevent the non-Orthodox from driving through their neighborhoods on Shabbat. Or, they would throw rocks at women passing by in sleeveless or immodest clothing. They would call these ladies a "*prutza*" (immodestly dressed woman). In my eyes, this was the wrong way to react. Besides violence, there are other ways to teach. The secular Jews and Gentiles need to be taught why the chassidic Jews dress differently, why we must observe the Sabbath and holy days, and why modesty is so important in the Jewish faith. Meah Shearim needs to open a tourist center where all tourists must enter for a brief educational session. It should be operated by professional educators. By doing so, the Orthodox community will be able to reach more tourists and will be respected for their way of living. It can also be a source of income for their community. There is no proof that violence is the answer for education.

As soon as the Sabbath was over, we would wait outside the *shul* (synagogue) to find a man to make *havdoloh* (the prayer that separates the Sabbath from the rest of the week). Mr. Zinger, a short toothless man, and a father to an orphan, always felt honored to recite the *havdoloh*. He used to read it so funny, so we named him Uzi because in the *havdoloh* we read "*Ki Ozy Vezimmras Ko*" and he pronounced it "Ki Uzy" and the children would get a kick out of him. His daughter eventually asked the girls to stop making fun of her father, and they did, but he still had his nickname. Then Tova went to the kitchen to wash all the big commercial pots that were much bigger than she was. On Saturday night, the *Shabavnikim* (Hasidic Jews who refuse to follow Jewish law, yet dress like Hasidic people) would go out to war against the rabbis and their own people. They would attack elderly people with sticks and nails. They set fires and stepped on innocent people; nobody seemed to be able to control them. The same people would rape girls and beat them up if they opened their mouths. They had no respect or dignity, and never showed remorse.

The holidays were also a great time in the *mosad.* Each holiday was something special, giving us the opportunity to celebrate and be happy. While they could be very depressing for those children who did not have a home to go to, the girls learned to overcome their pain and make the best out of the situation. For Sukkot, the children kept busy making decorations for the *sukkah* (booth). On Hanukkah, we all gathered around the menorah after Rabbi Naftali Rosenfeld lit the candles and we danced and sang Hanukkah songs. We put on a play and exchanged gifts. Hass-Neiny served donuts, we received Hanukkah *gelt* (money), and each girl received a bag filled with candies to play the game of dreidel. During Hanukkah week we were off from school.

On Tu B'Shevat, which is the new year for all the fruits, we had a party in school as well as in the *mosad.* We received bags filled with the best fruit. When we came home from school on the holiday, the tables were covered with white cloths; next to each plate was a little white bag with fruit in it, and we had a hot festive meal. Most of the time we would put on a play, and many people from the community came to watch. We also had a bazaar and raffles for the community to defray some of the *mosad*'s costs.

On Purim, we celebrated for a whole week. Our teachers and counselors invited us to their homes, and we had a party and play in school and in the *mosad.* We also got to choose where to hear the Megillah reading. Rabbi Rosenfeld read the Megillah at the orphanage, but many girls preferred to hear it read in shul. We used to watch the rabbi crack up when he saw us in our costumes. Each child sent *mishloach manot* (Purim goody bags) to friends, teachers, and counselors. We also picked out grab bags, where we had to buy presents for those whose names we selected. I always bought a beautiful present for the girl that I had picked, but never received any while I was in the *mosad*. Hass-Neiny also prepared many portions of cooked food for the poor and the homeless, and would prepare a table for those who wanted to eat in the kitchen. She helped the poor throughout the year, but prepared food even more nicely for them on the holidays. In the afternoon we would go out to deliver *mishloach manot,* and would see people dressed in costumes, dancing and singing in the streets. I liked to go to the hospitals and bring baskets for the sick. I would go to the childrens ward as well as visit the elderly. Hass-Neiny knew that I liked to perform this mitzvah, so she prepared baskets for me to take to the hospitals. I also went to visit children in mental institutions to cheer them up and put them in the Purim spirit.

The *mosad* also prepared a seder and provided for those children who did not have a place to go for Pesach (Passover). Whether the children left for the holidays or stayed in the orphanage, we cleaned our rooms, our closets, the storage rooms, the kitchen, the cellar, roof, clubs, and the hallways. Some girls went to their parents' homes, while others "to an aunt", counselors, or strangers who wanted to share their holidays with us. Tova and I went home to our loving family.

Lag B'Omer was the nicest holiday in Jerusalem, but especially in Mea Shearim. Bonfires burned in the backyards of all the *shuls* (synagogues) , and thousands of people danced around them and sang songs related to the father of Jewish mysticism, Rabbi Shimon Bar Yochai, as well as other Jerusalem songs. Music blasted from every corner and fathers, grandfathers, brothers, and uncles would put their young on their shoulders and rejoice. Many people went to Meron for the custom of giving their three-year-old boys their first haircut. Others went to *shul* (synagogue) and gave their sons a haircut, after which they put a *yarmulka* (skullcap) on their heads and *tzitzit* (a garment with strings hanging down from four corners that every Jewish boy must wear) under their clothing. These little boys looked like little rabbis in their new white *yarmulkas* (skullcap), white shirts, shiny colored coats, three-quarter length pants, white socks, and black shoes. Their happy fathers and grandfathers picked them up on their shoulders and danced with them for many hours to music while their female relatives stood in the women's section wiping their tears and sighing from *nachat* (joy).

One week before Shavuot, our teacher used to take us to the fields to pick flowers (a custom of the holiday), and to sing songs. (Our teachers had a song for every game or activity we did.) After a long field trip, we returned to school and started to decorate our classrooms with flowers. In the *mosad*, we also went with our counselor to pick flowers two days before Shavuot; some girls liked to pick little branches with leaves to enhance the flowers' appearance. Others carried little trees. Each child picked whatever she wanted. When we came back from our field trip, the girls would decorate their rooms, the dining room, the hallways, and even the offices and clubs. The building looked like a botanical garden.

Tisha B'Av, which observes the destruction of the First and Second Temples in Jerusalem, as well as other tragedies, was a particularly emotional holiday for the *mosad*'s children. Before undertaking our twenty-five hour fast, we prepared ourselves for the reading of *Eicha* (Lamentations). Every girl changed her shoes and put on a pair of sneakers, slippers, or stockings. She then turned the chairs upside down and sat on the floor in the main dining room to wait for the reading. The children cried, feeling their own pain at the destruction of the holy Temple.

Tisha B'Av was a time when many children cried because the day reminded them about the destruction of their own homes; others cried because their friends were crying, or because some girls would pinch or smack them. The readings of both *Eicha*, which is done in the evening, and *kinot* (elegies) which is read in the morning, took place in the dark, but we were allowed to light a candle. Every child who reached her twelfth birthday had to fast, but would be forced to eat something light by Hass-Neiny if she seemed to be too weak. Hass-Neiny was a very smart woman with wisdom and love for G-d and his children. She let us stay in bed and rest the whole day. The girls spread out mattresses on the big second-floor terrace, where we rested and spoke about the *Hurban* (destruction of the Temple), or questioned why we had sinned. We spoke about how badly we wanted to be friends and love one another so that the Messiah would come and rebuild the holy Temple again. We actually thought that it was our fault that the Temple was destroyed; I have never seen anybody mourn the Temple the way we did. As we lay on the terrace, a cool breeze came in from the west and we all felt great. Hass-Neiny came out to check on us to make sure that no one had a headache or felt sick.

In the evening, when the weather cooled off a little bit, we would go outside and pick acorns from the trees and throw them at each other. We called it "Bobkalach". Before we knew it the fast was over and we were able to eat. In 1959, while we were playing with the acorns, an eight-year-old girl, Chava'le, fell under a car and hurt her legs. She thanked G-d that she survived this accident, believing that the pain she went through was a result of not mourning enough for the Temple's destruction.

The month of *Elul* preceding the High Holy Days was a time to prepare ourselves for G-d's day of judgment. Stands and vendors filled the streets selling holiday greeting cards, while shoppers crowded the stores to buy *shofars* (ram's horns), *machzorim* (High Holy Day prayer books), *taleisim* (prayer shawls), new shoes and clothing for their families, and food. People tried to push through the heavy traffic and mobs of shoppers. The *shuk* (market) was so busy and crowded that it was hard to see where the stores were located.

In school we learned about *teshuvah* (repentance) and, as part of the holiday observance, were forced to ask for forgiveness from one another. We were scared to commit any more sins before the holidays, so forgiving each other was one step we all readily took. From the first day of the month of *Elul*, we woke up in the morning hearing the sounds of the *shofars* that were blown in the synagogues, the loud voices of men and boys learning Torah, and the reading by girls and women of *Tehillim* (Psalms). One week before *Rosh Hashana*, we got up for *selichot* (prayers of forgiveness) services before sunrise. Old men used to walk around the narrow streets of Jerusalem, calling the citizens to wake up for *selichot*. Men, women and children of all ages got dressed in two minutes and filled the streets running to the synagogue. We were even up before the cackling of the roosters. The fear coursed through us to such an extent that we felt as if we were about to stand on trial.

During the week of *selichot*, we were off from school. Tova and I went home the second day of *selichot* and stayed home until the beginning of the month of *Cheshvan*. It was a sad and depressing time for the *mosad's* many orphans. On *Yom Kippur* and other holidays where *Yizkor* (memorial services for the dead) is recited, a counselor or one of the older girls would stand near the stairs, and call out, "*Yizkor*! All the orphans please come to the front of the building." When I saw this horrible scenario for the first time, I was in tears and cried the whole day. Children ages two and up would be dressed in festive clothes and in sneakers. We lined them up and marched to *shul*. (I always liked to go to *shul*, so whenever I did not go home for a holiday, I would take the children with me.) The girls would have been okay, but the congregants who stayed in *shul* for *Yizkor* cried instantly when they saw how many orphans there were. Many children who said *Yizkor* never even had the chance to meet their parents. After services, the children would get a *pekale* (little goody bag) for behaving and reciting *Yizkor* so nicely.

There were plenty of celebrations at the *mosad*, too. The nicest were the weddings that were held there. The hall, which was decorated very professionally, looked great. The finest food would be served, and spirits were high. Although not all the girls were invited to the weddings, everybody participated in one way or another. The ceremony took place outside on the round, large terrace, so we were able to look out from our bedroom windows, or from the picture windows near the *moadonim* (clubs). After dinner, many girls would get dressed and go down to the hall to dance with the bride and make her happy. We were a real family, and we loved our sisters. There was no music, but the girls were better than any band, singing, dancing, and drumming on pickle cans and on pots. Each wedding was special. As soon as we saw the bride dressed in her white wedding gown, we hugged and kissed her, and gave her our blessings. Every wedding was a gesture of hope for us, and we always felt better, believing that one day we would get married and have a home of our own. It gave us a refreshing zest for life.

Most girls received two thousand dollars from the orphanages' sponsors as wedding gifts to set up their new homes. (Tova and I did not, because our parents were better off.) Also, each bride received instruction on marriage and domestic life. We learned the laws of family purity, and how to cook, clean, sew, bake, and even raise children. It was a lesson in responsibility and independence.

Not everything was perfect, though, because the girls were married so young. The marriages were arranged by the *mosad*'s principals or by people in the community. Many girls, while emotionally and physically in good shape, were often married to men with certain disabilities because of their orphaned status. Very often, girls were married to mentally ill men, and their lives turned hellish. One girl named Tuby was a good-hearted and hard-working girl who would do anything to help a friend. Tuby came from a broken home. She had two sisters in the *mosad* and one sister who was slightly retarded and wandered the streets. Tuby spoke like a little girl because she needed to be loved.

One evening, we got a phone call from her that she was engaged. All of the girls gathered in the lobby and started to sing and dance until our bride arrived. It was a surprise to all of us, not to mention the bride and groom, because of *ein hara* (evil eye), the Hasidic custom not to reveal an imminent engagement, and because parents or guardians would make the decision on their behalf after only one short date. Tuby went to America to live with her new in-laws so that they could prepare her for her wedding. Because she was an orphan, they thought they could control her and her groom's mother could physically discipline her. Tuby was smart enough to return to the *mosad* before she got married. She soon found another man with whom she now lives, very happily. Other children in similar situations were not as smart as she and they let themselves fall into bad marriages.

I believe that we learned a lot in the *mosad*, but there was one very sensitive issue that was ignored when it came to the girls' physical development, namely, their menstrual periods. Because of this omission, the girls were unprepared when the time came. Some counselors were more open than others, but they would often wait until a girl came forward to approach them. Some of the girls were so ignorant about what was happening to their bodies that they were ashamed to speak about it openly. As a result, some of the girls would steal cotton from other girls to use as menstrual protection. Our counselors did not realize how important it was to be educated about our bodies until one of the girls started bleeding profusely and had to be rushed to the hospital. The girls often did not have money to buy supplies for themselves, or were too shy to walk into a store and ask for them.

Other girls would also ridicule their peers as their breasts grew larger, until one day, Rivka Rein, one of the older, intelligent girls decided to go into each girl's room and privately discuss the maturity of a woman's body. She insisted that no girl should suffer any ridicule. Our principal finally followed through with an intense lecture on hygiene, how to keep clean, prevent bodily odor, and deal with excruciating premenstrual pain. She also advised the girls not to announce their monthly visit to others, but at the same time, to seek advice when needed. The girls were very thankful.

HELP ME, I AM DYING!

The story of my abuse at the hands of orphanage officials begins in 1961, after I returned to the *mosad* following a nine-month vacation at home with my parents. I had been trying to have a normal life with my family; I went to school and managed to make a lot of good friends.

While at home, Ima became very ill. She started to suffer from seizures and would often pass out; at times, she also would suffer from headaches and confusion. Around the same time, I also started to pass out, and suffered from an extended bout of pneumonia. My parents blamed themselves for my illness, and were afraid that something was going to happen to me.

Recognizing their physical and emotional instability, I decided to return to the orphanage where I had lived for four years. I took my eight year old brother with me to Jerusalem. Tova, now twelve, and I decided to place him in a boarding yeshiva. Our home environment was not good for us, and I was willing to do anything to make it easier for my mother.

Once I arrived at the *mosad,* I began to look for my sister. I walked through the back gate, and I saw a few children sitting and staring into space. Hoping to see her, I walked into the building and passed through the *machsan* (clothing room), dining room, and then out the front door to the front porch. In one corner I saw a gorgeous three year old, red-headed autistic girl who was sitting down. She was turning her head back and forth and doing strange things with her hands. On the front lawn stood a five year old girl, pretending to be a teacher. There were many chairs lined up just like in a classroom, but no students were sitting on any of them. The girl was playing and talking to herself. I walked out to the front of the building, where I saw Tova and her friend Leah peering into Berman's bakery. (The smell from the bread attracted anyone passing by. I used to spend a lot of time watching the bakers bake bread.)

Tova was happy to see me, but informed me that we had a new *menahelet* (principal), who was not a nice person. Tova was afraid of her, but when I told her about our home situation, she said that I did the right thing by coming back. Tova hugged Motty and me. After getting some food for our frightened eight-year-old brother, Motty, we went to look at three yeshivas before he was accepted at one of them. We promised him that we would come to check on him every day, and we did. We also went to visit him on Friday nights after our Sabbath meals. Once he was settled into the yeshiva, and after his rabbi introduced him to some other boys, Tova and I left.

It was time for us to eat, so Tova directed me to my group and to my counselor, Yehudis Hershkowitz, whom I knew very well. During mealtime, our new *menahelet* walked from table to table and looked into our faces. She did not offer one smile and looked like a member of the Gestapo. When she reached my table, she looked at me and told me that I looked like her daughter, who was killed by Hitler. Tova looked at me, and when Cahana moved away, asked me not to pay attention to her. She was strange looking in her white hat, coat and shoes, and heavy glasses. She looked like a strange doctor. She was demanding, unpleasant, abusive, and miserable, and she projected her anger toward the innocent children.

After dinner, Cahana called the girls into a meeting, and said she was going to change all the rules of the orphanage. Before she came along, our biggest problem was having lice; otherwise, we had a good life. The staff was nice to us and we loved them very much. Her first order for me was that I would no longer be permitted to sleep with my sister in the same room. She divided sisters, and she treated us in a manner similar to what she had seen in communist Russia. (She spoke German, as most other staff members did; and also Russian.) We all knew that we were in trouble with such a policewoman ruling over us. It was worse than being in the army. My only comfort was the lessons of my very special mother, who taught me to have faith and hope that better days would come.

Cahana was a very disturbed woman. She would often mention to us that she had lost a daughter in the concentration camp; only one son survived. The loss of her child made her so disturbed that she literally destroyed other childrens lives. I was one of them. Almost immediately after my return to the *mosad*, she began hitting me.

Since the day I met Cahana, my life completely changed. Everything looked negative to me, and my face looked so sad that I felt as if it was hanging like a turkey's neck. I lost my appetite, and all I did was feel sorry for Tova and myself. I constantly looked up to the heavens, and asked G-d (*Hashem*) to help us. I developed a fear of sleeping at night, so I used to sneak into or hide under Tova's bed. Tova always knew when I came into her room, so she gave me a pillow and blanket and let me sleep holding on to her hand or leg for security. Tova would be wheezing the whole night and would get so sick from her asthma attacks that I had to help her pump air into her mouth. Her asthma was out of control, and I was very concerned about her health.

One month after returning to the *mosad* I suddenly felt an unusual tiredness come over me during class. I felt as if I were being pulled to sleep. I put my head down on the table and fell asleep. During recess, my friends invited me to play with them. Ordinarily, I excelled in every game and sport; but on this day, I was unable even to lift my head. I grew sicker every day; I was unable to eat and was running a high fever. I was always underweight, but now I was disappearing altogether. I felt like vomiting and my skin color was pale. Everybody was concerned about me. I did not tell anyone that I already had pneumonia for three months; I knew something else was developing. I kept on telling my teachers that I was tired without revealing my medical condition.

I was only able to fake feeling well for a few days, until one day I developed a very high fever and began vomiting on the way home from school. My headaches were so severe, and I was unable to speak. When Hass-Neiny found out about my poor health, she put me into the infirmary under the care of our female house physician, Dr. Tzitron. She first diagnosed me with pneumonia. A few days later I developed the mumps on both sides of my face; three weeks later, while I was still in the infirmary, I had the chicken pox. I acquired so many diseases at once. My throat was aching and I was unable to swallow. I was coughing, and the chicken pox made my whole body itch.

On Wednesday evening, March 21,1962, the eleventh day in the Jewish month of Adar, two days before Purim, I had the most devastating experience any child could undergo. The weather was sunny and on the warm side, making the whole world appear to shine brightly. Because the weather was so nice, Dr. Tzitron gave me permission to go out onto the terrace for the first time in three months. I called to the girls who were playing downstairs, to my sister who sat outside on the stairs watching others play, and to the counselors. As soon as Tova saw me outside, she immediately came up and stayed with me on the terrace. I put my head on her, and she read a story to me and combed my hair. The two of us were very happy to breathe in some fresh air.

The time passed by quickly, and before we knew it, the sun started fading away. Hass-Neiny asked me to go back to bed in the infirmary. Four other girls were staying in the infirmary, Sarah Lipsker, Hana Bulgary, Rivkah Herman, and Yehudith Rappoport. One had a stomach virus, one had a sprained leg, and one had a sore throat. I was blessed with pneumonia, chicken pox, and the mumps. The white brass beds were nice and clean, and the room was sparkling. The same evening, Hass-Neiny decided to give me a bath because I was sweating from a fever. After my bath, she gave me fresh pajamas with little colorful flowers printed on it. Tova combed my hair again and I felt great. I really believed that this was the best day I had enjoyed in my life to date. Before we ate our supper, the girls and I were discussing what our favorite foods and games were, which subjects we liked in school, and so on.

While we were talking, one of the girls told me that she was very jealous of my being sick and able to stay in the infirmary for so long, while she could only remain for a few days. I told her that I did not like to be sick and that I preferred to play and go to school. Believing that I was receiving a lot of attention, she started cursing me, telling me she hoped I would die. I decided not to respond to her, and turned my body toward the wall. I made believe that I was asleep, until I eventually was.

Hass-Neiny woke me when she came in with supper at seven P.M. We had the most delicious tomatoes, my favorite food, along with olives, hard-boiled eggs, fresh rye bread, fruit, tea and a biscuit for dessert. Yehudith did not like tomatoes so she gave them to me, and I gave her my slice of bread. We all ate in bed, socializing and laughing. I ate my dinner with a good appetite.

Without warning, it became dark and I could not see anything. At first I thought the light was turned off, but the others told me that it had not been. I became scared, especially when one of the children called out that I was very pale. Just a few minutes later, I felt a weakness on the right side of my body and I was unable to breathe. Out of fear I screamed, "Hass-Neiny, I am dying!" I tried to look at my fingers but could not see them.

Hass-Neiny ran in immediately and took me into her arms, and with a broken voice she asked me: "Ahuva'le dear, talk to Hass-Neiny, and tell me what is happening?" I told her that I could not see, and that I felt weak on one side of my body. In the meantime, I started feeling a tremendous amount of pressure in my eyes, and I was choking. Tova came in as soon as she heard from the other children what had happened. She hugged me and begged me not to die.

Hass-Neiny ordered the other children to leave the infirmary, but many children stood behind the door and imitated the way I was screaming, making fun of me. Hass-Neiny told me not to pay attention to them, and asked one of the counselors to take all the children away. Tova took me into her arms, and Hass-Neiny called for a doctor. Dr. Cohen was on call, so he came right away. He asked me a few questions and then examined me. He looked into my eyes, listened to my heart, and examined my hands and legs. Then I heard him tell Hass-Neiny to call an ambulance to take me to the hospital. I also heard him tell her that it appeared that my brain was swollen, which was why I could not see. He was concerned, and told Hass-Neiny that the problem had to be taken care of right away. I had a high risk of going into a coma.

Tova, who was only twelve years old, asked Hass-Neiny to rush me to the hospital, but our housemother was so afraid to do anything without permission that she decided to call my mother. The problem was that Ima did not have a telephone in the house, and neither did any of her neighbors. Mrs. Rothblatt, the owner of the post office, had a telephone but the post office was closed at night; in any event, Ima was working in a catering hall at night and Hass-Neiny did not have the telephone number there. She ended up sleeping next to me the whole night, just as a mother would have. Ima did not get the message until the next morning.

I started to feel a little more relaxed from the injection Dr. Cohen gave me. I slept very little, and Hass-Neiny kept on checking my breathing and skin color every few minutes to make sure I was not slipping into a coma. At exactly eight A.M., Ima showed up at the infirmary, crying and hugging me. She was not able to ask me a single question. Tova and Hass-Neiny explained to her what had happened. Ima asked Hass-Neiny to give her a basin with warm water and soap, and she washed me, combed my hair, and dressed me.

In the meantime, Hass-Neiny called a taxi and the three of

them took me to see my doctor in the Kupat Holim (medical center). The doctor examined me and ordered many tests and an injection of steroids. The laboratory results showed that I was severely anemic. He ordered the nurse to give me a shot of iron. Because my body temperature was so low, he had the nurse put me into a heated barrel to raise it. After the x-ray and more laboratory tests came back, the doctor decided to immediately send me to Hadassah Hospital. Ima carried me in her arms into a taxi. On the way to the hospital, Hass-Neiny convinced Ima not to take me there because she was afraid that the doctors might do experiments on me, and other bad things if I were to slip into a coma. Ima was convinced that Hass-Neiny was right. She decided to wait a little longer and see if the steroids would help improve my condition and if my brain swelling would lessen. Hass-Neiny called Dr. Tzitron and told her about my condition. She came over right away and told us she could give me daily iron injections if anemia was the problem. If I needed blood, she could arrange for my mother to donate it in her clinic. Ima was very happy to oblige and even happier to find out our blood types matched. Hass-Neiny promised to cook healthy food for me that she would blend so I could swallow. Because it was Thursday, they all believed that it would be easier for us to stay home for the Sabbath, rather than waiting around in a hospital.

Ima did not return to work, but stayed with Tova and me. Hass-Neiny cooked for me and tried to feed me but I was choking and unable to swallow anything, even liquids. The children tried to break into the door, calling me names. This upset Ima, Tova, Hass-Neiny, and me. The counselors knew about it, but did not do anything to remove them. Hass-Neiny covered up the windows and gave a key to Ima. I was too weak to fight back, and my young heart could have stopped just realizing that the same children who were making fun of me were the ones I fed and gave lots of love to. They were my friends, and I did many good things for them; now they were rebelling against me.

My breathing got heavier, and I felt like I was choking to death. My vision came back for a brief interlude and then I went blind again. I fainted several times during the day. From one episode to the other I heard the voices of the children calling me "*hatkafot*" (attacks). This became my nickname until the day I left the *mosad* for good. As the night approached, my condition worsened, and at two A.M., I went into respiratory distress. This is when Ima insisted on calling an ambulance to take me to Hadassah.

In the ambulance, the paramedics put an oxygen mask on my face. They inserted an IV line into my arm, took all my vital signs, and asked me to stay awake. Ima and Tova sat next to me, holding my arms as the ambulance made its way to the hospital. I felt as if I was sinking into a ditch and I passed out.

On Friday, March 23, 1962, I woke up at eight A.M. to the smell of coffee, which I liked very much. One of the nurses placed a breakfast tray near the crib I was lying in like an infant, and Ima was sitting with her head next to me, trying to get some rest. The smell of the food was great, but when Ima tried to feed me, I choked on it. A nurse named Rinah came over and introduced herself to me. She was dressed in a light blue uniform with a white apron and a white cap with three blue stripes. She told me that she was going to be my private nurse and would look after me all the time. She wheeled me up to the children's intensive care unit. Then she transferred me to another bed, washed and weighed me, took my vital signs, combed my hair, and took me into the examining room on a stretcher. There I was introduced to Dr. Sabo, a very fine man. He got up from his chair and came over to me, with a smile beneath his mustache. With one hand he lifted my head and put his arm under it, and he gently asked me what had happened to me. He had a lot of information from the doctors who saw me prior to my hospitalization, but he wanted to hear the story directly from me. He gave me a complete examination and told me he wanted me to meet another doctor who had come into the room. The other doctor was an ophthalmologist. He introduced himself to me and asked for permission to look into my eyes. He looked into my eyes with a little light, pressed on them, and then asked me to count his fingers and to look in the center of his fat nose. He told me that he would order a whole set of tests and promised to see me the next day. The eye doctor left the room with Dr. Sabo, and the two of them talked behind the door about my condition. They came back inside, and Dr. Sabo looked into my eyes.

The eye doctor told Dr. Sabo in English that I have papilary-edema (a swelling of the optic nerve caused by pressure from swelling on the brain. Papilary-edema can be caused by a swelling on the brain, a brain tumor, or by excessive pressure from the spinal fluid. In my case it was a swelling of the brain and excessive pressure of the spinal fluid also known as Pseudo Tumor. My impression of Dr. Sabo was that he was a very caring doctor who took each situation seriously. He wanted to help me, and I knew that I would be able to trust him. After my visit with Dr. Sabo, he wheeled me into the children's activities room, where there was a Shabbat and Purim party. Most of the children were dressed in costumes, and the activities leader was singing Shabbat and Purim songs with them. She played all kinds of games with them, and each child left with a bag of refreshments. Dr. Sabo got a little bag for me too, and I asked him to give one to Ima; he did. This little bag helped cheer her up, as she was so hungry and tired.

After the party, Dr. Sabo wheeled me into a private room with walls made out of glass. On one side of the room was a twenty-one-year old female with no muscles who did not talk, move, or eat. She was fed by a feeding tube. Her body was so skinny that I was able to see the outline of her bones, and her skin looked like thin paper. She was connected to a respirator. She looked like a dead person to Ima and me. How she lived for twenty one years remains a mystery to me. On the other side of my room was a five-year-old girl, also connected to machines. The nurse told Ima that this little girl was born premature and never completely developed. She seemed to be the size of an infant. No one came to visit her. The unit was filled with creatures, none of them looked like human beings. They were all deformed, and it was scary to look at these children, who were unlike those I had seen at the Sabbath party. Everybody was lying in bed, and nobody was able to walk, talk, or move. Nurse Rinah was assigned to take care of me each night; during the day, another nurse was watched me.

Just a few minutes after moving to my room, a nursing supervisor entered. She was dressed in a white uniform with a white cap and a picture of a red star of David in the center. She told me that she had to bring a machine into my room in case I slipped into a coma and suffered respiratory failure, which the doctors believed could happen. She then hooked me up to a heart monitor, and put an oxygen mask on my face. She wanted to insert a tube into my nose but I refused. Another technician came in to do an EKG to test my heart; I also had an EEG for my brain and x-rays for my head, chest, abdomen, and kidneys. My vision continued to play tricks on me; I would get it back for short periods before it disappeared again. Occasionally I would slip in and out of a coma, but each episode lasted for only short periods of times, similar to seizures. The doctors were firmly convinced that I might go into a permanent coma at any time. I was afraid that I was going to die.

I felt so weak that I could barely tell if I was alive. In order to reassure myself that I was, I pinched myself, blew air on my hand or up my nose, shook my leg, and did the strangest things just for reassurance. During my hospitalization, there was construction taking place on the hospital's grounds. The builders used explosives in the surrounding mountains; they were drilling and the noise was intolerable. I was so scared that I thought every noise that I heard was coming from my body or from the machines in my room. I wanted to live because I knew that death was what my mother was most afraid of. She had lost so many family members, and now she was facing another trial in which she might lose her ten-year-old daughter. I was frustrated that I was unable to walk, and my breathing became more labored. I was also unable to eat. I kept my eyes closed most of the time because my blindness episodes scared me, and I became afraid of the dark. I fainted a lot, and felt sick from the blood transfusions. I looked around at the other patients and started to picture myself in their situation. I was afraid to stay in bed because I did not want to look like the other children around me. I wondered what would happen to my mother and my sister if, G-d forbid, I ended up in a phlegmatic state? How would I be able to forgive Cahana, whom I blamed for my brain swelling because she repeatedly hit me on the head; and the counselors, who hit my face on the stone floors, causing a swelling of my face and bruises on every part of my little body? How would I forgive the children who made fun of me? In case I did come out alive from this frightening situation, how would I be able to return to the orphanage, when I knew for sure the children would continue making fun of me? Would my parents' lives become totally destroyed? Would my father lose his mind completely after finding out that I was in such serious condition and in the intensive care unit? He already lost his oldest daughter to Hitler; how could he deal with another child dying? I was not concerned about my brothers because they were doing fine, but I was worried about my sister, who raised and took care of me.

The truth was that no one could give me any answers to my questions, not even the doctors. When the nurse came in to check my pulse, I asked her to squeeze it hard so that I could feel my heartbeat. I felt as if I were losing my mind before dying. For Ima, this was a hard ordeal. She was sitting next to me day and night and was afraid to fall asleep. She held me in her arms, kissing me, caressing my head, and providing love and reassurance. She tried to feed me baby food from a baby spoon, but I was afraid even to swallow that for fear of choking. Ima prayed to *Hashem* (G-d) that whatever we were going through was only a test; she was positive that G-d would help us.

In the intensive care unit, there was another doctor named Dr. Simcha. He was a tall, fat man who thought that he was G-d's gift. He treated his patients and their families like trash. There were times when I felt very sick, and whenever I asked him for help he would make fun of me and tell me that he would come into my room, but never did. My mother was very angry at him for his attitude, but he could care less. When he did come to see me, I told him, "Thank you, but Dr. Sabo is my doctor." I told him that one day I would laugh at him. He didn't like it, and asked me to allow him to listen to my chest. I told him that if he could not do it when I really needed him, I refused to have him listen to my chest now. I told him that there were times when all I needed was a doctor to tell me that I was okay and that I was not going to die.

On Monday, March 26, I asked Dr. Sabo to have me evaluated by a psychiatrist. I was so frightened that I needed to have doctors tell me that I was fine. He had a psychiatrist and a neurologist come together to evaluate me and see how they could help. They both sat down next to me, and the psychiatrist asked me why I was in the hospital and wanted to see him. I told him what was happening to me, the fear I was experiencing, the crazy things I did with my breathing and my legs, and how I was pinching myself to make sure that I was alive. The neurologist asked me to walk and checked my eyes and my reflexes. He asked me to touch each of our noses, squeeze his fingers, smile, show him my teeth, and move my head in every direction. I thought that my eyes would be permanently twisted. He also asked me to drink a glass of water, but I choked on it immediately. At the end of his exam, he ordered an angiogram. Both doctors promised that they would take care of me.

But as soon as they started to walk out the door, I called back the psychiatrist and told him about the abuse I had suffered in the *mosad* and my fear of returning there. He promised to return the next day and take notes of everything I had told him, and that he would take care of the situation. He also reassured me that my behavior was normal for my condition.

Nurse Rinah continued to be nice and took me out daily to see the construction taking place, since I was frightened every time there was an explosion on the mountain. She wanted me to see where the noise came from so that I would not think it was from my own heart. The doctors also asked the builders to let the ICU nurses know when they were going to explode dynamite.

My mother sat next to me for a whole week, except for one day that she went home to shower, change clothes, collect her mail, pay bills, and rest for a few hours. On this day, Tova and some of her friends came to visit me and Tova brought me a book of *Tehillim* (Psalms). I used this book daily for many years.

All this time, my father knew that Ima was in Jerusalem, but he had no idea that I was sick until the doctor called him to find out why he did not come to visit me. He came to the hospital immediately, and I believe that he looked worse than I did. He went into a panic attack when he saw how I was hooked up to monitors, IV fluids, medications, vitamins, and oxygen; how I was unable to sit or walk; and how my vision was playing with me. He was nervous and very angry that nobody told him about me, but my mother knew that he would not be able to cope with it, especially if I died. She did not believe he needed to know that his daughter might be on her way to the other side. He was hysterical and crying. I told him that I was anemic, which was why I felt so weak. Aba sat next to my bed and asked the nurse if he could put me on his lap. The nurse gave him a gentle smile and helped me sit on his lap. He wanted me to eat some food that he brought for me, but I told him my throat was hurting me. Aba sat next to me the whole day, knowing that I had not told him the truth about my condition. I was sure the doctors told him already since he did not ask many questions. I fell asleep in his arms and knew he was kissing me and crying because I felt his tears.

I have no idea whose idea it was to call in a psychic for a

reading of my situation. As I rested comfortably in my father's arms, the nursing supervisor asked Aba to bring me into another room. She disconnected my IV and got a wheelchair for me, and together we went to meet this specialist. My father, the psychiatrist, the neurologist, and Dr. Sabo were present during this reading. I was asked to sit facing this dark-skinned, partially bald man of medium height. When I was in the correct position, he asked me to drink a cup of coffee. I told him that I could not drink it so he told me to take some sips, and spit the rest out into a basin if I could not swallow it.

After I emptied the little coffee cup, he read the lines inside and came up with the idea that a black cat scared me, which was how I became sick. I told him that I was not afraid of any cats. He wanted to tell me that I made the whole thing up. I believed that it might have been my father who hired this man to tell me that there was nothing wrong with me, and that I made up my illness, but I could have been wrong.

My mother arrived at the hospital at that moment, and when she saw me sitting in front of a witch, she got angry and sent him away. She became angry at the doctors for allowing such a thing to happen; no one ever told us whose idea it really was. I told the doctors that I might be weak and frightened but I was oriented enough to know that the whole cat business was wrong. When Ima saw that the doctors were playing around with me and starting to put wrong ideas into my head, she decided to have them discharge me from the hospital. She wanted to take me back to the *mosad* because she knew that Hass-Neiny would take better care of me than any doctor in the world. The doctor asked my mother to wait a few more days for the spinal tap and other tests to be completed, and ten days later, Ima took me back to the *mosad*.

I refused to go back, though, because I was afraid of Cahana, and I was afraid that the children would continue making fun of me. But where else could I go? I was also brave enough to know that I would have to try hard to ignore these evil people, but if they continued to abuse me, I preferred to die than exist through such hell. I remembered learning in school that before the Jewish people crossed the Red Sea, they were afraid of drowning, but Moshe told them to trust *Hashem* (G-d). I, too, decided to return to the *mosad,* hoping that *Hashem* (G-d) would watch over me.

Before we left, Dr. Sabo called us into his office and told us that I was still very anemic. He suggested that I get daily iron shots and have my blood checked frequently. He also told me that I would need more blood transfusions in the near future.

When I returned to the orphanage, I planned to keep my illness private and tried very hard not to discuss my problems with anybody, not even my brothers or parents. As much as I needed help, I was very well taken care of by my sister; I wanted to leave the rest in the hands of G-d. Tova and Ima came with me from the hospital, but on the way I asked Ima to go home in the same taxi we were in so she could rest and go back to work. Ima decided to take a bus from the central bus station, which was cheaper than a taxi, and Tova and I continued to the *mosad.*

As we stepped out of the taxi, Tova held my hand and we walked into the building quietly, trying to avoid everybody. My friend Hana Mikler noticed me and ran toward me to snap some pictures of us. I wanted to stay in Tova's room, where I hoped to have some peace and quiet. But as we were walking up the stairs, Cahana approached us, and without saying hello, or wishing me a *refuah shleima* (full recovery), asked me why I put a knife in Aviva's bed; she was another student. I told her that I had just arrived from the hospital and had not seen anybody yet.

She looked at me with the eyes of a murderer and told me that she would hurt me unless I admitted to her that I was her daughter who was killed and resurrected from the dead. She made Aviva believe that either Tova or I had placed a knife in her bed. What I wished for was for somebody to shove a big knife down

Cahana's throat and shut her up for good, but I was not so lucky. This evil woman continued to harass me and destroy the lives of my sister and me. She embarrassed me in front of the other children and counselors, hit me with objects and with her hands, and made me so sick that I wished for my death. She separated me from my sister and friends, and had me sleep with the mentally retarded children. I was not afraid of this devil, but I hated her so much that every time I saw her or was reminded of her, I wanted *Hashem* (G-d) to make her disappear. I wanted to live a normal life.

At this point in my life I only needed Tova for support, and to get stronger, but it was impossible to live. It was painful for me to know that the other principals were aware of the situation and did nothing to stop it. I refused to eat and was unable to swallow any food because I would choke. The iron injections were hurting me so much that I decided to stop them. Because I could not see a brighter future, I decided to stop my treatments and asked G-d to let me go to sleep and never wake up again. Only ten years old, my life already seemed too long to bear such heartaches. I asked G-d every single night to come to me like a thief and take me to him. I knew that Tova would miss me but would be glad that I was not suffering anymore.

What allowed me to keep fighting for my life was Hass-Neiny. She understood me and always took me into her arms and spoke to me with words of encouragement. She invited me into her studio apartment, cooked food that I would not choke on, let me sleep in a room next to hers, and always checked on me at night. Yet even with all the love I received from her, I was unable to recapture my life. My childhood was gone. Some kids called me names and made fun of me, and Cahana did not allow anyone to play with or even talk to me. Sarah, Ronit, Aviva, Rachel, Chava'le, and Ruti basically destroyed me for life. The things these girls did will remain with me forever. They caused me so much pain by laughing at me, calling me names, telling Cahana things I never said, and following me everywhere.

But what strikes me the most is that even while these girls hurt me, they would invite me to play on their sports teams because I was very good and always helped their team win. I have a personality that forgave people regardless of how much pain they caused me; at the same time, I could not forget what they did. I was always their friend, but they were my enemies for the way they treated me, put me to shame, and called me names. Those actions will hurt me forever. I lost my self-esteem, and I still suffer a great deal from it. I wish I could ask these girls to speak to their children and tell them what they did to me, and how wrong their behavior was. They should teach them not to repeat the same mistakes, and if they do, to tell them it is wrong. I was so hurt by these children that it could have cost me my life.

The next morning, I got up very early and washed, got dressed, and went to school. The schoolyard was very quiet, because I was the only one there at seven A.M.. The doors were still locked, so I sat down on the floor and read from the *Tehillim* (Psalms). I was praying so hard and cried so many tears that by the time I had to go to class, I was drained. I was very tired, and my little eyes were red and swollen, but even so, I wanted to go to school where I felt loved and cared for, and where my friends remained friends forever.

The first thing we did during the school day was pray. While praying I was crying so hard that everybody was able to hear me. The children and my teacher understood me and came over to me after prayers to hug me. My teacher Rachel Kopshitz asked us all to sit down and had the girls stand up and bless *Hashem* (G-d) for healing the sick. Each child came over to me separately, handed me a little gift and wished me a sweet welcome back. My teacher came over to me and said she would help me with anything I needed. These words of comfort made me feel better. I did not want to be treated like a sad case, but I knew that my friends in school were not fake and I loved them all for it. They were the best angels who stood by my side at all times. Another person who deserves to be thanked is Rabbi Moshe Ehrenthal, the school's founder and principal. I always wanted to tell him how grateful I was that his school was based on love, goodness and good character.

I cannot speak for other girls, but in the eleven years that I was a student in *Benot Yerushalayim* I loved school very much. It is true that the school did not offer much in the way of secular studies, but what they did offer was principles of compassion, love, respect, honor, modesty, and goodness. These qualities can never be replaced. This is the school that gave me a reason to live, and because of this place I hope that other children and parents will understand why a good education is important for our children. We need to uncover the spirituality that lies in our souls.

During class, I kept all the gifts I received on the teacher's desk, and when it was time to go home, Tova helped me take them back. She stored all my presents in her closet and locked it with her key so that nobody would steal them. But in the evening, right after supper, Cahana came up to Tova's room and asked her to hand over all of my classmates' gifts. I told her that these games belonged to me and that they came from my teacher and classmates, but she said that I stole them. She also warned Tova and me that she would not allow us to be together.

At first, I had no idea who told her about my gifts; later, I was told that Ruti, a very jealous Sephardi girl who was in my group at the *mosad*, and a classmate told her. (Ruti made fun of me day and night, embarrassing me constantly. She would ask me when I had an appointment with the psychiatrist and would do awful things to me, even though I had nothing to do with her.) Tova refused to open her closet and give my gifts to Cahana, so she took Tova and beat her up so violently that her face and eyes were swollen and her nose and mouth were bleeding heavily. I fought with her so that she would stop beating my sister; she grabbed me by my braids, threw me into a broom closet and locked me up. This windowless room was filled with ammonia and other cleaning materials, and the smell was awful. She attempted to leave me there for the night and went home, but this beast had no idea that Tova owned a key to this room and others because Tova was stuck doing the hardest jobs in the orphanage and needed a master key for all the doors. Before Cahana left, she beat up Tova again. The next day, my teacher and classmates came by to swear that they were the ones who gave these gifts to me, and that she had no right to take them away.

The same night, when I was getting ready to go to sleep, I noticed another child in my bed. I asked my roommates why there was someone else in my room. They told me that Cahana told them that I was moving to another room. This barbarian had moved me into a room with first graders, and some of them were retarded. I was very angry and cried alot.

As I was about to go to Tova's room, Cahana was standing there and forced me to go into my new room. I refused and became sick watching her walk back and forth like a Gestapo member. She kept on telling me that Hitler killed her child and she would take revenge on me until I admitted that I was her dead child. I would rather be abused by her than tell her that I was her child. My heart was palpitating, and my body trembled. My muscles were contracting, and I was unable to defend myself. Tova was afraid to hit this monster, but Cahana felt free to hit her for no reason. Normally, Cahana would go home at five P.M. every day; but today, she stayed very late. When she did not stop harassing me, I got out of bed and yelled at her with all my strength to get lost. She beat me up again. I started to pretend that nothing was bothering me; I then felt an extra burst of energy and gave her such a kick in her leg that she got stuck like a mouse in a trap. I ran out of the room to my hiding room near the bathrooms. I was glad when Tova found me and told me that this sick woman went home limping.

My hiding room was also my meditation room. Many good things happened over the years while I hid there. This room had a window, a door, a sink with water, and a mirror on the wall. I spent most of my nights there and some hours during the day writing in my diary. I invited friends to play cards or *kugalech* (Chinese checkers). I was able to speak to G-d, study, plan, and do arts and crafts. This was the room where nobody ever hurt me.

In my diary I wrote the following while hiding: "Dear Ima. Today is April 2, and I am hiding in my hiding room because Cahana is hurting me and I am afraid of her. You cannot help me, my father does not care about me, and Tova is being hurt by Cahana because she is trying to protect me. Would you cry if I die? I don't want to live but I am afraid to hurt you. Please tell me that I can die and that you will not cry." I had written another letter like this to my mother, which she kept and I only found it after she died. While writing my diary I both cried and laughed; most of all, I was able to escape from one situation to another.

This particular night I hid under a hamper so that Cahana would not find me. I was told by some girls that they called her husband and he came to pick her up. Thank G-d I could often go into Tova's room and sleep next to her, or even under her bed when I felt that there was not enough room. Tova gave me a pillow and a blanket and I had a decent nights rest.

Even though I liked my friends very much, I tried to stay away from any conversations. The only time I would get together with them was during playtime, meals, and in school. Cahana did not let anybody play with me, but I was so good in all games that they needed me to help them win. In school, I never felt lonely. It also helped me that I was a spiritual child, and was very close to G-d. The problem was that this devil was stronger than my spirit, and managed to break it to the point of making me feel useless.

Cahana also lied to my mother about my behavior, and she believed her. My mother could not believe that such things were happening to me, and asked me to listen to the *menahelet* (principal) and not cause problems. The European mentality was that children who were beaten up were always guilty. She also was not well and was unable to think rationally because of the seizures she suffered. I did not want her to have to deal with such a sick woman and decided that whatever stories she heard from Cahana, to let it be. She told my mother that I was crazy and having attacks, and forced me to go to doctors to back up her stories.

After a while, Dr. Sabo knew that something wrong was going on, so he asked Cahana to leave the room during a visit. He gave me an exam, and asked me to tell him the truth about what was happening. Thank G-d, he was willing to listen to my side of the story, and he treated me accordingly. I asked him not to call her and tell her when I had an appointment to see him, and that I could come by myself or with my sister. Dr. Sabo invited Tova and me to his home for regular checkups, and when he felt that I needed certain tests or had to be hospitalized, he would send me to the hospital. During my weekly visits with Dr. Sabo, I was able to tell him my life story and about the abuse and everything else that was happening to me.

One day Cahana got very angry when she found out she was no longer welcome at his office, so she found another way to abuse me. When I came back from school, I washed up and went down to the dining room, where I found a full plate of my favorite food, carrots. The cook made a special soup for me and treated me like a queen. But when I sat down to eat, Cahana stood near my table. She knew that I liked tomatoes, so she tried to force me to eat rotten ones with worms crawling in them. When I refused to open my mouth and eat them, she smacked me across my face, and screamed at me that she was going to call an ambulance to take me to a mental institution.

I actually hoped that she would follow through for two reasons. For one thing, I would be able to tell somebody about this abuse, even though I might not be believed; further, I might be doped up and would no longer feel the pain. Instead, Cahana held my head back, pushing it against my neck, and with her other filthy hand she pushed the rotten tomato into my mouth. When my best friend Hana Mikler saw what this woman was doing, she kicked my leg as a gesture for me to stand up. We then ran away to the home of her Aunt Goldie, who lived in Jerusalem's *Beth Hakerem* neighborhood. There, we were served the most delicious goulash with a cup of tea, and we had such a beautiful afternoon. After lunch, we went to her mother's home in *Givat Saul*, where we were surprised to see Aviva and Sarah waiting for us. They were spying for Cahana. One hour later, Cahana showed up with a taxi and pulled us into it. Hana's mother gave her a warning that if she touched me she would have her arrested and put away for good, but she let us go back because she was afraid her daughter might be Cahana's next victim. This is how I struggled; all I had seen in my young life was violence and I never felt secure enough to fight for my life.

I continued going to my doctors alone, and did not even tell Tova when I had an appointment because I was afraid that she would be forced to reveal where I was going. It was only one month after I was discharged from the hospital when I went to see the eye doctor for the first time. He looked into my eyes and immediately asked me to go back to Hadassah Hospital to have my eyes re-evaluated. He felt that the swelling on my brain was pressing too much against my eyes, and wanted to make sure I was okay. I thanked him for his concern and I left.

The worst thing for me was not having anyone to tell about my visit with the eye doctor. The weather was freezing, and I did not have a coat to keep me warm; yet, I decided to sit outside on a bench near the health center. I sat so long I almost froze to death. I could no longer feel my arms and legs, and my face was so frozen that I could no longer open my mouth to yawn or speak. I wanted to give up and hoped that G-d would have mercy on me and let me freeze into a state of permanent sleep.

As I was starting to doze off, I heard the voice of one of the older girls in the orphanage, a new immigrant from Russia. She was the only student there who was permitted to go to nursing school, so she picked me up in her arms and took me back to the *mosad.* She took me directly to Hass-Neiny, and the two of them started to revive me. Hass-Neiny put a blanket over the hot radiators, took off my cold clothes, and then wrapped me in a warm blanket. She put a pair of wool stockings on my legs and mittens on my hands, and kept me under the heavy blanket to increase my body temperature. I was frostbitten and had cold blisters all over my mouth and almost my entire body. Tears formed in Hass-Neiny's eyes, and she asked me what had happened. I told her, and she cried and told me that she would personally see to it that this abuse stopped. She decided to take me to Hadassah Hospital to have my eyes checked. The doctors who examined me believed that I was going to die and that there was nothing they could do for me. I was stricken by double pneumonia, was underweight, had chest pain, high fever, and my breathing became worse each day. The headaches and the pressure I had in my eyes was so severe that I was unable to sit up or even talk.

This is how I suffered for many years. Each day was a living hell. I could not breathe and was crippled by headaches. When my father found out what was happening, he hired a counselor to take me out of the *mosad* every day for a few hours. He felt that I needed one on one attention and he paid for it. He gave the counselor money to buy things for me, and she helped me with my homework. When I was sick, she would stay with me.

The Wolf & Sarah Weinreb Building

New Building

My Parents & Siblings

Ahuva age 15, Hana'le age 10
First autistic child I worked with

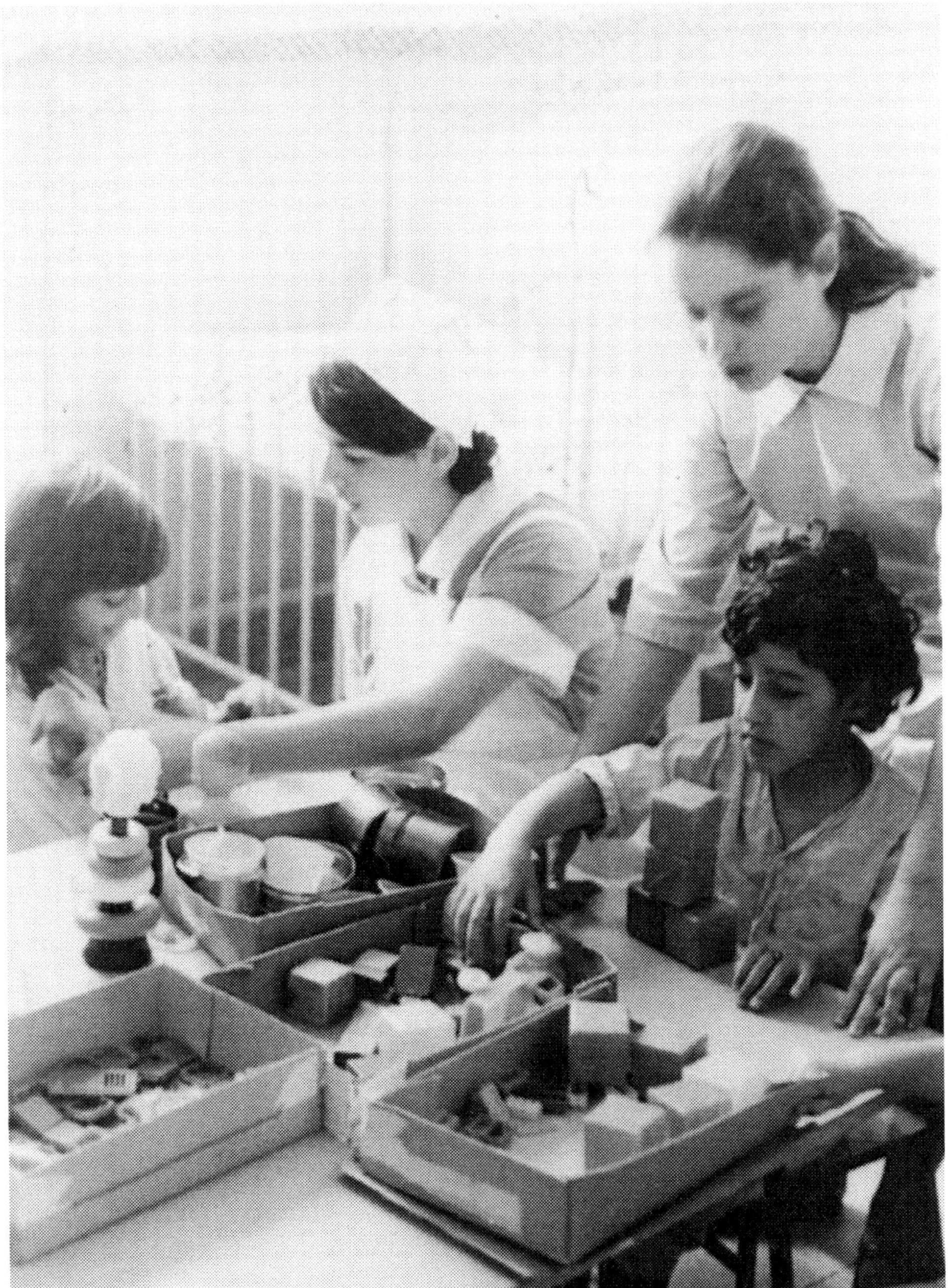

Ahuva age 15, volunteered in the infirmary, and Bikur Cholim

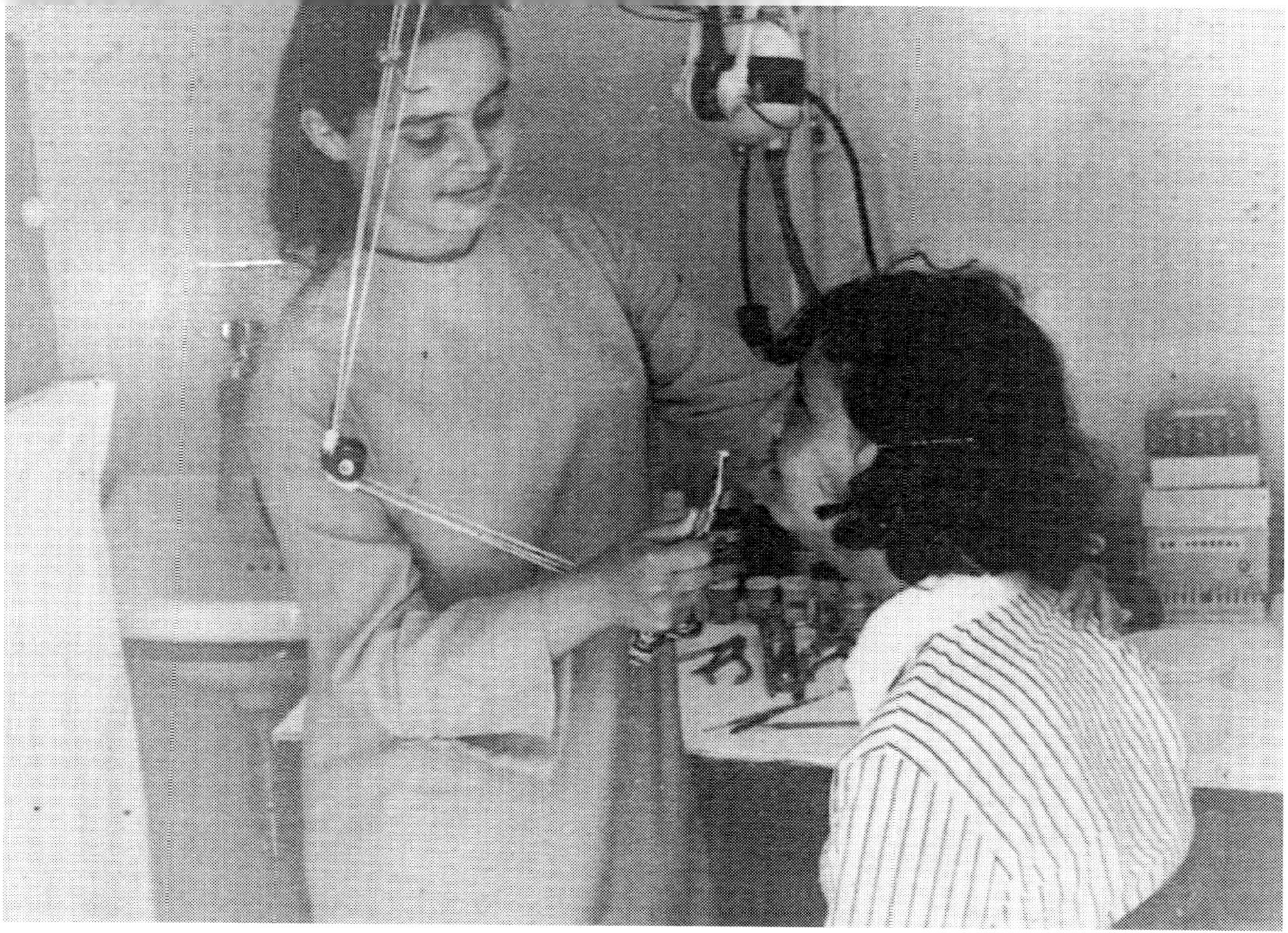

I volunteered for a dentist office. I make believe that I am treating Yonit.

Ahuva & Tova

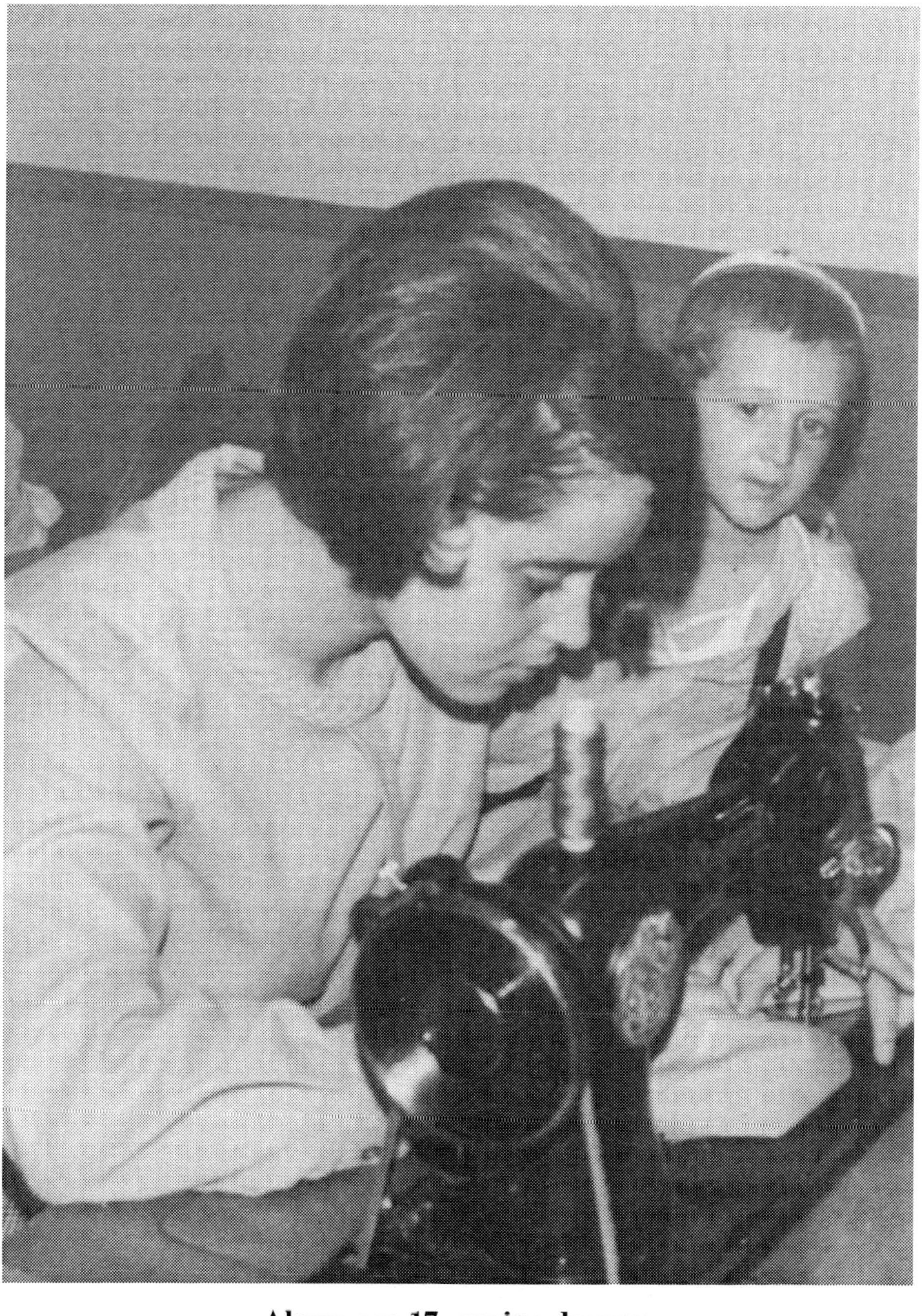

Ahuva age 17, sewing dresses for my wedding.

My Wedding

Mrs Cahana
Menahelet

Rabbi
Poppenheim

Rabbi
Rosenfeld

MY BAT MITZVAH

Tuesday, September 1, 1964, was my twelfth birthday. For this special occasion, Tova and I went home to our parents. Our two brothers also came home for the Sabbath. By this time, I was so weak and exhausted, physically and emotionally, that even my family was unable to deal with my condition. Tova was the only one who stood by my side and helped me fight.

My body looked dried out, and when I wanted to catch my breath I had to bend down to the ground. I was dizzy, my mouth was dry, and my tear ducts were all dried out. Because of this weakness I made many nervous movements with my shoulders, mouth, and other parts of my body. I had a choking sensation in my throat, and no matter how thirsty I was, I could not swallow even one sip of water. I hoped that if I stayed with my family until after the High Holy Days were over, I would get stronger and feel better.

But I did not receive the support I needed. My oldest brother Meyer impersonated me, my mother asked me to calm down and try to breathe normally, and my father kept on telling doctors that I was crazy; he wanted them to dope me up or take me away. My youngest brother, Motty, who was ten, felt sorry for me. He put his sweet little head on me and hugged me, telling me that he would help me. He was so kind to me, and was just like my sister in terms of helping me. Motty asked me to play cards with him and told me that my behavior did not bother him. He took me out for walks to the park and gave me a lot of encouragement.

I could not understand why my father failed to empathize with me; instead of helping me, he put me down and belittled me. At night, Ima took me into her arms and asked me to tell her what I was feeling. I was afraid to tell her because she was having seizures and was passing out herself, and I was afraid to hurt her. She wanted to know how she could help me breathe easier. Tova looked out for me, and if anybody started up with me she would open her mouth and shut them up. She yelled at my father and my older brother constantly, and asked my nosy neighbors to mind their own business. Since the day I was born, I always felt as if Tova were my sister and private guardian angel; without her, I would have been lost a long time ago. She loved me so much and looked out for me constantly.

On Saturday, Sept. 5, the twenty eighth day of the month of *Elul*, my father gave a *kiddush* (special party) in *shul* (synagogue) in honor of my bat mitzvah. He asked me to come with him to *shul* (synagogue) in the morning so that he could show off his *bat mitzvah* girl to his friends. But I was so small and my weight was only about seventeen kilograms. I was burning from fever and was too sick to sit up. I sat in a corner and covered myself with my father's coat because I had the chills. Everybody asked me if I was going to first grade; my father had to tell them all that I was the *bat mitzvah* girl.

When the ladies arrived, I went to Ima and she gave me some medicine to break the fever. She held me close to her and put my head on her shoulders, and kept on kissing me as tears rolled off her beautiful face. Everyone asked Ima why she was crying when she should be happy that it was my *bat mitzvah*, but my mother knew very well why. She believed that the two of us were awaiting our deaths; what she feared most of all was that I would be the one to go first.

My party itself was very nice, and all of the congregants, our neighbors and many of my friends attended. Ima invited many guests back to the house, where we felt much more comfortable. She prepared the most delicious Sabbath food, cakes, and drinks, and served the best fruits.

Yom Kippur is a day of atonement and a fast day. Now that I was officially twelve years old, I had to fast too. I wanted to fast not only because Jewish law commands it, but because I wanted to experience it like all my other friends did. They prepared themselves to fast, and I was going to do the same thing.

My father, however, was very concerned about my decision to fast. He called the doctor and asked him to tell me I was too sick and that it was very dangerous for me to fast. I was not going to argue with anyone, so I did not say anything. When *Yom Kippur* arrived, my father took a bag of food with him to *shul* (synagogue). But I was clever and went to services with my mother at another *shul* (synagogue), where I was able to *daven* (pray) with all my heart and soul. The day passed by so quickly, and I was so deep into my prayers, that before I knew it, the day was over and we all survived. We remained home until the end of the Jewish month of *Tishrei* and then returned to the *mosad*. The boys went back to their *yeshivot* (boys schools). I made up my mind that I would not kill myself because Cahana was such a sick woman. I had to plan my life in such a way that I would feel self worth. I had self respect and was very modest. I was very attractive and petite; because of my small size I received a lot of attention from friends and other people in the community. I might have been tiny, but I knew that the world is big and full of good things and much potential. I was brave, intelligent and learned, and was outstanding in sports, crafts, and all games. I figured out that there was nothing wrong with me, I just needed to stay away from people who caused me harm.

I started to take daily walks instead of sitting in the orphanage and waiting to die. During my walks I learned to meditate. I talked to *Hashem* (G-d) and asked him to help me. I thought about why I had to be away from home, and understood that no matter how difficult it was for me to be in the *mosad*, at least I had many friends to play with. Even those girls who made fun of me would invite me to play with them after I returned from school, the doctor, or my daily walks. It was hard to understand that the girls who refused to be my friends inside the building were my best friends out in the playground. I always forgave the girls because I knew that my friends liked me, but Cahana did not let them play with me.

I wanted to be part of the living and make something of myself. I also helped and played with those children who were belittled and excluded by others. I always felt a responsibility to look out for the shy and broken children. To me, nobody was retarded, nobody was stupid, and nobody was ugly. Some were nasty and mean, but the majority were beautiful children. There was one sweet, smart, educated girl named Rochme. She was kind of short, with beautiful blond braids, big blue eyes, and a gorgeous face. She was a daughter of a very well-known rabbi in *B'nei Brak*. She had a heart of gold; yet nobody wanted to play with her because she was not very clean. She became quiet and isolated. Instead of the counselors teaching her to keep herself clean, take more frequent showers, brush her teeth, and change her clothes at least three times a week, she was left isolated in her filth. What attracted me to this special girl was when she noticed that I was put to shame because of my illness or the physical or emotional abuse I suffered, she would stick up for me and would physically come in between me and the abuser. I became her friend forever; all I saw in her was beauty and a heart of gold. She was the perfect friend for me. She was very charitable, and possessed the best characteristics any Jewish child could have. She seemed like an angel sent by *Hashem* (G-d) to watch over me.

Time passed quickly, and we were now preparing to celebrate *Hanukkah*, the Festival of Lights. Tova and I packed and got ready to go to our parents' home for vacation. When we arrived home, no one was there to greet us. Ima was at the post office where she worked, Aba was at work, and the boys were not home yet from *yeshiva* (boys school). Ima always made sure that we all got together any time we had school vacation.

I was not well, and I really wanted to get help. Tova and I sat on the front porch talking to one another, when suddenly an idea popped into both of our minds. We decided to visit our family doctor in the *Kupat Cholim* (medical center) and tell him what I was going through. I wanted him to know about the situation in the *mosad* and how I felt and for him to help me. The doctor listened to me patiently, and sent me to a laboratory to have some tests done. Dr. Eizikowitz knew my family very well, and was really determined to help me.

Tova and I went to his office, where I decided to tell him about all the troubles I had in my twelve years of life and in Tova's fourteen years. There were many things that my sister and the doctor did not know, and I was glad that I was able to open up and tell somebody how I was really suffering. The doctor got up from his seat and came over to me, putting his arm on my shoulder. With a broken voice he told me, "Ahuva'le, I will help you in any way and with whatever it takes." At this point I knew that I had somebody to rely on. He then told me to return to his office on Friday when all the blood results would come back, and he would see what kind of treatment would be best for me.

On Friday morning, right after eating the breakfast Ima had prepared for us, Tova and I went to the doctor. First, we had to wait in line for a number. While waiting in line, we were planning what we would tell the doctor, and how we would go about the course of treatment he would prescribe for me. We had to wait another thirty minutes before the doctor called us in.

While sitting near the office, we had a big surprise. Our father was there, also to see the doctor. He asked us to let him come in with us, but Tova told him that she needed medication for her asthma and that she did not want him to come in. Even though my father was a good hearted man, he often failed to understand his children; we felt that we would feel better going in on our own. When the doctor called me in, I closed the door and told him that my father was waiting outside to see him and wanted to come in with us, but we refused to let him in. I asked him to tell my father that we came because Tova needed her medications. The doctor gave me a big smile and promised to give my father that message.

The doctor asked us to take a seat, and he reviewed my blood work and all the other tests that were done. He lifted his eyebrows and then took a deep breath. He read through the results and told me the reason I felt so weak was because I had very little iron in my body and was very anemic. He was trying to figure out why I was losing so much blood and iron, and told me to take iron pills every single day. I told him again about my fears, my dreams, my life in the *mosad*, my doctor visits, the abuse I suffered, and everything that was bottled up inside me.

Dr. Eizikowitz listened with a lot of patience and let me talk as long as I wanted. He looked at me and at Tova and then told us that we were very brave girls and very smart for coming in. Because we had the courage to speak up and express our feelings, he would help us right away. He asked Tova to allow him to listen to her lungs and see how she was managing with her asthma. She was wheezing, so he prescribed medication for her and asked her to go see the nurse for an asthma treatment.

While we went for the treatment, Dr. Eizikowitz called another doctor in *Ramat Gan*. He gave him a little history, and asked him to see us that same day. Tova and I thanked the doctor profusely and took the bus to the other clinic to meet a psychologist, a neurologist, and a hematologist. We walked into a large white building, and were instructed to go to the second floor. A tall doctor opened the door, and with a smile on his face, invited us into his office. He asked me to change into a hospital gown, and told me that he was going to call in two other doctors, a team that would try to help me. Tova kept on telling me not to hide anything so that they could treat me properly. I was so anxious to be well, that I was even ready to check into a mental institution.

After I had changed and was ready to be seen by the doctor, a very sweet, middle-aged nurse came in and introduced herself to us. She told me that she wanted to take my vital signs and do some blood work; she also wanted to take an x-ray of my chest, head and spine and an IVP, a test to check my kidneys and urinary tract. I had no idea why she wanted me to have so many tests, but she explained to me that I was seeing the best doctors who needed to run more tests before they could diagnose and treat me. I had the tests, and when everything was finished, she asked me to follow her back to the doctors' office. The nurse took my weight and height, and then asked me to lie down so she could run an EKG test on my heart.

I asked the nurse to tell my sister to wait outside while the doctors were talking to me because I had many things to tell the doctors that I did not want her to hear. She had seen and heard more than any child should. I felt that I was old enough to speak for myself, and I had to learn to trust somebody else besides my sister.

The three doctors were standing behind the door discussing the conversation they had with Dr. Eizikowitz. They all came into the office, shook my hand and introduced themselves to me. Doctor A told me that he spoke to Dr. Eizikowitz, and he knew my story, but he asked me to answer all their questions and guaranteed that I would not go home disappointed. First, the psychiatrist congratulated me for having the wisdom and the guts to come forward and seek help. The hematologist told me that as soon as he could help me get my blood and iron levels back, I would feel stronger. The neurologist, however, was still concerned about the swelling I had on my brain and wanted to make sure that when I left his office, I would be able to go home to a safe environment.

Each of the doctors had a pad and pen in his hands ready to take notes. They also reassured me that they had enough time and that there was no reason for them to rush. I felt better already knowing that for the first time in twelve years some wonderful people were ready to listen to my story and take my problems seriously. I gave them a big smile, and told the doctors that if they had the time for me and were ready to hear and believe my story, I would tell them everything. I started by telling them where I was born and that I was a child of survivors. I told them how old I was when I was taken to the orphanage, when and why I was abused and about the horror I was going through. I told them about my illness and my vision, but most of all that my nerves were weak and that I was afraid to sleep or eat. I told them that the worst part of my illness was the strange things I did in order to catch my breath. I told them that my family was angry with me for my acting the way I did and that my brother was laughing at me.

I suddenly burst into tears, and Tova immediately came in. She did not ask me why I was crying, but simply took me into her arms and hugged me. She also started to cry. The doctors waited patiently for me to get my act together, and the psychiatrist told me that part of my healing had already begun. They all hugged me and promised to take good care of me. I told them that my throat was choking me, I had pressure in my eyes, my headaches were intolerable, and my breathing was heavy. I called out, "Help me, I am frightened; I want to go away where nobody will hurt me again."
The neurologist looked into and checked the pressure in my eyes. He also looked into my throat and squeezed it a bit, asking me to swallow. He asked me to drink some water and saw that I was choking. He tested my reflexes and agreed that I had weakness in my body. A lab technician brought in the report of my blood count, and the radiologist brought in my x-rays. The doctors asked me to get dressed, and then asked Tova to sit with me in the waiting room while they reviewed my test results.

After a half-hour wait, the nurse called me in and the doctors went over the results with Tova and me. The hematologist told me that I needed a blood transfusion; he also wanted me to get iron injections. He said he would refer me back to Hadassah Hospital, so I could be treated near the orphanage. The neurologist prescribed steroids for me; he also referred me to the hospital's neurological unit. The psychologist advised me to take one tablet three times a day, and wanted to see me before I went back to Jerusalem. He promised me that if I took the daily iron shots, had a blood transfusion, and took the medications he gave me, I would feel much stronger, and no one would laugh at me again. I did as he said.

I returned to the clinic to meet my psychiatrist, who did some exercises with me to ease my fears, and one month later, I felt much better. This was the best thing that could have happened to me.

Neither my parents nor my brothers knew about my visit with the doctors and the medications I was taking. Tova kept all of my medications in the bag where she kept hers. We got home about half an hour before the Sabbath began, and as soon as I arrived, I started cleaning the house. Tova and Motty went to do last minute shopping, and I set the Sabbath table and prepared the candles for lighting. When Ima got home from work, everything was ready for the Sabbath. The boys, having already showered, polished everyone's shoes, and Tova and I went to take showers. I even remembered to warm up the food Ima had cooked in the morning before she went to work, and I also prepared boiling water for Ima to have coffee on Shabbat morning.

Ima was so proud of us when she walked into the house, which smelled of food. The table was set, and all Ima had to do was take a shower and light Shabbat candles. I handed a towel to Ima and asked her to take a shower and lie down. She came home from work exhausted, dizzy, and with a headache, so Tova and I prepared a clean bed for her. Tova took off her shoes and socks, I placed a pillow under her head, and when the men went to *shul* (synagogue), we climbed into bed with her. She kissed us and fell asleep; we left her room and let her sleep until the men came back from *shul* (synagogue). After she rested for an hour, Ima felt better, and we had a great Sabbath, laughing, singing and playing. On Shabbat morning we all went to *shul* (synagogue) together, and in the evening took a walk to meet neighbors and friends. We had a great time and a great vacation.

I went back to Dr. Eizikowitz for a blood transfusion and for iron shots, and was set to return to the *mosad*. On Sunday morning we packed our bags, and went back to our respective schools and *yeshivas* (boys schools). Five weeks after returning to the *mosad*, I felt much better. I would visit my doctor in Ramat Gan and then go back to Jerusalem on the evening train. I was not as frightened as I was before, and started to feel more in control. The world seemed much brighter and the only thing that didn't was my rear end from all of my iron injections.

I never told anyone when I had a doctors appointment; the only people who knew about them were Tova and Hass-Neiny, since there were certain tests that I needed adult consent for. Cahana kept on making appointments for me to see Dr. Sabo, but I had an agreement with him that these appointments would be strictly between the two of us. He also received a letter from my doctors in Ramat Gan, so he understood my situation better and was willing to cooperate with me. When and if Cahana insisted on going with me to the doctor, he would ask her to sit outside, and told her that he knew my story and could handle the situation without any more input from her.

When the doctor finally realized with whom he was dealing, he looked at me differently; he too helped me look at life from a more positive angle. Whenever I had to go for a spinal tap or an angiogram, I would ask a friend or my counselor whom I loved and trusted to go with me. I did not want Tova to suffer so much from my problems, so I tried not to tell her too much. She had such a rough childhood, and I wanted her to have a decent life. I felt that it was time to look out for my sister, who had given up her childhood for me.

My visits to Hadassah Hospital were very exhausting, and the tests I had were painful. The students used to study me and used me as a guinea pig. I used to spend a minimum of eight hours in the clinic because the students wanted to learn. I begged them to leave me alone, but the professor would ask me to stay just a few more minutes. He always told me that by allowing students to study my case, I could help them find a cure for other patients who had the same disease.

I used to cry and get angry because I had no strength to stand for these hectic experiments. The doctors told me that my disease is usually one that they see more often in elderly people. Even though some children also suffer from papiledema, it is not as common, and they wanted to learn from my case by experimenting on me. But I must still thank the doctors, nurses, and even the unit clerks for helping me fight the disease and for being there to give me all the emotional and physical support I needed.

The doctors and nurses would often invite me to the cafeteria for a snack, and this was the perfect time for me to express my feelings and be open with them. The entire staff got involved with my care, and everybody was very anxious to help. I remember the slices of cheesecake they used to buy for me. I was always very shy to eat outside of my own environment, but these wonderful, good hearted doctors taught me to feel confident in whatever I did. By eating with them, I showed them what type of foods made me choke.

One day, I was invited by a dietitian to eat with her. She asked me to taste all kinds of foods, and then wrote up a diet and instructions for Hass-Neiny. The best food for me was cooked, blended carrots, which I loved very much. The cook was so kind and made me all kinds of carrot dishes. The eye doctor was glad that I ate carrots, and also prescribed vitamin E for my eyes. I must say that it worked.

But the food was not the main reason why I was excited to eat in the hospital cafeteria. What I liked about it was being able to sit at the table with normal human beings, and learning to eat with respect and class. I learned to speak more maturely and was no longer shy when speaking to people who were above my level. I was also glad that they asked me questions that I would have never volunteered information about otherwise, and they always gave me good advice. I was very thankful to G-d for introducing me to fine people with whom I was not afraid to share my painful secrets. I remember my mother telling me that it is not a shame to cry because tears heal. So even when I was crying, it was okay. When I learned to opened my heart, I learned to open my mind, and eventually my mouth.

When I reached the sixth grade, I had very funny teachers. One of my classmates, Sheva'le, had no patience to sit in class and would carry on. She told us to write down word for word what the teacher said from the minute she entered the classroom. The next day, when we had to read aloud in class, we repeated verbatim what the teacher had said the day before. One time she got upset, but my friend told her we did it to show her that we were listening to what she was saying.

Sheva'le used to cut her gums to make them bleed during class, and then would ask the teacher to allow another student to go with her to wash her mouth. Sheva'le liked me very much, and chose me to accompany her; instead of returning to class, she would take me to the ice cream store and get treats for the two of us. As much as I wanted to stay in class, I wanted to be with Sheva'le because I never felt sick in her presence. She made me run, play and eat; yet, we always did our homework. Sheva'le managed to turn a shy little girl with the lowest self-esteem into a wild, self sufficient and expressive individual. She was the best doctor I ever had.

Sheva'le could not tolerate our teacher Perl, because she used to sit with her head tilted to the side and always looked like she was falling asleep. One day Sheva'le became frustrated and asked a few girls and me to walk around the teacher's table until she got dizzy and fell asleep. We all did it, and told our teacher that she would have to sit with her head up or we would not come to class. The teacher also spoke slowly and in a very low voice, and it was very hard to hear her speak.

Perl was such a lovely and special teacher, but she was shy. I finally asked Sheva'le to stop making fun of this innocent teacher. She agreed to stop but she also avoided coming to that class. My friend, Hana, never did her homework, and was not interested in schoolwork. But during this school year, I made her study because I did not want any of my friends to distract me from my work. As

playful as I was, school was the most important thing in my life.
In 1967, our seventh-grade teacher was our sixth grade teacher's sister. Rachel was more alert and was able to teach our class better than her sister had. She tried very hard to be strict with the girls, but my classmates were born clowns. She burst into laughter every time she tried to yell at a child. Some of my friends did their homework and some did not, but I always did mine because I loved to learn. The only subject I did not like was geography; otherwise, I wanted to learn everything the school had to offer. Because my classmates did not want to learn, I got very bored in class. So, I would hand in my work and then leave class with Sheva'le.

Yehudith, the assistant principal, was also the eighth-grade teacher. I liked this woman very much, so I decided to visit her class during school hours and refused to leave it. She tried to send me back to my class, but I refused to go because I was bored and wanted to learn. When she got serious, I went back to my class. I was really upset that I did not have anything of importance to learn. I had homework that took no longer than ten minutes to complete. So, I decided to put my head down during class until I fell asleep. My teacher called Yehudith and complained about my sleeping in class. Yehudith decided to punish me, by making me go to her class. I was so happy that I jumped up and gave her a juicy kiss. She looked at me with her big eyes, and then gave me a smile and a hug and we walked together to her class. I stayed in her class for three weeks. I did all the homework she gave as well as the work from my seventh grade teacher. I participated in her class, and answered any questions that her students did not know.

Yehudith kept on reminding me that I was in her class as a punishment and that I would have to return to my class eventually. I told her that I knew that and was just trying to do my work. I also told her I was following all her assignments. During recess, she called me into her office and asked me what she should do with me. She knew that I was bored in school. I even took out my homework to show her that I did both her and my seventh grade teacher's assignments, which was not enough for me. The more I learned the more I wanted to know.

While sitting in her class, the girls behind me would play with my braids, which I loved. Aviva, who was one minute my best friend and the next my biggest enemy, was excited to have me in her class because I always knew the answers. She got in trouble for playing with my hair, but I told her to continue doing it because I liked it. I used to feel relaxed every time someone played with my braids.

Yehudith made me go back to my class because she did not know whether to let me stay in the eighth grade or not; once again, I refused and went back to her class. One morning, I stood near her classroom with a long face and tears in my eyes. When she came to class, she asked me why I was there. I looked into her eyes and hugged her, asking her permission to stay. I told her that I liked her very much, and that I needed to learn. I was so hungry to learn that I would do almost anything to get a better education.

Yehudith took my hand and walked me into her classroom. She asked me to sit down in the same seat where I sat the first time, and I began to learn with enthusiasm. At this time, the eighth graders were taking their final exams. I took the exams with them and scored one hundred percent on all of them. I even helped the other girls with their studies, especially my friend Rochme, who wanted so badly to pass her tests. I completed the year with the eighth graders; and while I got all A's, I was told to go back to school with my friends. In a way they were right, because I belonged with my friends; scholastically, however, I belonged in a higher grade.

MEYER'S WEDDING

During Passover 1965, Ima decided to stay with us. Hass-Neiny prepared a clean bed for her and for my baby brother Motty. Meyer also came to eat with us. My father went to stay with the Gerer *rebbe* (rabbi) in Jerusalem. Ima had cooked the most delicious food and brought it along with her to make us feel like we were home. Hass-Neiny had set up a table and chairs in Tova's room for a *seder* (Passover meal). Ima covered the table with a white tablecloth, flowers, candles, and our *seder* (Passover meal) food. Many children were pushing through the door to see us prepare a home cooked *seder* (Passover meal).

I got up to close the door so that my brothers would not feel strange among so many girls, but Ima cried and told me in a pleasant voice never to close the door on children or adults. She put some food on a big plate to give to the children to share. When I saw their eyes, I kissed my mother and told her what a beautiful thing she had done. The girls took the plate, and smiled joyously at my mother. One girl thanked her on behalf of all the children, and they left the room. This was an important lesson for me.

My brothers went to the Gerer *shul* (synagogue) for services, and then came to eat with us in Tova's room. My father ate with all his male cousins and friends who had come to see the *rebbe* (rabbi). Meyer made *Kiddush* (prayer over the wine) and started to read the *Haggadah* (the story of Passover). Motty, the youngest child, recited the *Ma Nishtana* (Four Questions). After sitting down to eat, Ima announced that our brother Meyer was engaged. This was the reason why she wanted the whole family to come together for the holidays. We did not know how to react because he was only eighteen years old and was still in the army, but we wished him "mazel tov" and gave him our support.

We enjoyed every moment of this Passover evening. After our meal, we all went together to escort Meyer to the Gerer *Yeshiva* (boys school), and there he slept in the same room with our father and other relatives. The men wanted a blessing from the *rebbe* (rabbi). Most of the rooms in the *mosad* were empty because the girls went away for the holidays; nevertheless, it was not appropriate for a grown man to sleep in a girls' dormitory. Motty was only ten years old, so it was okay for him to stay with us. We all slept in the same room.

On Aug. 9, 1965, Meyer got married in B'nei Brak. My mother helped his bride with her attire for the wedding, and Aba prepared Meyer in his cousin's house. Meyer was dressed in a black *beketche* (kaftan), a *spodik* (tall fur hat), and new shoes; he looked stunning. Ima dressed the bride in a beautiful wedding gown and jewelry she had purchased for her. She made their wedding a day to remember. Ima combed my hair and put white ribbons in my braids. I wore a white and light-blue colored dress, white stockings and black shoes. As soon as our neighbors saw the black shiny taxi stopping near our house, they all ran and pushed through the crowd to see and bless the bride. My brother left for the wedding from our cousin's house. We had a difficult time pushing through the crowd to get into the taxi, but we made it and went over to the hall. When we got there, the bride was sitting on her throne and the music was playing; slowly, the crowd filled up the hall.

There was something fishy going on, when it came time for my parents to lead the groom and bride (*hatan* and *kallah*) to their *chuppa* (wedding canopy). We noticed that my parents were standing behind strangers who would lead them. When we asked our parents why they were not leading Meyer to the *chuppa*, they called us aside and told us that they had gotten divorced. We were shocked because we had no clue about this. My father held a day and a night job for many years, and so did my mother. She would send us to our father so he could see us, and he kept on telling us wonderful things about our mother and how pretty she was. They were two beautiful people who loved one another, but ultimately we were not surprised about this chain of events because we believed they did it for our sake. They were both emotionally falling apart, and it was better for them to heal and go on with their lives as individuals. Their lives remained our lives, and we never felt that they were truly separated. The couple got married with dignity, and both of my parents, while they did not lead Meyer to the *chuppa*, stood underneath it without anybody noticing that there was a problem.

I did not have any fun at the wedding, because I was assigned to stand near the bar and watch over the presents. I was unable to dance, eat, or speak to anyone. Mr. Schwartz, the band leader, positioned his band near the bar, and the music blasted through my head the whole night. I would have been better off staying in the *mosad* than attending my brother's wedding, where I did not feel like a family member. There was not even one picture with me in it; the photographer refused to take one of me. Everybody else had a good time, but the musicians played the same songs over and over, and after a while I got bored listening to them.

After the wedding, I did not want to go back to the orphanage. I wanted to be in a school near my home and my parents. My father started to look into other schools, but they all refused to take me in because I came from a Jerusalem school that was considered to be one of the finest. We decided to look into a boarding school in the same city as my parents, but this institution would only take me in for the summer. I decided to stay there for the summer, hoping I would be allowed to remain longer. One week later, I decided to leave because there were bed bugs that made my body itch and I did not like the smell of the building, which was ugly and depressing.

I learned to appreciate the situation I had in Jerusalem, and decided to think about going back. My father wanted to leave me home, but my mother got mad and asked me to go back to Jerusalem. As a child, I did not understand why my mother, who loved me so much, wanted me to be away from home; she was so brave and wanted to protect me from harm. She was sick and worked very hard, and my father was emotionally not responsible for his acts. I belonged in Jerusalem, in the home where I grew up since I was five years old. My school there was getting ready to dismiss the children for a vacation that had begun a few days before *Rosh Hashana* and would continue until the end of the month.

As for Meyer and his wife, the young couple went to live in Gamzu, on a small farm near Lod. Meyer was still serving in the army, and his wife was a part time teacher for a few children who lived on the farm. Most of the time she was busy taking care of her obese mother who refused to get out of bed and insisted on eating in a horizontal position, as well as her six siblings who were still very young. Her elderly father worked on the farm, milking cows and selling them and their milk; when he came home, however, he hardly had anything to eat. Her oldest brother was the only one in a *yeshiva* (boys school) away from home; the others were herding the sheep, goats and cows. Her baby sister was a gorgeous girl with blond hair, blue eyes, and freckles on her tanned skin.

That same summer, the two of them invited me to visit them on the farm. I had a great time playing with my sister-in-law's siblings and with the animals. I got so attached to these animals that I spent most of the day herding the cows and watching her father work in the barn.

On the same farm lived a family that I knew very well. Their identical twin daughters, Chava and Libbe were in the same orphanage that I was. The girls were part of a beautiful family; yet they were in the orphanage because their parents wanted them to have a good Jewish education. The twins continually invited me to their house. We took walks every evening, and I would spend most of the Sabbath in their house, where I ate at least one meal. I really enjoyed when they took me on horse rides and we visited other farms. I enjoyed every moment I was there.

I stayed in my brother's house for two weeks, and then I

returned to Ima's house together with Meyer and his wife. When we got home, I served the cooked food Ima had prepared for us. While we were eating, I thanked my brother and his wife very much for letting me visit them, and told them that I hoped I could visit them again some day. But my sister-in-law did not like what I said, and became angry enough to hit me. I felt as if I had returned to my own little island and no one would give me a chance to have a life, a place to go to when I needed a change of environment. Without saying another word, I took my belongings, and went to Ima at work to ask her for some money so that I could return to the *mosad*. No matter how miserable my life was there, it was a place I was always able to return to. I felt that I was born with a mission and my mission began in the orphanage. I just needed to find out what that mission was.

Tova was supposed to come home the next day for her vacation. After she saw me and heard what I went through she decided to stay in the orphanage, where we celebrated the High Holy Days. After the holidays and after Meyer and his wife went back to the farm, Tova and I went home to visit our parents for a few days. On the first day of the month of *Heshvan*, I entered the eighth grade. This year, my favorite teacher Yehudith became one of the high school teachers. We had an excellent group of children, and had a lot of fun. When it came to school, I was the happiest person in the world. This was the only place I did not feel threatened and where there was nothing to fear. In the orphanage and wherever I went I experienced violence, but in school I felt as if I were in heaven. We started to study for our finals and to complete the work necessary to graduate from the eighth grade. Most girls were thirteen and a half or fourteen years old. I was only thirteen, because my birthday is in September. I was the shortest, skinniest girl, but I had a zest for life. Most children spoiled me because they thought I was cute and very small in their eyes.

After the first day of school, my friend Hana and I went to a photographer. When I look at that picture, I can see the difference between my size and that of the other girls. I looked as if I was ten years old. In school we played and learned and had a great time, especially when one of the girls in our class got engaged. She was only fourteen, and I did not like the idea of a child that age getting married and having kids. The other girls were not surprised at all. Her parents simply told her that she was engaged; she would only find out who the *hatan* (groom) was on the night of her wedding.

I knew that my staying at *Benot Yerushalayim* might not lead me anywhere in life. But the seeds and strong roots they planted in my mind and my heart would have an everlasting impact on me. I started to study on my own, going to the public library to learn English, which was against the rules of the school. I read all types of materials and started to wonder how I could become someone of value to society and the world.

I looked at my life during this time a bit differently than I did when I was younger. The idea came to me when I drank a bitter cup of coffee; when I added sugar, it became sweet. My life was the same. My life also seemed bitter; all I had to find was a little taste of something that would make my life more fulfilling and rewarding, something that would give me a reason to live.

For example, at the age of ten, when I first became sick, my father hired one of the counselors to take me out for a few hours and give me one on one attention. When she got married, another woman took over. She invited me to her house, and I taught her crafts and songs and told her many stories. She grew to like me a lot and we became best friends. At the age of fourteen, I did not feel that I needed a babysitter any longer, nor that my father should have to pay for one. I told her that if she wanted to remain my friend it was okay, but she should look for another job. She was disappointed but understood and was willing to stay friends. Slowly, I stopped visiting her, and started going my own way.

There was a girl in my class named Esther who sat behind me. One day we were taking an exam, and she kept asking me for all the answers. Our teacher saw her doing it but did not say anything. After a while, I got annoyed and screamed at her that I was up the whole night studying so that I would be able to pass the test; I asked her to study and take her exam. She got angry at me because I did not let her cheat, and cursed me out. I told her that whatever she was cursing me would come back to her. I got up from my seat and asked the teacher why she did not say anything when she could see how this girl was disrupting my concentration. She did not have anything to say in response, so I decided to leave the class and go back to the *mosad.* My friend Hana followed me, so our teacher came outside and called us to come back to school. We decided to ignore her and we continued walking. She called us again and wanted to apologize to me, but I continued to go on and let her scream. Hana felt bad for our teacher and asked me to say something to her. I turned around and told my teacher that I would be back tomorrow. I also told her that I would have to report this problem to the school's principal and that I would not let her get away with this incident. I was tired and I made sure to learn my material; this girl could have done the same thing.

Hana and I decided to climb a very high mountain instead of going back to the *mosad.* As exhausted as we were, we made ourselves comfortable on a big rock. We took out our lunches, and ate with hearty appetites under the sunny blue sky. We were so excited to spend the afternoon on top of the mountain that we did not realize we were baking in the sun. We found this out much later.

Hana and I recalled our ten years in the *mosad.* We laughed, cried, and talked with mixed feelings about the experience. We felt that we were beginning a healing process. I learned to speak up for myself, I was no longer afraid to tell others how they made me feel, and I was not going to let anybody belittle me. I was intelligent and a good student and I had a lot to offer this world.

I stood up and looked down the mountain. I saw the whole city of Jerusalem. The view was amazing. The whole world looked so bright and beautiful. I flashed a big smile, looked up to the heavens and praised *Hashem* (G-d) for creating such a beautiful city. Suddenly, an idea popped into my mind. I thought that if I was on a mountain and could see the entire city with my naked eyes, then G-d, who sits in heaven, must be able to see the entire world. We stayed on the mountain for four hours, and then went back to the *mosad*.

When we arrived back, we saw many girls gathered outside as if something had happened. We rushed into the crowd and discovered that Esther, the same girl who cursed me in school, had fallen and cut her hand very badly. She was taken to the hospital and received one hundred and fifty stitches. I felt very bad for her, but knew that *Hashem* (G-d) has his way of paying people back. In a way I felt guilty because she cursed me and I told her that the curse would return to her. But then I did not see any reason to feel bad, because I did not hurt her or anyone else.

That same night, while I was studying for exams in my hiding room, I started daydreaming. I saw my whole life as if I were watching a movie. I decided to forgive my mother for placing me in this home, and I forgave all the children who might have hurt me over the years. The only person I was unable to forgive was Gertrude Cahana, the woman who turned my life into a living hell. I was glad that my father was not mad at my mother for placing us in this home, and things started to seem better. I was so deep in my thoughts that I did not realize I was crying.

Suddenly, I heard a knock on the door, making me snap out of my dream. It was Tova. My dear sister wanted to check on me and see if I was okay. As I got up from the floor, I noticed a mirror on the wall behind the door. I looked into the mirror, and I saw a beautiful girl looking at me. I said hi to her, she said hi to me, and I told her, "I love you." She said, "I love you." Whatever I said, she said the same thing. Any gesture I did, she did. I suddenly realized that it was my own reflection in the mirror, and this reflection was my best friend. I learned that I must connect with my innermost and outermost feelings and create harmony within my soul, body, and spirit. I needed to love myself; instead of feeling sorry for myself, I should feel sorry for other children and help them. I did not need somebody else to take care of me anymore, I needed to take care of myself.

On Sept. 14, 1966, there was nobody to celebrate my fourteenth birthday with me. Today, Cahana decided to change my room, and placed me with a mentally and emotional disturbed girl named Lusha. At the age of fourteen, she would wet her bed and spit on other children, her clothes, the floor, inside the closets, on the beds, and wherever we went. She disgusted me so much that I ended up sleeping in my hiding room on the floor or sitting up. She used to put her wet underwear in my closet or on my bed; she also took off her wet linens and put them on my bed. I tried to tell my counselor about it, but she too was afraid of Cahana.

Lusha's sister Rachel was my sister's roommate, but she was a fine girl who was very neat and charitable. She told me that she would give me some space in her closet for my clothes, and invited me to sleep in her room. I shared a broken bed with Tova, but I had two nice roommates and liked them all. Tova slept on one side of the bed and I slept on the other, but our bottoms fell into the same hole. It did not matter to us how good the bed was. We had to push ahead and pray that we would come out alive from this place. I never had a full night's sleep and I was always tired, but I decided to take these sleepless nights in my hiding room to write a book. I kept a daily diary, but part of the diary was lost or stolen. But because I was very organized, I also had many notes written in my notebooks and was able to write down all my memories and experiences. Whenever I used to study or write in my hiding room, I always felt as if I was being watched by angels. I never felt alone or afraid again.

Nights in the *mosad* were very scary. We would hear the metal doors banging from the wind, and sometimes I would see a man running out of the building. Other times we were able to hear shooting from the army or from nearby Arabs; there were also troubled children who used to scare other children. I also saw children sleeping together and climbing into other children's beds for emotional support and because they were missing the warmth, touch and security of a parent or sibling. The counselors were locked in their rooms and did not care how we felt.

It came to a point where I did not want to disturb my sister, who needed to have her own space. I started looking for other girls who would let me sleep in their rooms. I was always afraid to sleep. It was obvious that the others did not want me in their rooms; even my best friend Hana, who spent days and nights with me, did not want me to be her roommate. There were many nights when I locked myself in my hiding room and, sitting against the wall, would fall asleep for an hour or less.

The good news was that I was not the only child who was afraid to sleep at night, so in that sense, I did not feel alone. I wanted to sleep next to my mother and put my head in her arms, to feel her heartbeat and warmth, but I had to stay in the *mosad* and hope that one day I would find a man who would give me a loving home. At this age it was very normal for the girls to think about marriage; many girls got married at the age of fifteen.

I stopped paying attention to Cahana, but she did not like that I was becoming independent and could take care of myself. A normal child would expect to be praised for her maturity and independence; Cahana, on the other hand, would beat me up without cause. She also sent Rachel Schwarts, Ita, and Malka, counselors who were orphans before they became *mosad* counselors, and other children who came from very dysfunctional families to go up to my room and Tova's room to find any clues that they could use against me. This was because I did not want to talk to her, and I refused to tell her about my doctor's appointments.

These three counselors used to come up every day to my room; they would tie me up and beat me until I was bleeding all over. Cahana stood by and was very pleased to see me all bloody. As they pulled my braids, the counselors would hit me against the stone floor.

One day, I tried to run away from them, but I felt chest pains. One of my friends took me to the doctor, who told me that I had pneumonia. When she found out that I had pneumonia, she told Cahana, who called my mother to tell her that I was making myself sick; she wanted her to come to force me to go to school.

Before my mother arrived, Cahana noticed that I had a fever. She pulled me out of bed and into the hallway near the stairs. Rachel Schwarts hit me hard and then threw me down a whole flight of stone stairs. I hurt my spine and my entire body. Tova fought them to stop them from killing me, but they grabbed her by her braid and beat her up pushing her face against the floor.

My mother came after the fact, and brought along a magazine, which had an article about how to survive in this world. She wanted us to become smart and know what was going on in this world. Ima saw what was going on, but she was ill and afraid to say anything to these people; all she did was ask us to read and act accordingly. These beasts waited until Ima left and then bruised my sister until she was unable to breathe. Although I was severely injured, I got up and took Tova's asthma pump, and pumped in some medicine to open her airway.

I looked through the newspaper and saw that Ima had circled names of agencies and organizations that could possibly help us. When we went to them, we discovered that they would place us in institutions where there was no religious atmosphere. We were afraid we were going to sin and that G-d would punish us for slipping away from our religion; we were that brainwashed. If the courts had known about this abuse, we would have been taken away against our will. Ima tried to do everything in her power to save our lives, but she was unable to do more than she already had done. We sat in our room on the bed, hugging each other and crying. The only ones who heard us were the same people who made us cry.

Our friends knew about this abuse, but were afraid to say anything or get involved. My friend Rochme was one person who was not afraid. She kicked the counselors back, bit them hard until she left a mark, and cursed them. She stood in front of us, and when anybody raised a hand to us, she blocked us and asked them to hit her instead. We lived day by day, minute by minute, and in between we prayed to G-d and hoped that we would be redeemed one day. Tova and I knew that the only way to survive this horrible life was to stay close and love one another, no matter what happened. At this time, I felt that if Tova died in the *mosad*, I would go with her; if I were to die first, though, I wanted her to run away and change her looks and identity so that nobody would hurt her again. But Tova knew that she was my older sister and that she had to stay strong for my sake.

Despite my miserable life, I was the kind of child who always smiled at everybody. I played with the children even when I was short of breath. I was very attractive, and deep inside, I had a very happy spirit. Each time a new child came into the *mosad*, she would look at me; in two minutes we became good friends. But as soon as Cahana saw me talking to a new friend she would separate us and that was the end of the relationship inside the *mosad*. At school they were my best friends, and we remained friends after we got married.

One night, one of the new girls, Shula, fell very ill. She had a high fever and stomach-ache and was vomiting. I sat on her bed with her and held her head on my lap; with my hands I massaged her belly. I was afraid to leave her alone, and she needed to get medical help. Shula was screaming because she felt so sick. I took a cold washcloth and applied it to her forehead, and I ran to Hass-Neiny for help. Hass-Neiny came immediately; in the meantime, I went down to the kitchen and brought up a pitcher with fresh tea, in case she needed a drink.

When I came back, Hass-Neiny noticed that I was crying. She asked me why; I told her my friend was sick and needed help. Hass-Neiny hugged me and said to us, "stay friends." Shula told her that Cahana would not let her be my friend, but Hass-Neiny responded that she should be strong and count on me as the best friend she could ever have. Shula remained my friend and no longer listened to anyone else. Hass-Neiny asked me to go back to sleep and told me that she would make Shula feel better. After Hass-Neiny left, I went into Shula's bed and stayed with her until she fell asleep and I saw that she looked better. The next morning, Shula was taken to the hospital with appendicitis and stayed in the hospital for one week. As soon as she felt better, she began to stick up for me and helped me overcome my pain.

One day, we had a play in the *mosad.* We invited the community to come to our show. In this play, I had a small part where I was supposed to be killed. But before my death, I had to call out, "I want the money, I want to live in peace, I want the money, and not to suffer and die." As soon as I said these few words, one of the soldiers pretended to put a knife into my heart. Then, I threw myself down on the floor, where I supposedly died. I was suddenly overwhelmed with tremendous fear, I felt as if I was really dying. Throughout my life, I asked everyone to just let me live in peace. I did not want to die, but other people wanted me dead.

At this point I had a flashback from the age of twelve, when one of my father's cousins asked me to come with him for a car ride. He took me to the cemetery and then opened the door slightly, driving fast in circles. I was screaming and I asked him to stop driving so fast. I told him that I was going to fall out, but he ignored me. I felt that he was trying to get rid of me. I never told anyone about the incident because nobody believed my stories. Even my own sister, who took such good care of me, did not believe me when I told her about other incidents that had happened to me. I believed that G-d was my witness and that I did not have to prove the truth to any human being. I kept many secrets because I was born a target for trouble, and did not need to cause more problems.

While I was on the floor, my hands and legs were shaking. I was anxious to get up to make sure that I was still alive, but I had to wait for the curtain to close. In the next part of the play, a little girl named Malka'le sang the song, "*Hamalach Hagoel Oti*," ("May the angel who redeems me from all evil bless all the children and may my name be declared upon them and the name of our forefathers Avraham and Yitzhak"). She had such a beautiful voice and touched everybody's heart. One very special heart she touched was mine. The song gave me new hope and strength.

We also had a group of very good dancers in the play. The children were very talented and creative. A female accordion player also performed. She played so nicely, and I felt jealous because I also wanted to play a musical instrument. I went over to her and asked her if I could play the accordion. She told me that she would be available the next day, and invited me to visit her in her home, where she let me practice on the accordion. I fell in love with this instrument, and I started to save money so that I could buy one for myself.

Passover, 1966 was just around the corner, and all the children started to clean their rooms and the rest of the facility. One day before school vacation, all the children lined up near the clothing room to receive new clothes and shoes for the holiday. Tova and I also stood in line, but when our turn came, Hass-Neiny told us that Cahana had ordered her not to give us anything. I moved away from the line and stood on the side, but my sister would not move until she got something. Hass-Neiny did her a favor and gave her a pair of stockings; the others each got a new dress, shoes, underwear, and stockings. Tova started to cry, and we decided to fight for our rights. I went to Cahana's office and spit straight into her ugly face, and my sister went to complain to Rabbi Rosenfeld. All he managed to give us was a pair of stockings for me and a nightgown for my sister.

I told my sister not to cry. We went up to our room and packed our belongings, and went to Ima's home for the holidays. On the train from Katamon to Tel Aviv, there were many other children who were going home or to visit a relative or friend. The girls were so happy to leave for vacation. They stood near the windows and sang, and they were laughing and having a great time. The girls called out from the train to the herds of animals and to the Arabs who worked on the mountains or farms. We saw cows, horses, donkeys, sheep, and goats. Little children were waving to us and the girls waved back at them. Tova and I were sitting on a bench, with our heads leaning toward each another.

On the train, when I tried to talk, I suddenly felt terrible chest pains and was unable to catch my breath. My sister got scared because I turned blue and started to pass out. Tova pushed two aspirins down my throat with some water she had taken along with her, and pumped in some medicine from the little device she used for her asthma. My chest pain was better and I was able to breathe again. She leaned her sweet head against mine and we sat close to each other until we got to Tel Aviv.

Because of the tension that was building up between my parents that was due to my mother's failing health, our Passover vacation was not the greatest, but we wanted to stay for the first few days before heading back to the *mosad*. When we did return the building was quiet and we had a room to ourselves. The rest of the children came back one month later, and the normal routine resumed.

REACHING THE HIGHEST SPIRITUAL LEVEL

Living in an orphanage for so many years was not a good experience. It did, however, give me many years to plan how to redeem myself from my misery. I had to stop pitying myself. I knew that I could take control by helping other children who really needed it. When I graduated from eighth grade I wanted to be in the teachers' program; the principal, however, wanted me to be in the sewing program. We learned some biblical studics in school; secular studies were not required and there were only limited offerings. I did not argue with anyone, because I knew that if I really wanted to learn, I would find a way to become more educated. Learning was my life. I loved school, and the ninth grade was a pleasure.

My teacher always had a sweet smile on her face, and was a delight, and I felt her love. Yehudith invited me often to her house, where together we would mark the exams. She always marked my exam and never showed it to me until she handed them out in class. She made me feel important and gave me a lot of respect, and I loved her for it. She made me want to live and look ahead to a brighter future, as well as to study and actually know what I was learning.
I never told anyone about the angel who learned with me every night because they would think I was hallucinating, but my gift of knowledge came directly from *Hashem* (G-d) and his angels. When I came to school I knew everything. As soon as school was over, I ran to do my homework, which I loved. I felt that learning was a challenge and it helped me get through life. I also liked to play alot and I was always chosen to participate in all the games. I was not a nerd, I was just in love with learning, and I knew that the faster I completed my work, the more time I would have to play. If I had to study for a test, I would first do my homework, then go to play; after supper, I would take a shower, lie down on my bed and study.

Most of the time I would help other children with their homework. Until the age of fourteen, I was the most popular girl when it came to sports, crafts, Chinese checkers, table games, and many other activities. I was also known as the best student. Every evening, many children would gather around me and I would give a lecture in biblical studies. I felt as if I had become a rabbi. I knew the Torah inside out, because I studied and because an angel used to study with me.

One evening, Rabbi Poppenheim held a lecture for the oldest girls in the sewing room. I wanted to hear what the rabbi had to say, so I stood on the side and listened to his beautiful lecture. I was caught by surprise when he told the group that he was very impressed to hear that one of the ninth grade girls had started to give Torah lectures. He said he wondered why this girl had such an influence over children who had never wanted to learn. One of the girls, who was also a counselor, called out and mentioned my name. She also told him that she had never heard a *d'var Torah* (words of Torah) from any female as she had heard from me. Another girl called out, "Rabbi Shlomo, she is a genius."

I felt great that I was recognized in such a beautiful area of my life. I was always known as the best in sports, ball games, and in school. I was rich with friends, love, beauty, and I was good-hearted and devoted to all who needed me. What went wrong, was being so severely abused by an individual who made people hate me for no reason. Although I was very social and outgoing, I always minded my own business and never attempted to talk about others. In fact, as soon as I heard anyone talking about other children, I would move away and go to Tova in tears, asking her why people liked to say bad things about others. I could never understand it.

The next day, Cahana attended parent teacher meetings that were held in school. When she came back, she called me into her office. Since I was afraid to be alone with her, I told her that she could only talk to me in the presence of my counselor or one of the rabbis. I started to walk up the stairs, and she followed me. She fell down. I stopped to see if she needed any help getting up; she looked at me and told me that she fell on her nose. I don't know why, but I started to giggle and could not stop. I thought that it was funny how she felt sorry for her nose. Cahana asked me to listen to what she had to tell me. She received a remarkable report from school, where everyone praised my wisdom. I thanked her very much for telling me the good news. Cahana then called me back and told me that she received a phone call and a registered letter from Hadassah Hospital, the neurologist wanted to admit me right away. He got back the results from an angiogram I had two days earlier, and wanted to run some spinal taps and other tests. I was not in the mood to go to the hospital because I did not see the point of letting the doctors poke me. I went only because Tova asked me to go. Tova called Ima, who came right away and stayed with me in the hospital for two weeks. She saw how the doctors tortured me like they would a guinea pig.

The day I came back from the hospital, some girls teased me about my health. They asked me if I was in the hospital because I had panic attacks. Cahana told the children that was the reason why I was in the hospital. I looked at them angrily and told them that one day they would regret what they were doing to me, and I walked away. Hass-Neiny made room for me in the infirmary because the doctor explained to her that I went through some difficult neurological tests; he wanted me to be observed for a few days.

I decided to rest in Tova's room so that no one would know what was going on. I went to the doctors appointment by myself, without telling anyone, and I asked the neurologist not to give the test results to anyone but me. I explained to him my situation with the beatings and still, no one was arrested for abusing me. During the day I suffered from severe headaches, and the nights seemed too long because I never slept. I sat in my hiding room all night. There I studied and prayed to *Hashem.* (G-d) I asked him to give me the wisdom and knowledge to overcome my difficult life. I asked him to send me angels to be my friends and give me words of comfort. At times I cried, and at times I laughed; at other moments I went into an hypnotic trance in which I reviewed all the events of my life. I was seeking answers, solutions and conclusions. I always had a pen and paper with me so that I could write down all my thoughts and goals. After I wrote down everything, I read it over carefully several times, making corrections each time. Whatever situation seemed terrible to me as I wrote it down the first time began to look better with perspective, and I put all my problems into focus. In my little room I thanked *Hashem* (G-d) for the positive things that had happened to me. My list was divided into two columns -- the positive and the negative.

POSITIVE

- I have my wonderful sister with me.
- I have wonderful, loving parents.
- I have three meals a day.
- I have many nice friends.
- I have a home to go to.
- I have clothes to wear.
- My doctors are kind to me.
- I have deep *bitachon* (faith) in *Hashem* (G-d).
- I feel *Hashem*'s presence all the time.

NEGATIVE

- I blame the Holocaust for depriving me, my sister and two loving brothers from having healthy parents and a normal family unit.
- I blame a Holocaust survivor for my health problems.
- I live in fear.
- I never sleep.
- I feel like a victim because I am a child of Holocaust survivors.
- I am being severely abused.
- My doctors' diagnosis scare me.
- I fear nightmares.

 Will I die?
 I fear that Ima's diseases will kill her soon.
 I fear my sister being left alone.

Writing this list made me realize that I have a lot to be thankful for, even if the bad things stand out more and are very painful and hard to live with. I also learned how to use these exercises as a healing tool by analyzing each situation separately to determine what was positive and negative. I kept myself busy with another healing method: writing down a list of things that troubled me and putting it in an essay form. I wrote down a list of twenty words in a row. The words I chose were the first ones that popped into my mind. For instance: *telephone*; *brush*; *shoes*; *teeth*; *table*; *window*; *children; fear; war; ear; drums; orange; strong; cross; brace; ringing; goat; sandals; hair; change.*
Here is the essay I composed:
The *telephone* rang while I was about to *brush* my hair. I grabbed my *shoes* in my hands and jumped off the *table* I was standing on and ran to answer the *telephone*. While talking on the phone, I noticed some *children* looking at me through their *window*. Somehow, I felt that they had something to tell me. I was suddenly caught by *fear* when I heard the sound of *war*. I said goodbye to my mother, whom I was on the line with, and removed the receiver from my *ear*. The sound I heard was similar to the sound of *drums*. Suddenly, I saw an *orange* ball of fire cross our *window*; a loud and *strong* explosion could be heard across the city. I went into the powder room and removed my back *brace* in case I had to run for my life. The bell was *ringing* and the sound of the siren warned us, so I knew that I had to hide in the cellar. At this time, the milkman arrived, bringing a few cases of *goat* milk, which the children liked very much. I directed the milkman to the people in charge of the food, and joined my friends who were already in the cellar. There, we all got to put on a pair of *sandals*, which made us feel lighter when we walked and kept us from making

noise with our *shoes* while the other children were sleeping. I was also able to *brush* my *hair* and *teeth* and *change* into more comfortable clothes.

This story sounds very much like it could be true. Even though only part of it is, I learned that the original twenty words did not mean anything to me when I first listed them, but with those words I was able to create a story that made sense. I also learned from this exercise that what seems impossible can become a reality if I make the effort.

When I read over my story, I realized that I was focusing on the orphanage and on the forthcoming (Six Day) war that I feared. I protected myself by bringing a milkman into the story because I was focused on survival and the fear of hunger. In the story, I finally became relaxed, combed my hair, and made myself comfortable by changing my clothes. I also learned that the words that popped into my mind corresponded to the environment I was in. The results differed depending on whether it was light or dark, and on whether others were around me or not.

It did not matter to me where I was, because I was able to balance my life and overcome anger by focusing on the positive. I learned my mission in this world, and knew that every word that popped into my mind while doing these exercises was a message from G-d. Each letter has a living soul. If we spell a word correctly, we can see that a word comes to life and has meaning. This stream of consciousness method was very therapeutic for me, and I thank *Hashem* (G-d) for directing me in this way. I was not ashamed to write whatever I wanted in order to express my feelings, and without having anyone criticize, laugh, or call me names. The exercise also did not cost any money and prevented me from spending endless time in a therapist's office.

I was amazed that one of my exercises even gave me a reason to live. I sat in a trance, speaking to my inner soul and hoping to connect it with my physical body in order to see life in a positive way. I remembered that my parents came from Hitler's destructive, bitter war. They were sick and they suffered from the loss of loved ones; they placed us in a home where they believed we would be safe and taken care of. They visited me constantly and were there for me whenever I needed them. They protected us from the missionaries who were stealing Jewish children, and from *kibbutzim* that did not teach children Torah values. They wanted us to be among other children while they were working day and night so that they could provide for us and eventually marry us off with dignity and respect, all of which was against Hitler's plan. They themselves needed help, and wanted to live without letting anyone break them apart.

The orphanage was a good place, with the exception of some disturbed people hired to work there. I knew that I had to cope with the difficulties and hope that better days would come. I am sure now that someday I will come across the people I had to deal with, and with G-d's help, I might be able to help them too.

I was happy that Meyer was married and had a baby boy to look after. Tova was now a mature, sixteen year old girl, and the matchmakers were looking for a mate for her. I did not want her to get married at such a young age because I felt that I would be losing her, but I knew she would finally have a home of her own for me to go to. I knew that I would be next in line for marriage, and that I would also have a loving home for my parents and my siblings to visit. In the meantime, the orphanage was my home away from home. It was now up to me to better my life by taking on some work that would bring me feelings of accomplishment and success. If not for my own sake, it was for the sake of other children who needed me.

I learned so many creative things that helped me to go on with my life. Although my doctors did not believe that I was going to live long, I thanked G-d that I was able to walk on my feet and play and I made every effort to stay alive. I decided to channel my anger into happiness. I increased my activities by jumping more rope, and was involved with sports. I traveled a lot to parks where there was entertainment, dressed up for Purim, and laughed with my friends. I even laughed with those who were mean to me as much as I could. I was still slim and beautiful and had a great sense of humor. My friend Hana and I climbed mountains, walked on roofs, jumped down floors and stairs, took bus rides, and walked around the whole city of Jerusalem. We often made ourselves fresh pita bread sandwiches with butter and tomatoes and sat and ate them at the back of the building. Whenever we ate them, Rabbi Rosenfeld would see us and wish us a hearty appetite. He also warned us to stop climbing mountains in the heat because we always came back sunburned.

When I looked at the good things that I had in the *mosad*, I was able to push ahead with life. Tova and I were very close to one another and our love grew stronger day by day. We did not need strangers to love us; our siblings loved each other, and our parents' love for us was incredible. Our biological family was the most important thing because family is family forever. My family in the *mosad* was a temporary family; after I got married, it would be my choice to decide whom I wanted to stay in touch with.

One morning I woke up wheezing and short of breath. I did not tell anyone because I knew that person would tell me that I had made myself sick. As the day continued, I developed a high fever and was too sick to get out of bed. My counselor asked me what was wrong; I told her that I did not feel well. She asked me to go with her to the infirmary, but I refused to do so. I was sick and tired of being a grouch. The same afternoon, another counselor named Rachel came into my room to tease me. When I asked her to leave me alone, she slapped me across my face, pulled me out of my bed and dragged me to the hallway near the stairs. When I asked her to stop, she again pushed me down a whole flight of stairs. I got up and went to Shaare Zedek Hospital, where I told the doctors that I had chest pains. I hoped that they would examine me and see my bruises; instead, they just examined my chest and kept me in the hospital for a few days because I had pneumonia. I spent the first twenty four hours in the intensive care unit, and then I was moved to the pediatric unit. I felt much better just being away from the hands of sick people.

The same year (1964) my mother decided to come to Jerusalem to stay with us for the High Holy Days. My father and brothers went to their rabbi. When the holidays arrived, a Sephardic girl in the orphanage named Rachel was very anxious to know why I did not go home for the holidays. I asked her nicely to mind her own business, but she decided that she would not stop nagging me until I told her why I was not going home. After *Rosh Hashana*, Ima returned home.

After *Yom Kippur*, the children began to decorate the *mosad*'s big, beautiful *sukkah*. This was the first *Sukkot* I spent at the *mosad*, and everyone was looking forward to this beautiful holiday. The day finally arrived and we all sat in the *sukkah* for our meals. The first night went by very nicely. Rabbi Poppenheim made *kiddush* (the blessing over the wine and *challah*) and then went home to his family for the festive meal. We were all singing and dancing and it seemed to me like a beautiful holiday.

The problems began the next day when Rachel came over to me and continued to demand why I stayed there for the holiday. I told her that I did not ask her questions and did not need to tell her my business. She took my plate that was filled with boiling soup and spilled it on me. I refused to answer her or hit her back. I did not believe in fighting because those who abused me were so emotionally disturbed that they would become even more violent if I responded.

I was a very reserved child who was willing to accept pain and suffering, but would never hurt anyone or start fights. I would cry a lot in the privacy of my room, on the street, or whenever I was alone. I believed that G-d was testing me and that I was born to be a victim of this world. I moaned silently and prayed a lot. I hoped that G-d was listening to my prayers, and decided that even if he does not see or hear me, the prayers were still good for my spirit. I found comfort because I was able to cry during prayers. While in the *sukkah*, I recited, "*Al tira mepahad petom umeshoat reshaim ki tavo*," (do not be afraid from sudden fear and from the wicked who will approach you.)

Rachel thought that I was reciting the *benching* (grace after meals), and continued bugging me, but I kept praying. She did not like that I ignored her, so she pulled my hair and hit me until she left marks all over me and made me bleed. I pushed her aside, and headed to the kitchen to find safety with Hass-Neiny. Rachel called me names but I ignored her. In the kitchen I sat next to Hass-Neiny for a few minutes. She asked me to wash my face with cold water, and then I went up to my room, locked the door, and burst into tears. Right then a miracle happened. I heard my angel telling me to stop crying; my angel told me that the name *hatkafot* was given to me; it was a message from Hashem.

Hatkafot and *hatkufot* are spelled the same in Hebrew. *Hatkafot* means attacks, and *hatkufot* means a temporary time frame. All my suffering was only temporary. I felt better and looked ahead to the future. Some girls in my class were already engaged, and even though I did not want to think about marriage, I looked forward to running away to a brighter future.

Tova, who was not aware of what had happened to me because she was out with a friend, knocked on my door. When she saw how I looked, she cried out, "What do these wicked people want from my innocent sister; why do You, G-d, not watch over her?" Tova did not even see the burns on my legs from the soup. I told Tova that I wanted to see a friend from school and I left. I knocked at the door of my classmate Mindu, and when her mother opened it, I burst into hysterical tears. She invited me into her house and called Mindu, who was in another room. I assume that she told her daughter about my state. Mindu came out and hugged me and invited me into her room. There, she asked me what had happened, and called her mother, who looked at my wounds and burns and took care of them right away. She asked me to stay overnight; in the meantime, she sent one of her children to call Rabbi Poppenheim to come over. The rabbi came right away. He asked me to go back and promised to take care of the situation. He also told me to report to him everything that was happening to me. I knew, however, that he knew how severely I was abused and did not do anything to stop it, so I said I would not tell him anything anymore.

In February 1967, my friend Hana Mikler left the orphanage and went to America with her family. In the beginning I cried and was very sad about losing her, but with time I found another close friend named Yonit. Yonit was younger than me, but she was much taller and looked older. We would take many walks and visit her aunt and other relatives, and we had some great times together. One day she told me that her aunt got a television from America, and she wanted me to see it. I had never seen one before, and it was quite amazing for me to watch television. I thought that the TV was a radio with a window; when I went back to the *mosad*, I told everyone that I was able to see people talk inside the radio. How primitive I was.

Yonit liked window shopping, so she took me to department stores to see the fashion designs. By looking at the different designs I was able to progress in my sewing skills. Yonit also used to love to eat. She was such a hungry individual that she stopped in every restaurant and candy store to eat and drink. She persuaded me to eat all this junk too, which caused constant stomach problems and a sudden weight gain. Yonit not only ate in the streets but had me cook for her every single night; plus, she ate three meals a day in the dining room. We would go into the kitchen after midnight, where I cooked the most delicious soups and vegetables. I also baked potatoes or cooked whatever else I found.

Hass-Neiny, however, had a great sense of smell, and always came down to the kitchen to find out who was cooking in the middle of the night. We were very lucky that Hass-Neiny wore heavy brown shoes, and we could always hear her footsteps. As soon as I heard her, I would shut off the stove, grab the hot pot with a towel I had prepared in advance, and run straight up to my room with the pot.

Hass-Neiny heard us running, so she came up to each room and peeked into everybody's bed. She was anxious to find the gourmet cooks. We did not always have time to run out of the kitchen . We either hid in a corner and I would place the hot pot inside the oven, or I hid inside the storage room with the pot.

One time, Hass-Neiny insisted on finding us, and refused to leave the kitchen. She turned on the lights and looked everywhere. We had to hold onto a pipe on the ceiling. Suddenly, we noticed a rat staring at us. We were so scared of this rat that Yonit kept on pinching me. I asked her to stop; otherwise, I would have to jump down and Hass-Neiny would catch us. What I feared the most was that Hass-Neiny would be frightened if she heard a sound, especially if we had to jump down. I did not want to scare this innocent, holy soul. After she left the storage room, we walked out quietly and hid under a table in the dining room. After Hass-Neiny turned off the lights and went upstairs, we ate our food and then went to sleep.
When Hass-Neiny came into my room, she saw this innocent little girl facing the wall, pretending that she was snoring. All I needed was to burst into laughter, and this would be the end. As soon as she moved away, I started laughing. Hass-Neiny had the feeling that it was me, but she did not want to falsely accuse me. She came back toward me, so I made believe that I opened my eyes, and asked her, "Hass-Neiny, how come you are here?" She told me with a broken heart that she could not sleep because she smelled food cooking every night and she needed to find out who the cook was. I then asked her what time it was. She told me that she was going to wake up all the children, line them up and put an end to this catering business. Hass-Neiny showed up at 5:30 A.M., woke up all the counselors and turned on the electric wake-up alarm. In a few minutes, we were all lined up in the hallway against the wall. I asked Yonit not to stand next to me or laugh. As soon as I told her that, she cracked up and everybody started to giggle. Hass-Neiny had a hard time getting our attention, but the counselors put on serious faces and calmed us down. I did not laugh

at all because I felt guilty and knew that it was not right to keep such a devoted woman awake and who hardly got any rest. Hass-Neiny walked over to each child and looked straight into their faces, and everybody started laughing. I was the eighth girl in line, so when she came over to me, she stopped, looked into my eyes with her gorgeous, big blue eyes, and with a soft voice asked me, "Ahuva'le, did you see by any chance who is cooking every night? And did you see anybody running last night?" She looked so cute that I could not help but start to laugh. Because I felt guilty, I hugged her and told her that I was sleeping in the middle of the night, but if I knew who was doing it, I would let her know. Hass-Neiny told us all that if we were hungry she would provide more food for us, but she was very concerned with the cooking business.

This year's Purim was the best I ever had. I dressed up as a black housekeeper, and Yonit was a fancy madam. We hit the shops to celebrate. We first went into a barber's shop, where I swept the floor and collected all the hair. At first, the barber was afraid, but when we told him that we were just dressed in costumes, he let me continue and even gave me some money for the work. At first I refused to take the money, but he was pleased with my job and convinced me to take it. We went to other stores, and by the end of the day we came back with four hundred *lirot* (money).

After Purim I decided that as much as I liked Yonit, it was time to stop this nonsense of running around, eating in the streets and cooking at night in addition to having our three full meals a day. Not only did I put on a lot of weight in the short time I spent with Yonit, but our time together was not well spent. She owed me a lot of money for all the food she made me buy her. I finally told her that there were many other activities we could do besides running around and eating. She did not like that I confronted her with her nonsense, so we remained friends but did not go places together after that.

My goal was to do something special in my life. One day, when I came home from school, I decided to sit on the bench near the office. I started daydreaming and before I knew it, I was in tears. When I got my senses back, I noticed that my tears caused my vision to be foggy. Through this fog I noticed an autistic ten-year-old girl, Hana Weisenstern, sitting in a corner. She faced the wall and was turning her head back and forth. As I looked at her, an idea popped into my head. I got up from my seat and slowly walked over to her and sat down on the floor. She was in her own little world, but I said to her: "Hana'le, we are living in the same world, we live in the same orphanage, we are both from broken homes. You are biting and beating yourself, and I am being beaten by others, but we are both beaten up."

As I talked to her, I had the idea that it might be a good idea for me to take care of her, and that we would be best friends. I gave her a hug and a kiss on her sweet head and I got up from the floor. I looked at her again and saw someone with the most beautiful curly red hair, hazel eyes, a gorgeous face, and the perfect height for a ten-year-old, but a child who was very lonely and had no one to look after her. I looked over at Cahana's office, and for a moment I hesitated to knock on her door. I knew that in order to accomplish what I wanted to do, I needed to have the guts to speak up and I prepared myself for any response she might have.

Before I could knock on her door, Cahana walked out of her office. I walked over to her and told her that I would like to take care of Hana'le. She looked at me and immediately rejected my offer, telling me that she did not think she wanted to give her to me. I told her that I would give her only one day to give me an answer, otherwise, I would have to find a job outside the orphanage. I left her and took a walk outside near the *mosad.*

As I went out on the street, I met the daughter of my teacher Yehudith. She invited me to her house. I told Yehudith about my idea, and that I needed to do something special at this time of my life. I didn't know what I would do if Cahana did not give me this job with Hana'le. Because high school was not required for us, Yehudith advised me to get a job in school as a kindergarten assistant; she promised me that she would obtain that for me. I was very happy and continued attending school while awaiting the position.

When I got back to the *mosad*, Cahana was waiting for me. She told me that she had a conference with the other principals and my counselor, and everybody agreed that I was the right person to take care of Hana'le. She offered to pay me forty *lirot* (money) per month. I told her that every bad person has some good hidden in her too. I jumped up with happiness and then rushed up to Tova's room to tell her the good news.

With the first forty *lirot* (money) that I earned, I bought a melodica and practiced every single day until I was able to play music for Hana'le. I felt so fulfilled that I decided to volunteer in the children's infirmary. I fixed the little girls' beds, played games with them, and took them to the bathroom and helped them with their showers. I played music and read many stories to them, and if a child was admitted to the hospital I would stay with her in the morning or at night and during the weekends.

We had a girl named Ariela who was born with a split lip. She required corrective surgery several times. In the hospital, the surgeon asked me, a fifteen-year-old, if I wanted to assist him during surgery. I was so excited and said, "Yes." One of the nurses put a robe, surgical shoes, and a mask on me. She made me wash my hands, and when we were all ready, Ariela was put to sleep and the doctor performed the surgery. He explained everything he was doing; every time he asked me to hand something to him, the nurse would show me what it was. We talked and laughed, and in an hour, Ariela's surgery was successfully completed. She was transferred to the recovery room, where I was permitted to stay with her. Even though she was in pain, she was very glad that I was next to her when she woke up.

During the same period, a ten-year-old girl with juvenile polio, Rivka, had to have an appendectomy. She was a new immigrant from Romania, and needed me to stay with her all the time. I stayed with her every morning and then went back to the *mosad* to wait for Hana'le to come home. I also stayed with Rivka for Sabbath. When she was discharged, Rivka was placed in the infirmary, where I could stay with her for longer periods of time. The little girls there were so adorable. One was cuter than the next. I loved them, and they gave me a good reason to go on with life. Another special five-year-old girl with whom I got involved was Naomi, an orphan from Denmark, who suffered from typhus. She was so frightened from the injections she was getting, I decided to stay next to her day and night. I slept on a chair near her bed.

What about taking my friend Yonit to the dentist where I used to volunteer? While we waited for the dentist to come in, I teased her that I was going to drill her teeth. The dentist's wife liked our little comedy, so she grabbed her camera and took some pictures. When I look at myself holding the dentist's tools, I look and feel like a professional. I could be anything I wanted. I knew that one day, I would beat the odds and be an asset to society.

Just two months after taking Hana'le under my wings, I received many compliments from the counselors and the social services staff at her school for the great job I was doing. One day, a social worker came to visit us in the *mosad* to see what I did to help Hana's mental status improve so drastically. I helped her do many things. I taught her to play ball and jump rope. I trained her to go to the bathroom and clean herself and to clean off the table after she ate. I bought some sweets to give her to stimulate her performance; while she ate her snack, I would turn on music and she learned to clap her hands. I trained her to take showers and put soap and shampoo on her body and hair; she also learned to dress herself and brush her hair. Hana also learned that when I spoke to her, she was not allowed to turn her head back and forth, and I did many exercises with her to get her attention. She even learned to say her name. I often went to her school in Talpiot to meet her teachers and counselors, and I would show them some of the tools I used to improve Hana's quality of life.

I was not surprised when one day a woman came to the *mosad* to seek my help. She told me that she was referred to me by the Talpiot School. She had a five-year-old autistic daughter, also named Hana. She also had a three year old at home, and her husband was working in England, leaving his wife to deal with the two girls. This little Hana was also very pretty, and her mother was a doll. I worked for her on the weekends, and we treated each other with a lot of respect and got along great. When her husband came to visit, he brought beautiful presents for me. I remember the orange and white sweater he bought for me as well as many other presents. I did not want to take gifts from him but he asked me to. Within a short time, I had a group of ten children that I was working with. I became so busy helping these children that I did not have as much time to think about my own problems.

My main focus, however, was on the first Hana. I took her to the zoo, to doctors' appointments and on bus rides. But there is one trip I will never forget. One day when I came home from school, Hass-Neiny was anxiously waiting for me with tears in her eyes. When I saw the look on her face, I knew that something was very wrong. I hoped that nothing had happened to my sister. She told me that she called an ambulance to take Hana to the hospital. One of the children had poured kerosene on her body, trying to burn her. I dropped my briefcase on the floor and ran quickly to see my little angel. When I saw her, I burst into tears. She had major burns and blisters all over her body and was in a tremendous amount of pain. I asked Hass-Neiny to remove Hana's clothes, and I wrapped her in a clean white linen sheet. When the ambulance came I went with her to Hadassah Hospital.

This was such an awful thing to do to such an innocent little girl. The attending physician looked at this little girl's wounds and told me that he had to notify the police. I explained to him that another little girl did this to her. I did not care, though, if he wanted to report this case to the police because I hoped that such things would never happen again. The doctor asked me many questions, and in the meantime, we waited for a dermatologist. Hana was admitted to the hospital for two days and I stayed with her until she was discharged. Hass-Neiny and I took care of her day and night. The two of us wanted to make sure she would never be a victim again. She was a little girl who had never harmed anyone in this world.

The forty *lirot* (money) that I got paid for taking care of Hana was not worth the many hours I invested in her, but I learned a great deal from her and the experience. No university could teach what Hana had taught me. After this episode, Hana had major attacks where she would lie down on the floor, scream, hit herself, pull her hair and bite herself raw. I had no other choice but to tie her down until she calmed down; then, I would give her a drink and take her into my arms. These episodes became routine problems every night. No one was able to control her, so the house mother and the counselor would call me to go over to the nursery, where I spent my nights holding her in my arms until she fell asleep. I was no longer able to go home to my mother for vacations because Rabbi Poppenheim would call me to come back. As soon as she saw me, she calmed down and was happy. As hard as it was for me to handle her, I felt honored to be so successful in an area in which older people and professionals could not help. I would wash off her face with cold water and hold her in one arm, and with the other I caressed her head. I would also sing to her until she calmed down.

This was the first time I knew what my mission was in this world, and it gave me a reason to live. In *Kohelet* (Ecclesiastes), King Solomon writes that there is a time for everything. The truth is that I wanted to earn some money; even more so, I needed to fill in my empty cavities with good deeds by helping very special children like Hana. I worked with her for two and a half years until I left the orphanage. At that point, I had to leave her behind and go on with my life.

THE SIX DAY WAR

In November 1966, my seventeen-year-old sister got engaged. I did not like her fiance because he was a religious fanatic and I knew that Tova would have to change her looks and her lifestyle if she married him. But I was happy that she could finally move out of the orphanage and start a new life in her own home. She had a beautiful engagement party in the hall of the orphanage, and many relatives and guests came to take part in her *simcha* (celebration). We spent the year of her engagement busily preparing for her wedding. We had to sew dresses, shop whatever she needed for her new home, and look for an apartment. My parents had to work overtime to have the money for the wedding. As excited as we were, though, we felt political tensions building up in Israel.

In April 1967, we could feel the tension of war in the air. The Egyptians blocked the Suez Canal. The media announced that Jerusalem was in great danger and the rabbis asked us to pray for the safety of our holy land and for our soldiers and citizens. People started to prepare their cellars with water, emergency supplies, food, cordless radios, beds, tables and chairs. The Israelis were busy taping up their windows in the event that their homes were bombed. Everyone filled up sandbags that were used to shield homes, businesses, and each other from bombings. People emptied the stores as they bought food, tools and other supplies they needed in case of an emergency. Soldiers were spread out everywhere to ensure that civilians were properly prepared, and the radio sent out signals and codes to soldiers informing them when to report to their assigned stations.

As the month of June got closer, mothers and fathers had to say goodbye to their children, not knowing whether they would meet again. People were in a state of total panic; yet, the Jewish nation was so remarkable, knowing to trust in G-d whenever it faced danger.

From the nearby army base, we heard the soldiers' exercises, and the atmosphere became more frightening each minute. The residents of Jerusalem, especially the children in our orphanage, had no place to run to. We all had to stay put and await the upcoming war. The buses were taken away for the army's use; the country's trains and trucks were used for the soldiers and their supplies; airplanes were restricted from leaving the country; and the city of Jerusalem was put on hold.

The smell and the noise of war was everywhere. The streets were filled with soldiers carrying machine guns and Uzis, and tanks roamed all over. The overhead noise of the airplanes made it feel like war, a noise that went into our souls. In a way we felt as if the world were coming to an end; in another breath, we hoped that the Israeli army would recapture the Old City of Jerusalem and that everyone would come home safely. As much as I feared for myself and my sister, my thoughts were with my parents and my brothers who were not in Jerusalem at this time. There was no transportation. I feared for the soldiers and for their families.

The children in the *mosad* were very frightened, and many girls slept with their counselors or with older girls. The counselors were children themselves, but they were figures of power and were older than the residents. I was always afraid of many things, but now, I was only afraid for others. In the beginning I did not know why I was not personally scared of the war, but later on I understood better.

On June 5, 1967, in the morning, the sirens sounded. The war had begun. Hass-Neiny asked me to escort the preschool children to school. I told her that the war had started, and that we could not go out, but she insisted that I march down with a group of eighteen little girls in the streets of Jerusalem while bombs flew everywhere. She still did not listen, and forced me to take the children out.

As soon as we reached the bottom of the hill that led from the *mosad* to school, we were stopped by the soldiers, who screamed at me for violating the rules of war. I explained to them that I was forced to do so, and they made sure that we returned safely. On the way back, we saw bombs flying and heard explosions everywhere. War planes filled the sky and tanks crowded the streets. I asked the little ones to run, but they kept on falling and I had to make sure no one got hurt. We suddenly heard the soldiers call out, "Lie down on the ground." I pushed the children down and told them not to get up. The soldiers ran toward us and helped us. Between explosions, we ran until we arrived back at the *mosad*. Thank G-d, no one was hurt. I led the children down to the cellar under the building, and there I hugged, kissed and thanked all the brave little girls for listening to me.

I handed the children over to their counselor and went to search for my sister. I looked everywhere for her and when I was unable to locate her, I asked the girls from her group if they knew where she was. One girl told me that Tova went to the beauty parlor with her friend Malka Adler, who was scheduled to leave for America. I was surprised that the airlines did not notify her about their cancellations, and I assumed that the beauty parlor must have been closed. I had no idea where the two girls would end up hiding and how safe they were. I was scared and I asked Rabbi Poppenheim to locate them and bring them back. Rabbi Poppenheim called the army immediately; the girls were found a few hours later hiding in a cellar.

The first few days of the war were very scary. The children in the orphanage were crying and shaking, and they needed a lot of reassurance. The older kids took care of the younger ones. I loved to hold the two-year-olds and give them the attention they needed. They were so innocent and beautiful. Every time I took a baby into my arms I would burst into tears. What struck me the most was hearing these orphans cry out, "Ima'le" or "Mommy." Children were calling their own mothers, asking them to rise from their graves. Rabbi Poppenheim and his wonderful family stayed with us during the war and gave us all the support and love we needed. Even his mother, sisters and nieces stayed with us. Hass-Neiny was busy preparing meals for us, and Cahana, the cooks, and all the counselors also stayed with us.

From the first day of the war, I decided to help Hass-Neiny. I felt that G-d had given me strength, and that I should help take care of the *mosad*'s many orphans. Hass-Neiny and I went to each floor and spread out mattresses, blankets and pillows so that the children would not sleep on the floor. I helped out daily in the kitchen, and when I had free time, I would look after the children who did not feel well. I am sure the reason I felt so secure was because my parents were the only ones who called three times a day to see whether we were okay. Tova and I were busy running to the phone every time it rang because we knew that it was our parents who were calling. Every call we got broke our spirit, because our parents were crying and felt bad that they were unable to be with us during such a difficult time. We reassured them that we would be okay. We felt their love and knew that they had already gone through one miserable war; we felt bad that they feared that all wars were similar to the one they lived through during the Nazi era.

As we spoke on the phone, we could hear bombs going off in the background. The situation grew out of hand, so Rabbi Poppenheim asked my parents not to call so often because it was too dangerous for us to be in the office during this time. He promised them that he would let us call a few times a day when it was calmer; if we did not call, it was because it was unsafe for us to leave the cellar, where we did not have a telephone.

Most of the children and staff were afraid to sleep at night. It was pitch black outside, but bombs lit up the whole city. The windows were shaking and cracking as if there was an earthquake, and the building was so shaky that we feared it might collapse at any minute. We prayed day and night, and the children said the *Shema Yisrael* (Hear O Israel), which is the last prayer one recites before death.

Cahana also feared for her life. She kept on telling us that it looked like the Arabs were trying to bomb our building. She asked us not to be afraid, but she was so scared that she frightened us more by telling us that we were being bombed. When I saw how frightened Cahana was, I was very glad because for the first time I learned that she had feelings after all. Whether she feared for her life or ours, it did not matter. She had feelings and she cared. Somewhere inside her she was finally able to say, "I am afraid."

All the children, from the youngest to the oldest, said *tehillim* (psalms) all day long. Rabbi Poppenheim tuned in to the radio all day, listening to the news. We wanted to know how long the war would go on and what the outcome would be. The army came to visit us daily; sometimes they would come a few times a day to check on us and give us food and medical supplies. If a child had to be transferred to a hospital, they provided ambulance service.

Having had an appendix attack, Tova was the first one to be transferred. The hospitals were so crowded with wounded soldiers that if a patient's situation was not life-threatening, they would discharge him. It appeared that Tova's appendix could hold off from rupturing if she applied ice and stayed on a strict diet. She came back to the orphanage the same day, and Hass-Neiny monitored her closely to see that she did not develop a high fever, vomit, or feel an increase in pain. Rabbi Poppenheim and his family were angels sent by G-d to watch over us. With their help and the help of *Hashem* (G-d), none of the children got hurt.

On the second day of the war, I went upstairs to the kitchen to help Hass-Neiny prepare the meals for the children. There, I saw my friend, Yentu, sitting all alone near the door, depressed and in tears. She was wishing for her death. I called her name to let her know that I was there for her, but she responded, "Leave me alone, I want to die." I went over to her and sat next to her without asking any questions. Yentu was such a sweet child and we all loved her. She came from Romania and had juvenile polio, and she was a child of Holocaust survivors. Her parents told her all about World War II, and she feared the same war was threatening us.

I told Yentu my life story, and that I often felt the same way she did. We both looked out and saw ammunition flying before our eyes, along with a miracle: G-d directed the bombs away from us because he did not want to hurt the children of Israel. Yentu was afraid, and all she wanted was for someone to hug her and tell her, "I care." I took Yentu into my arms and gave her my shoulder to cry on. I asked her to get up and come with me into the kitchen, where she could help me prepare breakfast for the children. As much as we endangered ourselves by standing in the kitchen, I felt *Hashem's* presence and protection. Yentu felt better, and when we finished cooking, we took the food down to the counselors, who were watching the children in the cellar; there we ate breakfast with all the others.

By the third day of the war (June 7), the situation grew easier for all of us as we became used to the sounds of war. The Poppenheim sisters studied with the children in order to occupy their minds with good thoughts. Children wrote letters, the little ones spent time coloring, and others read books or played games. We did have some kids who were crying, but that was no surprise considering that children do not like to be locked up in one place, especially when the noise of war is so great. We heard the cries of fear, the cries for father and mother, the cries to be held and supported, and the cries of tiredness. It was hard to rest and most children did not sleep at all during the war.

It was interesting to see soldiers show up with some local citizens who wanted to volunteer. We had enough volunteers, but these women had their own motives: some were looking for food, some sought shelter, while others felt unsafe in the bunkers where they were hiding. Everyone knows that the army watched out for the children in the orphanages, so these women felt safer staying with us. Because the administration in *Bayit Lepletot* was so kind and charitable, they allowed strangers into the home and made them feel comfortable.

What shocked me the most was that while many soldiers were

dying and getting hurt, many children in the orphanage stole clothing and whatever else they could get. Our teachers taught us not to steal, but many children simply could not control their desires to take something, whether they needed it or not. Hass-Neiny realized that many things were missing from the storage room, but she found the girls and made them return the items to her.

On June 11, Rabbi Poppenheim came down to the cellar and asked us for our attention. He said he heard on the news that the Israel Defense Forces won the war, and that we won back the holy Old City of Jerusalem. He asked us not to forget that many soldiers were killed and many others were severely injured. He told us in an emotional voice that after the war we would be able to visit Jewish holy sites such as the Western Wall, the *Cave of Machpelah*, and the burial places of King David and our foremother Rachel.

His announcement seemed like a dream to us. Until this time we had learned about these people and places only from the *Tanach* (the Hebrew Bible) and the Torah; now we would actually be able to visit them. The children burst into tears of joy, and we all thanked G-d for restoring to us part of the holy Temple. We had to continue praying to *Hashem* (G-d) to help us win the complete city of Jerusalem (when the Messiah arrives) and that He should return to His home and His children, who have patiently been waiting for Him.

The rabbi turned on the radio so that we could hear the good news ourselves. He still was concerned about mines left all over Jerusalem, and told us that no one could leave the building until the army told us that it was safe. For security purposes, we were ordered to stay in the cellar until June 13. We started taking back all the mattresses and our personal belongings to our rooms and prepared ourselves physically and emotionally to visit the holy places for the first time. As soon as public transportation was restored, my parents came to visit us and to make sure that we were okay. Ima brought baskets filled with fresh fruits and sweets to hand out to the soldiers on the way to the *Kotel* (wailing wall) as a token of appreciation.

One week after the war ended, we received permission to go visit the holy sites. Most of the girls went to the Western Wall on the first day. One could still see soldiers everywhere, and they were keeping people from going to dangerous places. When we looked down at the rubble and the remains from the Temple, we felt the aura of holiness. It was painful to see all the ruins, but we also knew that G-d could restore the Temple very quickly. It took Him only six days to create the world and all of its creatures; He could rebuild His holy Temple in the blink of an eye

My dear mother went with us to the holy places. We went to the *Kotel* (Western Wall), the Tower of David, the *Cave of Machpelah*, and Rachel's Tomb, and we went to see the towers and gates that circle the city. She kissed every soldier she saw and gave them her blessings. She was so emotional and thankful to *Hashem* (G-d) and his messengers that she made everyone cry.

As soon as I arrived at the Western Wall, I threw myself against it and felt a vibration pulsating through my entire body. There was no doubt about it, the smell, the look, the whole aura was holy. It was a dream that came true. I cried my heart out, and when I looked up, I saw thousands of people leaning against the wall. Every single Jew was overwhelmed and their eyes were filled with tears. I was even more amazed to see Jews and gentiles standing near each other. All of us felt the same; we all prayed to the G-d of Abraham, Isaac, and Jacob. There was unity and beauty, and it was overwhelming to look around and see the whole city.

My mother pushed through the crowd until she reached the *Kotel*. As soon as she touched it, she was filled with joy. She threw herself on the ground, and leaned her head against the wall. She immediately burst into tears and thanked *Hashem* (G-d) for the victory of the children of Israel. She asked *Hashem* (G-d) to redeem her children and all the children of Israel from this bitter exile, and to reveal himself and dwell among us. Ima looked up at the blue skies and asked *Hashem* (G-d) to show us the miracles, just as he did in

Egypt.

I sat on the floor in a corner, leaning against the wall and crying hysterically. It was okay because everyone else was crying. I had the urge to scream out loud and bring up all of my pain that sat on my chest since the day I was born. Other people were not ashamed to cry out loud and thank *Hashem* (G-d) for the beautiful Jerusalem he had given back to us. We wanted the complete, peaceful Jerusalem that only the Messiah will usher in, but we still appreciated what we had. I cannot describe the beauty of the scene and how the holy city of Jerusalem looked the first time I saw it reunited. It was different than any other city in the world. I felt the spirit of holiness in my bloodstream, and sensations of electricity shook my body. The air smelled and felt different, and our hearts were filled with joy.

I remember the first *bar mitzvah* that was conducted at the *Kotel* after the war. The guests cried with their eyes and rejoiced with their hearts, body and soul. They invited everybody who came to pray, to share a piece of cake and to make a *l'chaim* (toast). I was also moved by the traditional outfits that the Arabs wore, and the way they rode their donkeys, camels, goats, and sheep. The smell in the *shuk* (open-air market) was incredible from their coffee and pita bread. Many Arab men sat in coffee shops drinking, playing table games, and smoking pipes, while the women sat on the floor by the entrance of the Mandelbaum or Sh'chem (Nablus) gates nursing their young ones.

Indeed, thousands of Muslim Arabs, Jews, Christians, and tourists pushed through the narrow streets of the Old City, particularly through the *shuk* (open-air market). Everything looked just as I remembered from pictures at school. One could hear the sounds of prayer from mosques, churches, and schools, and from both Arabs and Jews. We even went into a mosque to see what it looked like and how the Arabs pray. The mosque was huge, and many Arabs dressed in uniforms stood in straight lines. They all kneeled together and bowed their heads down as one unit. Bells were ringing, people were singing and dancing, it seemed to me as if redemption was definitely at the door.

We were so anxious to see all of these places in one day that one would think we were looking for food after a hunger strike. From every shop, school, clinic, home, bus and on the street, the radio blasted with music written during the war. All of the songs were related to Jerusalem; the most famous were: "*Yerushalayim Shel Zahav*" (Jerusalem of Gold), "*Hakotel*," "*Lach Yerushalaim*," "*Sisu Et Yerushalaim* and other songs related to the victory of the war and to G-d's return to Jerusalem and the hope for a full redemption.

After the war, I continued to work with autistic children as well as with the children in the infirmary. At this time there was a virtual epidemic of children being struck with appendix attacks. The hospitals were filled with our children. I decided to visit them and give them physical and emotional support. On the weekends I also went to the hospitals to stay with the children. No one asked me to do it; I always felt that it was my job to help everyone.

There was one special child named Devorah, who came to the *mosad* as a gorgeous little ten-year-old girl. I loved her very much. I felt very close to her and to her sisters from the moment they entered the orphanage. Her mother was a very special woman and we felt as though we were blood sisters. Her smile was worth a million dollars. I liked to take care of Devorah, play with her, and spoil her. She often became ill with tonsillitis. One time she sprained her ankle, and the doctor had to correct it surgically because the bone came out of place. She also had an appendix attack and was operated on in Shaare Zedek Hospital. I sat next to her day and night, and did everything for her. I cried when she was in pain and made her laugh so she would heal faster. When she was healed, she went back to the *mosad* and stayed in the infirmary until she grew stronger.

On Monday, July 17, 1967, the ninth day in the Hebrew month of Tammuz, shortly after the war ended, I too had an appendix attack and was operated on in Shaare Zedek Hospital. I had troubles with my appendix for two years, but Cahana would not let me see a doctor. (A counselor had privately taken me to one, who placed me on a strict diet and treated me with ice compresses.) On this particular day, I became very sick while I was working in the infirmary. I told Esther, the house mother for the preschool children in the old building, about the pain I felt on the lower right side of my belly; I also had a fever and was vomiting. She told me to apply ice and rest. When I started to feel really sick, I returned to the new building and sat outside the office, hoping that somebody would have mercy on me and take me to see a doctor. Cahana came toward the office and asked me why I was sitting there. I told her that I was having an appendix attack and that I needed somebody to take me to the hospital. She yelled at me and told me that if I left the building, she would personally punish me. I remained seated on the bench near the offices and waited for someone else to show up that hopefully would call Tova or my counselor, Gittle. Two minutes later, Bashy Turner, a girl from my group, showed up. I told her that I felt very sick and needed to go to the hospital. I asked her to call my sister and my counselor. She was so good hearted and started to cry when I told her that Cahana would not let me leave the building.

Bashy ran immediately for help, and my counselor and my sister arrived soon after. My counselor went to see Cahana and told her that she was taking me to the hospital. Cahana still would not give her permission to take me there, so Gittle told me to go with my sister and take the elevator to the back entrance, and she called a taxi to take us to the hospital.

Because the hospital was so busy with injured soldiers, they sent me to *Magen David Adom* (Israeli Red Cross) to be evaluated. My counselor decided to walk with me to the *Magen David Adom* station because she did not have enough money for the taxi. On the way, my appendix ruptured. I was unable to walk but the two of them helped me. When we got there, I was seen by Dr. Shuster, a surgeon. When he saw the situation I was in he ordered an ambulance to rush me to the nearest hospital, which was Shaare Zedek. I was taken into the emergency room for blood and urine tests, and the nurse took my vital signs. At one A.M., just a few minutes after I arrived, I was rushed into the operating room.

In the morning, after I woke up from the surgery, I saw Tova standing near the window crying. I turned my head to one side, and there was my holy mother sitting next to me and crying hysterically. She held my hand, and when she noticed that I was awake, got up from her seat and fell directly on my face. She kissed me and wiped the tears from my face. I still had a very high fever and was vomiting. The pain was horrible. Dr. Adler, the surgeon, walked in and told Ima that he had to open the stomach up wide because the pus was everywhere; I was lucky to be alive.

Later in the morning, I noticed my father standing behind the door crying hysterically. I asked Tova to call him in. He came to me, his eyes and cheeks wet, and hugged me. He took my head into his arms and cried out, "Why is she burning from a fever?" He asked what had happened to me and why I waited so long to get help. I told him that Cahana had threatened to punish me if I had left the building. I also told him that I was having attacks for two years, but nobody paid attention to me; if anything, people believed that I pretended to be sick. Nurse Tziporah came into my room every three to four hours to give me an injection for the pain, which in and of itself hurt. Once in a while, Ima, Tova, or Aba would wet a cloth and wash off my lips and my face. Tova was exhausted, but she was not going to leave me.

Five days after my surgery, the nurse took me out of bed for the first time. I asked her to place me near the door so that I could see some action in the halls. But with my luck, I only saw beds filled with young soldiers who were injured during the war or from exploded mines. One of them was in a one piece cast that covered his entire body; only his eyes were uncovered. An eighteen-year-old had burns across most of his body. Others were missing body parts and limbs. One beautiful nineteen-year-old even lost his eyes and his arms; the others were indescribable. It looked worse than anyone can imagine.

My heart went out to them. I lifted myself slowly from the recliner and, while holding on to the side rails, set out to visit the young victims. These children screamed from pain and fear; their panic attacks were indescribable. One of the soldiers even thought he saw a machine gun; it was only the cleaning lady passing by with her wagon. He started to scream and cry. They were in such bad shape that even their parents were unable to look at them. I don't know why, but I felt as though I had known them forever, and I was determined to help. As hard as it was for me to look at them, I asked the nurse to bring me a wheelchair, and I wheeled myself slowly toward each one of them to offer my blessings, comfort and hope. This was a perfect time for me to appreciate my health and life, and I knew that I had to do something to get stronger so that I could help others. I could not have my health fail me because there were people sicker than I was, and they were supposed to be the focus of attention during the critical post war period when they were fighting for their lives. Some of them lost their siblings during the war, and I had to help them to stay alive.

I learned that my mission was to help the orphans and the sick. My illness was just a path for me to find others who needed help. I was a messenger sent by *Hashem* (G-d); I just wanted Him to lead me to these people painlessly so that I could be of assistance to them. My sister Tova was already engaged, and she would soon leave me and go on with her life. It was time to grow stronger and follow the rest of my life's path to future adventures. I pictured myself looking out a window, where I was able to see the real world.

On Friday, July 21, I was surprised by my teacher Yehudith. She came to visit me in the hospital and told me that she was waiting for her daughter to come too. She had prepared everything for me for the Sabbath, *challah*, a malt drink, fish, grape juice, chicken soup with noodles, a piece of chicken, gefilte fish, a piece of cake, fruits, and chocolates. She also got a card game for me, and a book of *Tehillim* (Psalms) so that I could pray for myself and for others who were sick.

The fact that I knew that people cared about me made me feel better. It gave me a good reason to live and look for solutions that would help me overcome any anger I had toward those who had hurt me and made me sick. I knew that it would be hard for me to forgive certain people, but I decided to forgive, not forget. My past would remind me how to teach my future children, friends, or even students, clients, or patients. I had many prophetic visions that told me that I would be someone very special if I survived my diseases, the brutal abuse I endured in the *mosad*, and the destruction of war.

There were three other women besides me in my room: Libby, a seventy-four-year-old with a cast on her leg and a fractured hip; Bella, who had her hemorrhoids removed and was not the nicest person; and Shushana, a nice lady who had surgery on her veins. Libby was the most fun of the three. I asked Shushana, who was able to walk around, to help me set a Sabbath table. On Friday night, I made *Kiddush* for all of us. The nurse brought in the *challah* and the food, and we all celebrated Shabbat. As sick as we were, we sang *zemirot* (Shabbat songs). After our meal, I asked the nurse to help me get off the bed, and I went to wish the young soldiers "*Shabbat shalom.*"

I was discharged from the hospital on Wednesday, July 26, and Tova took me back to the *mosad*'s infirmary. There I stayed for one day, and in the meantime, Tova packed all of our belongings. We went to Ima's home, where I was able to recuperate from the surgery. We also had to get ready for our baby brother Motty's *bar mitzvah.*

I was under the care of Dr. Eizikowitz, and he saw to it that I would get stronger. Tova had made me a beautiful pink dress with black pearl buttons for this special occasion. I bought a new pair of stockings, and wore pink shoes to match my dress.

On Friday night, July 28, I developed a high fever again and felt terrible pain in my legs. I was so sick that I was unable to go to the *bar mitzvah* or attend the party that took place the same Sabbath in the *Gur Yeshiva* (synagogue) that Aba used to attend. On Saturday morning, when I woke up, Ima noticed that I had a rash all over my body. She gave me medications for the fever, and called a babysitter to look after me until the party ended. She then took me to see the doctor, who told her that I had measles.

Ima felt very bad that I was unable to attend my brother's *bar mitzvah*, so she planned something immediately afterward. She invited all of our adult relatives and neighbors who already had the measles and made another, smaller party for Motty that I could attend. I was too sick to walk or even sit up straight, so she put me in a reclining position for a few minutes while my brother gave a little speech. I was very thankful. All of the guests kept me company as I lay in bed. They all wanted to see my incision, but I was burning off a fever and was not in the mood to show my belly to anyone. And besides, why would anyone want to see a little belly with a huge scar, with twenty four pins holding my stomach together?

My problem began when the incision became infected and did not heal properly, a probable result of the measles that I got right after my surgery. I had to return to the surgeon, who tried to cure my infection; when my fever continued to rise, he decided to open the incision and let the pus drain. I was in so much pain and agony, but Tova and Ima stood by my side and took very good care of me. They bought ices for me and gave me everything I liked to eat. Motty played games with me and kept me busy so that I would only think about good things.

Only one month after Motale's *bar mitzvah*, and six weeks after my surgery, my father decided that it was time to find a *shidduch* (match) for me. He wanted to get rid of me at the age of fourteen and a half. He made me so angry that I threatened to rebel against him and run away if he pushed me to do such an inhumane thing. Here I was trying to put my life together and overcome all of the negative forces that were causing me to consider suicide or to run away, and all I needed now was for my father to add more stress to my already weak soul.

One day he arrived at the *mosad* and told me that he had come

to buy shoes for me. I was shocked because my father never invited me to a store to buy anything; only my mother took care of such needs. He took me first to the *Mea Shearim shuk* (open-air market). Whenever I liked something, he told me that he first wanted to go to other stores before he could decide what to buy me. He then took me to the *Mea Shearim yeshiva* (boys school) and asked me to wait outside for a few minutes. I stood like an idiot against a tree, away from the *yeshiva* (boys school) , because it was not appropriate for a girl to stand near a boys' *yeshiva* (boys school). I waited until one of the rabbis came out with my father. The rabbi, a teacher, told me that he had a very good match for me. My first question was if the boy had already celebrated his *bar mitzvah*. He replied with such an affirmative, "Of course, he had his *bar mitzvah* almost four years ago." I looked into his eyes angrily and told him that I was glad that this little *schmeker* had his *bar mitzvah* almost four years ago, but it was only two and a half years since my *bat mitzvah* and I was still in diapers. My father got so mad at me, telling me that nobody had to know my age. I told him that it was good enough that I knew it.
The matchmaker saw that I was hard to deal with, so he told my father that he would stay in touch with him. I told the matchmaker that he had no right to meddle in my life, and that if he had something to say about me, he should say it directly to me. The matchmaker did not like my attitude, and this was the last time I ever heard from him. Aba continued schlepping me from store to store; again, whenever I saw a shoe I liked, my father would tell me he wanted to keep looking. After a while I told him that I did not need shoes, and I refused to go with him to any more stores.

We finally reached a restaurant on Geulah Street, across the street from the *Gerer Yeshiva* (boys school). Aba ordered a meal for the two of us. I told him, "Aba, you did not come to buy shoes for me, you came to find a husband for me." As soon as we finished eating, Aba told me that he had an appointment with a man on Rechavia Street, and that he was in a hurry. I told him that he could go wherever he wanted, but that I was ready to go back to the *mosad*. He begged me to come with him because this other matchmaker wanted to see me. I told him that I refused to show my face to any man and said goodbye.

I went back to the *mosad,* crying hysterically. I was very upset. Since I was twelve, my father and his cousin Chazkel had been teasing me with the prospect of marriage. I got so sick of their remarks that I hated them both. My father needed some help for his bizarre actions; I was only a helpless child. I felt belittled for growing up in an orphanage, and for the abuse I suffered there. My own father, who was so antiquated in his opinions, had some nerve to tell me that I had an appendix attack because I needed to get married. I cried day and night and asked *Hashem* (G-d) to have mercy on me, impart wisdom into my young mind and give me the strength to overcome all the obstacles that were in my way.

MY FIFTEENTH BIRTHDAY

Another year had passed, and thank G-d I was still alive. My fifteenth birthday was on Thursday, the twenty fourth day of the month of Elul. Based on my father's philosophy and that of *Bayit Lepletot*, I was considered a very old bachelorette. These people needed to work hard to find me a husband; otherwise, I would remain an old maid that nobody would want to marry. Rabbi Poppenheim called me into his office and told me that he had a very fine young man who would make a nice groom for me. The little stinker was seventeen-years-old, with *payes* (hairlocks) dangling to his waistline, and he was physically handicapped. To justify this beautiful match, the rabbi started to point out my faults, hoping to convince me that I should be happy if anyone were to marry me. I saw that these *Yerushalmim* (Jerusalem residents) were very sick, and I told him that it appeared that this crippled boy would be a perfect match for his beautiful blond daughters. I then walked away. This was the first and last time that Rabbi Poppenheim looked for my soul mate.

My seventeen and a half-year-old sister was busy getting ready for her own upcoming wedding. She ran around looking for clothing, linens, and dishes. She took me along with her to look for an apartment, furniture, and drapes, and we were busy day and night. I was not sure what kind of life she was going to have because she was talked into a match with a man from the ultra-Orthodox *Neturei Karta* sect in Jerusalem. To marry him, she would have to give up her beauty and be dressed in black clothes and socks and a *tichel* (head scarf) as a reminder of the destruction of the holy Temple. She would essentially be sheltered from any world outside of *Mea Shearim.* Nobody asked her if she wanted to marry this guy; she only did what she was told. All I could tell her was either to put up with wearing this garb or leave him; however, I did give her my blessings that her future husband would be normal and good to her and that she would be happy for the rest of her life.

Tova got married in the orphanage on Thursday, January 21, 1968, the nineteenth day of *Kislev*. My parents and brothers, uncles and aunts, cousins, friends, teachers, counselors, Tova's in-laws from England and relatives and friends from the groom's side all participated in the wedding. The *Toldos Aharon rebbe* (rabbi) and *rebbetzin* (rabbi's wife) participated too. Even though the wedding was beautiful, I was worried about how Tova would feel afterwards. The crowd to whom her husband belonged was not for her. My parents were much more modern and were very much involved with the real world, and I believed Tova was entering a cult that would prevent her from living a normal life.

I loved Tova very much, but I knew that I would not be able to spend much time around her or her fanatic husband. I became more modern in my outlook, and at this point, did not want to have anything to do with *Hasidic* Jews or their lifestyle. I liked my friends from the orphanage and school as well as my teachers and counselors who were kind to me, and I planned to stay friends with them for the rest of my life. I was not willing to marry a man from their crowd, however, nor change my looks or personality. I wanted to stay religious but also be able to relate to the rest of the world.

After Tova's wedding, I continued to work in the infirmary and with young and autistic children. In the evenings I practiced music, and went twice a week to the *Bais Yaakov* School For Girls to study *Tanach* (the Hebrew Bible). On the weekends I volunteered in hospitals, where I met many friends. Many nurses and doctors used to invite me to participate in lectures; they even advised me to sign up for a nursing course. I knew that I could have succeeded in this field, but was afraid to do so because I did not want to hurt the people in the *mosad*, my friends or my family. Also, I did not want them to turn against me.

I had the option of moving into the nurses' dormitory, but because I was drifting away from the *Hasidic* world, I was afraid that I would stop being religious altogether. Therefore, I had to stay strong and continue to do what I was doing without hurting others or myself. In my mind I wanted to emulate the nurses, but inside my heart, I felt as if a little person was there to remind me who I was and where I came from.

At this time I rebelled against the fanatics by changing my hairstyle, from two long braids to one. Instead of wearing long-sleeved tops that reached my fingers, I folded the sleeves a little higher than my wrist. I changed from wearing dark to lighter colored clothes. As soon as Cahana saw me at the *mosad* sporting one braid, she slapped me across the face and hit me violently. I then told her about her son, who was wearing a bolero with a penny-sized *yarmulke* (skullcap) and was hardly religious, while in the *mosad*, she had the nerve to beat children. She had nothing to say, and continued hitting me.

If this was not enough, I had a new Gestapo member ruling my life. My new brother in law wanted me to change back to wearing long black dresses and two braids. It reminded me of the stories my mother used to tell me: that the Jewish people were killed by the Nazis because they believed the Jews were different than they were. They wanted all human beings to be of one race. In the *Hasidic* world it is the same. Anyone who looks different from them is not considered a Jew. This is where hatred comes in, and is the cause of destruction.

I did not take my brother-in-law's comments personally because I had the choice of whether or not to talk to him or visit his house. I did not owe him anything. He did not raise or support me. My parents were proud of me because they knew that I was intelligent, educated, open-minded and down to earth, all while following G-d's commandments. I dressed just like my mother did and did not rebel against my family. What did hurt me was that I loved Tova and wanted to continue being in her life as a token of appreciation for what she did for me all those years in the orphanage; now, I had the opportunity to help her. (I continue to remain close to Tova and her family and, despite our different lifestyles, I have managed to get along well with her husband.)

I also knew that the only way to get stronger was to ignore all obstacles and move on with life. I continued to work, and with time I grew physically and emotionally stronger. I knew exactly who I was, and in which direction I was going. I lived with positive goals. In the meantime, I occupied myself by helping other children in the orphanage. Those who wanted to be my friends were always welcome, and I respected those who wanted to distance themselves from me because Cahana told them to. They were children and I was never angry at anyone. The world is round and it had many good things to offer me and everyone else.

One day, a girl named Yehudith got very sick. Hass-Neiny did not feel that her condition was serious enough to warrant taking her to the hospital. But when I saw that her joints were red and that she had a high fever for more than three days and was unable to eat or drink, I decided to take her to see Dr. Polak in the health center. The doctor sent us to the laboratory for some tests; when the blood count came back, she asked me to take Yehudith to the Bikur Cholim Hospital in Jerusalem. There she was evaluated by the emergency room doctor and was diagnosed with rheumatic fever. She was admitted to the pediatric unit. Yehudith was very frightened, so I sat with her in the hospital from three P.M. until midnight. I spoke to her and promised to visit her daily. I even held her in my arms. She was not much younger than I was, but six years made a big difference for children living in an orphanage.

It was about ten P.M. when Esther Hershkowitz, the house mother for the preschool children, and Frieda Grossman, a counselor, showed up at the hospital to check on Yehudith. I stayed with them for an hour and then told them that I was going to speak to the nurse in charge and ask her to look after Yehudith. By the time I got back to the room, the two ladies left.

At this late hour I was afraid to walk back by myself to the orphanage because it was not safe at night, so I waited in the hospital until some of the nurses finished up their evening shift and could take me home. The nurses finished their job at eleven P.M., but when the night shift came, they had to make rounds and hand the reports over to the next shift, so it took even longer for me to get home. Among the nurses were two male residents who worked on the pediatric unit. They were all kind enough to take me home. On the way, I noticed some *Hasidic* people who lived across the street from the *mosad* looking out their windows; not only did they see me walking with non religious people, but I was accompanied by two males.

In front of the entrance, I was welcomed by Cahana, Esther Hershkowitz, Frieda Grossman, my counselor Gittle Rosenberg, and Tova. As soon as I walked into the building Cahana slapped me across the face. She accused me of going out with men and non-religious nurses, which was against the rules. At first I looked into the eyes of Esther and Frieda, and asked them why they left without me. They told me that I did not come back right away. In the meantime, one of the nosy neighbors had called the *mosad* and accused me of going out with a group of low lives. I reminded them that I was trying to help a sick child I had brought into the hospital. I asked Esther, was this what I deserved for working for her without pay in the infirmary for two years, helping her with the children every time she needed me and watching over other children at the hospital without getting any sleep? And now, after being exhausted from a long day, I had to get beaten until my nose bled?

I tried to ignore them and started to walk up the stairs to my bedroom. Cahana chased me and beat me up for walking away. This sick lady was on my case day and night. Tova wanted me to come to sleep at her place, but I refused to go. I wanted to go to sleep and never wake up. I did so many good things by helping other children and taking care of them, but nobody wanted to listen to the truth.

That same Saturday night, my sister's friend Pninah Geller, who became my friend after Tova got married, invited me to go with her to Geulah Street to buy ourselves a falafel, with our counselors permission. When we returned, we decided to walk on Strauss Street, which was better lit, instead of Chaye Adam Street, which was dark and very scary to walk on at night. But Aviva and Sarah spied on us and reported to Cahana that they saw us near a theater; they thought we went to see a movie. Once again, without asking us the facts, Cahana called us into her office. Without asking us questions, she beat up Pninah like a terrorist. She was unable to defend herself. I called to her, "Murderer, leave my friend alone," but she kept on beating us. I told Cahana that our counselor had given us permission to go out and buy a falafel, but she wouldn't listen. I then told Pninah to run out of the office, and when she did, I gave Cahana a kick. She was shocked, but I told her that if she lifted a hand to any child again, I would report it to the police. She thought that I was joking, but I meant it, and I was not going to let any child get hurt again. I was willing to take all the abuse, but I did not want anyone else to experience a tragic life at the hands of a sick beast like Cahana. I left her office, but Cahana continued calling me back. I refused to listen to her, and Pninah and I went into the *moadon* to read some books.

There was a girl at the orphanage named Chaya. This child was a nebbish. Children used to laugh at Chaya, who had a very bad odor coming from her body. She had crushes on counselors and other girls whom she adored alot, but they could not stand her. The only girls who would be her friends were Tova and me. When Tova got married, Chaya was already twenty-one-years-old, the oldest of all the children there. Girls her age already had a house full of children, but who was going to marry this mentally retarded person? Nobody knew, that she was not as retarded as she appeared. She came from a very poor family. Her father was crippled from the waist down, and her mother took care of her sickly husband. Because of the difficulties her parents had, her poor mother had to send her children to orphanages, where they could get the care they needed. Chaya had crushes on other girls and counselors because she needed to be loved and hugged, and she needed someone to guide her on how to dress, bathe, and groom herself like the other girls. She was old in age, but very childish in mind.

After Tova's wedding, I decided to move into the room with Chaya. Only the two of us shared this room. This girl was bored, so I decided to make her into a real person. I went to Cahana, and asked her to give Chaya a job to help her feel important. Instead of listening to me, she smacked Chaya across her face, and told her that she would have to stay put in her room. I was no longer going to tolerate and give in to this barbaric, sick animal, so I called the police and filed a claim of abuse. She received a warning, but as soon as the police left, she told me that she was not afraid of them and she threatened to hit Chaya again. I assumed that I was her target, but since I would give it right back to her, she decided to turn her anger or frustration on my friends and hit them instead.

I hugged Chaya and took her up to our room, and I told her that I had a plan for her. I decided to cut her hair. I asked her to take a warm shower and I sprayed her with a touch of cologne. I asked Hass-Neiny to give her a nice dress. My plan was to take her in the morning to the employment office and begin looking for a job for her. Chaya was all excited about my idea, and she did as I told her. The two of us went to sleep early and in the morning, we cleaned our room and fixed our beds, and I opened the windows to air out the room. I took her into the powder room to brush her teeth, and I combed her hair and sprayed it with a little bit of hair spray. She put on nice clothes and black dressy shoes with little heels that I had bought for her.

After all the girls went to school, Chaya and I went to the employment office. Before we went in, I put some makeup on her face and sprayed a drop of cologne on her so that she would smell good. When it was time for our interview, she looked just like a typical twenty-one-year-old girl. I was not very surprised how intelligently she answered all the interviewer's questions. She had a beautiful smile on her face and felt like a million dollar lady. The man sent us to a garment factory, where Chaya was hired.

I also took her to the hospital to visit the sick. It made her feel good and very important. When I went to pick her up from work, Chaya was so happy. Her eyes looked so bright, and she smiled and called out happily, "I cannot believe that I have a job." She realized she was not crazy and could do everything they asked her to do. I gave her a hug and with tears, I told her, "Chaya'le, you are old enough to take care of yourself. If you have a problem, learn to help yourself because you are your best friend, and no one knows what you really need." My plan was great, and the girl was happy, but not for too long.

One week later, when Cahana found out that Chaya was working, having finally found a resolution for her miserable life, she waited for her at work and forced her to leave her job. The girl went into a major depression, and cried day and night. She no longer got dressed in nice clothes, nor put on lipstick, or smiled. This was the worst thing I had ever seen. She was yelled at or smacked every time she passed by Cahana. I decided to go back to the police and file another claim of child abuse. Cahana received a written warning. She kept on teasing me, but I did everything in my power to protect the innocent children.

In the morning, I went down to the dining room to eat lunch. On this day we had five South African sponsors. Rabbi Poppenheim gave them a tour around the facilities, and then they came down to tour the dining room. When these guests passed by my table, they looked at me. One man asked me how old I was, and I told him I was sixteen. A lady asked me how long I had been in the orphanage; I told her eleven miserable years. Another lady asked me if I was going to high school. I told her that I was out of school for two years, but was working for two schools and in the infirmary and did volunteer work in the hospitals. I added that high school was not required in the orphanage. Rabbi Poppenheim was very disturbed by my answers and tried to shut my mouth. Why didn't he call his guests away if he did not like my answers? These people kept on asking me more questions, but I told them that I had a very busy schedule. Besides working for so many hours, I was taking music lessons and attended Torah studies at the *Bais Yaakov* seminary every Wednesday night.

This was the first time that anybody in the *mosad* knew my schedule. It was forbidden to study music there, but music was my best friend and I needed an outlet to express my anger. I was not going to take drugs to calm me down, so I kept myself busy doing good things. I was still very active in sports and crafts, and could not sit still and do nothing. These guests were very impressed about what I had told them, but Rabbi Poppenheim looked very disappointed.

By this time we had another *menahel* (principal) named Yitzhak Stern. (We called him *pukid*, or secretary.) Later he was given the new title of Rabbi Stern. Everybody in the *mosad* knew that I played the melodica very well, but I never told anyone that I took music lessons. I was always yelled at or smacked when I practiced my music. But today, Rabbi Stern asked me to play music for the guests. I refused and told them that I could not play because I would get beaten up, but Rabbi Stern begged me to; he knew that he was one of the people who stopped me from playing, and he felt hurt. These visitors were very smart. They felt that I was very intelligent and had many things going my way. They were impressed with what I had to offer and wanted to see what they were paying for.

I finished eating and then went up to my room to get some rest. Rabbi Stern came to visit along with his guests, who waited for me to invite them in and to play for them. I had the feeling that they knew that I was in distress; I also knew that if I displayed my talents, they would give a nice amount of money to the *mosad*. Yet when they left, I would continue to be abused and tortured. *Pukid* begged me to play just this one time. I felt bad for him and took out my melodica.

They all sat next to me and I played for them. It did not take long before I burst into tears and was unable to catch my breath. One of the ladies hugged me and asked me to tell her why I was so bitter. I wished that they would just offer to take me with them, but I did not want to say anything else. They all kissed me and had tears in their eyes.

I got up and went to Tova's house to cry my heart out to her. She asked me to go back to the *mosad* and pack my belongings, and she invited me to move into her house. I used to visit Tova daily since her marriage. Her husband went to *shul* (synagogue) very early in the morning, and while Tova was still asleep, I would come into the house to clean it and prepare breakfast for her and her husband. I know that she appreciated everything I did for her, which is why she invited me to live with her. Tova had a very nice, large apartment. She had a huge hallway at the entrance. On the left side of the house was one bedroom, the kitchen and the bathroom, and on the right side was the living room and another bedroom. I would not have been in their way, but I knew that it was not right for me to live with such a young couple.

But I did as Tova asked me just to get out of the concentration camp I lived in for eleven years. I went back to the *mosad* and packed all my personal belongings, leaving behind my friends and the place I called home. Before I left, I went down to the dining room to eat lunch because I wanted to sit next to my friends. The tables were set very festively with white tablecloths; next to each setting was a little white bag with the nicest fruits for *Tu B'Shevat*.

After lunch, I went to see my counselor, Gittle, whom I loved very much. I gave her a kiss and told her with a broken voice that I had decided to leave the *mosad*. She asked me where I was going, and I told her that I was moving into Tova's house until I found another solution. She gave me her blessings and a warm hug. I called a taxi and planned to leave the orphanage for good, without saying goodbye to anyone else. I made up my mind this time that nobody would ever send me back to this place. If anyone tried to convince me to return, I would either run away or have to kill myself. I had had it.

While waiting for her car, Cahana came over to me and asked me where I was going. I told her that it was not her business, and politely added that I would never forgive her for what she did to my friends and me. I also told her that she would have to turn over in her grave to seek my forgiveness and, pointing at her, that I would never forgive this devil.

I suddenly remembered that I had to see Hass-Neiny, our house mother, so I ran up quickly to her studio and fell right into her arms. She did not know why I was there nor why I was crying in her arms. It took me time to thank her for being so understanding and being an excellent mother to all of the children. When I told her that I was leaving, she tried to convince me to stay. I told her that I was afraid that Cahana would cause me to do stupid things; it was now the right time for me to leave. We kissed each other and she gave me her blessings.

In the meantime the taxi arrived. I loaded my bags into the trunk and off I went to Tova's house. Because I did not know how long I would be able to stay with my fanatic brother-in-law, I had to plan immediately where my next home would be. I quit my jobs and seminary classes and was left with memories of my years in exile that would continue to haunt me for the rest of my life.

I lived with Tova for only three weeks. Even though we got along well, and despite the fact that I helped her all the time around the house, went shopping, and accompanied her wherever she wanted to go. I felt I had to leave because it was not right for me to live with a newlywed couple and my brother-in-law constantly made remarks about my dresses, shoes and hair. He would not even walk into the house if, G-d forbid, he heard me singing. It was his house and he had the right to tell me how to act there, but it was my choice either to accept his chronic criticism or leave.

Before I left Tova's house I went to look for a *kibbutz*

(collective farm) where I felt that I could work and earn my meals and clothes. The *kibbutzim* were not Orthodox, but it was the religious people who kicked me around and failed to make me feel welcome, loved, and understood. What else could I do? I tried to go to another orphanage, a *kibbutz*, or even a community school, but I was rejected because I came from a *yeshiva* in *Mea Shearim*. Even people from an Orthodox school like *Bais Yaakov* believed that I was rebelling by leaving such a place.

I went to the office in Tel Aviv that arranged *kibbutz* stays for children and told them my situation. They gave me two options. I either needed consent from an older caregiver or had to wait until I was seventeen before they could accept me without notifying anyone where I was. I was ready to join one, but did not want to hurt my mother. I asked them about *Kibbutz Chafetz Chaim*, which is an Orthodox *kibbutz*. The office manager called my mother, who came and asked me not to follow my weakest instincts. She promised me that I would regret doing so. I hugged her and gave her two options. She should either take me home without making me feel guilty for leaving the orphanage or register me at a *kibbutz*. I was no longer going to put up with any abuse. Politely, I also gave her another option, that I would find a home in the streets.

Ima took me into her arms and asked me what I would do at home all day long. I told her that I wanted to work and help her around the house. I could go to evening school and make money from selling my needlepoint. She told me that she was sick and did not want me to see how she suffered, but I wanted to be there for her and help the woman who always took care of me. In sickness and in health, and in rain, heat, wind, snow, and hail, she came to visit us. Ima took me by the hand and said, "Let's go home." We decided that Ima would go back home, and I returned to Jerusalem to pick up my belongings from Tova's house. I came back the same night to Ima's house.

The next day, Ima took me to meet an employment counselor, who found me a temporary job in an architect's office processing pay stubs. After work, Ima took me to the *Histadrut* to register me for sewing classes. I felt great and so did my "*Yiddishe mame*"(Jewish mother). Every single day, she either picked me up from work or I went to get her, and we took the bus home together. We were the best of friends. My brother Motty came home every Sabbath, and we were very happy. Meyer already had a baby boy, so his family also came, and when Tova heard that Meyer was coming, she and her husband decided to join us.

Once I was home, my father started putting pressure on me to get married. I refused to do so because I was only sixteen-and-a-half years-old and was still a child. I wanted to grow up, make more friends, and have a life. The European mentality was so old-fashioned, and he believed that as soon as a girl reached puberty, she had to get married. Whether I liked it or not, I had to give in; right after Purim 1969, I got engaged without my consent.

MY BINDING LOVE WITH MY HUSBAND

My husband Avraham was born on the last day of Passover, the 20th day in the month of Nissan, 1948, in Iasi, Romania. Both of his parents were Holocaust survivors. His father, Morris, Z"L, lived through both World War I and World War II. My father-in- law was the older son and has one brother who is still living in Israel. Morris's mother died in 1972, at the age of ninety six, and his father died many years ago. Avraham's mother, Liebbe, Z"L, was one of six children. All her siblings died at a very young age after very long illnesses, leaving many orphaned children. Only one sister is still alive. She is living in Israel but has been estranged from the family.

Morris lived through many difficult times in the eighty six years of his life, but his experience during World War II brought him a lot of pain. He lost his first wife, the mother of their three children, Yissi, Yehoshuah, and Judith. She was sprayed with bullets for saving a woman and her hungry children. After his wife's death, Morris was left to take care of his three orphaned children and to see to it that they would have a safe life in the promised land. Yissi, the eldest of the three children, left Romania and safely reached Israel, while Yehoshuah, who went to Israel with a youth organization, did not arrive at his destination because the British army, who was governing Israel at that time, intercepted him and sent him to jail in Cyprus. There he stayed for six months until one of the rabbis who had accompanied the children on the boat helped free him.

In 1942, Morris married a young woman, Liebbe, who had a one-year-old daughter, Batsheva. Six years later, my husband was born and in 1951, came to Israel with the rest of his family. Their family was sent to an immigration tent encampment in *Shaar Ha'aliyah*; a few weeks later, they were transferred to a transit camp in *Or Akiva*, Caesaria. Life for Morris and his family in Israel was very difficult because they were placed in a tent without water, electricity, and bathrooms, and there was no employment or immediate schooling for the children. They also did not speak the Hebrew language.

In order to meet the needs of their children, the parents had no other choice but to place the two girls in a boarding school. Yissi was an adult who had a permanent job. Yehoshuah went to learn in a *yeshiva* (boys school) and he grew up to be the founder of a *yeshiva* in the southern part of Israel. He was the only one who went into the desert and turned the land into a blossoming city for the learning of Torah. For my husband, life in Caesaria was very hard because his father wanted him to grow up in a true torah environment, and the only Orthodox school there was for Sephardic children. They did not like the Ashkenazi children, and bullied him because he was the only Ashkenazi student in the school who did not speak the language yet.

It got to a point where his parents had to move to *B'nei Brak*, a city where most residents are Orthodox and of European origin. In his new home, Avraham made a lot of friends, but was not able to invite them into his home because his family was very poor, living in a one room apartment in an abandoned building without windows, a shower or bathtub. A broken stairway led to their apartment, and the roof leaked. In the summer, the heat was unbearable, and in the winter they suffered from the elements pouring into the house through the roof and missing windows. The children became very sick with colds and rheumatoid arthritis.

In 1952, Morris and Liebbe were blessed with another son, Daniel. At this time, Morris worked for the city cutting and planting trees and working on the roads or wherever else they needed him. These jobs were temporary; the city officers were just playing with him. He would work for a week, and then be unemployed for many months. He was unable to provide even for the basic needs of his children. Morris, eventually gave up looking for work and retired. As the baby grew older, Liebbe got a housekeeping job at a *yeshiva* in *B'nei Brak*. Avraham went to the local *talmud torah yeshiva*, where he tried to learn to the best of his capability. His older brothers were independent, and his parents were not learned, so he never had any help with his studies.

During his first year of high school, Avraham went to learn in a local *yeshiva*. That same year his mother became sick with esophageal cancer, and in 1963, died at the age of forty two. She left behind her two young sons who had to raise themselves. His older brothers and sisters were all married and had their own families, and his sixty-two year-old father was retired and had no strength to raise a fifteen-year- old and an eight-year-old child. My dear husband, who was left to fend for himself at such a young age, had to quit school and go to work to bring in some money for himself, his younger brother, and his retired father.

Until the end of the eighth grade, Daniel continued to learn at the local *talmud torah yeshiva*; for high school, he studied and lived at the *Ramat Hasharon Yeshiva*. With his high motivation to learn and the financial and emotional support of his older brother, who encouraged him to continue his studies even when he wanted to quit, he completed the highest level of learning at the *yeshiva* in *Kfar Hasidim*, a farm near Haifa. Daniel was ordained and founded a *yeshiva* in *B'nei Brak*. With his outstanding talents, Daniel was introduced and married Shifra, a true woman of valor, who is a charitable, righteous, pleasant, and soft-spoken woman. I love her very much and she is a special kind of sister-in-law that respects the privacy of family. These two wonderful people were blessed with Torah-loving children who emulate their parents. With the help of his wife, Daniel followed his brother Yehoshuah's path, and he too built a talmudical school, which houses six hundred students. He also works for the Rabbinical Court in Israel.

After his mother's death, Avraham needed to do something to fill the void besides working all day long to support his family. He decided to buy himself a clarinet and a saxophone and started practicing many hours a day until he became an outstanding clarinetist, playing Jewish and klezmer music. At the age of seventeen, Avraham was already performing. Besides working as a jeweler during the day, playing music at night, and playing soccer every Friday, he also attended evening classes at the Belz Seminary.

On Feb. 3, when I left the orphanage, I returned home to live with Ima. One day a man named Mr. Frankel approached my parents with the prospects of introducing me to a boy. As I have already said, I was not in favor of this idea because I was only sixteen-and-a-half years-old and wanted to continue my education. Mr. Frankel was very adamant and forceful about what he wanted, making continual nightly visits to the point that my parents were forcing me to meet this boy.

As a joke I told everyone at the table that evening that I only wanted a boy named Avraham, and that he should be a musician. Low and behold, a few days later Mr. Frankel returned, all smiles, and said, "I have an Avraham for you who plays the clarinet." I said I was only joking and had no intention of getting married at this point in my life. Nobody took me seriously.

They found out that Avraham was playing at a wedding, so behind my back they set up an appointment for me to go to the hall and meet him. I refused to keep the appointment, so my future father-in-law was sent to meet me at my home. My father-in-law met me coming out of the shower dripping wet, barefoot, and with sopping wet long hair; he immediately commented that it was very impolite of me not to wear shoes. I looked at him and said that in my house I did what I wanted. I then walked away. I had an impression that he left our house disappointed.

On Saturday, March 8, 1969, just three days after Purim, I was told that I was having a visitor come see me later in the day. I was not informed about this appointment, and no one asked my opinion. My future father-in-law and the matchmaker returned to my home with Avraham, with the intention of making the match. When she saw him walking up the steps, my mother loved him immediately. Everyone left the room except Avraham and me. The door was left open for modesty purposes. Avraham sat on one side of the table and I sat on the other. Ima put out some leftover cake from Purim and a cold drink, and while we were talking, our parents were sitting in the kitchen, trying to listen to our conversation.

At first we were both shy, and neither of us knew how to start the conversation. I was the one to ask him what his name was, and then he asked me mine; this is how we got acquainted. I did not realize that this was the Avraham the matchmaker had in mind. My first impression was that he looked much older than I was and too tall for me. Because he was so shy, I was unable to judge his personality, goals, or thoughts. He asked me if I knew how to cook and sew, and I asked him if he knew how to repair a leaking sink or fix other broken things in the house. He said, "Yes, I do." I told him that I could cook and sew.

I wasn't interested in Avraham, so I told him all of my negative personality traits with the hope that he would lose interest and leave. But he told me that he liked me and my personality. After an hour, my mother suggested that we all take a walk together. During that time our shyness began to disappear, giving us more time to talk to each other. I actually found myself having a pleasant afternoon. My nature is to be daring and risky; little did I know that Avraham has the same nature. A little comedy entered our walk. The adults were walking ahead of us, and suddenly, Avraham saw a caterpillar crossing the street. He said to me, "Let's stop and see how long it will take for the caterpillar to cross the street." Meanwhile, the adults were out of sight, not realizing we were not behind them. Avraham said, "Let's pull a trick and hide behind the bushes." Suddenly, the adults realized that we were not behind them. As they were walking back to find us, Avraham and I ran up the road to get ahead of them. My mother then noticed us, and we finally came together. The adults said a few more words and we parted.

On Saturday night, March 22, I was very surprised to see three of my neighbors sitting in my living room when I returned home from my friend's house. Ima laughed when I asked her why our neighbors were in our home. An hour later, Avraham, his father, and the matchmaker came to my home, and I was very puzzled. I saw my neighbors signing some kind of paper, and I asked my mother what they were signing. She laughed and continued to watch the signing. Suddenly, there was a shout of "mazel tov," and I asked what this was for. I did not realize we were engaged. No flowers, no ring, and no pictures. I became upset, crying and threatening my parents that I would run away for good. I was only sixteen and a half years old, and I was not ready for marriage. I hated everybody in the room, especially my father, who was the one who arranged the match. I told my father that I would never forgive him for such an ugly thing he did to me, and I kept my promise. The European mentality was so old-fashioned, and children like ourselves were helpless because we could not give our opinions. We did not argue with our parents. Whatever they did and said was holy, and if we did not listen to them we were punished.

I realized that Ima loved my groom from the first moment she saw him. She pitied him because he never had a decent home, three square meals a day, clean clothes or a clean bed to sleep in; he did not know the meaning of love. My mother decided that he needed a home and a wife to take care of him, so she chose her daughter against her knowledge and permission. My dear mother invited him to our home for all the meals, including the Sabbath and holidays. Could it be that Ima wanted us to know each other? She gave him a mother's love. She gave me money to buy him food and supply him with additional pocket money. She also made sure that he had clean towels when he showered in our house. My mother's actions with my groom made me angry because I wanted to be supported by a husband and not have to give him money for a bus ride.

When my mother saw that I was upset, at a time when most girls are happy to be engaged, she started to cry and told me, "He is an orphan and we have to help him." I was thinking to myself that if my wonderful mother wanted to help this poor boy, why did she have to include me in her *mitzvah* (good deed)? Today, girls would tell their parents to mind their own business and never do such a thing behind their back. Which culture was healthier?

At this juncture, I would like to point out a very serious problem in today's worldly culture. During the time when my marriage was arranged, love was not a factor; the European mentality was that as a couple grows together they will learn to respect and love each other. Today, love and instant gratification is the name of the game. As a result of this instant love, children coming from broken homes suffer, and the divorce rate is horrendous. In the 1800s, a Jewish bride and groom first met under the *chuppa* (canopy), and it was an excellent match because they both came from the same town and prayed in the same synagogue. Their mothers cooked the same food, and they had the same religious practices and language. There was no adjustment to be made. Everyone married within his or her social class. And do you want to know something? They celebrated their fiftieth anniversary together with their extended family, who followed the ways of their ancestors.

From the day Avraham became part of our family, the Sabbaths in our home were the most spiritual celebrations in town. He was always singing and attracted all the neighbors, and everybody used to compliment his voice. We used to watch Rabbi Weiss and his wife and the other neighbors standing on their terrace enjoying themselves and singing along with him.

On Sunday, Oct. 12, the thirtieth of *Tishrei*, we got married in the Viznitz Hall in *B'nei Brak*. My siblings, parents, many friends from the orphanage, the founder of the orphanage and his wife, and many neighbors and relatives participated in our wedding. Avraham's siblings, his father, and many of his friends and relatives attended as well. The party was beautiful, but I was bored and wanted to go home. The women wanted to watch the men dance and forgot about me.

After my wedding Ima started to arrange all the papers she needed to immigrate to the United States. She had always wondered what it was like to live, work and pray in a free country. She sold many things, including her apartment, so that she would have the money to start her new life in a new land. Avraham was very upset when Ima told us that she had set the date to leave Israel. He felt as though he was losing another mother, whom he loved.

Ultimately, I am thankful to G-d and to my parents for marrying me off, because I cannot imagine the kind of life I would have without my own family. I have a fine, hard working husband, and three very special children. My responsibilities helped me mature and understand life better.

EPILOGUE

I am sitting quietly in my living room and looking with deep love at pictures of my wedding and my wonderful children and grandchildren. My eyes slowly pass to a picture of the group of girls that I spent eleven years with. I thought we were a large, happy family like sisters should be. But when you started to reject and make fun of me, and when I had shortness of breath because I was hit on the head by one of our sick counselors, you continued to make fun of me instead of helping me through my seizure. What was in your mind when you made fun of my suffering? Why didn't you comfort me instead? Could it be that you were jealous of my being the center of attention, or that you thought I was very beautiful and popular?

Years have passed, and now that we are all adults, do you still have that childish inadequacy? What makes people jealous and act in a vengeful manner? You all know who you are. You left me with scars that cannot heal, but I have to go on with my life and I have a wonderful family that needs me. Do you have the same scars as I? What kind of role model are you to your kids?

I then turn the page of the album and see a petite, beautiful woman who was and still is my role model, my Ima. With tears in my eyes, my thoughts flash back to when I was five years old. I silently ask *Hashem* (G-d) how I endured my life. How did my mother, who was my beacon of strength, survive? How did my people survive and then return to having normal, thriving, religious Jewish communities? The saying "people are stronger than animals" comes to mind. How did other nations survive terrorism and madmen? I can only speak for myself when I say that I never for one minute forgot *Hashem* (G-d). The *Shema Yisrael* and the *Ani Ma'amin* were always on my lips; G-d was my strength.

Today I pray for my biological family and for my sisters from the *mosad* to have the *z'chut* (merit) to welcome the coming of the Messiah, so that all nations can live in total peace and harmony. As our prophet *Yeshayahu* (Isaiah) predicted, "The lion and the lamb will stand side by side in peace." Amen.

Now that my book is completed, I can sit back and breath easier. I can finally work towards my goal of helping children and mothers who might live in a similar environment as I did. My first step is to form a non profit organization named Kool Society for Children, Camp Chava, an outreach program that will provide advise, therapeutic education, and maybe even build an all year round camp/ orphanage/ home for children to turn to. This organization is named after my righteous mother Chava Z"L who sacrificed her life to save children during and after World War II, She was a woman who sacrificed her life to save her own children out of the hands of the missionaries and from the hands of people who would have taken her children away for good. Her love for children made it obvious to me that this is what she wanted me to do. "Save the children." With such a name attached to a facility or organization, children would be proud to tell the world where they are going and where they come from. However, in order to build such a nice loving home, I need help from many good hearted people. My husband, Rabbi Avraham Goldenthal, who is the leader of the Kol Rinah Orchestra, and who is well known to the *Kashrus* (Kosher Supervision) Industry, and my righteous children Chaya, her husband Asher, and their children, my exceptionally talented son Yankey who is a partner with his father in the band, and my youngest son Eli, who is well known to do *chesed* (good deeds) with elderly people, and who today calls himself "DJ Gold," are willing to help me fulfill my dream. Our loving, good hearted family who has experienced so much pain wants to help children and mothers learn how to cope with their own pain.

I can finally face reality, and confess that marriage was the only alternative for me at that time. Today, with the knowledge I now know about modern life I would have chosen to move in with a family

Len Platt has produced a ground-breaking book. *James Joyce and Education* is a forensic exploration of how Joyce's work engages with both the social and psychological aspects of schooling. Platt exposes how the structure of schooling and education at the time Joyce was writing, produced hierarchies and elites – something that endures within the education system of the here and now. This scholarly account is highly informative, readable and often amusing. This is a text not only for James Joyce scholars but for all who are concerned with how education policy and practice work to maintain social order and the status quo.

– **Rosalyn George**, *Professor of Education*, *Goldsmiths*, *University of London*

James Joyce and Education

James Joyce and Education is the first full-length study of education across the Joyce oeuvre. A new account of how the politics and aesthetics of the Joyce text is informed by historical contexts, it is the latest contribution to the growing contemporary debate about education, late modernism and literary innovation.

This highly original account reads *Dubliners*, *A Portrait of the Artist as a Young Man*, *Ulysses* and *Finnegans Wake* in new and challenging ways. It produces the Joyce text as a complex and comic devotion to the representation of schooled education – an exemplification of the elitism that state schooling was historically designed to reproduce and a devastating undoing of the epistemologies it was designed to sustain. Chapters explore a range of themes, including Joyce and radical education, the impact of Nietzsche's writing on Joyce and women and education.

The book will appeal to researchers, scholars and postgraduate students in the fields of literature in education, pedagogy, Joyce scholarship and modernism.

Len Platt has published widely on modernist literary culture, especially on the works of James Joyce. He is also a leading expert on early musical theatre and on the exchange and transfer practices that made it a characteristic culture of conservative popular modernism at the *fin de siècle*.

Literature and Education Series
Series Editors- David Aldridge and Andrew Green

Editors' Introduction

Dr Johnson, in an essay in *The Rambler* (31 March 1750), acknowledges the potential powers of literature. Because of the imaginative hold they exert over readers, he suggests that literary works enjoy formidable didactic potential, and 'may perhaps be made of greater use than the solemnities of professed morality, and convey the knowledge of vice and virtue with more efficacy than axioms and definitions'.

The aim of the Routledge *Literature & Education* series is to address the multiple ways in which education and literature interact. Numerous texts exist that deal with literary issues for educational purposes, serving the schools and higher education markets. Within the academic field of educational studies, there are works on the value of literature for moral formation or for the broader humanistic development of students of all ages. Within literary studies, there is a range of works that discuss the ways in which authors, texts or literary movements address educational themes. However, comparatively little has been written that specifically explores the complex notions of how literary texts function educatively, or what happens to them once they are brought into educational spaces and used for educational purposes. Additionally, limited attention has been paid explicitly to the ways in which literature can be a resource for educational thought or can nurture and inspire educational change.

This series provides a space for these issues to be explored. It presents scholarship working at the intersection of literary and educational studies and seeks to define an important and emerging area of interdisciplinary enquiry. Titles in this series engage in significant ways with what happens when an intermediate space opens up between the study of literature and the study of education. The series proposes a broad understanding of literature and education that is not bound by particular national, pedagogical or political contexts, and titles address one or more of the following themes:

1 Literature as education

> This theme connects discussions within educational studies and literary studies about the extent to which literature can or ought to be considered as educational.

2 The co-construction of literature and education

This theme addresses the various ways that the fields of literature and education have historically, theoretically and imaginatively served to co-construct one another, for example the relation of the literary canon to the literary curriculum, and the formation of literature as a school and university subject.

3 What literature can teach us about education

This theme addresses the ways that educational questions have been explored by different writers, literary movements and genres, drawing on the combined theoretical and interpretive resources of literary and educational studies.

Our hope is that this series will encourage thinking about the relationship between literary texts, readers and educators, providing an opportunity for creativity, investigation and debate. By forging new interconnections between literary and educational studies, it is our aim to encourage and open up fruitful new areas of thought and practice through which readers will be inspired to reconsider their understanding of both literature and education.

Books in this series

George Orwell and Education
Learning, Commitment and Human Dependency
Christopher Hanley

Literature and Understanding
The Value of a Close Reading of Literary Texts
J. W. Phelan

James Joyce and Education
Schooling and the Social Imaginary in the Modernist Novel
Len Platt

For more information about the series, please visit www.routledge.com/Literature-and-Education/book-series/LITED

James Joyce and Education

Schooling and the Social Imaginary in the Modernist Novel

Len Platt

Routledge
Taylor & Francis Group
LONDON AND NEW YORK

First published 2021
by Routledge
2 Park Square, Milton Park, Abingdon, Oxon OX14 4RN

and by Routledge
52 Vanderbilt Avenue, New York, NY 10017

Routledge is an imprint of the Taylor & Francis Group, an informa business

British Library Cataloguing-in-Publication Data
A catalogue record for this book is available from the British Library

Library of Congress Cataloging-in-Publication Data
Names: Platt, Len, author.
Title: James Joyce and education : schooling and the social imaginary in the modernist novel / Len Platt.
Description: Abingdon, Oxon ; New York, NY : Routledge, 2021. | Series: Literature and education | Includes bibliographical references and index.
Identifiers: LCCN 2020039460 (print) | LCCN 2020039461 (ebook) | ISBN 9780367859664 (hardback) | ISBN 9781003016045 (ebook)
Subjects: LCSH: Joyce, James, 1882–1941—Criticism and interpretation. | Education in literature.
Classification: LCC PR6019.O9 Z78215 2021 (print) | LCC PR6019.O9 (ebook) | DDC 823/.912—dc23
LC record available at https://lccn.loc.gov/2020039460
LC ebook record available at https://lccn.loc.gov/2020039461

ISBN: 978-0-367-85966-4 (hbk)
ISBN: 978-1-003-01604-5 (ebk)

Typeset in Goudy
by Apex CoVantage, LLC

Education . . . hallows so many lies.
Friedrich Nietzsche, *The Joyful Wisdom* (1910)

Contents

Abbreviations

D	*Dubliners*, the corrected text with an explanatory note by Robert Scholes and fifteen drawings by Robin Jacques (1914; London: Jonathan Cape, 1967).
FW	*Finnegans Wake* (London: Faber & Faber, 1939).
P	*A Portrait or the Artist as a Young Man*, edited with an introduction and notes by Jeri Johnson (1916; Oxford: Oxford University Press, 2000).
SH	*Stephen Hero* (London: Jonathan Cape, 1944).
U	*Ulysses*, the corrected text, edited by Hans Walter Gabler (1922; London: The Bodley Head, 1986).

Acknowledgments

> One of the many uses of our public schools is to confer an aristocracy on boys who do not inherit it.
>
> William Sewell, founder of Radley College (1872)

In 2001, I published a book called *Aristocracies of Fiction: the idea of aristocracy in late-nineteenth-century and early-twentieth-century literary culture*. In it I explored what I saw as a dominant trope in literary culture at the *fin de siècle*, a turn to aristocracy occurring at a time when traditional elites of the landed class were losing power in the real world on all fronts. After almost a century of being consigned to the margins – margins of narrative, politics, morality and philosophy – traditional aristocracy was making a comeback; not in the real world, far from it, but in the aristocratic imaginaries created in novels, plays and poetry. From the popular fiction produced by such writers as Emma Francis Brook, Arthur Conan Doyle, Elinor Glyn, H. Rider Haggard, Baroness Orczy, Mrs Humphrey Ward, Stanley J. Weymann and P.G. Wodehouse, through to the Edwardian realists and early modernists – Henry James, George Bernard Shaw, H.G. Wells and Vita Sackville West – literary cultures at the end of the bourgeois century were mounting a remarkable figurative comeback, a defensive attempt, as I saw it then and still do, to offset the immanence of 'mass' culture with a new conditioning of fantasies of distinction.

High modernism, shaped under the influence of Nietzsche, was exemplary of the dynamic but in very particular and often extreme ways. An explicit and probing assault on modernity as bourgeoisification, it sometimes imagined the modern incarnations of traditional aristocracy in terms of tortured animism. Wyndham Lewis's *Tarr* (1918) and the struggles of its central character Kreisler would be illustrative here, as would Robert Musil's remarkable *The Confusions of Young Torless* (1906), a school novel that renders bourgeois young men trained in the humanist culture of traditional aristocracy as brutal sadists. More typically, however, modernism transferred the will to distinction into an aesthetics of text, producing writing designed to be so difficult, so mystificatory, that it would always operate beyond the reach of the 'masses'.

The Joyce text in this account was placed in the position of both confirming that schema and at the same time mounting a fundamental challenge to it. As I understood things then, Joyce was the arch practitioner of aristocracy of form, the maker of texts so complex, so demanding that they could easily be taken to exemplify Pound's notion of an art that defies 'the mob'. Yet the very same texts also seemed deeply antithetical to cultures of aristocracy. Here traditional aristocracy was seemingly *not* typically associated with nobility, authenticity and stability or linked with any sense of organic community. These unresolved tensions and ambiguities return in this current book where they get a very different treatment.

Joyce and Education: Schooling and the Social Imaginary in the Modernist Novel began as a lecture given at a colloquium held at Oriel College, Oxford, in 2018 organized by the Society for Educational Studies and entitled 'Writers and their Education'. The organizers aimed to 'bring together scholarly and literary-professional examination of conceptions, perceptions and representations of education in the life and works of writers across all genres of literature'. They wanted to 'take a fresh look at the influences of education, broadly conceived'.[1] One of the keynote speakers was a superbly dressed Homi Bhabha, who, as far as I recall, said very little that could be described as being on this subject, however conceived. My own much more sober contribution was to open up discussion about the ways in which education might have been important to the mature Joyce aesthetic. As a result of that event, I was asked by David Aldridge and Andrew Green to contribute to their series *Literature and Education*. This book is the result and my first acknowledgment goes to them for initiating and encouraging it.

The contention of the talk was that education was more than a biographical 'background' to Joyce's life and writing. I also thought that a fully developed version of the formulation 'Joyce and education' could contribute to a historical understanding of education cultures in the late nineteenth and early twentieth centuries, making for a more intimate, contingent relationship than is usually achieved – certainly in literary studies and perhaps in education research too. Such ideas remain very much alive in this book. At its broadest, the aim here, too, is to establish new lines of communication between the politics of radical modernist literary aesthetic and both schooling and 'informatics' – the social and technological transformations in the late-nineteenth and early-twentieth century that reproduced knowledge as commodity on a scale hitherto unknown. In both versions, education figures as a central text of modernity, just as *Dubliners*, *A Portrait of the Artist as a Young Man*, *Ulysses* and *Finnegans Wake* have also figured as central texts of modernism. To this extent, *Joyce and Education* is concerned with the making of modernity and with the modernism that was so much a criticism of the modern world.

The project was hampered in some ways by the fact that it comes out of a long career working on Joyce. I studied Joyce as a third-year undergraduate and wrote a dissertation on Joyce and Parnell way back in 1978. My PhD was written on Joyce. It was examined nearly 40 years ago in 1983. Likewise, my first full-length book – *Joyce and the Anglo-Irish* – published in 1998. In 2007, I published *Joyce, Race and Finnegans Wake.* Four years later, I published a general introduction to Joyce entitled *James Joyce: Text and Contexts.* It is fair to say that my views on Joyce had been well and truly formed by the time I came to this book. The rethinking this book required could not have happened at all without new research into education as a historical culture and a revival of interest in education and literature registered by Natasha Periyan's 2018 account, *The Politics of 1930s British Literature: Education, Class, Gender.* More specifically, the past few years have seen the emergence of a new interest in how Joyce's status as a modernist might be thought through education and schooling, a trend exemplified by Elizabeth Switaj 's *James Joyce's Teaching Life and Methods* (2016) and Ramsey McGlazer's 2020 book *Old Schools: Modernism, Education, and the Critique of Progress.* My second acknowledgment, then, is to the scholars who have fuelled such debates and made it possible to engage again with Joyce on new terms; especially to Ramsey, who sent me a copy of the relevant chapters of his book when COVID-19 prevented my local bookshop from obliging in more traditional ways.

This book is also the work of a teacher – I have been teaching since 1978 – someone who currently works, and has done since 1998, first in a university continuing education department and then in an education department. I would like to make acknowledgement to the colleagues with whom I work directly and to students in what is now my department, especially my research student, Philippa Campbell, who was working on the contemporary campus novel while I was working on Joyce and education. Our ideas evolved together in some respects, and our difficulties in formulating them were, I hope, mutually beneficial. I also want to thank my colleagues in the Education Department – Tara Page, who read drafts of some early chapters, and Rosalyn George, who read virtually the whole manuscript before publication and made many useful observations on it. Both have continued to support the project over many hours of discussions. John Clay, once a school inspector and now an education academic, made useful observations as the work developed and put up with endless attempts of mine to work through ill-thought-out ideas. My colleague Anna Traianou, an expert on education in 'neo-liberal' times, was especially encouraging. Patrick Ainley, Professor of Training and Education at the University of Greenwich, read an early chapter of the book and gave me some excellent advice on its theoretical orientation.

I also want to thank my old friend Peter Bailey, one of best historians of early popular culture ever turned out of Oxbridge in my view – although, as Peter will be quick to point out, he was probably singular in this respect. Not many Oxbridge graduates in the 1970s would have taken much serious academic interest in the Aly Sloper cartoons, the modernity of the musical comedy stage or the aesthetics of a Loie Fuller dance. Whatever, Peter's 'jottings' on an early and incomplete draft of this book provided the most useful, funny and self-indulgent commentary I am likely to get anywhere.

Finally, during the course of researching and writing the book, I was contacted out of the blue by Luke Davis, a poet who, among other things, writes poems to order on a manual typewriter outside Tate Modern, and Ben Watson, music journalist, author of a book on Frank Zappa and a member of the current incarnation of the legendary AMM Allstars. Both Luke and Ben are devoted readers of *Finnegans Wake* and its worlds. I would like to thank them for their enthusiastic support of my earlier books on Joyce, their encouragement of this one and, especially, for their work on the epic track 'Summoning Lense Platypus', designed to get me out of the ivory towers of New Cross and into a pub in Deptford. Musicians performing on the epic 59-minute-long invocation/rain dance include Graham Davis on bass, koto, shakuhachi, kokyu, koririko and fireworks; David Black on guitar and Paul Shearsmith on trumpet. According to another old friend of mine, this strange but hugely generous act means that my work on Joyce, whatever its reception elsewhere, can claim the status of a very, very, small cult following. For anyone who wants to listen to this remarkable piece of music, here, as we say, is the link – https://archive.org/details/SummoningLensePlatypus23I-i-019.

Note

1 Society for Educational Studies, 'Writers and their Education' – annual colloquium, Oriel College, University of Oxford, (2018), (np).

Series editors' introduction

In *James Joyce and Education: Schooling and the Social Imaginary in the Modernist Novel*, Len Platt has taken on one of the true giants of the modernist canon. Beginning with the early texts (*Dubliners*, *Stephen Hero* and *A Portrait of the Artist as a Young Man*), often read as autobiographical representations of an Irish educational system that is both highly class-bound and highly politicized, Platt argues for a wider view as nations across Europe, including Ireland, sought to develop modern and modernizing systems of education fit for the purposes of the twentieth century. Against this backdrop of educational 'progress', Platt establishes a range of means by which we can engage with education in these early works, using these as a foundation for our understanding of the radical educational subversion of the later Joyce (*Ulysses* and *Finnegans Wake*), in which the literary text seems to pit itself in battle against traditional formulations and representations of knowledge.

In charting the unresolved (and in many ways unresolvable) tensions and ambiguities of Joyce and education, Platt provides us with a vision of the author and his work that is rooted in the shifting educational beliefs and practices of his times and that harnesses (and often ridicules) these beliefs in the service of high art. Platt presents us with a Joyce who, immersed in education and educational literature, uses his work self-consciously to reformulate his personal experiences and views in the service of high-status (and high-stakes) canonical literary education. The Joyce we see in these pages is a man profoundly troubled by (but also curiously accepting of) the systems and philosophies of the education that formed him and trying to make sense of this representationally.

Platt argues that Joyce's treatment of education emerges in relation to a uniquely framed Irish inflexion of mainstream European modernism. He explores the ways in which the Joyce of both the early and the later works engages with the modernist tendency to romanticize older iterations of elite educational systems, placing Joyce within a literary and philosophical tradition that seeks to reinforce an elitist literary–educational project. Joyce emerges as a writer exercised in an almost Bourdieusian sense by the ways in which schooling produced and reinforced distinctive elites, as it was designed to do. Joyce's writings, Platt argues, insist on the centrality of 'cultures of schooled knowledge', but such representations of cultures of education are inherently problematic; as varied schooled knowledges collide in the literary text, readers encounter a kaleidoscopic effect, as often a source of misremembrance and uncertainty as it is a source clarity. Moving on to *Ulysses* and *Finnegans Wake*, we encounter a literary world where education, and particularly elite schooling, cease to be simply a representational domain but become in themselves elements of the works' textuality.

Platt also reads the 'Europeanizing', modernist tendency in Joyce against and in relation to the demands of Irish educationists such as his contemporary, Patrick Pearse, who pursued an alternative, Gaelicized project of nationhood and an education system fit for Ireland. Against these and other contexts, Platt explores the emergent conflicts and idiosyncrasies of Joyce's work with admirable clarity, tracing an educational historiography beginning with the Victorian Intermediate Education Act of 1878 that so shaped the author's own education at Clongowes through a sequence of Edwardian reforms and into the interwar years with their radical overhaul of state education systems across Europe. Platt's account demonstrates the extent to which the forms and functions of education – and particularly Irish education and Joyce's work – were shaped by competing forces of nationalism and imperialism and by conflicting sectarian ideologies.

Joyce has what Platt calls 'an obsessive political determination to bring education culture into systematic alignment with a wider and changing social order'. Platt delineates Joyce as a writer for whom education is a practice that shapes every aspect of a society. For Joyce, Platt argues, 'the schooled mind in all its dimensions – its wit and its ambition but also its pretension, divisiveness, and ambiguous and contradictory relations to State and Church – becomes an important domain'. Platt's book creates a strong case for reading Joyce's work as inseparable from the educational contexts and practices from which it emerges and with which it so obsessively deals. In this project, the representation of education and schooling – the terms are not synonymous – is a central feature not only of the early Joyce text, but also of *Ulysses* and *Finnegans Wake*, in which we encounter a fictional world that constantly returns to the idea of knowledge and the means by which knowledge is encountered and consumed. Developing educational technologies and a growing social demand for knowledge inflects both the fabric and the form of Joyce's work.

In this, Platt demonstrates the extent to which Joyce's later work is shaped by a nascent culture of information and the ways in which popular publications such as *Tit-Bits* and *Answers* – alongside a vast array of references to more formal educational publications such as textbooks and examination papers – forge both its epistemological and ontological domains. Joyce appears as a writer steeped in and endlessly responsive to the shifting cultures of education and educational practice that characterized the *fin de siècle* and the emergent modernist era. Pushed to their ultimate in *Finnegans Wake*, engagement with learning and the uses of education appear not merely as meaningless routines but as processes that actively combat and at times strip out meaning. Moving beyond the technical experiments with educational concepts and educational forms that characterize *Ulysses*,

Platt asks us to see *Finnegans Wake* as a work that forcibly deconstructs and re-forges the relationship between the literary text as known and knowable entity.

James Joyce and Education: Schooling and the Social Imaginary in the Modernist Novel charts a new way of considering the figure of Joyce and his engagement not only with the places of education, but also with a variety of other 'spaces' for education, including the literary text. In his own words, Platt 'argues for a much more central role for education in our reading of both the early and the late Joyce text, and in our conceptualization of their reception'. Platt's book contributes a wealth of insight not only to hardened Joyceans but also to the more general reader of Joyce, developing lucid historical understanding of educational and literary cultures in the late nineteenth and early twentieth centuries and making for a more intimate and contingent relationship between Joyce and the world of education than is often found. In the spirit of the *Literature and Education* series, Platt has brought his extensive experiences both as a literary studies and as an Education academic to bear on his subject, combining these two bodies of knowledge in challenging and fruitful ways.

Andrew Green and David Aldridge

Chapter 1

Contexts and their problematics

> Think of the harm Nietzsche could do to the half-informed minds of some of our undergraduates.
>
> Oliver St. John Gogarty, *As I Was Going Down Sackville Street* (1937)

Literature and education

What is involved in the idea 'Joyce and education'? The question is not as straightforward as it seems. On the one hand, very little work has been done on the issue of reading literature in the contexts of the structures and technologies in which formal education takes place. Although the history of forms of literature, the novel in particular, has routinely been related to capitalism and the development of the nation-state, questions about the relations between literature and one of the most characteristic institutions of the modern state, the education system, have had very little purchase.[1] It appears that 'literature' takes place in one domain and 'education' in another, although we know this cannot be the case. On the other hand, the place of literature in the classroom has been much theorized, not only in terms of the effective teaching of reading and writing but also in the development of such high-status but hard-to-define notions as 'creativity' and 'imagination'. Such debates are in turn related to connections sometimes made between literature and what is imagined as the emancipatory impact of education, its capacity for challenging social inequality. Highly contested arguments about the impact of canonical literature on learner confidence and, ultimately, performance and success in the world are part of everyday life and figure regularly in the media. From this perspective, canonical literature in all its variations can be perceived as both an alienating imposition of hegemony and a liberating affirmation. The importance of such positions rests on the idea, also highly disputed and largely untested, that educational achievement is contingent on how modern educational institutions and their pedagogies manage what we now call 'identity'. We know that students' 'backgrounds' have an impact on their achievement. Sometimes particular backgrounds are considered impairments to educational achievement; sometimes rich heritage to be exploited. How far and in what ways educational institutions can build on opportunity, or address the 'gaps', however, is not at all clear.

James Joyce and Education: Schooling and the Social Imaginary in the Modernist Novel is about a writer whose work was and is ambiguously related to 'literature and education'. In terms of the status of his writing and how it came out of an educational establishment, critical tradition has insisted equally, or at least simultaneously, on Joyce's radical rejection of orthodoxy and on a Joyce aesthetic informed by the orthodox. In an early piece of Joyce biography/criticism produced in the 1950s – *Joyce Among the Jesuits* – Kevin Sullivan argued that, however much Joyce's writing railed against 'the plague of Catholicism' (*SH*, 173), it was somehow condemned to be everywhere instantiated with the signs of a Catholic education. 'Joyce's early familiarity with Catholic ceremony and ritual', Sullivan wrote, 'so richly invested with symbolic gesture and meaning, constituted a sort of novitiate in which the embryo artist was prepared'.[2] Some 40 years later, Peter Costello, in his biography of the 'foundational' years of Joyce's life (1982–1915), declared the writing which has become synonymous with radicalism and innovation as being both continuous with literary tradition and an outcome of the Jesuit curriculum. 'The essential nature of Jesuit education', he claimed, 'aside from its system, was its literary nature; it depended on reading and translation from Latin and Greek into English and vice versa. From his earliest days literature became for Joyce the basis of everything'.[3] This kind of registration, in which Joyce's challenging fiction finds itself stamped with traditionalism and clichés sometimes racialized as Irish or Catholic – whether in its revolt, its 'spirituality' or its apparent devotion to high-status learning – has figured over and over in Joyce criticism ever since.

More recent approaches to 'Joyce and education' have taken position in relation to these orthodoxies. Andrew Gibson's work (2013) in this field is largely an extension that understands 'Joyce and education' in terms of a highly refined temperament struggling to come to terms with the imperative to revolt against Anglicization and colonization. Elizabeth Switaj's *James Joyce's Teaching Life and Methods* (2016) circumnavigates the idea of the classicist Joyce with the manufacture of a Joyce whose aesthetic radicalism is reconvened as a commitment to progressive pedagogy. Ramsey McGlazer's *Old Schools: Modernism, Education, and the Critique of Progress* (2020) argues precisely the opposite – that the modernism of the late Joyce text, represented by the late chapters of *Ulysses*, is characterized by 'enforced repetitions and formative wastes of time' constituting a radical appropriation of *traditional* methods of pedagogy, what he calls a 'counter progressivism' deemed, not without difficulty, necessary to proper schooling and formulated against the progressive turn represented by such figures as John Dewey.[4]

In terms of the status of his writing *in* education, the situation is just as confusing. Joyce's early fiction frequently appears on school and college curricula. In some ways it is part of the orthodox canon; in other ways not. It is both classical modernism, as it were, and experimental in terms of an aesthetic still frequently conceptualized as a recentring at the decolonizing 'margins'. It is a current institutionalized orthodoxy and, at the same time, remains radical innovation. The issue becomes even more problematized in relation to Joyce's later works. The reading of these texts is now substantially located in universities – some would say this is the only place they are read – but neither *Ulysses* nor *Finnegans Wake* are widely taught in the modern university, certainly not at undergraduate level. Their 'difficulty', their extraordinary performance of 'complexity', connects them to the very apex of cultures that have infinite capacities for reproducing hierarchy. Here they have special status and as such are rendered up in profoundly select terms. From this perspective, reading the mature Joyce text is much more than just reading. These works amount to a 'new times' fiction that, *pace* Adorno and Lukács, appears to be neither an assault on the commodification of modern life nor an enactment of its dark meaninglessness. Indeed both *Ulysses* and *Finnegans Wake* have often seemed so much a flouting of contemporary urban culture – of its energy, its 'polyphonic' nature, its 'carnivalesque' – that they could be said to be aspiring to a reactionary version of modernity, although Joyce figures most prominently as not just an aesthetic radical but a political one as well, as if the two were somehow interchangeable. Certainly, these fictions are, whatever else, elitist, both by design and in terms of reception, and their status in the world is inextricably tied up with their reserved nature. Those famous Eve Harding photographs of Marilyn Monroe seated on a child's roundabout in shorts and a brightly coloured top, reading not at the beginning of *Ulysses*, where so many of us get 'stuck', but at its end, makes this point in a kitsch way but with great confidence nonetheless. Reading these texts denotes a connection with contemporaneity, even now, and it denotes membership to a select club. From this perspective, Virginia Woolf's sense of Joyce as an 'under bred' writer, a Shemish figure flaunting himself 'like some callow board school boy' has seriously back-fired. The genuine distinction deemed to be possessed by the 'self-conscious and egotistical' Joyce text has largely prevailed, and something of its status rubs off on his fans.[5] The 'real' Joyce aficionado – not the everyday reader who has 'only' read *Dubliners* and *A Portrait* and begun *Ulysses* many times, but the devotee 'Joycean' who has laboured with late *Ulysses* and the monstrosities of *Finnegans Wake*, commands a distinction framed by a familiar social logic. This is reproduced both in the work of professional 'Joyceans' committed to the decoding of the Joyce text, which inevitably means maintaining its hermeneutic status, and in social hierarchies sustained by education in terms of 'intelligence' and differences in intelligence.

The question of the relations between education and emancipation *in* the Joyce text is framed by parallel contradictions. Their open, polysemic nature rescues them from the authority and authoritarianism of the master reading, but only to those who can read their difficulty in such terms in the first place. More specifically on the matter of schooling and *its* capacity for emancipation, the early Joyce text in particular is much devoted to schooling. It is sometimes imagined as 'autobiographical' in this respect and coterminous with Joyce's real life, as if it were somehow being written while it was being lived. In fact, it is a representation of schooling, the schooling of elites, written a long time after the event and engaging with the ways in which schooling was culturally reproduced. It draws on forms of radical education also contemporary with Joyce, the terms of which are configured in the dissent of his central character, Stephen Dedalus. It is, in almost all ways, a critique of the modernization of schooling. At the same time, it makes no commitment to the idea of education as emancipation. Indeed, this is one of the central points about the representation of education in Joyce. Its critique is on the grounds of the rights of the individual rather than social good or fairness and it is powered more by egoism than by a sense of social justice. The later texts *perform* as elitist literature, flouting their own schooled knowledge in such fields as grammar, rhetoric, language, literature, history and made-up subjects like 'arithmosophy' and, indeed, in 'Wakese' (*FW*, 134.14–15), effectively a made-up language. The earlier ones re-enact the conditions under which a singular elitist is made, or, perhaps more accurately, tries to make himself.

The impact of these complexities and contradictions and the way we now receive them is partly dependent on the gap between the early 1900s which saw the beginning of Joyce's publishing life, and now, 2020, a period still centrally framed by the 1960s for people of my generation. Among much else, this was a time when sociology appeared on the point of discovering the workings of power and locating its mechanism in hierarchies of schooling. By the 1960s, schooling was perceived to be everywhere, and it embodied a central contradiction which attracted widespread attention from across the social, cultural and political spectrum. Schooling was held to be a mechanism for promoting social equality and at the same time functioned as the primary mechanism by which social inequality was engineered or 'reproduced'. In France, that paradox, constructed now not as failure but as structural principle, had a profound influence on the development of new philosophy. It was taken up by Louis Althusser and Michel Foucault and informed the influential sociological work of Pierre Bourdieu and Jean-Claude Passeron. It also shaped the anti-philosophy of Jacques Rancière which, however pitched specifically *against* the sociologizing of learning, was likewise devoted to an explication of how social cohesion and consent was embedded in relations between schooling and the state.[6] Unsurprisingly, the same paradox has shaped some of the most central education narratives of our time, including the contemporary narrative that constructs 'neo-liberalism' as a rolling back of the radical sixties, or of what some still regard as the post-war settlement.

None of that history was available to Joyce, of course. Schooling in the 1900s, as in the 1930s, was less than a century old and a seriously incomplete project. In the earlier part of the period as in the latter, working-class girls typically were excluded from education, state-funded or not, at any level above primary, as were the vast majority of working-class boys. Intermediate education was the preserve of a gendered elite; university education of an even smaller one. The situation was considerably exaggerated in colonial Ireland but not substantially different. In 1879, just 4,000 students took the Irish intermediate examination; by 1899, the figure had doubled to 9,000, still a very small proportion of 16-year-olds.[7]

The position was not much changed by the formation of the Republic. Not least for this reason of scale, education did not register in the same way as it does now, especially in relation to the issue of social justice. Until the end of the First World War, formal education much beyond 12 or 13 years old, however much it might have been aspired to, was in many ways a novelty rather than an everyday reality. The state's authority over education's governance was in its relatively early days. Such facts are not a prelude to an apologist account of Joyce but a simple reminder both that history matters in reading literature and that historical readings are just as problematic and provisional as any other – just as liable to 'error'.

Education and the modern

Until fairly recently, education featured in the 'background' of Joyce studies, as important biographical context and a social reality reproduced in such texts as *Stephen Hero* and *A Portrait of the Artist as a Young Man*. The publication of the books by Switaj and McGlazer changes that. With them, education moves to the centre of the things, which means that education now becomes important to understanding the late Joyce text too, the aesthetic upheaval famously sloganized by Eugene Jolas as 'the revolution of the word'.[8] In this sense, *James Joyce and Education* joins ranks with Switaj and McGlazer. This book also argues for a much more central role of education in our reading of both the early and the late Joyce text and in our conceptualization of their reception. It takes issue, however, with both Switaj and McGlazer, in relation to starting point and rationale. As was indicated previously, in important respects, these two writers are diametrically opposed, but they both share the idea that education is important to the Joyce text because of what they see as the central conflict between progressive and conservative techniques of education which becomes overwritten as a dynamic across tradition and modernity. In Switaj the late Joyce text (*Finnegans Wake*) becomes itself exemplary of progressive pedagogy, constituting 'an extended (and successful) language lesson in Wakese', conducted 'at the extremes of the antiauthoritarian pedagogy'.[9] In McGlazer the 'Ithaca' and 'Oxen of the Sun' episodes of *Ulysses* become an exemplary deployment of conventional pedagogy which ties Joyce into a commitment to tradition. For both, however, the modernity of Joyce's treatment of education turns almost entirely on the position it takes in relation to progressive education.

This account is much less interested in progressive education and sees it as being much less important to the 'Joyce and education' formulation. The reasons for that will become clear, but first I want to address the obvious and more pressing point. If 'Joyce and education' does not much implicate the progressive/traditional debate, what does it write to? What is the nature of its investment? How *do* we relate the modernity of the Joyce text to education and its histories? At one level, the answer to such questions is quite straightforward. Education, or to be more precise, schooling, is itself a modern phenomenon. The capacity of education to register both progressivist historiography and traditions of social order so powerfully meant that by the end of the nineteenth century, education discourse had reached a high-tide mark of circulation and prominence, much of it easily recognizable in terms of the discourses of today.[10] Progressive education was an important but nonetheless marginal aspect of this modernity.

The general currency of the bigger picture can be illustrated with reference to the flourishing exhibition culture of Victorian and Edwardian Britain. A dedicated education exhibition was opened in London by the Prince of Wales in January 1900 – a dry run for inclusion in the Paris Exhibition to be held later in the year – although education technology had been represented at all major exhibitions since the Great Exhibition of 1851 and first appeared even earlier. In 1854, an exhibition held at St Martin's Hall in Long Acre – once a concert hall and used for political meetings and lectures – illustrated how far the modernization of education was constructed in terms of innovation. It was seen by *The Times* as an 'appropriation' of space by 'a collection of objects illustrating the methods and appliances of education'.[11] Typically displayed in exhibitions like this one was a world of modern things: current designs in school building and school furniture, the latest changes to blackboard design, charts and educational maps – which apparently Germany excelled in. Their catalogues included globes, blocks and forms for teaching arithmetic and geometry, peg boards, clock dials, toy money, coloured fraction discs, tellurians, examples of 'Fröebels' gifts' and so on. In later exhibitions, reading apparatuses like the Spelling Stick, sciopticons, magic lanterns and stereoscopes would have been on show, all suggestive of the kind of links made between education and the modern world. The aim behind the 1901 exhibition was to illustrate 'the progress in public education that had been made in the nineteenth century, especially the remarkable developments of popular elementary education and the education of girls and women'. It emphasized 'still more the growth of technical training', although *The Times* insinuated that this was more hype than reality. If education was advancing so rapidly in Britain, it asked, why were the 'experts making so much fuss about organization and complaining so loudly of our educational deficiencies'?[12]

Currency was also evident in new scales of press coverage. Writing in 2014, sociologist Ansgar Weymann suggests that in no period before or since has education attracted as much widespread public attention and engagement and it did so in ways that would be familiar today.[13] Across national newspapers in the West, education, however undergrown by twenty-first century standards, was widely perceived to be crucial to both national standing in the wider world and social cohesion at home. At a time when the West was reigning supreme in terms of world power, the education performance of the nation emerged as a central concern. The August 1900 edition of *The Publishers' Circular* carried an article linking relative school achievement to what was perceived to be the practical application of philosophical training – 'Germany is beating England out of the field', the writer claimed, 'because German education enables the German people to study things at their roots and to see things as they are, and to adapt their national methods to their national needs'. League tables, it turns out, were in place *avant la lettre*, even if the terms of the accompanying narrative now seem to belong to a more remote age. The writer of this piece, for example, continues:

> The blood and racial instincts of the English people are probably superior in quality to those of the Germans. English colonizing capacity, courage, equanimity in defeat, and terrible power when raised all point to the essential soundness of the middle classes, if only their energies were directed in accordance with the modern needs of empire.[14]

In Ireland, likewise, education was of central importance not least to the 'Irish question' which on the one hand was not expected to be resolved 'by a people who are behind the rest of the world in intellectual training and information' and yet on the other was framed by the 'Efficiency of Irish Schools and their superiority to English Schools'.[15] Here, 'places of education for Irish boys' 'proved and explained' Irish readiness for Home Rule. The establishment *Freeman's Journal* perceived new reforms to primary education proposed at the beginning of 1900 to be 'vital to the industrial progress of Ireland'. The recommendations of the Commission on Practical and Manual Education, arguing for 'improved industrial, technical and scientific education' and for the implementation of drill and physical exercise in Ireland's National Schools, as in Britain and the West widely, were similarly related to modernizing and nationalist agendas. In Ireland, as in England, comparisons were made with 'Continental educationalists' and Germany especially, where the wisdom of separating 'practical and commercial education' from 'the literary and professional side' was being questioned.[16] Here, too, from all sides of the political spectrum, education policy was broadly understood in highly contemporary terms as 'a core element of the modern state's sovereignty and autonomy', and indispensable to 'improving political power and legitimacy through meritocracy, and fuelling and stimulating economic growth via human capital investment'.[17]

At the same time as colonial Ireland embraced education as the route to the formation of a empowered Catholic middle class and national independence, it also constructed education rhetorically as an alien colonial imposition. Some of the most central and characteristic nationalist discourses of the post-Parnell period celebrated the Irish boy in terms of a purity and heroism seen to be endangered by the Anglicized school and its English curriculum. The link between the formation of a new nation state and the emergence of a new Irish system of education was made over and over again, explicitly so and with considerable force in the work of radical nationalists such as Patrick Pearse and D.P. Moran. The latter excoriated the 'sound English education' that many Irish families wanted for their sons as

> one of the graves of Irish initiative and prosperity. What do the people of Ireland want with a curriculum suitable to the needs of England . . .? The effect is the very opposite to the aim of true education, for it tends to turn

> out imitators, shallow despisers of their own nationality, simperers, prigs and bounders instead of men and Irishmen.[18]

As Chapter Two of this study shows, the link between nation building and masculinity produced a flourishing boy culture in late-nineteenth-century Ireland, one which often seemed to 'mirror' English models.[19] From this perspective, the formation of the League of Columb in the late 1890s and the resurrection of Cuchulain as a national hero were specific responses to a school reform movement designed to produce 'manly Christianity' from the public schools of England. Likewise, Baden-Powell's Boy Scout movement, one of the most characteristic institutions of English 'boyology', was reproduced in the Irish equivalent – Fianna Éireann.[20] In the early twentieth century, J.S. Sheehy, a priest at the elite Castleknock College in Dublin, made the point explicitly. Highlighting the cultural absence of an Irish rival to fight off the influence of the English boy hero, he embraced the heroics of adventure novels by such writers as G. A Henty, books he deemed 'excellent for *English* boys, whether they are Catholic or Protestant' on the grounds that 'they show forth types of healthy-minded, brave, truthful, open-air boys'. But he lamented the fact that they were

> essentially English. Thus unconsciously, Irish boys, during their plastic years, are being West Britonized. Their heroes are English warriors of the past, or English public school boys of today, or English adventurers and detectives. . . . I am anxious to get the Irish boy to look at home for his models, to see in Irish boys, like himself, examples of bravery, truth, 'playing the game', culture, self-respect, also fun and diversion, as well as among English boys.[21]

Such debates were not just about what Irish boys were reading but about what they would be in the future and what part they would play in the formation of a new nation state. They would have been reproduced everywhere in the cultural environment of Joyce's day and in the schools where he was educated, schools which played out what it meant to be a Catholic schoolboy in colonial Ireland on a daily basis, in social as well as educational and spiritual ways.

For all the distance in time then, there are continuities between Joyce's world and our own. They were the product of a common long-term history where schooling became a key signifier across the period of state formation and central to the modernizing project. Indeed, from some perspectives it simply *was* that project, entirely freighted from its beginning with the progressive discourses of the Enlightenment and simultaneously bureaucratized to ensure continuities of tradition. The kind of education Joyce experienced in Ireland in the 1880s and 1890s, propagandized variously as the education of an intellectual and/or genetic elite, was modern and, at the same time, a particular form of the return to aristocracy that so characterized literary culture in Britain from the 1880s to the 1920s and beyond. As such, it was typical of modern education at the turn of the twentieth century and embodied its essential contradictions.[22]

Traditionally, the transformations in educational provision taking place in the second half of the nineteenth century had been understood as a technocratic rationalization, taking 'a loosely connected set of private foundations with idiosyncratic curricula, teaching methods and assessment practices' and developing them into something more closely representing an education 'system', a convergence perceived to be bringing secondary and higher education into closer interaction with the 'occupational system of the high industrial era'.[23] In reality, the evidence pointing to a genuine alignment of this kind was significantly absent, even in nation–states often understood to be advanced in terms of technical education. In France and Germany, too, the historical record clearly showed that the rising classes, industrial or otherwise, were not by and large choosing to have their sons educated in new technology and science. On the contrary, their ambition was to see them turned out as 'gentlemen' schooled in the classical education of a traditional – that is, landed – elite. Across the West, there was a high correlation between prestige schools and universities and traditional curricula that privileged the humanities in its oldest of forms. Whilst there was some demand for curriculum modernization, the far stronger impulse was for traditionalism.

The modernization of schooling in the nineteenth century was constituted by a sustained period of reform – commission report followed by parliamentary act at each level of schooling in Britain. This produced a stratified structure into which all forms of education, aided by state funds or not, were made to fit. In this way, seemingly democratizing developments in education history served to sustain and condition social hierarchies. German historian Detlef K. Müller, drawing on the work of Bourdieu and, more substantially, Weber, called this 'systematization', the process whereby a 'diverse collection of vaguely defined schools' became transformed into a highly defined system which reproduces social inequality.[24] As the system developed and complete hierarchies of schooling became elaborated, all aspects of school life from governance and management through the marketing of schools to pedagogy, curriculum and assessment were shaped by the same systemizing principle. The rank order of qualifications they offered 'came to define a corresponding hierarchy of occupations. . . . With little exaggeration, one can speak of an "educationalization of the occupational system", not an industrialization of education or a functional adjustment of the educational system to the economy'.[25]

The dominant narrative of the nineteenth century for most education historians, the organization of education into a single system, was the product of powerful social imaginaries fundamental to the formation of state schooling, privatized or otherwise. In the nineteenth and early twentieth centuries, as now, education was typically constructed in terms of modern, democratizing futures and yet structurally organized to reproduce elites classed and gendered in traditional ways, so much so that by the end of the nineteenth century, schools, in Ireland as elsewhere, rather than 'channels of family and influence', had become the central means by which social hierarchy was reproduced and their importance in the world grew proportionally.[26] For revolutionary France, responsible for the earliest and most radical experiments in the organization of education by the state, elite schooling become the crucial mechanism through which the new order was managed and loyalty to it maintained. Speaking in 1795 at a time of great crisis, the Revolution articulated its dependency on the nationalist fantasy that superior children belonged first and foremost to the schools of the Republic 'and only secondly to individual families. Without this principle there can be no republican education'. Its new military academy, the École de Mars, was established to educate 'three thousand young citizens, the strongest and most intelligent' and expected to 'devote their blood to their country'.[27] In a more sober but equally heavily freighted Victorian configuration, nine elite schools at the top of the educational system in mid-nineteenth-century Britain – Eton, Harrow, Winchester, Westminster, St Paul's, Charterhouse, Merchant Taylors', Rugby and Shrewsbury – with a combined roll of just 2,696 pupils, were credited with exercising an influence exceeding far beyond the powers of executive management.

> It is not easy to estimate the degree in which the English people are indebted to these schools for the qualities on which they pride themselves most – for their capacity to govern others and control themselves, their aptitude for combining freedom with order, their public spirit, their vigour and manliness of character, their strong but not slavish respect for public opinion, their love of healthy sports and exercise. These schools have been the chief nurseries of our statesmen . . . and they have had perhaps the largest share in moulding the character of an English gentleman.[28]

What Switaj and McGlazer see as 'traditional' education, then, was in fact a modern phenomenon. The point of this current study is to raise the question of how the Joyce text articulates both within and against this modernizing dynamic which is also a dynamic of modernity – within, because Joyce was educated by prestigious schools as a member of a new Catholic elite; against, because this was a subject position that his writing both instantiated and yet effectively overwhelmed. In doing so, *James Joyce and Education* makes the claim that the idea of education as system enters Joyce's fiction at every stage of its organization and is the central context through which the idea of knowledge and modernity is framed. There are, in Joyce, forays against styles and instruments of education, but these are always contingent on a deeper critique, an unravelling of an education system which becomes symptomatic of modernity not perhaps in the worst of its forms but in some of its most troubling and characteristic ones – as technocracy, bureaucracy and commodification. The following chapters of this book show how the systemization of education in the nineteenth century becomes a dominant narrative of the Joyce text. It is entwined and caught up with the biographical experiences that are such an important part of all Joyce's writing. At the same time, it is centred in contemporary political cultures of the late nineteenth and early twentieth centuries and radical responses to those cultures.

Radical education

Radical education is a complex concept, awkward in many ways and often conflated with progressive education. The terms overlap so much that they have become virtually interchangeable, although distinctions have been made between the two and they are drawn upon in this account.[29] Progressive education is often seen as being primarily concerned with pedagogy and connected to ideas of child- or student-centredness in teaching and learning. It is itself a kind of technocracy and frequently *progressivist* in nature. It often assumes that education 'failure' is an organizational problem that can be overcome by improvements in technique. Radical education, however, speaks directly to the system of education which it regards as constituent of the political and social world. Thus Rancière's insistence that his book *The Ignorant Schoolmaster* (1989), although it might be mistaken for a quaint investigation into a strange moment in the history of pedagogy, is in fact 'a philosophical reflection on the way in which pedagogical logic and social logic bear on each other'.[30] It does not propose a practice that can be co-opted to the cause of emancipation – far from it. Jacotot, the post–French Revolution schoolteacher at the heart of the book, is driven by the revelation that 'all men have equal intelligence'. That certainty cannot tell us about *what* will be learnt – 'nothing maybe' – or how.[31] It is concerned with capacities only. But it is emancipatory nevertheless; indeed, emancipatory for that very reason. It is also tied, however obscurely, to historical materialism.

Progressive education operates very differently. It is not anti-philosophy – far from it. But it positions itself in a distinct tradition, one often traced back to the most romantic of Enlightenment philosophers, Jean-Jacques Rousseau. Figures important to its articulation – Johann Pestalozzi, Friedrich Fröbel, John Dewey and Maria Montessori – are drawn upon specifically to challenge what are perceived as traditional modes of teaching and learning. It has no relationship to Marxism and notionally operates outside any specific or precise politics.

The above might be taken to suggest that radical education in contemporary times is typically linked to the politics of the left, but this is not and certainly was not always the case. In the forms that Joyce knew it, radical education developed from across the political and cultural spectrum specifically as a set of responses to the modernization of education, its 'systemization'. It appeared in the writing of figures contemporary with Joyce, some of whom joined him to form a loose literary clique important to the development of European and American literary modernism in its first and classic formulation, so much so that there is a good case for constructing literary modernism generally in relation to education. Ezra Pound, who had no instinct for the political left, has been described as 'obsessed with learning' and yet was completely hostile towards the education institutions of his day, especially universities which he dismissed as 'beanaries'.[32] In things like 'How to Read' (1928), *ABC of Reading* (1934) and *Guide to Kultchur* (1938), he devised alternative curricula and radical learning goals for a new culture that also had the capacity for transforming society. In the 1930s, he used anthologies such as *Profile* (1932) and *Confucius to Cummings* (1964) to construct counter-canons and, at the beginning of the 1940s, wrote to American philosopher George Santayana, inviting him to collaborate on a volume on the 'ideal University or the Proper Curriculum'.[33] The third figure in that proposed project was T.S. Eliot, like Pound a Joyce supporter, one whose political instincts imagined tradition as a natural order to which 'individual talent' was mysteriously programmed to reconcile itself. *After Strange Gods* (1934), *The Idea of a Christian Society* (1939) and *Notes Towards a Definition of Culture* (1948) are all devoted to the maintenance of genuinely elitist forms of education as a defence of 'culture' against what was imagined to be the modern degeneration of reform. All three texts advocate for the preservation of an organic intellectual elite. In 'Modern Education and the Classics' (1931), Eliot, as reluctant a modernist as ever, reimagines this elite, 'in Christian civilisation', as a clerical order tasked with the 'preservation of education within the cloister, uncontaminated by the deluge of barbarism outside'.[34]

There was no logical connection, then, between radical education and the left in the late nineteenth and early twentieth centuries. Indeed, it spanned the political spectrum, from high conservatism through to anarchism, producing texts from writers politically diverse and often at odds. Some of these figures, as the previous examples suggest, were more important to Joyce than others and for different reasons. The relation between nationalist Patrick Pearse and Joyce is a case in point. The figure of Pearse, iconic in modern Ireland as a founding father of the Republic but also now somewhat kitsch, is a kind of negative image in the Joyce text, present but demeaned and diminished as the patriot 'Hughes', who sneers his way through *Stephen Hero*, and as the Shaun figure in *Finnegans Wake*, Shem's twin and rival brother and the 'chief celtech chappy' behind the great historical turn to a new order in a new Ireland that is a *return* (*FW*, 237.20).[35] Pearse's passionate plea for a Gaelicized education modelled on the ideal of a 'Gaelic polity nearly two thousand years old', underpinned by complete loyalty to the Catholic Church and a 'service to nation' – a 'love', 'so excessive as to annihilate all thought of self, a recognition that one must give all, must be willing to make the ultimate sacrifice' – is a reversal of Joyce in almost every respect.[36] The only thing Joyce shares with it is the rhetorical figure of the school and the university operating as a kind of machine turning out commodities. In his polemic 'The Murder Machine' (1915), Pearse had imagined contemporary education in colonial Ireland as a dehumanizing force, 'an elaborate piece of machinery devised by highly salaried officials for the purpose of turning out citizens according to certain approved patterns'.[37] But this was no necessary indicator of a common broad position. By 1910, the metaphor was already a cliché, found everywhere in radical education literature and by no means used exclusively against education in Britain. Joyce could have found it implied or directly used in several volumes contained in his own library in Trieste – Tolstoy's *Essays and Letters* (1904), Benjamin Tucker's *Instead of A Book By A Man Too Busy to Write One* (1897), Bakunin's *God and the State* (1882) or Bertrand Russell's *The Principles of Social*

Reconstruction. None of these authors was Irish, of course, and none was writing in these particular volumes specifically about colonization and traditional empires. They were writing about what they saw as a modern world already in the process of 'moving on' in new and dangerous ways.

The role of Nietzsche in relation to Joyce and radical education, however, is a very different story. Nietzsche's place in Joyce criticism has gone through great shifts since the 1950s, from a time when biographer Richard Ellmann could confidentially assert that 'at heart Joyce can scarcely have been a Nietzschean any more than he was a socialist' (1959) to Joseph Valente's elegantly devised argument that 'the hermeneutical collapse Nietzsche heralds' is reworked in the aesthetics of the 'revolution of the word' in the later Joyce text (1987).[38] The complete about-turn parallels upheavals in the broader Western intellectual tradition and the radical revaluation of Nietzsche produced again by French anti-philosophies in the 1960s and 70s. But for all the impact of the transformation in epistemology, Joyce studies have yet to consider the importance of Nietzsche in relation to Joyce and education – partly because the full appreciation of just how central education was to the development of Nietzsche's philosophy is itself a relatively recent field of study as yet of limited impact.[39]

Almost 40 years before Pearse attacked 'English' education in 'The Murder Machine', Nietzsche produced a series of lectures later published as 'The Future of Our Educational Institutions' (1872). Speaking from the borders of Basel at a time when Germany's modernization of education was the envy of the world, he delivered a powerful critique levelled against all Germany's chief institutions of post-primary learning, from the Realschule through the gymnasium and the university – not on the grounds that they were insufficiently national, as in Pearse, but because they represented a democratizing of the 'rights of genius', an avoidance of the 'hard necessity' of 'working for that genius, of making him possible'.[40] Here, reformed education, the best the West could devise, became nothing less than a cheap sham and an exploitation of youth by the state – the turning out of 'useful officers' trained to be unconditionally obedient 'by means of excessively severe examination'. In the dialogue of 'The Future of Our Educational Institutions', a student admonished by his philosopher/teacher on the grounds of supposed tardiness articulates the awful paradox he sees in modern education, describing how in it two antagonistic tendencies, 'equally ruinous in effect and eventually converging in their end results', combine. The first 'is the drive for the greatest *expansion* and *dissemination* of education, the other is the drive for the *narrowing* and weakening of education'. The former is supposed to 'reach the widest possible circle', the latter compels education 'to give up its highest, noblest and loftiest claims and content itself with serving some other form of life, for instance, the state'.[41]

Thereafter, education figured largely in Nietzsche's work. Contemporary education was used to illustrate the absurdities, the dangers and the failures of liberalism and progressivism. The antidote for the modern was signposted over and over by the figure of 'an antithetical type who is as little modern as possible, a noble, an affirmative type' who could only be properly educated in a kind of institution not yet existent, a real '*school for gentlemen*' (italics in the original).[42] This intervention, a harmonizing of iconoclasm with romantic traditions of personal heroism, resonated powerfully across European modernism, and so it does with the Joyce text. The versions of a 'paralysed' Dublin Joyce constructs in texts like *Dubliners*, *Stephen Hero* and *A Portrait of the Artist as a Young Man* is everywhere framed by Nietzsche's account of a paralysed Europe. Stephen Dedalus's antinomianism is likewise strongly framed by Nietzsche's version of 'the antithetical type'. The same applies to Shem in the *Wake*, like Stephen a rebel of schooling and yet a product of it too, one who, according to his brother, has badly let the side down – 'what under the canopies of Jansens Chrest would any decent son of an Albiogenselman who had bin to a university think' (*FW*, 173. 12–14). How Joyce takes such figures of the artist – are they heroes or failures? – has historically been a controversial issue in Joyce studies. How far the search for distinction passes over into the impossiblist aesthetic of the late Joyce text is perhaps becoming an important issue too. It is here that it looks as though a process of revaluating Joyce may be beginning. The signs are there in McGlazer's recent account. In the 1970s and 1980s, it used to be argued that Joyce's politics were left, linked to socialism and anarchism. In the 1990s and 2000s, the focus was on the postcolonial Joyce in which politics and aesthetics were linked to histories of Irish nationalism. Now it has apparently become possible to make the case for Joyce the traditionalist, whose extraordinary technical innovations become a product of a 'counter progressive' restoration of pedagogic tradition.

Such are the starting points for *James Joyce and Education*. It is clear that, whatever else, Joyce's fiction is not a history of education but it is unusually mediated by the politics and culture of education. Modernity is made manifest in the Joyce text not in industry or even science and technology, but in social systems of knowledge formation, of which schooling is one – certainly not the only one, but a primary one for sure. This shapes not just the contents of texts from *Dubliners* to *Finnegans Wake* but the forms it takes. It is sometimes suggested that this concentration can be somehow negatively explained with reference to the Ireland of Joyce's youth and adolescence – neither much industrialized nor much invested in science and technology it is claimed. *James Joyce and Education* argues that the locus of the Joyce text in this respect, foundational and central to the development of the Joyce aesthetic, is an active intervention rather than the product of some kind of deficit and it is centrally implicated in the versions of modernity that his fiction formulates.

Notes

1 For the novel and the state, see Patrick Parrinder, *Nation and Novel: The English Novel from Its Origins to the Present Day* (Oxford: Oxford University Press, 2006). For new shoots in relation to literature and education see, for example, Benjamin Conisbee Baer, *Indigenous Vanguards: Education, National Liberation, and the Limits of Modernism* (New York: Columbia University Press, 2019).

2 Kevin Sullivan, *Joyce Among the Jesuits* (New York: Columbia University Press, 1958), 10.

3 Peter Costello, *James Joyce: The Years of Growth 1881–1915* (Cork: Roberts Rinehart, 1992), 84.
4 Ramsey McGlazer, *Old Schools: Modernism, Education, and the Critique of Progress* (New York: Fordham University Press, 2020), 4.
5 *The Diary of Virginia Woolf*, edited by Anne Oliver Bell, assisted by Andrew McNeillie, vol. 2 (1978; Harmondsworth: Penguin, 1981), 199.
6 Rancière argues that the logic of new sociology was that of 'rewriting its realm, legitimising its specificity as a science through a naturalising objectification of the other'. See Kristin Ross, 'Translator's Introduction', in Jacques Rancière, *The Ignorant Schoolmaster: Five Lessons in Intellectual Emancipation* (1987; Stanford, CA: Stanford University Press, 1991), xii.
7 Brendan Walsh, '"Injurious to the Best Interests of Education": Teaching and Learning under the Intermediate Education System 1878–1922', in Brendan Walsh (ed.), *Essays in the History of Irish Education: Past, Present and Future Perspectives* (London: Palgrave Macmillan, 2016), 129–79 [135].
8 Eugene Jolas, 'Manifesto: The Revolution of the Word', in *transition* 16–17, reprinted in Jolas (ed.), *transition workshop* (New York: Vanguard, 1949), 173–4.
9 Elizabeth Switaj, *James Joyce's Teaching Life and Methods: Language and Pedagogy in 'A Portrait of the Artist as a Young Man', 'Ulysses', and 'Finnegans Wake'* (London: Palgrave Macmillan, 2016), xiii, 133.
10 See, however, Natasha Periyan's recent account *The Politics of 1930s British Literature: Education, Class, Gender* (London: Bloomsbury, 2018). Periyan makes the case that the 1930s were particularly characterized by the 'pressing nature of the pedagogic' and suggests that 'to those perennial symbols of the decade – the gramophone and the loudspeaker, should be added the textbook and the blackboard'. Writers in the 1930s, claims Periyan, seemed to be increasingly turning to teaching as a profession and at the same adopting forms of writing, like the lecture and the essay, which were suggestive of pedagogic purpose [2].
11 *The Times*, August 12, 1854, 7.
12 *The Publishers Circular*, January 13, 1900, 3. *The Times*, January 6, 1900, 7.
13 See Chapters 6, 7 and 8 of Ansgar Weymann, *States, Markets and Education: The Rise and Limits of the Education State* (Basingstoke: Palgrave Macmillan, 2014). Weymann analyses newspaper reporting of education in four national newspapers – *The Times*, *The New York Times*, the *Frankfurter (Allgemeine) Zeitung* and *Le Figaro* – from 1900–2006. The beginning of the period, from 1900 to 1914, is seen as an education heyday. Front-page coverage of education issues was frequent and continuous in this period, with a maximum of 106 articles per year and an average of 42 devoted to this topic. In the second half of the century, coverage halved, showing a diminishing interest in both domestic and international education issues.
14 'English and German Methods of Education', *The Publishers Circular*, August 18, 1900, 147.
15 The first quote comes from a book anonymously authored by 'Jacques' and entitled *Irish Education as It Is and as It Should Be* (Dublin: Gill, 1906), [4]. The second is the title of a pamphlet written by Maurice C. Hume and published in London by Simpkin & Marshall in 1889.
16 *Freeman's Journal*, February 7, 1900, 4; September 3, 1900, 4.
17 Weymann, *States, Market and Education*, 1.
18 *The Leader*, September 1, 1900, 7.
19 For historical research on Irish masculinities and nationhood see, for example, Joseph Valente, *The Myth of Manliness in Irish National Culture, 1880–1922* (Urbana, IL: University of Illinois Press, 2011) and Aidan Beatty, *Masculinist Power in Irish Nationalism 1884–1928* (London: Palgrave, 2016).
20 See Gail Baylis, 'Boy Culture and Ireland 1916', *Early Popular Visual Culture*, 13/3, 2015, 192–208.

21 J.S. Sheehy, 'The Need of an Irish "Boys" Paper', *The College Chronicle*, *Castleknock* 2/24, June 1909, 32, quoted in Ciaran O'Neill, 'The Irish Schoolboy Novel', *Eire-Ireland*, 44/1/2, 2009, 147–68 [151].

22 For an account of this return and its relations to literature, see Len Platt, *Aristocracies of Fiction: The Idea of Aristocracy in Late-Nineteenth-Century and Early-Twentieth-Century Literary Culture* (Westport, CT: Greenwood, 2001).

23 See Fritz Ringer's introduction to Detlef K. Müller, Fritz Ringer and Brian Simon (eds.), *The Rise of the Modern Educational System: Structural Change and Social Reproduction 1870–1920* (Cambridge: Cambridge University Press, 1987), 1.

24 Ringer, 'Introduction', in *The Rise of the Modern Educational System*, 5–6.

25 'Introduction', *The Rise of the Modern Educational System*, 7.

26 Hilary Steedman, 'Defining Institutions: The Endowed Secondary Grammar Schools and the Systemization of English Secondary Schools', in Müller, *et al.*, *The Rise of the Modern Educational System*, 111–34 [117].

27 The quote comes from a plan for a military academy put before the National Convention in 1795 by Bertrand Barère de Vieuzac (1755–1841). See Colin Jones (ed.), *The French Revolution: Voices from a Momentous Epoch 1789–95* (London: Guild, 1988), 222.

28 Derek Gilliard, *A History of Education in England*, www.educationengland.org.uk/documents/clarendon1864/clarendon1.html

29 See Jacques Rancière, 'On Ignorant Schoolmasters', in Charles Bingham and Gert Biesta, *Jacques Rancière: Education, Truth, Emancipation* (London: Continuum, 2010), 1–24.

30 Rancière, 'On Ignorant Schoolmasters', 1.

31 Jacques Rancière, *The Ignorant Schoolmaster*, 18.

32 See the introduction to Steven G. Yao and Michael Coyle (eds.), *Ezra Pound: An Education* (Orono: University of Maine, National Poetry Foundation, 2012).

33 For an account of Pound and Santayana, see Martin Coleman, '"It Doesn't . . . Matter Where You Begin": Pound and Santayana on Education', *Journal of Aesthetic Education*, 44/4, 2010, 1–17.

34 T.S. Eliot, 'Modern Education and the Classics: A Revision of an Address Delivered to the Classical Club of Harvard', in *Essays Ancient and Modern* (London: Faber & Faber, 1936), 161–74.

35 Hughes appears only a few times in *Stephen Hero*, but each time he is sneering, on one occasion at Stephen Daedalus's paper 'Drama and Life' which he sees as 'a moral menace to the people of Ireland'. See *SH*, 53 and 89.

36 Patrick Pearse, 'The Murder Machine', in *The Collected Works of Padraic H. Pearse: Political Writings and Speeches* (Dublin: Phoenix, 1917), 24–5.

37 Pearse, 'The Murder Machine', 26–7.

38 Richard Ellmann, *James Joyce* (New York: Oxford University Press, 1959), 147; Joseph Valente, 'Beyond Truth and Freedom', *James Joyce Quarterly*, 25/11, 1987, 87–103.

39 For Nietzsche and education, see David E. Cooper, *Authenticity and Learning: Nietzsche's Education Philosophy* (London: Routledge & Kegan Paul, 1983). Illustrative of the more recent interest are Thomas E. Hart (ed.), *Nietzsche, Culture and Education* (London: Routledge, 2017); Mark Jones, 'Overcoming *Ressentiment*: Nietzsche's Education for an Aesthetic Aristocracy', *History of Political Thought*, 34/4, 2013, 669–701; Allen Ansgar, 'Awaiting Education: Friedrich Nietzsche on *the Future of Our Educational Institutions*', *Philosophical Enquiry in Education*, 24/3, 2017, 197–210.

40 *Anti-Education: Friedrich Nietzsche: On the Future of Our Educational Institutions*, translated by Damion Searls, edited with an introduction by Paul Reitter and Chad Wellmon (New York: New York Review of Books, 2016), 26.

41 *Anti-Education – Friedrich Nietzsche*, 27.

42 Fredrich Nietzsche, *Ecce Homo: How One Becomes What One Is*, translated with notes by R.J. Hollingdale with an introduction by Michael Tanner (1908; Harmondsworth: Penguin, 1979), 82.

Chapter 2

'Pinocchio! Oh Pinocchio! You're a boy! A real boy!' – boyology and stories of childhood in Pearse and Joyce

> Consider the Irish speaking child. He is the fairest thing that springs up from the soil of Ireland, – even more beautiful than any flower, more graceful than any wild creature of the fields or woods, purer than any monk or nun, wiser than any seer.
>
> Patrick Pearse, 'The Irish-speaking child' (1907)

> Some laughed again: mirthless but with meaning. Two in the back bench whispered. Yes. They knew: had never learned nor ever been innocent. All. With envy he watched their faces: Edith, Ethel, Gerty, Lily. Their likes: their breaths, too, sweetened tea and jam, their bracelets tittering in the struggle.
>
> James Joyce, *Ulysses* (1921)

Boys and men – education and the representation of masculinity

George Mosse's study of modern masculinity, *The Image of Man* (1996), begins with a statement about the pervasiveness of 'distinctive images of masculinity' in Western culture, images through which men 'assert what they believe to be their manhood'. These are symbols of 'personal regeneration', but they are also deeply implicated in the construction of national identities. For Mosse, there is an intimate relationship between masculinity and the formation of modernity, a chronological contingency that permeates every aspect of life and crosses ideological differences of the most fundamental kinds. In this historiography, 'manliness', with its beginning in the second half of the eighteenth century and the Enlightenment, is a modern phenomenon. In his scoping of the topic, Mosse explains that 'examining the manly ideal means not only dealing with nationalism and fascism, usually regarded as "masculine", but also with socialism, communism, and above all, the ideals and functioning of normative society'.[1] Critically, manliness is part of the fabric of ordinary, everyday life, which is why its image appears so natural. Masculinity here becomes a stereotype but by no means a negative one. On the contrary, the fit and proper male is a profoundly prestigious and elevating social imaginary, not just positive but constitutive of a hugely powerful culture engine driving 'the nation and the society' – a 'Bygmester Finnegan' or a Here Comes Everybody writ large in *Finnegans Wake* (*FW*, 4.19) – although Mosse emphasizes that 'the existence of a negative stereotyping of men who not only failed to measure up to the ideal but who in body and soul were its foil' had a lasting effect on sustaining the authority of the positive stereotype – and tragic consequences for the modern world.[2]

Elsewhere in this introduction, Mosse outlines the agencies and agents through which the masculine stereotype was reproduced as social ideal. He refers, for example, to the roles of science, theology, art, social and political movements and so on. Curiously, education receives slight treatment in the book, although it is clear how fundamental it must have been in this respect.[3] Nineteenth- and early-twentieth-century education in Europe and America was a matter of educating boys, producing class elites that would govern, administer and police. In England the creation of that elite was firmly linked to the work of a handful of public schools and perhaps its most characteristic ordering system, the prefect system, a system that 'gave the senior boys a taste of the exercise of power and put them on their honour not to abuse it'.[4] If, as Mosse says, the positive masculine stereotype existed against 'a background of cosmopolitan Enlightenment', the institutionalizing of education must have been key to its formation. It is in this spirit that Mosse references Friedrich Ehrenberg who wrote that 'the image of true masculinity must be easy to read because it sets the goal for man's education' and uses Fröebel to show how the goal of education, even at the edges of early radical pedagogy, was fundamentally spatial, territorial and masterful – 'the boy forms for himself his own world; for the feeling of his own power implies and soon demands also the possession of his own space and his own material belonging exclusively to him'.[5]

This current chapter takes its wider terms of reference from Mosse's analysis. It also draws on accounts of masculinities as they were formulated specifically in colonial Ireland, especially versions of masculinity emerging out of both Irish revivalism and Catholicism. The central point is made in a 2008 essay by Joseph Nugent entitled 'The Sword and the Prayerbook: Ideals of Authentic Irish Manliness', which shows how the Catholic Church in the latter half of the nineteenth century responded to secular models of the nineteenth-century hero 'by refurbishing its saints'. The League of Columb, established in 1899, was key to the new calibration and had 'inordinate impact'.[6] In *Ulysses*, Stephen Dedalus recalls a time when he could see himself doing 'wonders. . . . Missionary to Europe after fiery Colombanus' (*U*3,192–3), a reformist fantasy taken up by Shaun in the *Wake*. By 'sacralising the discourse of Irish nationalism . . . , the clergy deeply inflected the trajectory of Irish manly development', a process made manifest in school textbooks and revisions to the *Lives of Irish Saints*. As a result of this work, the priests 'delivered to the young men of Ireland a model of patriotism thenceforth inextricably entangled with the mysticism of the Roman Catholic Church'.[7]

This chapter is a reading of the stories of childhood in Joyce's *Dubliners*, positioned in the context of nationalist and postcolonial discourses of masculinity and expressed through boy cultures. It seeks to situate the 'Joyce and education' formulation in relation to Joyce's early fiction and the nationalist politics cultures current in the Ireland of Joyce's day. The central strategy in the reading is to place Joyce's stories against a series of stories written by Patrick Pearse around 1905 and published together as a collection two years later, all this close to the time Joyce was writing 'The Sisters', 'An Encounter' and 'Araby'.

The comparison is problematized by the fact that there is an obvious distinction to be made between these texts. The Pearse stories were written for children and young people; Joyce's stories became infamous for offending adults, notably Grant Richards's printer and, subsequently, the publisher's lawyer, who advised against publication of 'An Encounter' on the grounds that if attention were to be drawn to certain passages with enough force, prosecution might follow.[8] There is a further complication in that there is no direct textual link between Pearse's work and Joyce's in this respect nor any suggestion that Joyce could have even read Pearse's stories before writing his own. They did not appear in translation until the Dundalgan Press edition of 1916, and Joyce's knowledge of Gaelic was limited. Neither is there any evidence that Pearse knew of Joyce's stories – only 'The Sisters' could have been available to him before 1905.

That said, there are compelling reasons for reading Joyce against Pearse. The general point is that Pearse's stories were an important part of the cultural environment that produced *Dubliners* and that Joyce's stories write to. Joyce's realism in *Dubliners* is substantially the reverse side of a generic romanticism which Pearse's stories relate to and exemplify – the realism in these stories, that is, is precisely formulated as an antidote to Pearse's revivalism. More specific to the themes of this study, the fact that the *Íosagán* stories were written *by* Pearse remains significant outside any consideration of direct intertextuality, because Pearse was both a leading Irish Republican Brotherhood member who became a founding father of the Irish Republic and an education radical. The two roles were forged together in Pearse's life and bound up with each other. This gives to the relation between Pearse, the great nationalist, and Joyce, the great iconoclast, a kind of totemic status. Whatever separated the two writers, and a great deal does, there is a kind of inevitability about bringing them together in a study of this kind.

According to Desmond Ryan, writing in the first of several biographies, although Pearse was trained as a barrister, he never practiced law because he refused to take part in what he came to consider 'the most wicked of all professions'.[9] He became instead a committed teacher–activist, dedicated to the cause of the language revival and the complete de-Anglicization of the education system in Ireland. In 1909, he founded *Sgiol Eanne* (St Enda's School), sited first at Ranelagh then at the Hermitage, Rathfarnham, which is now a museum to Pearse administered by the Office of Public Works. Under his leadership, the school educated a small number of fee-paying Irish boys in a hybrid style, a combination of pragmatism and militaristic national idealism. The sister girls' school, St Ita's, was short-lived, closing shortly after its inauguration because of financial difficulties, but it was organized on similar lines. Pupils were taught Gaelic alongside English, French and Irish literature and performed in ceremonial plays that celebrated mythological Irish heroes. At the same time, they were prepared for intermediate exams if parents requested it, with the boys being schooled in scouting cultures that appeared modelled on Baden-Powell's scouting manual, a charge Pearse struggled to manage:

> Our programme includes every element of a military training. We are not mere 'Boy Scouts', although we teach and practise the art of scouting. Physical culture, infantry drill, marching, and the routine of camp life, semaphore and Morse signalling, scouting in all its branches, elementary tactics, ambulance and first aid, swimming, hurling, and football, are all included in our scheme of training; and opportunity is given to the older boys for bayonet and rifle practice. This does not exhaust our programme, for we believe that mental culture should go hand in hand with physical culture, and we provide instruction in Irish and in Irish history, lectures on historical and literary subjects, and musical social entertainments.[10]

In *Pearse's Patriots: St Enda's and the Cult of the Boyhood*, cultural historian Elaine Sisson constructs the school as a bizarre amalgam of Wagner, Montessori and Cuchulain, all framed in a Gaelicized curriculum which reinvented 'imperial pedagogical and cultural forms', including the English public school in some respects, 'for an Irish audience'.[11] In this latter respect it figures as a classic postcolonial institution and one likely to appeal only to a distinctly classed minority, although such a view has been challenged by modern Irish historians, notably Brendan Walsh.[12]

Three years before the Rebellion, Pearse had been hailed in the *Irish Review* as an Irish Montessori, partly because of his reputation as the headmaster of St Enda's, but also because during his period as editor of the Gaelic League's periodical *An Claidheamh Soluis* (*The Sword of Light*), between 1903 and 1909, he wrote a series of pieces amounting to what some saw as 'an informed' and progressive 'promulgation of Irish language literature teaching methodology'.[13] Shortly afterwards, he began writing a series of observations about education politics first published in the school magazine at St Enda's. These were published more widely in 1915 as 'The Murder Machine', a blistering attack on education in Ireland under the empire. 'To invent such a system of teaching and persuade us that it is an education system', Pearse wrote, 'an Irish education system to be defended by Irishman against attack, is the most wonderful thing that the English have accomplished in Ireland, and the most wicked'.[14] Here Pearse argues that education 'is the most grotesque and horrible of the English inventions for the debasement of Ireland', a parasitical, invading imposition designed for substituting 'mere things' for 'men and women'. Education becomes a manufacturing process. 'Our children', says Pearse, 'are the "raw material"; we desiderate for this education "modern methods" which must be "efficient" but "cheap"; we send them off to Clongowes to be "finished"; when "finished" they are "turned out"; specialists "grind" them for the English Civil Service'.[15]

Dubbed 'the 'schoolmaster of all Ireland' in an anonymous poem written in 1916, Pearse is himself a powerful embodiment of just how connected state formation and schooling had been and continued to be. Although education historian Norman Atkinson insisted in the 1960s that, 'the educational philosophy which he [Pearse] preached . . . [was] largely ignored, and has made remarkably little impact on the school structure of the Irish State which he did so much to create', the symbolic association between Pearse and education has been important.[16] Indeed, in more recent times, the resurrection of Pearse as an educational progressive has been seen by one historian as 'a case study in the mechanics of Irish nation building'.[17] Whilst Pearse's political legacy as a militant, conservative nationalist may remain contentious for a modern liberal state, Walsh has pointed out that the idea of Pearse as a 'truly progressive educationalist' can be taken as something very different – confirmation of 'Ireland's modern progressive status'.[18] This is one reason why the alternative view, which insists on linking Pearse with proto-fascism, has been so strongly contested.

From this position, Pearse and his boy stories register vividly and in still contemporary ways against *Dubliners*. They show just how far the nebulous discourses of 'boy culture' converged around rhetorical concepts of schooling – not just in Ireland of course, but throughout the West, where heroic versions of masculinity shaped state formations across a range of otherwise determinedly distinct nationalisms, albeit not without risk.[19] In this respect they are important to the registration of education culture in the age of Joyce.

Íosagán agus Sgéalta Eile

In 1907 the Gaelic League published four short stories intended primarily for children and young adults. Set in the Gaeltacht and illustrated by Beatrice Elvery, they were written in Gaelic under the title *Íosagán agus Sgéalta Eile* (*Iosagan and Other Stories*). As Anne Markey, their modern editor, points out, the volume responded to a precise and immediate educational requirement. In 1908, Irish was adopted as a compulsory matriculating subject which created a demand for sympathetic texts that could be used in the study of the language. At the same time Pearse worked a seemingly counter-intuitive aesthetic agenda, at least in his literary essays.

Pearse was fervently anti-modern. In 'The Murder Machine', he was to argue that 'there can be no such thing as "sound modern education" – as well talk about a "living modern faith" of a "serviceable modern religion". It should be obvious that the more "modern" an education is the less sound, for in education "modernism" is as much heresy as in religion'.[20] Nevertheless, in 1907 he wrote in anticipation of a 'modern' national literature that '*cannot* (and if it could, should not) be built up on fairy tale'. It should engage instead 'with the mind of contemporary Europe' and be 'modern not only in the sense of freely borrowing every modern form which it does not possess and which it is capable of assimilating, but also in texture, tone and outlook'.[21] The context to this unexpected alignment was the conservatism of academy Gaelic leaguers like Richard Henebry, advocating for the continuation of an aristocratic literary culture based on seventeenth-century forms and modes rather than on the language of 'the people'.[22] Pearse's plea for a modern Gaelic literature implied not the incorporation of Ibsen-like forensic as it did for early Joyce, but something quite different – the continuation of a living tradition set against the curating of a dead one. It was in this sense consistent with Pearse's insistence on the spirituality of the Irish people and his celebration of the living Irish boy who, for Pearse, was the embodiment of the authentic nation and the predestined incumbent of the modern Irish world to come. The assimilation of the modern, then, served as a riposte to those who argued that the retrospection of revivalism was nothing more than fantasy and nostalgia.

All four stories in the collection were centred on children. One of them, 'Barbara', is atypical to the extent that its main character is a little girl, but the narrative is gendered in traditional, orthodox ways nonetheless, and in this way is a confirmation of conventional boyology. The central characters are Brideen and her two dolls. The first is a rough, local toy that Brideen's mother gifted her. Brideen falls in love with it at first sight – 'I'll have a child of my very own now, – a child of my very owneen own! Brideen will have a child!'.[23] The doll is named 'Barbara' after Brideen's aunt, and Brideen takes her everywhere she goes, even to church, where she imagines that the blessing she receives from the priest is in fact for Barbara.

The second doll, 'Niamh Goldy-Head', is a newcomer described as 'a native of Dublin'. A modern, sophisticated toy that says 'Ma-ma', it is a present from a visitor arrived in rural Ireland to learn Gaelic. The new doll, imported from the city, instantly usurps the old, traditional one in Brideen's affections, until one day she falls asleep by the fire with her new doll beside her and her clothes catch alight – 'There wasn't a soul in the house to protect the darling little child. . . . Nobody knew her to be in peril, but only God – and Barbara'. It is only the old doll mysteriously falling off the sideboard that alerts Brideen's mother, who saves her 'from the death that was faring on her'.[24]

The ostensible point of the story is Brideen's understanding that 'Barbara' is more 'true' to her, a privileging of tradition that implies the rejection of urbanization, the new and the metropolitan mind. But the orthodox moralist frame carries further codes, constructing girls as naturally fickle, for instance, and characteristically at risk until the world teaches them otherwise. As Markey suggests in her introduction, the choice over dolls is really no choice at all. Either way, motherhood is 'the highest aspiration that a little girl can have'.[25]

The other three stories are centred specifically on boy characters which would potentially link them to boyology cultures characteristic of the early twentieth century, although their roots go back a little further.[26] In America, the ur-texts of the tradition would have been Twain's *Tom Sawyer* (1876) and *Huckleberry Finn* (1884), homosocial quest narratives and celebrations of the freedom of boys to roam. This kind of narrative figured everywhere in late-nineteenth- and early-twentieth-century Britain – in the developing traditions of the public-school novel, for example; the high status and huge popularity of a writer like G.A.

Henty; the formation of institutions such as Baden Powell's Boy Scouts – a backwoodsman culture addressed to boys who 'want to help' their country and 'other people' as 'all the best men are out to do' – and in early psychology, such as Granville Stanley Hall's *Adolescence* (1904).[27]

Pearse's work as an educationalist and nationalist was characterized not least through his militarization of the Cuchulain story from Irish legend. The stories in the *Íosagán* collection, however, are very different. They are typical of boyology in that they imagine boyhood as a special, privileged state set apart from the world of adults, but the special kind of 'primitivism' elevated in traditional boyologies, not least through masculinist rough and tumble, is almost completely missing from them. Here the perfection of Pearse's boys is drawn up in terms of innocence, physical beauty and spirituality. The first of them concerns an old man who appears to have lost God in all respects except one: 'the love he has for the cleanest and most beautiful thing that God created, – the shining soul of the child'.[28] In Pearse's fiction, boys are perfect, innocent and true – indeed, 'Iosagan' imagines Christ as a Gaelic-speaking child in a pastoral Connemara paradise who appears only to other children and the one adult given the grace to see him. Likewise in 'Eoineen of the Birds', an especially sentimental narrative which gifts the main character special powers of imagination, language and the ability to commune with nature. This is the beautiful 'Irish-speaking child', called to an early death and rebirth 'in the country where it does be summer always'.[29]

The most interesting, and certainly the strangest, story in the collection, 'The Priest', instantiates this idealizing version of boyhood and the central role that spirituality has in Pearse's conception of masculinity. It begins with a disconcerting image of a 'priest' being stripped of his clothes and washed by his mother, who is 'rubbing and scrubbing every inch of his body'. She kisses him, too, because she cannot 'keep her mouth from a wee, red moutheen as sweet as Paraig's (Paraig's my Priest's name, you know)'.[30] At this point what appears to be a deeply twisted narrative rights itself to become a not-quite-straightened one. Paraig, it turns out, is not an adult priest at all, but an eight-year-old boy inhabited by the fantasy of becoming a priest. Much to his mother's consternation, he has a new game which involves him dressing up in her clothes and pretending to be a priest reading Mass. His mother's 'red bodice' becomes pretend vestments and 'a little Gaelic book' stands in for the missal. Alarmed by what she fears may be her son's transgression, she confides in the local priest, a calm, refined, self-possessed figure who visits the house and secretly witnesses for himself the 'queer sight' of the boy acting out his fantasy in a mixture of Latin, Gaelic and made-up language. The priest is kind, authoritative and 'manly'. Taking the boy aside, he tells him that he is too young to serve and advises that he may never experience the joy of leading a real Mass – 'it's not granted to anyone but to God's priest to say the Mass'. That caution aside, he is encouraging and asks whether the boy would 'like to be serving Mass on Sunday?'[31] Fantasy takes a few steps towards becoming reality and horizons widen as boy becomes altar boy. The story ends with the boy's mother fantasizing that Paraig could indeed one day become elevated to bishop.

Except that this is more a tale of predetermination than fantasy – Pearse's preface to the collection tells the reader Paraig's fate: he is 'serving Mass now'.[32]

The point of the story is again the association of the Irish boy with spirituality, achieved here through a vivid illustration of the power of the priest image as masculinist model. The story is in part based on Pearse's own life. In reality, he himself was possessed by the same fantasy in which his character indulges. Pearse, too, used to dress up in his mother's clothes as a boy and pretend to be a priest – biographer Ruth Dudley Edwards comments that his serious expression and preference for black clothes as an adult 'made him look like a young clergyman'.[33] He also was especially devoted to his mother. The stranger implications by which eroticism, incest and transvestitism get caught up with the transforming power of the cross, however, are left un–worked out, and, indeed, unformulated at any level outside the unthinkable. Order is restored by the agency of the priest. Paraig's mother has some concerns that her son has no breeches or brogues for his new role. Indeed, she thinks him too young to be put in breeches. But the priest is able to reassure her. There is no call for breeches; a 'little cassock' can go over his coat and he knows where a pair of brogues is going spare. 'We'll dress you right, Paraig', he says, 'no fear' – and any sign of *fin de siècle* gender trouble becomes properly righted.[34] What remains is a story irresistible to the queering it works so hard to render unsayable.

The collection was overall well received. It ran into five editions by 1915. Reviewers praised the narratives precisely for their 'simplicity' and 'the perfect knowledge of the Gaelic juvenile mind which they betray' – possibly 'portray' was intended here, although the slippage, if it is one, is telling.[35] The review in *An Claidheamh Soluis* likewise appreciated both the representation of childhood in the stories and their appeal to children – 'they are children's stories, or rather, stories of child life, but they are drawn with a touch of charming delicacy, and a sympathetic insight into the ways and manners of children which is quite uncommon'.[36] But there were dissenting voices in the reception. Writing in D.P. Moran's *The Leader*, Henebry took issue with the heroic and spiritualized boy culture with which Pearse had meant to challenge 'Anglo-Saxon' versions of masculinist heroism. Against the comparison made with conventional Anglicized Irish literature as 'the talk of big, broad-chested men', Pearse did not come off well. For Henebry, Pearse's stories were likewise Anglicized, but differently geared towards 'the frivolous petulancy of latter-day English *genre* scribblers' and, worse, ill-bred and effeminate – 'their utterance is as the mincing of an under-assistant floorwalker of a millenary shop'.[37] Far from celebrating Irish masculinity, Henebry saw Pearse's stories as a 'vile' affront to be 'shunned in thought, in feeling, in outlook, in word, punctuation, everything'.[38] This extract from 'Eoineen of the Birds' illustrates the kind of thing Henebry would have been objecting to. Here the boy Eoineen is delighted to see the first swallow returning from the 'Southern World':

> 'O, my love, my love you are!' says Eoineen, taking it in his two hands and kissing it on the little black head. 'Welcome to me from the strange

countries! Are you tired after your lonely journey over lands and over seas? *Ora*, my thousand, thousand loves you are, beautiful little messenger from the country where it does be summer always! Where are your companions from you? Or what happened you on the road, or why didn't ye come before this?'

While he was speaking like this with the swallow, kissing it again and yet again, and rubbing his hand lovingly over its blue-black wings, its little red throat and its bright, feathered breast, another little bird sailed from the south and alighted beside them.[39]

Henebry's dismissal might have been sharp, even homophobic, but it is not difficult to see why he would have thought this kind of thing more twee, effete and sentimental than authentically Irish. It played straight into the hands of a prestigious and influential English raciology that had signposted Irish literature as a feminizing culture. Here the Celts became 'passionate in everything' but incapable of the manly self-regulation that 'would give strength and stability to the sentimental parts of their disposition'.[40] In Pearse's account formal, institutional schooling, for Brideen as for Paraig, has been erased to the extent that it barely figures at all. The strongest debt here, however, is not to *Emile* and nineteenth century European traditions of romanticism seeking to preserve the natural boy from the evils of the world, but, rather, to a history of the Catholic Church in Ireland in the nineteenth century which saw the recoding of self-regulation as manly Catholic denial.

Joyce's stories of childhood

A version of the first of Joyce's stories of childhood, 'The Sisters', was written in 1904 and published that year in *The Irish Homestead*. 'An Encounter' was written in 1905 and 'Araby' finished in 1906. The history of the long delay to full publication of *Dubliners* is well known – a complete version could not appear until 1914 – and 'An Encounter' played a particular part in that history. It is true that there are echoes of Pearse's short stories in *Dubliners*. The strange priest in 'The Sisters' who becomes 'a disappointed man' after breaking a chalice (*D*, 16), for example, seems prefigured by the dying old man in 'Iosagan' who 'wouldn't go to the Mass. People said that he didn't believe there was a God in it'.[41] But these are superficial and usually fraught. For the most part, the movement from Pearse to Joyce is nothing less than a journey to another world. Joyce writes a story entitled 'A Mother' and Pearse another called '*The* Mother', both writing to a figure central in Irish literary culture as in many others. They do so, however, in quite antithetical ways. In one, motherhood is idealized and spiritualized in a rural Gaelicized idyll; in the other, it is socialized and psychologized in modern urban life. There is a fundamental dissonance that permeates virtually all points of potential comparison between the stories and that shapes the versions of boyology they respectively construct. One group is 'simple', 'straight-forward' and 'innocent' in this respect, the other self-consciously complex, ambiguous and knowing – a configuration of superiority just as intentionally positioned in relation to revivalism and nationalist historiographies as was Pearse's articulation of innocence.

Both authors work the central significance of the role of the Church in the construction of boy culture and education. But in Joyce's case, the priest is only one of many models for boys, specifically associated in 'An Encounter' with the authoritarian and censorship, which makes it not so strange that Joe Dillon, imaged as a boy capering 'round the garden, an old tea-cosy on his head, beating a tin with his fist and yelling – Ya! yaka, yaka, yaka!', turns out to have a vocation for the priesthood (*D*, 18). Orthodoxy is consciously assimilated to inappropriate and sometimes dangerous contexts so that the entanglement of spirituality with sexuality, submerged in Pearse's stories, is, in Joyce, if not in the open at least strongly implied. In 'The Sisters', the old priest is suspect, at least to the adult men in the story. Old Cotter says ominously that he 'wouldn't like children of mine . . . to have too much to say to a man like that' (*D*, 8). In 'An Encounter' the threatened dispensation of school punishment at the hands of priests is wickedly conflated with sexual pleasure through the figure of 'the pervert' excited by the prospect of 'Murphy' being chastised, 'whipped and well whipped' (*D*, 27). In 'Araby', a narrator remembering himself as a boy in love merges secular courtly traditions with a priestly performance:[42]

> I imagined that I bore my chalice through a throng of foes. Her name sprang to my lips at moments in strange prayers and praises which I myself did not understand. . . . I did not know whether I would ever speak to her or not or, if I spoke to her, how I could tell her of my confused adoration.
>
> (*D*, 31)

In the same way, Pearse's idealized image of the young, wise, selfless and authoritative priest serving his community and acting as a model of Irish masculinity is traduced in Joyce's figure of the priest as dying old man in 'The Sisters', whose body is decaying and whose mind is running out of control. The narrator recalls his dream of this figure in grotesque terms of the 'heavy grey face of the paralytic'; he remembers his earlier self puzzling over 'why it smiled continually and why the lips were so moist with spittle' (*D*, 9). Later in the story, the old priest's sister reveals that 'his life was, you might say, crossed'. It was known that something had 'gone wrong with him' when he was discovered 'sitting up by himself in the dark in his confession-box, wide awake and laughing-like softly to himself' (*D*, 16–17). For all this dark mystery, however, and in part because of it, the priest retains respect and distinction in a culture of deference. Here his status is untouchable, whatever the gossip. He possesses deep knowledge of the most prestigious kind which both mystifies and impresses the young narrator. Taught 'to pronounce Latin properly', 'the meaning of the different ceremonies of the Mass and of the different vestments worn by the priest', the narrator becomes 'annoyed' at himself that he should feel 'a sensation of freedom' at the priest's death (*D*, 11). For his part, teaching the boy gives the old priest a twisted kind of pleasure:

> Sometimes he had amused himself by putting difficult questions to me, asking me what one should do in certain circumstances or whether such and such sins were moral or venial or only imperfections. His questions showed me how complex and mysterious were certain institutions of the Church which I had always regarded as the simplest of acts. The duties of the priest towards the Eucharist and towards the secrecy of the confessional seemed so grave to me that I wondered how anybody had ever found in himself the courage to undertake them; and I was not surprised when he told me that the fathers of the Church had written books as thick as the *Post Office Directory* . . .
>
> (*D*, 11)

The further transgression here is that the 'spiritualism' of the Irish boy, so much a part of national identity in Pearse's formulation, becomes aligned not with selflessness and love of God and country but something much more performative and self-interested, much more 'social' – the desire for status, distinction, authority and control. The 'great wish' that the old priest is said to have for the boy in 'The Sisters' plays into his desire to be distinguished from those around him – from old Cotter, a 'tiresome old fool', an insult later developed in 'tiresome old red-nosed imbecile' (*D*, 7, 9), and from his uncle and Nannie, whose skirt is hooked 'clumsily' at the back and cloth boots are 'trodden down all to one side' (*D*, 13). It also shapes the dream in which the boy appropriates to himself the authority to forgive the old priest – 'to absolve the simoniac of his sin' (*D*, 9). The result of education into the mysteries of the Church is to fuel such fantasies of distinction and social power. Stephen Dedalus's vocation in *A Portrait of the Artist as a Young Man* works in similar ways.

These respective treatments of the Church are central and separate Pearse out from Joyce in fundamental ways, but they are, in these stories, products of a broader disarticulation between quite different, and opposed, conceptions of the nature of both boyhood and socialization. It is here that we see, for the first time in Joyce's writing, the great subtlety of his representation of social and cultural processes and the extent to which this positions him so clearly at the contemporary margins in relation to orthodox Irish nationalisms. This is almost certainly the real reason why his stories took so long to reach the public domain. The sexual 'connotations' are the tip of an iceberg of potentiality for offence positioned everywhere – not least in relation to boyology. Perhaps the most significant indicator in this respect is the way in which these stories violate what most then contemporary versions of boyology, including Pearse's, sought to preserve at all costs – the separateness of boyhood. Although classic boy culture is deeply supervisory, it simultaneously protects the boy–adult divide, celebrating the boy identity as a distinct state, a 'kingdom' contiguous to adult life but separate from it. The American writer on children's literature, Kenneth J. Kidd describes it as 'a world of harmless pranks and reverie just slightly removed from the world of adults'.[43] The overall effect is to render up boyhood as an impermeable condition. Like Pearse's stories, all three of Joyce's are written from the perspective of anonymous narrators – adult men – but Joyce's narrators specifically look back on their own life. From such a position, boyhood can only be notional from the outset – a tale told by adults who constantly mediate and intrude. This has the effect of making the formulation of boyhood simultaneous with its erasure, a contradiction thoroughly exploited by Joyce. Each of the stories are characterized by stops, halts, frustrations and interruptions which reinforce the sense of blurred borders and overlapping zones and are invariably the result of adult work – Old Cotter's 'tiresome' interventions in 'The Sisters'; the uncle's late return from the pub which threatens to derail his nephew's trip to the Araby bazaar and the tawdry reality of things when he finally gets there; Father Butler's censorship of the boys' reading in 'An Encounter'. Indeed, the latter story, most conventionally framed as a traditional boyology, concerned with 'doors of escape', fleeing the 'restraining influence of the school' and the desire for 'real adventures' (*D*, 19–20), is centrally focused on arrested boyology, and what makes it so finally is the alarming meeting with the 'queer old josser' (*D*, 26), an adult encounter that threatens boy space and the freedom-to-roam narrative with the most unthinkable kind of invasion.

In Pearse's version of things, it is critical that boyology remains disguised to itself, otherwise the spell is broken. The main aim of his boy stories is to instantiate a highly racialized and romanticized version of the boy condition as the real. The Joyce texts, however, are entirely knowing about the boyology that operates in them, which is not least a fabricated product of commercial modernity. This explains the impact of 'An Encounter' which opens with reference to three boys' magazines that existed in reality – *The Union Jack* (1894–1933), *Pluck* (1895–1933) and *The Halfpenny Marvel* (1893–1922), 'chronicles of disorder' that pass into real and unruly boy games played away from institutions and set in sharp contrast to 'the peaceful odour of Mrs Dillon . . . prevalent in the hall of the house' (*D*, 19, 18). As several Joyce commentators have shown, the cultural history behind the magazines was complex and multiple.[44] In Joyce's story contemporary modernities are established through the coding of the magazines as 'American', partly through the 'Wild West' content but also because the narrator distinguishes himself from his friends by preferring 'American detective stories which were traversed from time to time by unkempt fierce and beautiful girls' (*D*, 19). Typically, however, these particular narratives were set in what were then still colonial spaces, including Canada and South America, and they imagined traditional and highly Anglicized versions of masculinity, the kind of gender imaginary – 'plucky', stout and honourable – seen in boyologies everywhere at this time. All three publications were published in England by Alfred Harmsworth, an Anglo-Irishman born at Chapelizod in Dublin County, who went on to become Viscount Northcliffe, the magnate behind Amalgamated Press and publisher of the *Daily Mail* and the *Daily Mirror*. A subsidiary company, the Education Book Company, produced *The Harmsworth Self-Educator*, *The Children's Encyclopaedia* and the *Harmsworth Universal Encyclopaedia*. At the time there would probably have been no single figure better able to represent how boyology figured as commercial product in the cultural mainstream of the real world.

At the same time Joyce's 'boy stories' share space with other modern supervisory discourses, linked to adult worlds of education, psychology and sociology. Again, 'An Encounter' is highly suggestive in this respect. It begins by constructing a familiar typology of boys distinguishing between the 'idle', the 'fierce' and the 'timid'. Deploying the categorization later picked up on by 'the queer old josser', the beginning of the story describes the narrator in his younger days as 'studious'. The 'adventures related in the literature of the Wild West' are 'remote' from his 'nature' and conflict with his claims on the genuinely literary. The opening also registers psychological anomalies between what individual boys are and their development in later life. As we have seen, Joe Dillon plays rough, is rowdy and dominates. And there is a focus on the group psychology of the boy peer group where under the influence of 'a spirit of unruliness', 'differences of culture and constitution were waived' and the boys band together – 'some boldly, some in jest and some almost in fear' (*D*, 18–19) – like a kind of 'tribe'.

Contemporary versions of boyology often characterized the boy as a wild figure who had to be constrained and trained into civilization – school life was supposed to tame the 'feral' boy without ruining him. The schoolmasters in Rudyard Kipling's *Stalky and Co* (1899) visualize their charges as 'Brutes! Barbarians! Savages! Children!' The narrator of the same novel – a self-proclaimed expert in boy psychology – explains that 'outside his own immediate interests the boy is as ignorant as the savage he so admires; but he has the savage's resource'.[45] The connection to racist theories of recapitulation was sometimes explicit. Here biogenetic law was held to confirm that human ontogeny (human growth from embryo to maturity) refigured the adult stages of phylogeny (species or racial development).[46] The white middle-class boy was imagined as exemplifying in his growth to maturity a development from barbarism to civilization. Misbehaviour, aggression and wildness became a throwback to a racialized past. The narrator of F.W. Farrar's public-school novel, *Eric: Or, Little by Little* (1858), for example, explains how 'I have often fancied that there must be in boys a pseudo-instinctive cruelty, a sort of "wild trick of the ancestral savage", which no amount of civilisation can entirely repress'.[47] Baden-Powell's *Scouting for Boys* imagines the civilizing impact of scouting as exploiting the natural inclinations of boys for reformist purposes. Here scouting puts boys into 'fraternity groups which is their natural organization, whether for games, mischief or loafing'.[48]

Such ideas figure largely in 'An Encounter', where they combine with the racism which sometimes depicted the Irish boy as a particular version of the primitive. Percy Hetherington Fitzgerald's 1867 public-school novel *Schooldays at Saxonhurst, By One of the Boys* represents a relatively mild version of the tradition in the character 'Paddy', a 'free-and-easy . . . half-buffooning, half dangerous fellow'.[49] Joyce's 'Paddy' is Mahoney who 'goes in for games' and has 'three totties'. He is 'a very rough boy', a more 'Irish' sort of boy given the false name 'Murphy' by a worried narrator who significantly takes the stereotypical English name of 'Smith' for himself (*D*, 25–7). Here Joyce indicates how gender stereotypes and class stereotypes are overlaid with raciality and shows an Irish boy reconciled to being headed off from what turn out to be dangerous potentialities. Deceived into intimacy with a troubling man who plays on his interest on higher-order literature, the narrator concludes this story with an agitated version of his younger self bidding the strange man 'good day' and walking away. He does so 'calmly' but his 'heart was beating quickly with fear'. Now he calls to his friend, 'Murphy', who eventually comes 'running across the field' to join him. 'And I was penitent; for in my heart I had always despised him a little' (D, 28). He has been returned to a familiar masculinist order, and at the same time frightened out of the dreams of distinction that so characterize him.

Some have seen Joyce's story as an assault on homosexuality itself. Writing in 1998, Margot Norris saw it as a homophobic text where 'the homosexual is figured as a sinister and sadistic predator of young boys'.[50] She has a point, but a presentist one which ignores how the past perceived certain types of child abuse as everyday and maintained complete silence over others. The stronger insistence is on the disciplining dimensions at the heart of boyologies which links erotic fantasy with the supervisory restraint of the school. The role of adults in all this gives Joyce's stories their decisive critical edge and takes boyology out of the elevated realms its more conventional signification seeks to inhabit – 'the pervert' is one of those adults. Here, boyologies do not embody the true unsullied state they typically purport to in Pearse and elsewhere. On the contrary, boyologies are fully exposed as naïve and ideologically informed social imaginaries. In Joyce's boy culture narratives, the colonial traffic of boys' own adventure travels alongside the boy narratives of Catholic hagiography to produce a complex and multiple cultural environment. With astonishing economy, these stories are established within a set of discourses – moral, religious and philosophical as well as psychological and sociological – all of them connected in some way to the development of boys into men. English models mix and merge with American discourses, these conflated by and in Irish gender typologies, which illustrates their ubiquity and cross contamination in the modern world. In this way, the boy culture mystified in Pearse's stories becomes uncoupled from its essentialist moorings, to be reinstated as a series of social and cultural constructs. For all these reasons, Joyce's 'stories of childhood' take position as a kind of gateway, not just to his developed representations of the school but to his engagement with the representational orders that once framed 'education' and a bigger cultural politics.

Just to make the point absolutely clearly, there is no evidence that either Joyce or Pearse was aware of what the other was doing in relation to short story writing. The stories are thrown into counterpoint because of the cultural environment that produced them and the history that followed in their wakes. From that position they are highly suggestive of what were completely antithetical versions of boy culture. To the extent that all 'boyologies' must somehow manage the impact of socialization on boyhood's end, they become illustrative in the debate, critically important to historical versions of modernity, of what it means to educate boys into men.

Notes

1 George Mosse, *The Image of Man: The Creation of Modern Masculinity* (New York: Oxford University Press, 1996), 3–4.
2 Mosse, *The Image of Man*, 6.
3 There are just a handful of references to education in Mosse's book, and these are to systems established in England and Germany. See 134–5, 138–42.
4 Jeffrey Richards, *Happiest Days: The Public Schools in English Fiction* (Manchester: Manchester University Press, 1988), 12.
5 See *The Image of Man*, 7. The Ehrenberg reference is to *De Charakter und die Bestimmung des Manne* (Hildburghausen and New York, 1834), 14–15. The Froebel quote is from, *The Education of Man* (1826; New York: Appleton & Co., 1887), 106.
6 Joseph Nugent, 'The Sword and the Prayerbook: Ideals of Authentic Irish Masculinities', *Victorian Studies*, 50/4, 2008, 587–613 [599].
7 Nugent, 'The Sword and the Prayerbook', 607.
8 See Richard Ellmann (ed.), *Letters of James Joyce*, vol. 2 (London: Faber & Faber, 1966), 309. Joyce's solicitor wrote, 'magistrates are directed to hear such cases in private and the Executive as much as possible endeavours to prevent its even being brought before the Public – and I might quote Gibbon's "Decline and Fall" to show how much the subject is loathed "I touch with reluctance and dispatch with impatience this most odious vice of which modesty rejects the name and nature abominates the idea."' (306).
9 Desmond Ryan, *The Man Called Pearse* (Dublin: Maunsel, 1919), 27.
10 Patrick Pearse, 'To the Boys of Ireland', in *The Collected Works*, 114. Baden-Powell had written to Pearse in 1909, inviting him to set up the Boy Scouts in Ireland, an offer which Pearse declined.
11 Elaine Sisson, *Pearse's Patriots: St Enda's and the Cult of the Boyhood* (Cork: Cork University Press, 2004), 9.
12 See Brendan Walsh, 'The Progressive Credentials of Patrick Henry Pearse: A Response to David Limond', *History of Education Review Bundoora*, 35/2, 2006, 32–44.
13 Walsh, 'The Progressive Credentials of Patrick Henry Pearse', 33. For the comparison to Montessori see Dáire Keogh, 'Patrick Pearse: "Studies" and the Birth of Revisionism', *Irish Quarterly Review*, 100/40, 2011, 421–32.
14 Pearse, 'The Murder Machine', 16.
15 Pearse, 'The Murder Machine', 6–7, 12.
16 Norman Atkinson, 'The Educational Ideas of Patrick Pearse, 1879–1916', *Comparative Education Review*, 11/1, 1967, 68–74 [68].
17 David Limond, '"The Schoolmaster of All Ireland": The Progressive Credentials of Patrick Henry Pearse 1879–1916', *History of Education Review*, 34/1, 2006, 63–73 [67].
18 Walsh, 'The Progressive Credentials of Patrick Henry Pearse', 33. Limond's essay is a powerful rebuttal to the claim that Pearse's educational writings were 'by any criteria . . . significant, original, extensive and progressive'. [66] It insists that he was fundamentally opposed not just to criticality but to any kind of genuine dissent.
19 For a different angle on some of the issues handled in this chapter, see Christopher Michael Elias, 'What Makes Them Dubliners? James Joyce's "An Encounter" and the

Foundations of Masculinist Nationalism in Ireland', *Journal of Men's Studies*, 24/3, 2016, 229–40.

20 Pearse, 'The Murder Machine', 18, 22.

21 Patrick Pearse, 'About Literature', *An Claidheamh Solais*, 26 May, 1906, 7.

22 See Patrick Pearse, *Short Stories*, with an introduction by Anne Markey (Dublin: University College Dublin Press, 2009), xvii.

23 Pearse, *Short Stories*, 24.

24 *Short Stories*, 28, 32.

25 Markey, 'Introduction', *Short Stories*, xxv. Markey continues, 'In Pearse's stories, women are born to be mothers while boys are born to be loved and revered'. See 'The Priest' in this collection, in which a mother dries her son after his bath: 'He was a lovely picture, standing there, and the firelight shining on his well-knit body and on his curly head, and dancing in his grey-laughing eyes' (15).

26 For an account of boyology and its development in America see Kenneth B. Kidd, *Making American Boys: Boyology and the Feral Tale* (Minneapolis: University of Minnesota Press, 2004).

27 Robert Stephenson Smyth Baden-Powell of Gilwell, Baron, *Scouting for Boys: A Handbook for Instruction in Good Citizenship Through Woodcraft* (London: Horace Cox, 1908), 7. The full title of Hall's influential book was *Adolescence: its psychology, and its relation to physiology, anthropology, sociology, sex, crime, religion and education.*

28 Pearse, *Short Stories*, 8.

29 *Short Stories*, 47. See Patrick Pearse, 'The Irish-Speaking Child', *An Claidheamh Solais*, 5 January, 1907, 7.

30 *Short Stories*, 14.

31 *Short Stories*, 17, 19.

32 *Short Stories*, 4.

33 Ruth Dudley Edwards, *Patrick Pearse: The Triumph of Failure* (1977; Dublin: Irish Academic Press, 2006), 24.

34 Pearse, *Short Stories*, 20.

35 Anon, 'Íosagán agus Sgéalta Eile', *An Chonnachtach*, March 1908, 12.

36 E Ua M., 'Children of the West', *An Claidheamh Solais*, 23 May, 1908, 7.

37 Richard Henebry, 'Revival Irish', *The Leader*, 6 February, 1909, 588.

38 Richard Henebry, 'Revival Irish', *The Leader*, 30 January, 1909, 565.

39 Pearse, *Short Stories*, 39.

40 J.A. Froude, quoted in Valente, *The Myth of Manliness in Irish National Culture*, 15.

41 Pearse, *Short Stories*, 6. See 'The Sisters', 16–17.

42 For a much fuller handling of religious imaginary in 'Araby', see Harry Stone, '"Araby" and the Writings of James Joyce', *The Antioch Review*, 25/3, 1965, 375–410.

43 Kenneth J. Kidd, 'Boyology in the Twentieth Century', *Children's Literature*, 28, 2000, 44–72 [47].

44 See, for example, R.B. Kershner, *Joyce, Bakhtin and Popular Literature: Chronicles of Disorder* (Chapel Hill, London: University of North Carolina Press, 1989), 31ff.

45 Rudyard Kipling, *The Complete Stalky and Co*, edited with an introduction and notes by Isabel Quigly (1899: Oxford: Oxford University Press, 2009) 65, 80.

46 See Kidd, *Making American Boys*, 16–17.

47 F.W. Farrar, *Eric: Or, Little by Little* (1858; New York: Rudd & Carlton, 1859), 36.

48 Baden-Powell, *Scouting for Boys*, 11.

49 Percy Hetherington Fitzgerald, *School Days at Saxonhurst, by 'One of the Boys'* (Edinburgh: A.C. Black, 1867), 176. See also 221.

50 Margot Norris, 'A Walk on the Wild(e) Side: The Doubled Reading of "An Encounter"', in Joseph Valente (ed.), *Quare Joyce* (Ann Arbour: University of Michigan Press, 1998), 19–33 [20].

Chapter 3

'Is it with Paddy Stink and Mickey Mud?' – systemization and portraits of the artist as schoolboy

> A century ago, a rich land owner, the manufacturer, even the lawyer or the doctor – unless by chance he could produce a pedigree – held little place in the social scheme, but today his granddaughters flaunt it with the best.
>
> Katherine Cecil Thurston, *The Fly on the Wheel* (1908)

There is a further comparison to be made between the *Íosagán* collection and the Joyce stories. Narrative voice in Pearse is an extension of other elements in the story – its characters, its landscape and its cultures. It invites the reader into a shared community with an everyday invocation which assumes a familiarity that can never exist in reality. In an attempt to register oral cultures and folk traditions, the fictions are ascribed the status of conversation, so that 'The Priest' begins by talking directly to the reader, as if addressing a figure in the story itself. In this way, the line between fiction and reality is notionally erased. 'It's in yon little house you see in the glen below you, and you going down the road from Gortmore to Inver, that my Priest lives. Himself and his mother, and his little sister and brother – those are the family in it'.[1] The literary shaping of the story resides almost entirely in such devices and the reproduction of an everyday world characterized by the ease of its readability which is also a kind of openness. The complete absence of guile and deviousness poses as anthropological but is in fact textual – or, put another way, it is a worked literary effect. On the rare occasion when its truth and clarity are offended against, as when the narrator of 'The Priest' mischievously leads us to think that his story begins with an adult woman bathing a naked priest, this can only be as a joke, an exception to the norm, and the misdirection is immediately corrected.

The *Dubliners* stories are not just different in this respect. They are self-consciously antithetical, specifically detached, ingenious, clever and over-determined. Even in the stories of childhood in which the conceit is that the narrator and the subject are one and the same person, the narratives remain 'above and beyond' the events they relate and aloof from them. The meanings of the stories, perhaps especially these early ones, are famously 'gnomic' and unrevealing. Clarity is not just deferred, it is emphatically refused, as if meaning was never there, never offered, in the first place. Joyce's brother, Stanislaus, was the first to highlight what many were later to see as an obtuseness that stands in stark contrast to the open play of Pearse's stories. Writing in October 1905 in relation to 'An Encounter', he questioned the meaning of writing 'one half of a story about "Joe and Leo Dillon" and the other half about a sodomite, named by me for convenience sake "the captain of fifty"? To call it "An Encounter" will hardly link the two parts together'. He added though that for all his misgivings, he 'would not wish for a good deal that this type were missing from *Dubliners*'.[2]

This chapter, if it were focused on the *Dubliners* stories, would read this stark contrast in narrative styles in relation to the seemingly unrelated fact that Pearse, son of a stonemason, was educated by the Christian Brothers at a school in Westland Row, and James Joyce by the Jesuits at Clongowes Wood. The point is not that these texts are somehow predetermined by the education histories of these two famous alumni, of course, but rather that their characteristic and wildly divergent aesthetics make sense in relation to the very different positions in systemized education structures that their respective authors were fortuitously placed as children and adolescents. If even that clarified claim, returned to later in this chapter, seems not just excessive but downright strange, it might be worth making the point that it is hard to overstate the importance of reformed education to nineteenth-century Europe. This chapter begins properly with another iteration indicative of why that was so at the general level.

The social and cultural effects of modernizing education were genuinely wide ranging. In practical terms, it was essential to the administrative efficiency of the modern state. It was also central to the development of higher-motive narratives. In a brutal age of industrial transformation and empire consolidation on a massive scale, education was the means by which nineteenth-century ideologies of progress and civilization were made manifest and authorized in the real world. The historiography that accompanied the development of education was itself an illustration of the civilizing mission of reform. Here the rationale for cleaning up the ancient schools and universities of Europe was self-evident in the decadence and decline they were said to be reproducing in the traditional landed classes.

In social terms, the new 'systemization', a stratified structure into which all forms of education, state funded or not, were made to fit, served to sustain and condition social hierarchies. It gave the new middle classes access to a set of transformed elitist institutions and effected an institutionalization of borders that would confirm their own distinction in relation to a radicalized working class, a 'lower order' that typically – tragically in some ways – read education in emancipatory terms. Education historian Brian Simon, examining the process in Britain, related it to the work of a series of Royal Commissions appointed between 1850 and 1870 which together amounted to a reform of all levels of education from 'elementary schools to the ancient universities'. The central agenda behind all the activity was how to provide schooling for the 'various strata of the middle and professional classes, gentry and aristocracy', not as a matter of right and social justice but in relation to the maintenance of social order at a time of dynamic political and economic change. Each commission led to an act of parliament and constituted a restructuring brought about by the direct intervention of the state, even though little additional financial support was offered 'either for secondary or university education'.[3] The 'background' to this was the rise of the new middle classes, the increasing radicalization of the working class and perceived inadequacies in the old institutions.

> To put the matter simply (and no doubt, crudely) there was, on the one hand, a growing pressure for reform from sections of society (middle and working classes) that wanted change and modernisation and who were demanding access to a set of transformed educational institutions, and, on the other, a growing realisation on the part of dominant sections of the social hierarchy (gentry and aristocracy) of the urgent need for reform if the traditional institutions of the country were to preserve their hegemony and not be supplanted by new institutions representing the interests and aspirations of new social classes.[4]

State intervention in Ireland followed the same path of creating a system out of a patchwork of private schools, except that here the early Royal Commissions – 1806 (reporting 1809–1812) and 1825 – took with them a secularizing agenda resisted by both Protestant and Catholic establishments. The former expressed itself through a Protestant evangelism which regarded proselytization as a right and responsibility; the latter through the ultramontanism of Archbishop Paul Cullen and the 'devotional revolution', the term coined by historian Emmet Larkin in the 1970s to describe the process by which religious practice in nineteenth-century Catholic Ireland became transformed. Against that highly charged background, the National school system was introduced into Ireland in 1831, a state funded system, overseen by a National School Board and organized at the local level. The intention was that these schools should deliver 'primary' education to working-class children, although in practice a minority sometimes stayed on beyond 11 to the ages 12 and even 14 as the nineteenth century wore on. There was no element of compulsion, however, until 1892, and even then the measure was very limited. Children between the ages of six and 14 were required to attend for a minimum of 75 days a year, with many exceptions – rural areas, for example, were excluded from the requirement altogether. For most children in nineteenth-century Ireland, that would have been the full extent of formal schooling. It was at this level that the Catholic episcopate worked with extraordinary determination to establish a regime of denominational instruction belonging entirely to the Church.

Intermediate level education was likewise established on denominational lines, although many families of both Catholic and Protestant elites had their sons educated outside Ireland in England or on the Continent. These schools, 'public' or otherwise, also delivered schooling to younger children, but they were seen as part of a private domain and 'a matter of concern for the middle classes who, if they saw fit, should buy it as a commodity'.[5] The numbers of pupils attending these schools were small in comparison with the numbers attending National schools, and less controversy was focused on them than on national education.[6] Crucially, Catholic intermediate/public schools were in the hands of religious orders like the Jesuits, which meant a higher degree of independence and relatively little interference from the Catholic episcopate.[7] There were four Irish schools that charged 'prohibitively high fees and deliberately targeted the wealthiest Catholic families' – Clongowes, Castleknock College, Blackrock College and Tullabeg.[8] The latter closed in 1886, its students transferring to Clongowes. Research on school magazines like *The Clongownian* and *The Belvederian* has been used to show how elites at such schools were taught to share many of the 'racial and cultural assumptions of the European classes'.[9] What one historian calls 'imperial attitudes' apparently 'suffused the whole group'.[10] Certainly these schools imagined themselves and the boys they turned out operating on a world stage, which meant a colonial stage:

> There are Belvederians to be found in the Far East, near the rising empire of Japan; there are Belvederians in the Far North, where Canadian crops are ripening. Australia and Africa, too, have sent us records of our past, and when we add the news that has come from the Rockies and Argentina we find that our Alma Mater is represented the whole world over.[11]

Full systematization, however, was delayed in Ireland until the Intermediate Education Act of 1878. This legislation notionally maintained the non-denominational principle by curriculum and examination alignments shared across Catholic and Protestant schools alike but did nothing to alter the fact that nearly all schools in the country were either Catholic or Protestant.

Joyceans have known that education is registered everywhere in Joyce's early fiction, but the context of its modernization and contradictory relations to tradition has not been appreciated. The attitudes by which middle-class parents and their sons and daughters distinguish themselves in relation to schools established for the working classes and the poor – National schools, for example, and Christian Brothers schools – belong to a system of education that has been modernized. In 'Araby', for example, North Richmond Street is quiet except when the school day is over at the 'Christian Brothers' School' and the superior narrator and his friends have to run 'the gauntlet of the rough tribes from the cottages' (*D*, 29–30). In 'An Encounter' Father Butler is appalled at his pupils' interest in boys' magazines. 'I could understand it if you were . . . National School boys' (*D*, 19). The class prejudice is picked up again and again in this story, combining with gender prejudices when Mahony chases a crowd of 'ragged girls, brandishing his unloaded catapult'. It reappears almost verbatim as an imagined riposte when the 'queer old josser' asks whether Mahony gets whipped often at school: 'I was going to reply indignantly that we were not National School boys to be *whipped* as he called it' (*D*, 21, 27). In 'The Dead', Gabriel Conroy also is a product of modernity and the commodified versions of education it brings to market. The grandson of a 'gluemaker' – in fact a factory owner who makes a poor job of emulating his social betters – Gabriel establishes his own social status on firmer ground.[12] He takes a degree at 'the Royal University' and becomes a teacher; his brother is a 'senior curate in Balbriggan' (*D*, 213). From this position he acts out an inflated sense of social superiority, in relation to the Gaeltacht, the 'vulgarians' of his own family and to Molly Ivors, the sharp-witted revivalist who threatens his sense of natural order and who he imagines as being representative of a new 'hypereducated' generation. This attempt to distinguish himself from a new contamination 'growing up in our midst' (*D*, 232) and to identify with a more authentic, cultured version of education is both a sign of the currency of traditionalism and deeply ironic. He and Molly, the obvious representative of the new times he has in mind, are of the same educational generation. Their careers run parallel and are products of the same system, except that as a woman she is especially exceptional.

Again, the traditionalism and social snobbery attached to modern education are apparent in *A Portrait* where from the earliest pages, Stephen is taught the importance of associating with 'fellows' of the 'right kidney' (*P*, 77). His arrival at Clongowes involves a rigorous checking of his social credentials by a fellow schoolboy. Nasty Roche asks him, ' – What is your father?' Stephen replies, '– A gentleman'. Stephen has presumably been schooled in this answer, but it puts him on unstable ground. Nasty Roche responds with a further challenge: 'Is he a magistrate?' (*P*, 6). Later, Stephen is to pity his father because he is not a magistrate, to wonder why he was sent to a school where high-status boys have fathers who are (see *P*, 21) and to fantasize that his father has become elevated 'higher than a magistrate' (*P*, 16). The same obsessional linking of school and social status lies behind Simon Dedalus's relief that he has somehow managed to get Stephen into Belvedere despite the poor state of family finances. This means his eldest son will not be educated with the Christian Brothers along with 'Paddy Stink and Mickey Mud'. He will instead be remaining with the Jesuits, themselves an elite, 'a very rich order', 'Fedup, by God, like gamecocks' and well placed to help their students secure their futures. 'They'll be of service to him in after years. Those are the fellows that can get you a position' (*P*, 59–60). Simon Dedalus's own educational life has instilled in him old-style aristocratic values and attitudes but not given him access to the kind of material wealth he needs to maintain himself in that style. As a young man, Stephen's mother tells him, his father used to spend 'all his time out after the hounds or rowing on the Lee'. Even when he is penniless, he thinks he has 'castellar rights' and despises his wife's family name which puts her so much in 'the burgher class' (*SH*, 72, 96–7). These are attitudes that have been cultivated through an elite education.

It is not difficult to add to these examples. In 'A Little Cloud', Little Chandler, however acutely he envies Gallagher his 'vagrant and triumphant life', consoles himself with the thought that he has the potential to outdo him because 'Gallagher was his inferior in birth and education' (*D*, 88). In 'Grace', Tom Kernan agrees to attend a Jesuit retreat in part because he knows the Jesuits are 'an educated order' with a refined congregation. They 'cater for the upper classes', which means educating their students in the classics and Latin, the kind of accomplishments that cannot be got from 'the penny-a-week school' (*D*, 184–5, 190). In *Ulysses* the same system shapes the warm and personal response of Father Conmee to Belvedere boys, and, a few lines later, the cooler acknowledgement of a scruffy looking 'band of satchelled schoolboys' who 'raised untidy caps. . . . Christian brother boys' (*U*10, 41–5; 76–7). Likewise in the *Wake* where Will, Conn and Otto are 'free boardschool shirkers' (*FW*, 51.11) and the 'little folk' creep 'on all fours to their national school treat' (*FW*, 178.19), while 'Belvederian exhibitioners' pose in 'their cruisery caps and oarsclub colours' (*FW*, 205.5–6). In the same text Issy asks the readers to excuse her brothers' swearing on the grounds that 'theyre christianbrothers irish!' (*FW*, 301, fn.2). These illustrations establish the importance of reformed education, both in the construction of social order and the formation of social consciousness. The ways in which they operate in Joyce's early fiction especially is entirely consistent with the image of himself he presented to potential publishers of *Dubliners*. Here he figures, like his character Stephen Dedalus, as a detached observer of Dublin life, reporting on its 'paralysis' with all the objectivity of a European naturalist or, indeed, a kind of social scientist.[13]

But Joyce was more than an observer of Dublin, not least in relation to education. His first biographer, Herbert Gorman, claims that the first school he went to was where 'the life of James Joyce may properly be said to begin'.[14] This was also a school with a particular place in the hierarchy – at its top. To imagine it as 'middle class' in any contemporary sense would be understandable but misleading. In the opening year of its foundation it was charging fees of 50 guineas a year; some 30 years later, in 1841, per capita incomes in Ireland still stood as low as £16 per annum.[15] The school had gone through modernization some 15 years before Joyce enrolled and in both biography and fiction, the process is understood directly in relation to change and 'progress'. The representational figure Stephen Dedalus, then, is imagined in terms of the systemization that has produced him, as is Joyce himself in the Gorman biography. From this perspective, the literary reproduction of education becomes less a report on the conditions of the social world and more a case of a potential entanglement of biography and fiction which, like *A Portrait* itself, has a more complex relationship to truth and the real than perhaps has been realized. It is from this basis that the rest of this chapter explores how the impact of systemization on self-formation operates in the representational order of *A Portrait*, primarily in the first chapter of this novel.

Joyce and Clongowes

After less than two years in attendance, Joyce had to leave the first school he attended, Clongowes Wood College, because his father could no longer afford the fees. Afterwards, just before his father managed to get him into Belvedere, again a prestigious school run by the Jesuits, he spent a period with the Christian Brothers This was the religious order positioned at the forefront of resistance to attempts to proselytize the Irish working class and the battle against 'bible schools', where 'children were exposed to scripture without adequate interpretation'.[16] No account of the period exists anywhere in Joyce's writing and he never mentioned it to his biographer, Gorman. For the writer so frequently imagined heroically confronting the conditions of his society, this is a strange avoidance. Richard Ellmann, a later biographer, points out that the stay with the Brothers was Joyce's 'one break with the Jesuits', and thinks the silence unproblematic. It is suggestive of his sharing his 'father's view that the Jesuits were the gentlemen of Catholic education and the Christian Brothers . . . its drones', which seems only natural enough, at least to Ellmann.[17] Whatever the case, it is clear that Joyce must have been significantly shamed by his spell with 'Paddy Stink and Mickey Mud', so much so that he attempted to bury the fact completely.

Clongowes Wood College, however, where Joyce boarded from September 1888 to sometime after Parnell's death in October 1891, was another matter. It figures largely in Joyce's writing, most notably in the first chapter of *A Portrait* but also in *Ulysses*, where it resurfaces in virtually every episode in which Stephen figures. In 'Telemachus', Stephen, cleaning up after Mulligan, sees his life in terms of servitude: 'So I carried the boat of incense then at Clongowes. I am another now and yet the same. A servant too. A servant of a servant' (*U*1, 310–12). In 'Proteus', he remembers the strategies by which he attempted to register social position at the school: 'You told the Clongowes gentry you had an uncle a judge and an uncle a general in the army' (*U*3, 105–6); in 'Aeolus' a chance remark by newspaper editor Myles Crawford throws Stephen back in time to the class where he is accused by Father Dolan and falsely punished: 'See it in your face. See it in your eye. Lazy idle little schemer' (*U*7, 618). The punishment scene and Conmee's intervention returns in a Circean 'hallucination' much later in the novel:

> **FATHER DOLAN**
>
> Any boy want flogging? Broke his glasses? Lazy idle little schemer. See it in your eye.
>
> (*Mild, benign, rectorial, reproving, the head of Don John Conmee rises from the pianola coffin.*)
>
> **DON JOHN CONMEE**
>
> Now, Father Dolan! Now. I'm sure Stephen is a very good little boy!
>
> (*U*15, 3670–6)

Clongowes is deep in Stephen's heart and mind. It also figures in *Finnegans Wake* and likewise plays a prominent part at the beginning of the 'definitive' Gorman biography. Herbert Gorman's role in helping Joyce readers appreciate the importance of this institution is acknowledged, and mocked a little, in the *Wake* where his name morphs into the school name as 'King Gores Wood' (*FW*, 348.21).

In the real world, then as now, places like Clongowes were marketed as exclusive institutions. In *James Joyce: a definitive biography*, published in 1941 – the year of Joyce's death – Gorman characterizes the class of 1888 as being 'a fairly representative group from the greater part of Ireland', but socially the students were all male and would have been highly privileged.[18] They were attending what was considered to be the most fashionable school in Ireland. Some 60 years on from its founding in 1814, Timothy Corcoran, S.J., later Professor of the Theory and Practice of Education at University College and powerful influence on the Education Department under the Free State, could reflect on the school's achievement in terms of the remarkable successes of ex-boys, like himself, who had gone on to occupy important public positions in Irish life, such as:

> Lord Chancellor, Lord Chief Justice, and Lord Chief Baron, Chairman of the Irish Parliamentary Party, President of the Royal College of Physicians, Governor of the Bank of Ireland, President Commissioner of National Education, Chairman of the Intermediate Education Board, of the Chamber of Commerce of Dublin and Cork, and of the Ports and Docks Board of Dublin.[19]

Ten years later, the school magazine, *The Clongownian*, was reporting that no less than seven current Westminster MPs were ex-students. Two former boys received knighthoods in the same year. One of them, John Lentaigne, had been surgeon to the household of the Lord Lieutenant for the previous 13 years.[20]

Clearly the links between such schools and the English establishment were strong, but the extent to which they were Anglicized was, and still is, highly contestable. Ciaran O'Neill's 2014 history of the education of Catholic elites in Ireland argues that the modelling of Irish schools was obvious enough but took place at a 'superficial' level, cultivated for 'the sake of the market target'. Beneath 'the Eton suits and cricket creases', O'Neill continues, 'lay schools that constantly strove to instil Catholic values in their students', a view that Joyce agreed with and was proud of in some ways, although he always made the distinction between rank-and-file Catholicism and the Jesuit order responsible for his own education.[21] Famously, he told his friend Frank Budgen that for the sake of accuracy he should refer to him not as a Catholic but as a Jesuit.[22]

In making such points, O'Neill writes back to radical nationalists active at the turn of the nineteenth century for whom public schools like Clongowes were reactionary, regressive institutions. D.P. Moran, writing in *The Leader*, ridiculed Castleknock as a 'cricket and ping-pong' College that put 'a brake on the Irish wheel'. Clongowes specifically was 'an eminent Tommy Atkins College' where 'the spirit of the Seoínín' was 'much in evidence'.[23] Patrick Pearse likewise describes Clongowes in 'The Murder Machine' as a 'finishing school', designed to churn out candidates for the English Civil Service.[24] Although some Joyceans have attempted to reconcile Joyce with such views, both the fictional representation and the biographia associated with it tell a very different and more complex story underpinned by deep social attitudes.[25]

Far from being an alien imposition, the Clongowes of Gorman's biography is dramatized as a particular expression of Irish identity and Ireland's 'mythos'. The Castle and grounds are an embodiment of the 'bloodshed and religious fanaticism that underlies the entire structure and development of Ireland'. Clongowes figures as a seed-bed, where 'heroes and heroines of the dark and distant Ireland' are imagined rising up to greet a young James Joyce 'though the soil'. Associated with the Norman invasion; the aristocratic landowners of the settlement; the devastation of the commonwealth and, especially, United Irishmen, the school is positioned in close relation to a culture of heroic resistance to English rule, where a 'venerable old' retainer residing at Clongowes castle, Mrs Eustace, suffers her jaws to be smashed open by Cromwellian troopers rather than hand over the keys to a 'supposed secret stronghold, or priest hole' which she has hidden in her mouth. The derring-do of United Irishmen establishes 'a thrill of tradition' drawn on 'by generations of Clongowes boys', as it does in *A Portrait* where the exploits of Hamilton Rowan escaping British soldiers through the halls and connecting doorways of Clongowes fire Stephen's imagination.[26] Early issues of the school magazine, *The Clongownian*, were likewise freighted with references to United Irishmen and such figures as Wolfe Tone and Hamilton Rowan. The point helps to position Clongowes in relation to Irish political culture more finely. It was conservative but it was also patriotic. The versions of national identity it subscribed to would have been aligned to the school's sense of its own social standing and its aspirations for its students. The realities are surely captured by O'Neill again, who writes that school nationalism in this elitist institution 'depended a great deal on the antiquity of the event celebrated and the social class of the patriot celebrated. No mention was made of more controversial or proletarian forms of resistance, such as the land agitation or Fenianism'.[27]

In the Gorman account, then, Clongowes is not just a better school with contacts 'that can get you a position' (*P*, 59), it is also an Irish school imagined in terms of an encompassing of history: 'Ancient savagery, the hot romance of political struggle and the steel hand in the velvet glove that was the Church, all were there'.[28] The elevation is not exactly inconsistent with *A Portrait*, but it does sit oddly in some ways. It is true that Stephen Dedalus knows that he has been removed from his family life to a historic place with traditions shared at all levels of college life which soon intrigue and excite him. 'One day' when he is 'called to the castle', the butler 'shows him the marks of the soldiers' slugs in the wood of the door' where Hamilton Rowan was allegedly shot at, and he is given 'a piece of shortbread that the community ate' (*P*, 7), a ritual that has echoes of the Mass and enacts a kind of initiation. Although his status as a true Clongownian is challenged at various points, his right to attend is underwritten by the familial connection to a great figure in Irish history. His 'granduncle' had once presented an address to Daniel O'Connell, 'the liberator', at Clongowes College (*P*, 21). Questions may be asked about his strange name, but 'great men in the history had names like that', which again confirms his right to the distinction of being a Clongowes boy and how far that right is based on heroic and aristocratic versions of history (*P*, 46). His mind is thrilled and troubled by stories about the ghosts of men who received their death wounds 'on battlefields far away' (*P*, 15) – the figure behind this is the son of a Irish expatriate, Maximilian Ulysses, Count von Browne, who was killed at the battle of Prague in 1757. His father was a member of the Browne family, who had owned Clongowes Castle for successive generations.

For all the glamour of the place, however, the realities of everyday life at Clongowes are very different in the fictional account – not exciting, noble and aristocratic at all but, rather, a matter of dull routine, repetition and discipline. At its centre, figuratively and literally, is the iconic scene in which Stephen is beaten by Father Dolan. For many readers, this moment, more than any other, will be what most characterizes the life of Stephen at Clongowes, and which by extension so frames the lifelong dissent of the writer whose boyhood provided the original model. The act itself has little to do with heroism and adventure. On the contrary, if Clongowes is genuinely represented by it, then Stephen's formation at the hands of the Jesuits is a product of something quite different – mindless spite and brutality. How does that sit with the pride that Stephen Dedalus has been taught to associate with this place?

The Intermediate Education Act (Ireland)

How we read Stephen, and Joyce, at Clongowes is strongly framed by an event in education history referenced by both literary text and biography. Indeed, Gorman's account gives a full description of the legislative instrument that managed the systemization of Irish education at the secondary level and of its full implementation at Clongowes. The legislation appeared later in Ireland than parallel interventions in England, but its connection to the wider agendas of education reform outlined at the beginning of this chapter is unmistakable.

From some perspectives, the range of the Intermediate Education Act (Ireland) (1878) was limited and heavily circumscribed. The Intermediate Board it established could not provide capital funds for building or equipping schools; it had no role in training, monitoring or paying teachers. Nor did it possess any inspection function. It had no direct control over textbooks used in schools – an issue of great controversy in Ireland – and it did nothing to seriously challenge the authority of the Church over Irish education. The curriculum and assessment framework it established applied to Catholic and Protestant schools alike, but any impact on the denominational basis of schooling was no more than notional. Its sole function was to take responsibility for devising programs, setting examinations in them and dispensing funding to students and institutions on the basis of results – a relatively minor administrative intervention but one that had a major impact on reinforcing hierarchies of education. The payment-by-results system it instituted proved vital to the economic viability of elite schools because it functioned as a public demonstration of the relative positions individual institutions occupied. The predecessor of the Irish leaving certificate, this style of assessment, with its precise link to the building of school prestige, quickly became popular. It remained in place long after educationalists in England had moved away from its stultifying impact on a pedagogy already routinized by the prevalence of learning by rote, although attempts were made to reduce cramming and the impact of payment by results in Ireland in 1900. Results were 'annually trumpeted in the public press' as competing schools sought to outdo one another in securing enrolments, and it was on the basis of performance under the new regime that, as Gorman explains, Clongowes was confirmed 'at the top of the list of efficient Irish educational establishments'.[29]

The system is reproduced in *A Portrait* as the competitive culture which frames teaching in the classroom and leads ultimately to the pressure to perform in examinations rewarded by state prizes. When Stephen Dedalus, now at Belvedere College, goes to the Bank of Ireland to draw his orders for 'thirty and three pounds . . . the moneys of his exhibition and essay prize', the bank teller wishes him 'a brilliant career' and tells him that he is 'living in changed times and that there was nothing like giving a boy the best education that money could buy' (*P*, 81). The commodification the reform ushered in is echoed elsewhere in Joyce. In the *Dubliners* story 'After the Race', for instance, Jimmy Doyle's father, a butcher made good and now regarded as a Dublin 'merchant prince', feels 'commercially satisfied for having secured for his son qualities often unpurchaseable'. He does so by sending him to England 'to be educated in a big Catholic college' and afterwards 'to Dublin University to study law' (D, 48, 45).

Gorman goes to considerable lengths to insist on just how transformative the legislation was for Clongowes and how far it shaped the education Joyce would have experienced. It produces a new Clongowes order, set in complete contrast to what is perceived as the genuine traditions of the institution. The Clongowes that Joyce was to join 14 years after the legislation was passed is now a disciplined bureaucracy, organized through a system of schedules that placed 'all classes before the dinner hour, allotted increased hours to mathematical and scientific studies, regularized examinations, and otherwise established a timetable precision for the routine of the school'.[30]

It is true that some of the traditional features central to the identity of Clongowes can withstand what is presented as an onslaught. The 'time-honoured tradition' of the *Ratio Studorium*, for instance, remains a constant untouched by change – this was a Jesuit system of instruction compiled as part of the Catholic Counter Reformation. It was revised in 1832 but maintained an 'intellectual order and thoroughness' connected to a much more distant past. It is clear however, for all such survivals, that the new 'uncompromising' system of studies constitutes a dark, modernizing wave that threatens to overwhelm a traditional, 'gentler' school culture, when 'interests outside the study hall and classroom' were given free rein.[31] The same historiographical narrative is shared by *A Portrait*. Stephen Dedalus too has heard about a *laissez-faire* time when 'the fellows in Clongowes wore blue coats with brass buttons and yellow waistcoats and caps of rabbitskin and drank beer like grownup people and kept greyhounds of their own to course the hares with' (*P*, 21). Both texts set up a sharp critique of modern education. In an emphatic reversal of the familiar nineteenth-century historiography that imagined the modernization of schools as progress, they insist on a more authentic, libertarian Clongowes culture being placed under severe threat.

The historiography runs counter to orthodox education politics, especially to orthodoxies in Ireland, where it was widely held that the impact of the1878 reform was to show, 'once and for all', that 'it is not only Protestants who are able competently to educate their children'. Since 'the inauguration of the Intermediate system, the Catholic schools of the country have steadily moved forward until, taking into account their endowments – they are now easily the first educational institutions of Ireland'.[32] It also links Joyce to early-twentieth-century modernists, whose criticism of new schooling sometimes turned into romanticization of older forms, as in Pound and Eliot. There is, however, an even more controversial element in the Gorman account – the extraordinary importance it insists on giving to Father James Daly, the model for Father Dolan in *A Portrait*.

In Gorman, it is neither the English state; nor the Catholic hierarchy, who in reality helped draft the legislation; nor the school itself which must have been complicit in its implementation, that is held responsible for the modernization of Clongowes but, rather, a single individual – Father Daly.[33] He not only oversees the transformation but single-handedly performs the reforming work. He is enthusiastic, a zealot of modernization, so much so that he becomes nothing less than an embodiment of its nature, coded with specific reference to the historiography of change and drawn in sharp distinction to the College rector in this respect. If Daly/Dolan is modernizing and destructive, Conmee is 'a benevolent figure', a humanist 'of skill and tact' endowed with 'a distinct literary gift' and, again, a strong association with tradition. The social imaginaries implicated in the opposing descriptions are clear and stark.[34] The Rector, Father Conmee, is a gentleman, Dolan/Daly is not. An essential part of the latter's registration as a modern force is the corollary that he is also a social inferior, not working-class as such but a representative of what Wyndham Lewis called 'mass man' – Joyce reported that he was 'low-bred'; Gorman describes him as a plain-talking, blunt 'administrator'.[35] Significantly, Dolan/Daly, in both texts, is positioned on the margins of the school in which his inferior status becomes conflated with his taste for inflicting punishment. Although Father Arnall in *A Portrait* is chastened by the storm represented by Dolan's intrusion into in his classroom – he tries to help his boys with 'gentle words' and 'soft' voice – Dolan is unremittingly and irrevocably 'cruel' and 'unfair' (*P*, 43, 44). He is not 'decent', unlike the rector – 'the decentest rector that was ever in Clongowes'. (*P*,49).[36] Indeed, the implication is that Dolan/Daly is no genuine Clongownian at all, although in reality Daly served at the school for nearly 40 years. A 'born martinet' who knows 'his mind and made no bones about expressing it', he represents 'a type', chastised in Gorman for even being at post in the school. Daly 'should never have been with the Society of Jesus but rather with the Christian Brothers or the Fathers of the Holy Ghost'.[37] Here social identity becomes fixed and organic. Snobbism is routine, unexceptional and needs no explanation. The fictional counterpart to the sentiment is given to Stephen himself. In a place where family name remains almost everything, Dolan's name is mocked, even by the usually mild-mannered and reserved Stephen: 'Dolan: it was like the name of a woman that washed clothes' (*P*, 46).

The Dolan/Daly provocation

Joyce's fiction is specifically uninterested in the idea of the villain. The singular exception to that rule is Father Dolan as prefect of studies, stalking the corridors of Joyce's school in *A Portrait*. Straight out of the pages of Victorian melodrama, Dolan crashes into Stephen Dedalus's classroom at the beginning of a new term in Part Three of Chapter One, on the lookout for some 'lazy idle loafers' to punish. Falsely denounced as a liar and a 'Lazy little schemer', Stephen himself is one of his first victims. Barely seven years old, he is forced to kneel before his classmates and Latin teacher (Father Arnall) and submit to the terror and shame of a pandy stroke on each hand: 'His whole body was shaking with fright, his arm was shaking and his crumpled burning living hand shook like a loose leaf in the air' (*P*, 40–2). Dolan exits in a whirlwind, threatening his intention to return 'Every day. Every day' (*P*, 43). The reason why Dolan is so exceptional a figure in Joyce might appear to be self-evident, a product of the way a brute would have appeared in reality to a very small boy. We might speculate that Joyce himself must have been seriously wounded by this unjust punishment to recall it so vividly. The scene still feels compellingly real, however many times we read it. But, as we now know, there is also a complex contrivance in operation here involving powerful social imaginaries that shape Stephen Dedalus, just as they shaped Joyce himself.

All these associations between Dolan and modernity and the College rector and tradition are brought together in the action that has Joyce/Stephen appealing the punishment meted out to him. The sequence leading to that event is structural and circumscribes the whole of Part Three of Chapter One of *A Portrait* which operates on a singular trajectory. It begins with a group of schoolboys, including Stephen, discussing a vaguely defined but clearly serious transgression of school rules by a group of boys caught by 'the Hill of Lyons' (*P*, 33).[38] That excited exchange leads directly to Dolan's dramatic entrance into the classroom. His ugly pandying of Stephen represents a new regime of punishment designed to restore order. As the Gorman biography explains in some detail, punishment at Clongowes was one of the few traditional elements that had remained untouched by Daly's modernization. 'Simple and patriarchal', it is specifically identified by the complete absence of 'fagging' – 'that dubious tradition in English public schools' which, as Gorman points out, was anathematized by the elder Pitt, Earl of Chatham, for terrorizing every boy he had ever met who attended Eton. The marker is an important one. Rather than brutalizing the boys, traditional punishment at Clongowes is considered to be part of more humane regime designed to promote 'the independent personality'.[39] The beating dispensed by Daly/Dolan, then, is an offence against Clongowes and a Jesuit culture significantly formed around the idea of tradition. From this perspective, Dolan's punishment of Stephen is more than unfair. It is itself a transgression. This is why the complaint Stephen takes to the rector, although its importance is undermined in a later chapter, is of importance in real time to the school as a whole. In *A Portrait*, the schoolboys combine after Stephen's beating to form an alliance of 'the senate and the Roman people'. They have a collective stake in the fact that Stephen has been 'wrongly punished'. The corollary is that Stephen's determination to be 'quiet and obedient' in his victory and not in any way 'proud' represents a convergence of his nature with his understanding of the imperative that he must behave like a gentleman at all costs (*P*, 44, 49). As he makes clear, it is no part of his intention to instigate a rebellion. On the contrary, he has advocated for the restoration of a traditional order.

In this way the historiography that looks backwards to a golden age and expresses so deep a social animus in Gorman's text converges with Chapter One of *A Portrait*. In their respective but related realms of the real, both biography and fictional narrative share the same dispositions. Here, highly prestigious values like benevolence, kindness and refinement reside with tradition. Even more high-status concepts like justice, honour and courage are placed in the same framework of ideas and both are implicated with an education ideal. Modernity, characterized by bureaucracy and commodification, is associated with vulgarity and low social status. Modern education, typically seen as the means by which a rising Catholic middle class achieved emancipation in Ireland, is reimagined here as a kind of betrayal. Such alignments have wide implications for reading Joyce. They indicate that Joyce's well-known respect for the Jesuits was historically contingent or, more precisely, seriously compromised by what he saw as their contamination by the modern world. They place him and this novel in closer proximity to a disposition of an intelligentsia that likewise defined the modern condition against traditional hierarchy and understood historical process in terms of conflicts between traditional authenticity and the cheap fakery of mass society. At the same time, they return us to the fraught issue of Joyce's politics and his relations with nationalism. To situate Joyce in education cultures in this way is to be reminded of the variety of positions that can be assimilated to different versions of late-nineteenth- and early-twentieth-century nationalism, and, again, of the great distance separating Joyce from Patrick Pearse, who writes of his own ideal school in terms of a relationship between a 'master and his pupils' modelled on 'Our Lord and his friends' and a 'Gaelic polity' nearly 2,000 years old. This once gave Ireland, Pearse claimed, a unique education system, 'the best and noblest that has ever been known among men'. Pearse insists on the fantasy that the aim of this Gaelic education was 'democratic', designed not to educate an 'aristocracy' but an entire 'people'.[40] In this respect, it is worth returning first to the biographical Pearse who was famously a product of the Christian Brothers so looked down on by Joyce and his family and second to the Joyce aesthetic, evident as early as *Dubliners* and continuous throughout the entire oeuvre. Here the 'personality of the artist', 'paring his fingernails' in a gesture of aristocratic disdain, becomes so detached that he becomes, in a telling phrase, 'refined out of existence' (*P*, 181).

Education in these texts, then – one fiction, the other biography – is bound up in complex ways with the modernization of education and the social identities attached to its systemization. Looking forward to later chapters of *A Portrait*, it seems likely that the development of radical individualism in the artist figure will become, ironically enough, not only inseparable from elitist social attitudes but contingent upon them. In *Stephen Hero*, Stephen's dissent is shaped by a snobbery that is ubiquitous and quite incidental, almost unconscious. He identifies Maddern eugenically by 'the peasant strength of his jaws' (*SH*, 18); the dress of one of the Daniels's girls is apologized for as being 'somewhat colleen' (*SH*, 36); he hates Emma Cleary's 'middle-class affectations' (*SH*, 57). It is also explicitly rendered in education terms. Stephen thinks Glynn, 'a young man who was by day a clerk in Guinness's Brewery and by night a student of mental and moral philosophy in the night classes of the college', a ridiculous fraud (*SH*, 103). He must guard against his own instinct in this respect. In *A Portrait*, the voice, the accent, even the mind of a student from Ulster offends him, which leads him to 'unkindness' – the thought that the student's father 'would have done better had he sent his son to Belfast to study and have saved something on the train fare by so doing'. The sentiment is quickly suppressed as something belonging to 'the comic Irishman in the bench behind' (*P*, 162), but Stephen has it nevertheless. In *Stephen Hero*, his own kind of intelligence is specifically identified as 'aristocratic', which might be a Catholic quality (*SH*, 182). When imaginary ambassadorial voices from the Church are sent to tempt him into religious conformity, Stephen hears them flattering his scepticism in relation to 'the enthusiasms of patriots'. The appeal is precisely to his sense of intellectual superiority. One voice points out that, whatever Catholicism is, it is not '*slovenly* in thought' or 'amorphous in ritual'. It has always been a friend to art. Another says directly that Stephen believes in 'aristocracy' – 'in the eminence of the aristocratic class and in an order of society which secures that eminence'. The voice continues: 'With us you can exercise your contemptuous faculties, when you are recognised as one of the patrician order' (*SH*, 182–3).

Stephen rejects these appeals, it is true, but he is hardly indifferent to them. On the contrary, the idea of authentic distinction and hierarchy is all but irresistible to him. The attraction to the superior is reproduced everywhere across these texts, a turn to aristocracy that has historically taken many forms in response to a diversity of historical circumstances. For Joyce and his early fictions, it is substantially a product of an obsessive political determination to bring education culture into systematic alignment with a wider and changing social order. In this way systemization becomes central to identity formation in these texts and the critique which puts education at the centre of social consciousness in the modern world.

There are two further points to make about the narrative sequence of false punishment and its rectification in *A Portrait*, and both have a significant bearing on how education in the Joyce text responds to modernization, tradition and social orders of hierarchy. First, although it is specifically rendered as a unique and heavily personalized event, the basic form of the storyline is entirely familiar. The motif of the schoolboy wrongly punished and appealing to a higher authority was repeated over and over in the school or public-school novel. Here it routinely figured, just as it does in *A Portrait*, as a liberty narrative, testing young elites in the workings of the adult political world. This narrative genre had well over a century of history behind it by the time Joyce came to write *A Portrait* and was part of the cultural environment that produced him. It has particular importance for the concerns of this present account because its development shadowed so precisely the systematic modernization of schooling in the real world. It provided the most direct illustration of how schooling operated in the symbolic domain, which is why the issue of its relation to *A Portrait* is returned to in a later chapter.

Second, the authority for the truth of the story behind Daly's beating of the young Joyce is strong but not cast iron, not least because exoneration of Stephen/Joyce from any transgression of school rules sits uneasily against the record of the Clongowes punishment book. This shows that in the hard-to-dispute reality of Jesuit chronicle, James Joyce was pandied on three separate occasions at Clongowes, none on the spur of the moment and all properly regulated by formal process. On the first occasion, he received two strokes five days after his seventh birthday. These were requested by Father Power, the sympathetic Father Arnall in *A Portrait of the Artist as a Young Man*, for the offence of failing to bring the appropriate textbook to class – this event close in some ways to the fictional one. In February of the same year (1889), six strokes were ordered by Jesuit prefect Andrew McArdle – McGlade in *A Portrait* – for wearing boots inside instead of house shoes. Finally, later in the same year, and also ordered by McArdle, Joyce received four strokes for using vulgar language; not the last time, as others have noted, he would be censored for that transgression.[41] The record does not say who dispensed these punishments. Writing in 2009, Bruce Bradley S.J., once a rector of Clongowes himself, admits the chance of an improvised beating not being recorded, but inevitably the other possibility is raised, too. In its most extreme form, there would be no fall on the cinder path, no broken glasses, no innocence and, whoever actually dispensed the pandies, no vicious, unpredictable, unyielding priest either. There can be no way of knowing of course, but, whatever the case, Bradley's research into the authorized archive means there can be no doubt either that Father Daly, out of all the Jesuits at Clongowes, was singled out for special treatment by Joyce. His nomination is exemplary of a social logic that Joyce knew very well because it was so much there in the conditions of his own schooling and the social framework of his upbringing.

Notes

1 Pearse, *Short Stories*, 14.
2 Ellmann (ed.), *Letters of James Joyce*, vol. II, 115.

3 Brian Simon, 'Systemization and Segmentation in Education: The Case of England', in Müller et al., *The Rise of the Modern Education System*, 88–108 [89].
4 Simon, 'Systemization and Segmentation in Education', 90.
5 J. Coolahan, *Irish Education: Its History and Its Structure* (Dublin: Institute of Public Administration, 1981), 53.
6 See Ciaran O'Neill, *Catholics of Consequence: Transnational Education, Social Mobility and the Irish Catholic Elite, 1850–1900* (Oxford: Oxford University Press, 2014), 9. The Dale and Spender Report of 1901 calculated that only about one in ten of those who 'entered the preparatory grade completed the senior grade'. See Coolahan, *Irish Education*, 55.
7 Norman Atkinson claims that intermediate schools in Ireland were relatively independent from Church hierarchy and the State, although this was to change after the Intermediate Education Act of 1878. See Atkinson, 'The Educational Ideas of Patrick Pearse 1879–1914', 68–74 [69–70].
8 Ciaran O'Neill, 'Education, Imperial Careers and the Irish Catholic Elite in the Nineteenth Century', in David Dickson, Justyna Pyz and Christopher Shepard (eds.), *Irish Classrooms and British Empire: Imperial Contexts in the Origins of Modern Education* (Dublin: Four Courts, 2012), 98–110 [100].
9 Timothy G. McMahon, 'Irish Jesuit Education and Imperial Ideals', in Dickson et al. (eds.), *Irish Classrooms and British Empire*, 111–23 [111].
10 O'Neill, 'Education, Imperial Careers and the Irish Catholic Elite', 103.
11 *The Belvederian*, 2/2, summer 1910, 209.
12 Patrick Morkan uses the work-horse that drives his mill to go out riding. When they reach the statue of King Billy, the horse begins to circle. Gabriel speculates that the horse might have fallen in love with the horse King Billy sits on or else 'thought he was back again in the mill'. Either way the attempt to emulate 'the quality' is not a success. See *D*, 237–8.
13 See the letter to Grant Richards, dated 5 May 1906, for example, where Joyce talks about the 'scrupulous meanness' which characterizes the style of *Dubliners* and the book's commitment to truth-telling. Ellmann (ed.), *Letters of James Joyce*, vol. 2, 134.
14 Herbert Gorman, *James Joyce* (London: John Lane The Bodley Head, 1941), 22.
15 See O'Neill, *Catholics of Consequence*, 29.
16 See Dáire Keogh, 'The Christian Brothers and the Second Reformation in Ireland', *Eiré-Ireland*, 40/1&2, 2005, 42–59 [53].
17 Ellmann, *James Joyce*, 35
18 Gorman, *James Joyce*, 32.
19 Rev. Tim Corcoran S.J., *The Story of Clongowes Wood AD 1450–1900* (Dublin: Catholic Truth Society of Ireland, 1900), 35.
20 *The Clongownian*, vol. 6, 1911–13, 114.
21 O'Neill, *Catholics of Consequence*, 65.
22 Ellmann, *James Joyce*, 27.
23 Quoted in *Catholics of Consequence*, 25, 46.
24 Pearse, 'The Murder Machine', 22.
25 See Andrew Gibson, *The Strong Spirit: History, Politics and Aesthetics in the Writings of James Joyce, 1896–1915* (Oxford: Oxford University Press, 2013), 123–42.
26 Gorman, *James Joyce*, 28, 23, 26.
27 O'Neill, *Catholics of Consequence*, 46.
28 Gorman, *James Joyce*, 28.
29 Walsh, '"Injurious to the Best Interests of Education"', 129–79 [137]; Gorman, *James Joyce*, 30.
30 Gorman, *James Joyce*, 29–30.
31 *James Joyce*, 29–30.
32 *The Freeman's Journal*, July 20, 1900, 4.

33 Fr William Delany S.J., the reforming rector of Tullabeg and the Holy Ghost Fathers at Blackrock, was much implicated in the drafting of the 1878 Act. For one historian, it was an 'Irish catholic invention'. See O'Neill, *Catholics of Consequence*, 16; 59–64.
34 Gorman, *James Joyce*, 30.
35 See Ellmann, *James Joyce*, 27; Gorman, 29.
36 Gorman, *James Joyce*, 30.
37 *James Joyce*, 29.
38 A place also associated with an aristocratic history. This was the inauguration site for members of one of three septs of the Uí Dúnlainge dynasty which rotated the kingship of Leinster between 750 and 1050. After that time, the family became Normanized as the FitzDermots.
39 Gorman, *James Joyce*, 30–1.
40 Pearse, *The Murder Machine*, 23–4.
41 See Bruce Bradley S.J., '"Allude to Me as Jesuit": James Joyce and His Educators', in María Luz Suárez Castiñero, Asier Altuna García de Salazar and Olga Fernández Vicente (eds.), *New Perspectives on James Joyce: Ignatius Loyola Make Haste to Help Me!* (Bilbao: Desuto University Press, 2009), 246–62 (247). See also Bruce Bradley S.J., *James Joyce's Schooldays* (Dublin: Gill & Macmillan, 1982).

Chapter 4

Early Joyce and radical education

Classical education! That sounds so distinguished!

Friedrich Nietzsche, *On the Future of Our Educational Institutions* (1872)

'Systematic compensation'

In *Stephen Hero*, there is a moment where Stephen Daedalus has a particularly tense discussion with one of his fellow students. Both attend University College, the Catholic University founded by John Henry Newman in 1853 and in Joyce's day still struggling for funding. A Universities Bill passed by parliament in 1879 had given it financial support but only as part of a Royal University framework that controversially placed Catholic university education in a secularized framework, linking it with other colleges in Cork, Galway and Belfast, the so-called 'Godless colleges'. This was the struggling, and in some ways embattled, institution that Joyce left in 1902 with an undistinguished degree. In the fictional scene, Madden (Davin in *A Portrait*), a committed revivalist and Gaelic Leaguer, is provoked by Stephen for no apparent reason. One day, he says, quite out of the blue, ' – I suppose these hurley-matches and walking tours are preparations for the great event'. Madden replies, darkly, that ' – There is more going on in Ireland at present than you are aware of – ', and so the argument kicks off. Stephen, perhaps offended by the idea that he is out of touch, or, worse, excluded, pointedly asks what use camàns (hurley sticks) will be in the battle to come and makes the suggestion that revolutionary purposes might be more efficiently pursued if Madden and his friends serve a period in the British Army, as many Irish schoolboys and graduates did in reality.[1] There, they would be trained in the use of 'modern weapons', drilled, fed, paid and sent home ready to meet their insurrectionary destiny. Madden is appalled by what he takes to be an absurd idea. He suspects that he is being mocked, which he is of course: ' – Do you mean to say you want young Gaelic Leaguers to wear the redcoat and take an oath of allegiance to the Queen and take her shilling too?' At this point, Stephen invites Madden to consider the case of Hughes, a patriot and Irish language teacher based on Pearse. 'One of these days he will be a barrister', Stephen points out, 'a Q.C., perhaps a judge – and yet he sneers at the Parliamentary Party because they take an oath of allegiance' (*SH*, 52–3). The heated debate continues with Davin defending Hughes with considerable force of argument, and Stephen responding in kind:

> — Law is law all the world over — there must be someone to administer it, particularly here, where the people have no friends in Court —
> — Bullets are bullets, too. I do not quite follow the distinction you make between administering English law and administering English bullets: there is the same oath of allegiance for both professions —
> — Anyhow it is better for a man to follow a line of life which civilisation regards as humane. Better to be a barrister than a redcoat —
> — You consider the profession of arms a disreputable one. Why then have you Sarsfield Clubs, Hugh O'Neill Clubs, Red Hugh Clubs? —
> — O, fighting for freedom is different. But it is quite another matter to take service meanly under your tyrant, to make yourself his slave —
> — And tell me, how many of your Gaelic Leaguers are studying for Second Division and looking for advancement in the Civil Service —
> — That's different. They're only civil servants: they're not . . . —
> — Civil be damned! They're pledged to the Government, and paid by the Government —.
>
> (*SH*, 53)

This is a staged performance, in more ways than one. It is constructed in terms of the social dramas that were being produced in the late nineteenth and early twentieth centuries to great controversy for the entangled transgressions of putting politics at the centre of aesthetics and contemporaneity at the centre of culture. Behind Stephen's detached analysis there are surely echoes of Shaw and, more substantially, of Stephen's great hero, Ibsen. It is one of many scenes in this fragment that position Stephen as an outsider, a 'detached' figure, subjecting the world around him to the logic of his critical and superior gaze.

The centrality of education to this dissection of Dublin is not much commented on. The pose of social rebel has usually been considered in relation to Stephen's attempts to fly by the nets of church, family and nation and his commitment to art, but the specific target of his anger and frustration is, again and again, an education system which seems representative of the modern world. He attacks a setup that produces both uniformity and conformity, condemning its subjects to emerge from their studies as lifeless commodified products. The texts speak loudly in registration of the grip of the Church over young Irish minds and the subservience of what is perceived as genuine intellectual achievement to the pursuit of social and economic status. In *Stephen Hero* especially, Stephen's attack reaches high levels of rhetoric. He spells out his disillusion as a student of University College, his sense of College life as a 'dull mechanical endeavour' (*SH*, 39), insisting that his contemporaries are trapped in ideological commitments to both Church and State:

'They admired Gladstone, physical science and the tragedies of Shakespeare: and they believed in the adjustment of Catholic teaching to everyday needs, in the Church diplomatic' (*SH*, 153). Their learning is obsessively concerned with the clock, examination results and future prospects. His own stylized laziness and tardiness becomes a way of resisting the conventional world he sees around him. In *A Portrait*, too, educational attainment is specifically, and wickedly, constructed in terms of state favour and the prospect of employment in the administration of empire: ' – Did you hear the results of the exams? . . . . Griffin was plucked. Halpin and O'Flynn are through the home civil. Moonan got fifth place in the Indian. O'Shaughnessy got fourteenth. The Irish fellows in Clarke's gave them a feed last night. They all ate curry' (*P*, 177).[2] Talk about examination success and failure is strategically placed in *A Portrait* as interpolation that frames Stephen's explanation of his attempts to carve out some kind of understanding that will help him develop as an artist, an endeavour which, as he points out repeatedly, is entirely unvalued by the world around him. The first part of Stephen's disquisition on aesthetics, explained to Lynch in terms of the apprehension of beauty, ends at a street corner where a 'fat young man' stops and salutes them with the report on examination results quoted above. The second, on the 'most satisfying relations of the sensible' which must correspond to 'the necessary phases of artistic apprehension' (*P*, 178), is directly followed by students 'talking among themselves' about 'two friends who had passed the final medical examination, of the chances of getting places on ocean liners, of poor and rich practices' (*P*, 181). The effect is to heighten the estrangement between Stephen and his contemporaries who, complicit with an educational system become bureaucracy, have 'leagued themselves together in a conspiracy of ignobility' (*SH*, 20). It produces packaged outputs, even in relation to the most spiritual of vocations. After a chance meeting with an old school friend now training to become a priest, the Stephen of *Stephen Hero* visits a seminary where he recognizes 'the martial mind of the Irish Church in the style of this ecclesiastical barracks'. The faces around him are 'cowed without being humble' (*SH*, 61). Likewise, his fellow students at University College 'all bore the same stamp of Jesuit training' and are permitted only the living of 'toy' lives (*SH*, 153, 166). The central point, one repeated throughout the early fictions, is that the elitism produced by modern education is a fraud – a cheapened, commodified imitation. Far from signifying the genuine superiority of a real elite, education figures everywhere in these texts as a matter of commercial exchange easily obtained. Its more mature, established products are likewise dismissed as cheap fakes. In *A Portrait*, they figure as men who think about 'army commissions and land agents: peasants greeted them along the roads in the country: they knew the names of certain French dishes and gave orders to jarvies in highpitched provincial voices which pierced thorough their skintight accents' (*P*, 200). In this respect, *Dubliners*, *Stephen Hero* and *A Portrait* together form a consistent domain of critique in which the bourgeoisie, produced under a modernized system of education, struggle to reach any level of authenticity, however qualified they may be. The position is an extreme one, largely removed from any concept of social justice, as it is in both

Eliot and Nietzsche. It offended many of Joyce's contemporaries, who challenged its realism. Looking back from 1968, C.P. Curran, contemporary with Joyce at University College, claimed to see 'nothing of Stephen's "shivering society"'.[3] But the fact remains that these texts are peculiarly charged in this respect, emphatic in their devotion to the playing out of the highly controversial and problematic idea that the privilege of elite schooling is a sham privilege not worth the having. In reality, even in the reality of a British colony, the advantages attached to being an educated member of the Catholic bourgeoisie would, for most, have been self-evident and hard to refuse, but Stephen rejects them. The extremity of his position is made up of many elements – the turning away from the Church, the refusal to be shamed by the body and sexuality or to romanticize family, the turn to art and so on – but it is also significantly configured in the challenge to the common-sense version of the world that imagines educational achievement in the institutions of the state as confirmation of a natural order.

Stephen's dispute with Madden, then, is part of a much wider contest which dominates the representation of university life in both *Stephen Hero* and Chapter Five of *A Portrait*, much more so than the 'University Question', important for Joyce's contemporaries and authorized histories of Irish education but by comparison ignored here. Stephen experiences higher education as a life spent living in a system, the surest and most consistent sign of radical education discourse, but not the only one. These texts are linked to political and social theory in other ways, too. The term Stephen Dedalus gives to the process by which his fellow students attempt to reconcile the contradictions he insists they inhabit is 'systematic compensation' (*SH*, 55). It does not derive directly from the writings of Marx or Bakunin, but it sounds as if it could have. It is clear that although Stephen in his undergraduate guise is famously disengaged from the debates that most occupy his contemporaries – on 'universal peace' for instance or, as one of his fellow students puts it, 'votes for bitches' – he repeatedly returns to the issue of modern education and its commodifying effects (*P*, 163). It is this that links him so centrally to discourses of radical education.

As we have seen, radical education discourse developed precisely in response to the modernization of education and was serviceable across a broad range of politics. Pearse talks about the iniquities of modern education as colonial invasion and an offence against the rights of nation; Virginia Woolf, otherwise indisposed towards discourses of social justice, makes a powerful commitment to women's inclusion at the higher levels of education. The aim of this chapter is to refine our sense of what version of radical education these early Joyce texts articulate. The method employed is to use the contents of Joyce's Trieste library to map out a landscape from the relevant material that Joyce had closest to hand, a landscape then related to the representation of education in the pre-*Ulysses* fictions. The procedure is far from exact, but it does show how education in these texts derives from a framework of ideas utilized in particular ways from particular positions – albeit one which will inevitably be aestheticized in Joyce's fiction, circumscribed, edited out and otherwise worked on.

The Trieste library

Joyce's Trieste library consists of some 600 titles collected between 1900 and 1920.[4] It is by no means self-evident which items among these count as being 'education' texts. What appear to be a quite random group of items – the odd school novel and a small collection of school textbooks, including a handbook on language teaching published by the Berlitz language school – are personal to Joyce and suggestive in a variety of ways. This group includes a copy of the first edition of his school magazine *The Belvederian* (1906), which contains a school story entitled 'Sassy', set around a cricket match being played in Australia, and a short feature on the history of the school building on Great Denmark Street, emphasizing its architectural features and linking with an aristocratic Dublin past. It also includes a list of achievements of former boys, near mandatory for elite schools. This draws attention to the achievements of such figures as the Right Honourable Christopher Palles, Lord Chief Baron of the Exchequer in Ireland and Chair of the Board of Intermediate Education from 1896; William Martin Murphy, 'the Tramway King' and politician who organized the lockout of Dublin's dock and transport workers in 1913; Sir Francis Richard Cruise, Honorary Physician in Ordinary to Edward VII, and General Sir Martin Dillon, who served in the Punjab Campaign, the Crimea, the Indian Mutiny and the Abyssinia War and was one-time military secretary in Bombay.

The library also contained a copy of John Burnet's *Aristotle on Education* (1903) which Joyce wrote a review of, published in Dublin in the *Daily Express* in September 1903. It is short to the point of dismissiveness but makes an interesting comment in relation to an Aristotelian theory of education that in Burnet's account is 'subordinate to his theory of state' and whose function is to 'recruit for a Greek state'. 'Individualism, it would seem', Joyce writes, with some circumnavigation because he has more than a sneaking regard for Aristotle, 'is not easily recommended to the Greek mind'.[5] Joyce also possessed a copy of R.S. Rait's *Life in the Medieval University* (1912), an account which opens by contrasting the modern corporate university given degree-awarding powers by the state with the informal gatherings of scholars which Rait takes to be typical of the early days of European universities. The sweeping narrative from genuine ancient scholarship to modern bureaucracy echoes the familiar story of Western decline evident in intellectual circles at this time.

Other items confuse and complicate the narrative around Joyce and education. Somewhat strangely, the library contained the first 173 Fabian tracts published between 1884 and 1914 – perhaps a leftover from Joyce's early interest in socialism. These included Tract 25, 'Questions for School Board Candidates' (Sidney Webb); Tract 52, 'State Education at Home and Abroad' (J.W. Martin); Tract 106, 'The Education Muddle and the Way Out' (Sidney Webb); Tract 111, 'The Reform of Reformatories and Industrial Schools' (H.T. Holmes); Tract 114, 'The Education Act of 1902 and How to Make the Best of it' (Sidney Webb); Tract 120, 'After Bread, Education' (Hubert Bland); Tract 146, 'Socialism and Superior

Brains' (George Bernard Shaw) and Tract 156, 'What An Education Committee Can Do (Elementary Schools)'. These are notable for articulating ways through the minutiae of education reform and make detailed practical suggestions about how activists can become involved in education work – how to become elected to school boards and school boards of governors, for example. They seem efficient and local, Bloom-like at some level and quite removed from the dramas associated with Stephen Dedalus and his dissent.

Other tracts, however, do deal with the big educational issues, often in terms that align with Joyce's fiction and the representation of Stephen in them. Tract 146, one of Shaw's, is a brilliant assault on the eugenicist fantasy that inequalities of wealth can be justified by the fact that they are deserved by the natural superiority of contemporary economic elites. Other tracts likewise deride modern versions of elitism. Tract 52, for example, argues that school inspectors, most of whom have graduated from Oxford or Cambridge, know nothing about education in the real world. Almost all these tracts attack the involvement of the church in education, again one of the most consistent markers of radical education literature at this time and evident throughout Joyce's fiction, albeit with much more personal investment and nuance than in the Fabian tracts.[6] Tract 25 advises that one question to ask school board candidates is: 'Will you take care that no questions of religion shall be allowed to influence any appointment by any committee on which you sit?' The same tract argues that secondary education is an 'Arcadia of private unregulated enterprises'.[7] Tract 52 puts the poor state of education in Britain squarely at the door of conflicting churches and attacks the religious cant that dominates teacher education. Tract 114 recognizes that the 1902 Education Act represents significant reform but warns that it will not prevent the placing 'of sectarian propaganda before public interest'.[8]

At the same time, the Fabians separate out from the Joyce text and Stephen Dedalus's analysis of modern education in central ways, most notably in the routine connections they make between the reforming potential of education and its capacity for redressing issues of social injustice. Several of them argue that the poor state of education in Britain is a result of its almost complete privatization at intermediate, or secondary, level and call for 'a democratic system of education' that will give 'every child free access to a school under public control'.[9] Tract 106, for instance, talks about 'the powerful social prejudice which resists any development of "primary" education beyond the preparation for a life of hewing wood and drawing water'.[10] In this respect they share territory with other late-nineteenth- and early-twentieth-century radical texts, again often operating from varied political and cultural positions.

Among the earliest of figures producing such texts, and certainly among the most well-known, would have been Tolstoy, who famously withdrew to his estates in the late 1850s and early 1860s to set up experimental schools for the children of local peasant families. These were free, non-compulsory and without fixed timetable or curriculum. Tolstoy taught at them for about three years, taking a period out to tour European schools in 1861. After the publication of *War and Peace* in 1869, he continued with his education work, producing good-quality textbooks for 'the people' including four levels of readers and the *ABC Book*. He took on the role of school inspector in 1874 and attempted to set up a college for teachers in 1876. Although Joyce's library has a number of items authored by Tolstoy, it has none of the standard writings on education – the account of the experimental schools he set up on the Yasinaya Polyana estate, for example, his report on education in Europe or the essay 'On Popular Education' which argues that 'every curriculum ought to be a response to questions posed by life'.[11] It does, however, include Tolstoy's *Essays and Letters*, a volume that includes a letter addressed to 'The Tsar and his Assistant'. In it Tolstoy argues a position central to his education theory, that 'all barriers to education, instruction and to imparting knowledge, should be destroyed' and no distinction should be made 'debarring people from any class from education'.[12] The same volume contains Tolstoy's 'Letter on Education', written in 1902 to a near relative belonging to the upper class of Russian society, whose 'children are generally sent to the high schools (gymnasia), where they are crammed with much knowledge, chiefly in order to pass examinations'. The relative has asked Tolstoy what boys should be taught. Whatever else, Tolstoy advises, they should be 'taught that others do for him what he naturally should do for himself', to 'understand that the chamber-pot he uses is emptied and wiped, without any pleasure, by a nurse or housekeeper'.[13] Without this understanding, the child will come to the only conclusion possible – 'that people are divided into two highly gendered classes: masters and slaves'.

Further examples of radical literature contained in Joyce's library make the same point about education and social justice in similar ways, once again often from very different political positions, some seemingly incompatible with the social organization of schooling in any sense. Bakunin's *God and the State*, for example, circumnavigates the complexities and contradictions of reconciling education with anarchism, beginning with the statement that 'Professors of the modern school . . . will necessarily become, some without knowing it, others with full knowledge of the cause, teachers of popular sacrifice to the power of the state and to the profit of privileged classes'. Does this mean, he asks 'the elimination from society' of 'all instruction'? . . . Far from it! Instruction must be spread among the masses without stint, transforming all the churches, all the temples dedicated to the glory of God and to the slavery of men, into so many schools of human emancipation'.[14]

For others, the limited extension of state education in the modern age was already sufficiently developed to raise serious doubts about what its further extension might bring, especially in relation to post-elementary schooling. This was the central issue distinguishing education radicals at this time, not always along predictable lines. Bertrand Russell is illustrative here, famously liberal and at some points in his life socialist. Nevertheless, he was deeply suspicious of the democratization of education which he interpreted as its extension to what he called, in an echo of Nietzsche, 'the herd'. This was because in his view, elitism represented a genuine intellectual order, not hereditary but somehow 'natural' all the same. 'The error of aristocracy', Russell wrote in the 1930s:

> lay, not in thinking that some men are superior to others, but in supposing superiority to be hereditary. The error of democracy lies in regarding all claims to superiority as just grounds for the resentment of the herd. In the modern world, much work which is necessary to the community requires more ability than most men possess, and there must be ways of selecting exceptional men to do this work. In general, if they are to be as well qualified as possible, it is desirable to select them while they are still quite young – say twelve years old – and to allow them to make more rapid progress than is possible to a class of average boys or girls. The feeling that it is undemocratic to single out the best pupil is one which leads to a great waste of good material.[15]

Most of Russell's writing on education was produced in the 1920s and 1930s. *Education and the Good Life*, heavily influenced by behavioural psychology, was published in 1927 and *Education and the Social Order* in 1932. Between them Russell experimented with his own version of education as headmaster of Beacon Hill, the progressive school that he opened in Sussex with his wife Dora. Well before this activity, however, *Principles of Social Reconstruction* (1917), the volume held in the Trieste library, established Russell's fundamentally individualist position on education and schooling. Here, in an attempt to imagine post-war governance informed by devotion to 'creativity' rather than the exercise of power for its own sake, Russell protested against a system created without what he calls 'reverence towards others'. Writing in the context of a post-war collapse of regimes, Russell explains that 'threatened institutions, while they are still powerful, possess themselves of the educational machine, and instil a respect for their own excellence in the minds of the young'. The passage goes on, 'the children themselves are not considered . . . they are merely so much material, to be recruited into one army or the other'.[16] In this way, again echoing Nietzsche, education becomes a product of 'machine-made cast iron systems' – 'militarism, capitalism, Fabian scientific organisation – all the other prisons into which reformers and reactionaries try to force the human spirit'. The result is 'a dead level of glib mediocrity'. When the individual *is* considered, Russell argues, it is 'almost exclusively with a view to worldly success – making money or achieving a good position'.[17] From this perspective, almost all education has a political motive, aimed at 'strengthening some group, national or religious or even social, in the competition with other groups'. It is this motive which determines 'the subjects taught, the knowledge offered and the knowledge withheld, and also decides the mental habits the pupils are expected to acquire'. Russell elaborates in relation to the teaching of history which 'in every country is so taught as to magnify that country; children learn that their own country has always been in the right and almost always been victorious', propagandism 'encourages strife and serves to keep alive a bigoted nationalism'.[18] He imagines competition in schools reflecting and reproducing the 'ruthlessness of capitalism', especially in middle-class schools which attract student numbers 'by advertising the successes of students'. The imperative to achieve results produces 'one long drudgery of examination tips and text book facts', which makes education a 'means of acquiring superiority over others', a system 'infected' with 'ruthlessness and glorification of social inequality'.[19] More insidiously, 'almost everyone who goes to Eton and Oxford is taught to 'worship' what Russell calls 'good form', the assumption that 'what is most important is a certain kind of behaviour . . . which minimizes friction between equals and delicately impresses inferiors with a conviction of their own crudity. As a weapon for preserving the privileges of the rich in a snobbish democracy it is unsurpassable'.[20]

The book was published too late to have any direct impact on either *Stephen Hero* or *A Portrait*, but it helps to establish the precise dimensions of an educational politics of individualism within which these texts operate. In many respects Russell's work on education finds echoes in *Stephen Hero* and Chapter Five of *A Portrait*, where it is 'a bad sign for a young man to show interest in anything but his examinations or his prospective "job"' (*SH*, 26). It informs the making of the Joyce avatar, Stephen Dedalus, especially in the post-school years where Stephen rails against the university, ridiculed as an inferior 'day-school full of terrorised boys, banded together in a complicity of diffidence'. Its students have 'eyes only for their future jobs: to secure their future jobs they will write themselves in and out of convictions', and 'toil and labour to insinuate themselves into the good graces of the Jesuits' (*SH*, 208).

Nietzsche is critical to this articulation of schooling in the Joyce text. In no other contemporary figure was education so central to the development of an anti-philosophy; nowhere else was such a powerful attack on the systematization of education saturated so thoroughly by individualism. Of the titles by Nietzsche that Joyce had in his Trieste library, *The Birth of Tragedy* (1909) has, admittedly, relatively little to say about education, apart from celebrating the divine justice that one day would call to account 'all that we now call culture, education', before a pagan authority, 'the unerring judge, Dionysus', although it is suggestive that Nietzsche makes the two terms 'education' and 'culture' synonymous and places both at the centre of his critique of the modern world.[21] In *The Case of Wagner*, he laughs at the idea that 'the eternal contents' of Wagner could ever be translated 'into the real, into the modern'. Imagine, he asks, Parsifal as a 'candidate in divinity with a public school education'.[22] *The Joyful Wisdom* (1910) gives an suggestive account of how education proceeds to do its work for 'the general good' and against the development of the individual. It imagines schooling as an iron system that 'endeavours, by a series of enticements and advantages to determine the individual to a certain mode of thinking and acting, which, when it has become habit, impulse and passion rules in him and over him, in opposition to his ultimate advantage but "for the general good"'. Nietzsche continues: 'If the education succeeds every virtue of the individual is a public utility, and a private disadvantage to the highest private end'.[23] Again, education is positioned as the antithesis of a drive central to Nietzsche's thought, the drive against the contemporary political state. In the same text, he makes a problematic but deep connection between education, gender and sex, an illustration of how far education is incorporated into Nietzsche's general philosophy, resonating across a wide range of issues:

> There is something quite astonishing in the education of women of the higher class. All the world is agreed to educate them with as much ignorance as possible in *eroticus*, and to inspire their soul with a profound shame of such things, and the extremest impatience and horror at the suggestion of them . . . . And then! To be hurled as with an awful thunderbolt into deadly knowledge with marriage – and indeed by him whom they most love and esteem; to have to encounter love and shame in contradiction. . . . There, in fact, a psychic entanglement has been effected which is quite unequalled.[24]

The third of Joyce's Nietzsche volumes – *The Case of Wagner*, *Nietzsche versus Wagner*, *Selected Aphorisms* – contains 'We Philologists', a classic of radical education literature. Written in 1874, close in time to 'The Future of Our Educational Institutions', this is a highly original assault on the modern curriculum that puts 'classics' at the centre of a systemizing order where it figures as a model of harmony, order and rationalism.

The teaching of ancient Latin and Greek language and culture was, of course, critical to the social logic played out within modern education in the nineteenth and early twentieth centuries. Thomas Arnold, archetypal headmaster and principal pedagogue of the Victorian age, thought the study of language somehow corresponded to structures in the mind and that since Greek and Latin were 'perfect', they must be 'the very instruments' for teaching boys.[25] Gladstone dispensed with the pseudo-science, baldly declaring to the 1864 Royal Commission on Public Schools (also known as the Clarendon Commission) that it was his 'firm conviction that only a classical education was, or could be, appropriate to that small section of the population destined to attend the leading "public" schools and then to assume responsibility for governing the country'.[26] From whatever position, the knowledge of the classics was the single most worked marker of an elite education and high social status in Victorian and Edwardian culture and beyond.

In Nietzsche, the teaching of classics in school becomes a laughable parody of genuine education, not because it has no bearing on the contemporary world but because it is taught in such a way that students can learn nothing from it. The 'philologists' who operate the system – 'teachers at public schools and professors at universities' – 'exploit the vaguely-felt dissatisfaction of modern man, and his desire for "something better", in order that they may earn their bread and butter'.[27] This is both a materialist form of study and a falsified one that cannot genuinely 'enter in antiquity' because, 'served up mixed with Christianity', it cannot be reconciled with the paganism of true Hellenism. It cannot substantiate its claims of being genuinely historical for the same reason, nor can it seriously deliver in relation to critical engagement. What Nietzsche calls 'the preference for antiquity' is absolute, which positions education in the classics as a kind of unchallengeable 'witchcraft', rendering it worthless in relation to meaningful pedagogy.[28] From this perspective, the education of elites and the education 'science' that Nietzsche dubs 'philology', far from exemplifying modern energy, is an exhausted pedagogy, falsely situated at the very centre of contemporary culture. 'In all those places where European culture has found its way', Nietzsche writes, 'people have accepted secondary schools based upon a foundation of Latin and Greek as the first and highest means of instruction. In this way philology has found its best opportunity of transmitting itself and commanding respect. No other science has been so well fashioned'.[29]

'Smatterings of Latin' – Nietzsche and the Stephen Dedalus persona

The terms of Nietzsche's arguments are substantially configured in Joyce's early writing, where classical education is reproduced as dull formula responsible for the production of schoolboys and College graduates whose knowledge of the classics is poor and facility in the languages of antiquity weak. John Dillon, co-author with Brendan O'Henir of *A Classical Lexicon for 'Finnegans Wake'* (1977), has reconstructed Joyce's own education in the classics, which would have been reinforced by the Church responses he learned as a child and shown its limitations. The most obvious general outcome of the system it represented, outside of leading to jobs in the civil service and elsewhere, is the schoolboy Latin used by its speakers as code and understood by those inside and outside their clique as being indicative of high educational attainment and gentlemanly status. When Stephen is taken to Cork on family business, one of his father's old friends 'in order to put his Latin to the proof had made him translate short passages from Dilectus' (*P*, 79). Nietzsche's analysis is reshaped in the cod schoolboy Latin used everywhere in the last chapter of *A Portrait* and in Stephen's understanding that he himself is a poor Latin scholar with only the faintest understanding of antiquity:

> The crises and victories and secessions in Roman history were handed on to him in the trite words *in tanto discrimine* and he had tried to peer into the social life of the city of cities through the words *implere ollam denariorum* which the rector had rendered sonorously as the filling of a pot with denaries.[30]
>
> (*P*, 150)

The materialist implication here is echoed in the fact that one of the first examples Stephen had learnt in Latin was one coded in imperial ways '*India mittit ebur*' (India sends ivory). Far from qualifying Stephen to lead or to rule, his education in the classics and Latin in particular are registered in terms of worldly practicality combined with an Anglicized version of aesthetic beauty ('the shrewd northern face of the rector who had taught him to construe the Metamorphoses of Ovid in a courtly English') – the Clongowes of Joyce's day used to hire specialists, a Professor Motley being one of them, specifically to teach students 'correct', meaning more Anglicized, speech.[31] Further characteristics of Stephen's education in the classics include trivialization (learning and teaching is 'made whimsical by the mention of porkers and potsherds'), heavy mediation ('He had learnt what little he knew of the laws of Latin verse from a ragged book written by a Portuguese priest') and, perhaps above all, the sense that something of vital importance has been entirely erased. 'The pages of his timeworn Horace', Stephen thinks, 'never felt cold to the touch even when his own fingers were cold'. He does not know in what sense, but he is certain 'they were human pages' (*P*, 150).

That entire sequence contains no specific allusion to Nietzsche and 'We Philologists', but it is difficult to see how it could have been written without that extraordinary text in mind and clear how Nietzsche's version of the classics in the modern system of education is configured in Joyce's comic dispersal of classicism in the classical correspondences of the *Ulysses* schema, as well as the representation of schoolboy Latin in use which continues to shape the showy performances of Stephen and Mulligan in *Ulysses*. The idea, however, that this is nothing more than 'tom foolery' or the survival of 'the schoolboy in Joyce', is both problematic, because it trivializes what such a survival might mean, and presentist – that is, written from a position where the role of the classics in everyday schooling, once a powerful orthodoxy, has been completely reconfigured, discontinued in most cases.[32]

'We Philologists' also helps to establish the broader terms of Nietzsche's influence on the early Joyce text. This is evident in the lines through which Stephen is drawn, his linking of real art with something pagan and instinctive, the 'ecstasy' that makes him want 'To live, to err, to fall, to triumph, to create life out of life' (*P*, 145), and his attempts to forge some kind of genuine epistemology as he 'spurned from before him a world of the higher culture in which there was neither scholarship nor art nor dignity of manners' (*SH*, 30) – the rhetorical figure here sounds like Nietzsche. The encounter with education orthodoxies highly suspicious of any theory of art that fails to 'instruct, elevate and amuse' (*SH*, 82) similarly reproduces Nietzsche's critique, specifically as it is formulated in 'We Philologists'. The College President at University College, concerned by the claims that Stephen makes for modern drama, declares with confidence that 'All the world recognises Eschylus as a supreme classical dramatist'. Stephen's response insists that the president's world is in fact a small one, only a 'world of professors' whom the great tragedist 'helps to feed' (*SH*, 83). Nietzsche also shapes the Stephen Daedalus who thinks people are 'ignorant of the value of . . . words' and who, 'as this indignity of life' forces itself upon him, becomes 'enamoured of an idealising, a more veritably human tradition' (*SH*, 20). It is significantly through Nietzschean logic that Stephen elevates his elitist attitudes into something more compelling, rendering the work of anatomizing his society and its culture as 'heroic' work.

Historically, Joyce criticism has always insisted on a problematic contradiction here. It has manifested in terms which try to gauge the ironic disposition of *Stephen Hero* and *A Portrait* and which claim that there is something unlikable about this character and his so-called heroism. It may be true that the social world Stephen Dedalus inhabits is consistently drawn around obsessions with social status, but likewise his own position in that world is centrally powered by his own drive for distinction at all stages of his development. As a child, the identification with historical figures like Rowan Hamilton and Parnell and the dark avenger in *The Count of Monte Cristo* who never eats 'muscatel grapes' (*P*, 52) aligns him with versions of aristocratic distinction. The awkward desire to be one of the 'chosen' drives his attraction to a vocation for the priesthood that will give him a power in the world beyond that of 'king or emperor' (*P*, 133), although he finds the injunction to 'merge his life in the common tide of other lives . . . harder . . . than any fasting or prayer' (*P*, 128). This is likewise with the admiration for the plays of Gerhart Hauptmann, for the 'cloistral silverveined prose of Newman', 'the dark humour of Guido Cavalcanti' and 'the spectral words of Aristotle and Aquinas' that protect him, folding 'around him like a mantle' so that 'in revery at least he had been acquainted with nobility' (*P*, 147–8). The desire to be so 'acquainted' itself has inescapable social dimensions, as does the clothing figure. The word 'mantle', though sometimes associated with the finery of wealthy women, more usually signifies a robe of state worn by and designed to register the masculine distinction of a prince, a king even, certainly a noble.

Some critics – Hugh Kenner writing in the 1950s is the classic example – have read the space between Stephen's engagement with the elite around him and his own drives and motivations as a kind of hypocrisy which Joyce mocks as the 'indigestibly Byronic'.[33] Others – the London Joycean Charles Peake writing in the 1970s, for example – insisted that the ambiguities were natural to adolescence and for that reason accepted in an irony that is not 'a destructive irony'.[34] Others still – Andrew Gibson writing in the 2000s – have circumnavigated the apparent contradictions, insisting that, whatever else, Stephen Dedalus remains a heroic figure.[35] The point being emphasized here is that for all the controversy once raised by reading *A Portrait* as the book of Stephen, the social logic engaged in its representation of the schoolboy/undergraduate is not just consistent but impeccable. That Stephen Dedalus figures as both a troubling challenge to convention and at the same time a traditionalist, a seeming radical who yet refuses to join in with any of the enthusiasms stirring his contemporaries – these are not contradictions, but, rather, designs cut from the same fabric. They are the result of a particular understanding of the 'rationalities' that had produced a modern education system built around ideas of hierarchy and distinction. Such dynamics converge in the later part of book, in Stephen's instinct for something genuine which must take place outside of formal education, the 'monkish learning, in terms of which he was striving to forge out an esthetic philosophy . . . held no higher by the age he lived in than the subtle and curious jargons of heraldry and falconry' (*P*, 151). These are both traditional markers of traditional aristocratic cultures of course, worlds away from the stultifying world of formal education signified in Chapter Five of *A Portrait* by the lecture on physics:

> – Plaitinoid, the professor said solemnly, is preferred to German silver because it has a lower coefficient of resistance variation by changes of temperature. The platinoid wire is insulated and the covering of silk that insulates it is

> wound on the ebonite bobbins just where my finger is. If it were wound single an extra current would be induced in the coil. The bobbins are saturated in hot paraffin wax. . .
>
> (*P*, 162)

Or are they? For many years Joyceans have attempted to make something of Stephen's aesthetic theories, the product of the self-education that gradually replaces his institutionalized learning in *A Portrait*. They have been significantly related to Joyce's so-called classicism and even used in attempts to identify an aesthetics operating in the book Stephen is in. But they can also be read, as Joyceans have pointed out, as dull, every bit as dull as the physics lecture Stephen attends in Chapter Five. What makes them so is the same stultifying pedagogy that allows both the professor to preside over his students and Stephen to effectively lord it over his friends. This is Stephen on the difference between lyric, epic and dramatic forms, differences he explains partly in relation to discourses derived from science and mathematics:

> Lessing, said Stephen, should not have taken a group of statues to write of. The art, being inferior, does not present the forms I spoke of distinguished clearly one from the other. Even in literature, the highest and most spiritual art, the forms are often confused. The lyrical form is in fact the simplest verbal gesture of an instant of emotion, a rhythmical cry as ages ago cheered on the man who pulled at the oar or dragged stones up a slope. . . . The simplest epical form is seen emerging out of lyrical literature when the artist prolongs and broods upon himself as the centre of an epical event and this form progresses till the centre of emotional gravity is equidistant from the artist himself and from others. The narrative is no longer personal.
>
> (*P*, 180)

And so on. There are not too many grounds on which the 'real' professor's lecture and Stephen's can be compared, but there is at least one. They are both striking examples of what Rancière calls 'explicatory' pedagogy, a method of teaching which has a profound bearing on social order partly because it is so predicated on the promise of distinction. 'This is the genius of the explicators', writes Rancière, 'they attach the creature they have rendered inferior with the strongest chains in the land of stultification – the child's consciousness of his own superiority'.[36] This is how it works here. More than anything else, it is Stephen's superiority that the speech confirms, which means that in some sense his aesthetics theory is a performance that only returns him to the social order he so despises.

Notes

1 See Timothy McMahon, 'Irish Jesuit Education and Imperial Ideals', in Dickson *et al.*, *Irish Classrooms and British Empire*, 111–13, [118].

2 In reality, no less than one-third of all recruits to the Indian Civil service were Irish, although only one in ten were Catholics – 'a near total reversal of the denominational demographic'. See McMahon, 'Irish Jesuit Education and Imperial Ideals', 103.
3 C.P. Curran, *James Joyce Remembered* (London: Oxford University Press, 1968), 21.
4 For the contents of Joyce's library in 1920, see Richard Ellmann, *The Consciousness of Joyce* (London: Faber & Faber, 1977).
5 James Joyce, *The Occasional, Critical and Political Writing*, edited with an introduction and notes by Kevin Barry (Oxford: Oxford University Press, 2000), 80.
6 There have been many accounts of the Joyce and the Church, most recently, Geert Lernout, *Help My Unbelief: James Joyce and Religion* (London: Continuum, 2010) and Chrissie van Mierlo, *James Joyce and Catholicism: The Apostate's Wake* (London: Bloomsbury, 2016).
7 Sidney Webb, 'Questions for School Board Candidates', Fabian Tract 25 (London: The Fabian Society,1891), 2.
8 Sidney Webb, 'The Education Act 1902: How to Make the Best of It', Fabian Tract 114 (London: The Fabian Society, 1904), 2.
9 J.W. Martin, 'State Education at Home and Abroad', Fabian Tract 52 (London: The Fabian Society, 1894), 2.
10 Sidney Webb, 'The Education Muddle and the Way Out: A Constructive Criticism of English Education Machinery', Fabian Tract 106 (London: The Fabian Society, 1901), 7.
11 Leo Tolstoy, 'On Popular Education', in *Tolstoy as Teacher: Leo Tolstoy's Writings on Education*, edited by Bob Blaisdell, translated by Christopher Edgar (New York: Teachers & Writers Collaborative, 2000), 177.
12 Leo Tolstoy, *Essays and Letters*, translated by Alymer Maude (London: Henry Frowde, 1904), 274.
13 Tolstoy, *Essays and Letters*, 339–40.
14 Mikhail Bakunin, *God and the State* (1882; London: Freedom Press, 1910), 21.
15 Bertrand Russell, *Education and the Social Order* (1932; London: Allen & Unwin, 1982), 55.
16 Russell, *Principles of Social Reconstruction*, 144.
17 *Principles of Social Reconstruction*, 144–6.
18 *Principles of Social Reconstruction*, 148, 150.
19 *Principles of Social Reconstruction*, 160–2.
20 *Principles of Social Reconstruction*, 153.
21 Friedrich Nietzsche, *The Birth of Tragedy*, translated by W.A. Haussmann (Edinburgh and London: T.N. Foulis, 1909), 54.
22 Friedrich Nietzsche, *The Case of Wagner, Nietzsche Contra Wagner, Selected Aphorisms*, translated by A.M. Ludovici (Edinburgh and London: T.N. Foulis, 1911), 34.
23 Friedrich Nietzsche, *The Joyful Wisdom*, translated by Thomas Common (London: T.N. Foulis, 1910), 68–9.
24 Nietzsche, *The Joyful Wisdom*, 104.
25 Anon, *Boys and Their Ways: A Book for and About Boys, by One Who Knows Them* (London: John Hogg, 1880), 59.
26 Quoted in Simon, 'Systemization and Segmentation in Education', in Müller *et al.*, *The Rise of the Modern Educational System*, 95–6.
27 Nietzsche, *The Case of Wagner, Nietzsche Contra Wagner, Selected Aphorisms*, 137, 146.
28 *The Case of Wagner, Nietzsche Contra Wagner, Selected Aphorisms*, 150, 123, 125, 151.
29 *The Case of Wagner, Nietzsche Contra Wagner, Selected Aphorisms*, 124.
30 The first phrase translates as 'in such a great crisis'. The second is translated in the second half of the sentence.
31 See O'Neill, *Catholics of Consequence*, 50. See also R.D. Anderson, 'The Idea of the Secondary School in Nineteenth-Century Europe', *Paedagogica Historica*, 40/1-2, 2004, 93–106.

32 John Dillon, 'The Classics at the *Wake*: Some Aspects of Classical Influence in Joyce's *Finnegans Wake*', *Classics Ireland*, 5, January 1, 1998, 9–29 [23–4].
33 See Hugh Kenner, *Dublin's Joyce* (London: Chatto & Windus, 1955), 109–33 [132].
34 C.H. Peake, *James Joyce: The Citizen and the Artist* (London: Edward Arnold, 1977), 109.
35 See Gibson, *The Strong Spirit*.
36 Rancière, 'On Ignorant Schoolmasters', 22.

Chapter 5

A Portrait of the Artist and the cultural politics of the public-school novel

'"No-o! That's oratio directa", said Stalky, shaking his head. "I like oratio obliqua."'

Rudyard Kipling, *Stalky and Co* (1899)

Fiction, biography, the school novel

Writing in 2009, Finn Fordham expresses his concern and irritation with the current state of Joyce biography which, he says, has reached a kind of impasse. This has been produced first because, until fairly recently, the James Joyce estate under the late Stephen Joyce had exercised such surveillance over the maintenance of the Joyce image that independent biographical research was rendered virtually impossible. Fordham himself was effectively prohibited by the Estate from publishing his own early work on Joyce. Second, the problem is compounded paradoxically by the issue not of constraint but overabundance. Fordham sees the sheer volume of relevant archival material to have emerged since Ellmann's 1982 revision of the 1959 biography as being close to overwhelming – too voluminous and too complex to process in any coherent version of a Joyce life. Finally, there is the obstacle of the authority of the Ellmann biography itself, lauded by Anthony Burgess, as Fordham points out, as 'the greatest literary biography of the century'. Fordham sees it sitting 'comfortably on the shelf next to Joyce's own works, as if it were part of the canon'. Given that degree of authority, it is difficult to see how new versions can ever emerge: 'Having been established for so long as part of the oeuvre, how can it be displaced?'[1]

The blockage is a particular issue for Joyce studies because Joyce's writing is considered to be so highly autobiographical. Control over the life threatens to give control over the reading of the work, which means that if biography is somehow blocked, so, potentially, is new critical reading. At this point, Fordham puts in a plea. Despite all the difficulties, he advocates for what he sees as a genuine evidence-based form of biography derived not from the singular narrative which is the assumed Joyce life, but from what we know now about what Joyce was actually doing, as a writer – what he was reading and how he was putting text together at any point of writing. In effect this is a call, from a genetic critic devoted to unravelling the history of a given text, for a 'science' that separates out the chronologies of the writing of a book from the living of a life and turns the former into the genuine domain of literary biography. 'Ideally', Fordham writes, this kind of biography 'would move . . . along just one wave of time, the present, in which writing would be acknowledged to form a central set of events in the life'. Thus, the time Joyce spent in Paris in 1902 'would not be interspersed with Dedalus' memories of Paris'. Joyce's time in Trieste in 1915, however, 'would be interspersed with the moments when memories were transferred to Dedalus', because this would be the time when *A Portrait* was being written. The ultimate result would be a definitive split where 'Dedalus and all the other characters would feature not as alter-egos or glosses on Joyce's life, because they are entirely different kinds of being, textual forms, open to radical reformation, not equivalent to anything human'.[2]

The call for a purity of reading is as old as literary studies, but Fordham surely has a point in posing the problems inherent in conflating textual life with flesh and blood, problems illustrated with particular force in *A Portrait*, a novel so autobiographical and yet at the same time so distanced from the events of Joyce's life as they would have happened. This version of Stephen Dedalus was written some 30 years after Joyce went to Clongowes. It would have been influenced by many events and experiences, including the readings of radical education that took place more than a decade after Joyce left University College and Dublin. As Fordham says, the complexities that characterize Stephen as a product of schooled learning are first and foremost 'textual'. Indeed, they possess a specific textuality re-enacted in the relations between *A Portrait* and the public-school novel. Just as Stephen is a rebellious product of a conformist school system, so *A Portrait* is an iconoclastic version not so much of a life lived in the past as of the school novel text and its search for the heroic schoolboy. Here, there is an overlapping both with the modernization of education and with the radical response to it, because the literary form was so closely related to the emergence of modern schooling in the nineteenth century.

Historiographies of the public-school narrative have often stressed its variations, its multiple forms – as short story, novel, comic strip, film and so on – and its wide ambitions. Although some have been not much more than exercises in nostalgia written by middle-class men, others have been motivated by powerful reformist instincts, including Irish ones in the work of such figures as Maria Edgeworth and much later, Helen Elrington, Shan Bullock, William Patrick Kelly and Canon P.A. Sheehan.[3] They have been related to nationalist idealism, the spread of democracy, changing versions of citizenship, formations of masculinity and the cultural and political history of adolescence. Written about as incarnations of a time when schooling had 'ferocious influence' and 'emotional importance' deriving from the intensity of the public-school experience and the school's 'isolation from the rest of the world', they have also been constructed as both microcosms of the adult world and gateways to it.[4] Despite the fact that school and college narratives, even tales of elite schooling, continue to figure largely in the contemporary world, they are almost always seen as narratives of a bygone age, associated now with versions of national decline and sometimes imagined in terms of an end-of-pier quaintness and eccentricity.[5] But for all this perceived diversity and variation, there rarely can have been a literary form so singular in its social mission. Alongside the material facts of institutions, curriculum, pedagogies and assessment, education was part of the symbolic order where elite schooling was characteristically imagined as building on nature to cultivate and civilize the free and privileged middle-class boy in fulfilment of his destiny to rule. School or public-school stories were the mainstream cultural manifestation of this social mission. Once read by adults and children alike, they were held in high esteem and considered 'energetic', 'functional' and artistic long after they became commercially reproduced as serials in magazines in the late nineteenth century.[6] The literary counterpart to the process of education modernization, these narratives were powerful signifiers. One of the central mechanisms through which the social meanings embedded in systemization were registered across wider society, they were important to the construction of a world where social distinction was imagined as a moral and genetic condition vital to the 'higher order' maintenance of nation, state and empire and the inevitable progressivist march of history. Their heroes were collectively and invariably idealizations of traditional social and cultural elites and, from this perspective, the English public-school novel joined ranks with much more prestigious nineteenth- century cultural forms, like the *bildungsroman* and the *Erziehungsroman*. The English gentleman, the *honnête homme*, the Humboldtian idealist of *Bildung*, these figures all inhabited idealized tales, operating as models to the lower orders of Europe and its empires.

The English form would have been entirely familiar to Joyce, of course. It is reasonable to assume he would have known versions of it from boys' magazines like the ones referred to at the beginning of the *Dubliners* story 'An Encounter'. However much the elite schools Joyce attended may have objected to these more 'vulgar' manifestations of the school narrative, there would have been some sense in which they cultivated a reciprocal relationship with the schoolboy heroics made manifest in them. These were, after all, heightened versions of the 'heroism' that made superior schools marketable. It was no accident that school magazines such as *The Clongownian* and *The Belvederian* drew on sports heroics and tales of empire exploits of ex-boys, just like the fictional versions of school life. More specifically, as a student at Belvedere College, Joyce played the part of the headmaster in a dramatized version of F. Anstey's *Vice Versa, Or A Lesson To Fathers* (1882), a comic variation on convention which, by using magic to place an adult in the body of a schoolboy, managed to show with comforting geniality just how ugly and bullying life at a public school could be and thus how distorted conventional versions actually were. Also, Joyce's Trieste library contained a copy of Kipling's *Stalky and Co.* Described by journalist and historian of the English school novel genre Isabel Quigly in terms of a new twist on an old story, this was the schoolboy novel designed 'as empire manual'.[7] Indicative of the form's continued vitality, it operated a masculinist riposte to the sentimentality and religiosity of something like Farrar's *Eric: Or, Little by Little*.

Here, the Irish schoolboy placed in the English public school appears as a Gaelicized and orientalized 'McTurk'. His father is a landowner who 'held many acres in Ireland'. In stereotypical style, he figures as the gifted but unruly romantic, waiting to be trained up in the ways of hard but civilized rule as the chief legal mind of Stalky's gang – this achieved only after his English friends have 'carefully kicked [him] out of his Irish dialect'.[8]

The school novel was nothing less than the fictional counterpart to the school system that produced both Joyce and his avatar Stephen Dedalus. A fantasy version of the real life Joyce lived, it had high cultural status, although that was already changing. By the time Joyce came to write *A Portrait*, many of the characteristics of the genre – its high sense of moral purpose, it sentimental vision of masculinity and its proselytization of Christianity – increasingly were coming under strain, a fact reflected in newer versions, like Anstey's and Kipling's. It also routinely elevated Englishness to a high state of heroism and, not infrequently, stereotyped the Irish as nothing more than sidekicks – or worse, abominations. In Farrar's *Eric: Or, Little by Little*, a boy arrives at Roslyn from 'one of the most ill-managed schools in Ireland'. Let loose as a 'pestilence' with the capacity for 'destroying the immortal soul', his effect is nothing short of catastrophic. Some of the Roslyn boys never forget for the rest of their lives 'the unfathomable flood of moral turpitude and iniquity' which he brings with him and the 'broadening tide of degeneracy' that follows it. Hardly 'one gentlemanly or honourable fellow' is left uncontaminated, although exactly in what sense is never fully disclosed. Ultimately, his crimes, whatever they are, are uncovered by the school authorities and he is made to pay, becoming that most despised figure of the fictional schoolboy imagination – the anti-self of schoolboy heroics – a coward who cannot take his punishment: 'At the first stroke he writhed and yelled; at the second he retreated, twisting like a serpent, and blubbering like a baby; at the third he flung himself on his knees, as the strokes fell fast, clasped Mr Rose's arm, and implored and besought for mercy'.[9] There is no evidence that Joyce knew this novel, although it was a best seller and is specifically mocked over and over in *Stalky and Co*, where 'to Eric' becomes a verb meaning to imitate the mewling moralizing of that character for strategic purposes. There can be little doubt, however, that Joyce would have understood that, in writing a hyper-realistic narrative about an Irish boy in an elite school, he was simultaneously breaking stereotypes and running the risk of confirming them. From such perspectives, it is not difficult to imagine how the school novel might have appeared to Joyce as a provocative prospect.

'Not a feature alike and the face the same' – the making of an extended [phenotype]

Ireland is inscribed on every page in *A Portrait* – in its geographics, its representations of the political world, its cultural framing and so on. At the same time, *A Portrait* is laced with the convention of a literary form uniquely associated with

Englishness, so much so that it is difficult to separate out facts of autobiography from literary cliché in Joyce's novel. This is not to acknowledge that, for most readers, *A Portrait* will seem worlds away from the stereotypical formulas of the traditional public-school novel. For instance, the first chapter of *A Portrait* is typically seen, for good reason, as technically challenging and innovative. It begins with a complex narrative style that seeks to incorporate the language and point of view of a very young child, and the style of the novel famously changes with Stephen's growth and development. There is a kind of organic predisposition to the novel which throws it outside the bulk standard and into the realms of the art novel. Indeed, the existence of the book is one of the reasons why some cultural historians have seen 'a symbiotic relationship' between literary modernism and literary adolescence, 'for characteristic traits of adolescence, such as the blurring of identity, rapid role changing and the merging of the individual into a group, can only be represented by means of those shifting narrative perspectives that had been developing since Flaubert'.[10] Joyce's handling of such techniques is undeniably 'radical', but it also responds to the central problem of perspective that confronted all writers of the traditional school novel: how could an adult represent the life of a much younger person convincingly? Some writers devised interesting ways to work this illusion – Anstey's reversal of adult and child identities in *Vice Versa* for example. Most, however, fudged it, and a good many struggled with what Isabel Quigly identifies as a complex of aesthetic problems. She explains how the school-novel writer had to put himself

> into the shoes of an age-group whose outlook and feelings were, or should have been, quite unlike his own, he had to be absorbed enough in what happened to make it interesting to himself, and so to others, he had to treat the relations between master and boy from the boy's point of view when he was in fact the age of the master, yet to keep enough detachment to make it sound right.[11]

Quigly speculates that the difficulties might have stunted the development of the school novel as a serious form. Whatever the case, the immersion of Joyce's narrative into these issues, while it does indeed signify the high cultural status of *A Portrait*, has no choice but to operate with reference to the traditions of the public-school story running alongside.

Equally standard to school novels was the opening that featured the arrival of the new boy feeling lost and ill at ease and often threatened by the sheer force and energy of the sports field. The game played at the opening of the novel might have been unfamiliar to some readers – according to Bruce Bradley, what is described here is not rugby, but a kind of football known as 'gravel football' because it was played on a gravel surface; it was also played at Stonyhurst, the elite Catholic school in England to which many prosperous Irish families sent their sons.[12] But the broad scenario would have been enough to evoke unpleasant memories, whatever the specifics of the game. In a letter published in the preface to the sixth edition of *Tom Brown's Schooldays*, a friend of Hughes complained about what he saw as the neglect of the true extent of public-school violence in the novel, asking the author to imagine the feelings of small boys being forced to play sports with bigger ones. 'Healthy exercise and games and sports' were a good thing, he wrote, but 'should bear some proportion' to strength and capacity. Imagine the terror, he went on, of a small boy forced to face 'the rush of a set of great fellows at football [rugby] or the speed of a cricket-ball sent by a strong hitter'.[13] In *A Portrait*, Stephen's sense of 'wide playgrounds swarming with boys' and of standing 'out of the reach of . . . rude feet' on the playing field, feeling his body 'small and weak', brings the narrative down to a small boy's level (*P*, 6).

For all the originality of the first chapter of *A Portrait*, it is impossible to read without reference to the standard plots of the public-school novel. The bullying which results in Stephen being shouldered into a ditch by Wells, the pressure put upon Stephen 'never to peach on a fellow', Stephen's unfair punishment – these plot elements were repeated over and over across hundreds of narratives (*P*, 7). The sick fellow confined to the infirmary, as Stephen is, fearful of dying, likewise was conventional, a reflection of poor conditions in schools and scandalous outbreaks of disease but also connected to the idea that schoolboys were especially vulnerable to being contaminated by bad influences, as well as beneficial ones – they were visualized as learning by imitation.[14] Similarly, the complaint to the head teacher about unfair punishment was a familiar trope explicitly related to the political motifs that ran through the form in demonstration of the schoolboy's right to rule. In *Public School Literature, Civic Education and the Politics of Male Adolescence* (2008), Jenny Holt speculates that Percy Hetherington Fitzgerald's *Schooldays at Saxonhurst, By One of the Boys* (1867), based on his time at Stonyhurst, becomes a particular case in this respect by making a special connection between Irishness and dissent, apparently reflecting the realities of Stonyhurst – 'nationalism among students, as well as a tradition of dissent, contributed to a politically charged atmosphere at the school'.[15] Certainly, political excitement is especially evident in this narrative. Something as innocent as 'the evening reading' becomes 'clamorously insisted on as a matter of right'; even material objects, a cruet stand for instance, become fought over as 'emblems of independence'.[16] A number of details build the familiar connection, a kind of over-politicization that gets close to confirming the stereotype of the 'turbulent' Irishman. A dandy named T.W. Bridges, who has the air of 'a *heroes de roman* about him', will later be 'engaged in ill-fated attempts to enfranchise Ireland'. Forces join in the face of a school authority that appears to assault the rights of the 'fifth' and 'sixth' and in protest against poor food described by school radicals as constituting nothing short of a 'famine'. The subsequent 'barring out', a foretaste of further 'troubles' to come, forms a defensive barrier against which no 'despotism' will be allowed to break through.[17]

But the radicalism here, as well as registering as something Irish, also registers as aristocratic and is universalized as protest against generic injustice. Sometimes it is linked with English radicalism – the father of one of the boys once worked with 'Horatio Hunt' – at other times with European republicanism in the traditions of United Irishmen. A schoolboy 'revolt' has a striking 'likeness to the events of the French Revolution' and the schoolboys become 'citizens'.[18] School leaders Bob North and Jack Malt stand in for Gladstone and Disraeli respectively and, in competition, represent the constitution of England against the revolutionary politics of republican France, a more contemporary version of the York and Lancashire teams who compete for favour in *A Portrait*. As the above implies, there is no real consistency here and no real politics either. The school is a safe environment in which to try out what are effectively political games, enacted against the understanding that these 'young gentlemen' – 'heroes' – will be taking their places among elites of the future and under the general principle that there are clear limits to what is a stylized transgression of school rules.

Alongside these play politics, the real politics of this novel are specifically framed by the emphasis on the future roles boys will be expected to fill. They arrive at an institution that from the outset distinguishes itself from the 'common, pedagoguish, birching, parlour-boarding sort of place'. The connection between institution and social status is everywhere inscribed in the tradition, as it is in *A Portrait*. Saxonhurst similarly is 'more a college than a school' and, in a telling phrase, 'quite a patrimony'. The new arrivals may be 'green' and uncertain, but bright, high-ranking futures are guaranteed for them from the outset: 'Never fear, we'll make a Lord Chancellor or Chief Justice of him'.[19] Their political education is underwritten by exposure to a well-connected culture in which political discourse and performance frame every relationship and dissent in face of injustice becomes a central narrative driver. In these respects, *Schooldays at Saxonhurst*, for all its Catholic setting, is positioned exactly as the standard school novel and so is *A Portrait*, with the important distinction that in the latter the idea of the school as political microcosm, 'that world in miniature', is compromised by the gap between the real political world outside, of which Stephen has little understanding, and the schoolboy politics on show, which he believes he can both read and have agency in.[20]

The issue of unjust punishment was also explicitly related to the political motifs that ran through the form. The whole sequence in *A Portrait* which leads to the Clongowes rector being urged to intervene and agreeing to restore a recognizable order of discipline was, as we have seen, standard in school novel narratology and part of the political culture in which it operated – again, a testing of the boundaries in which obedience and responsibility to concepts like justice and fairness were played out. In Farrar's *Eric: Or, Little by Little*, for instance, Eric intervenes with the school head to save his friend Wildney from expulsion; Oliver Greenfield in *The Fifth Form at St Dominic's* (1887) has to appear before the Head on behalf of his younger brother; in Kipling's *Stalky and Co*, Stalky gets bored by the sheer number of occasions he has to intervene on the schoolmates' behalf.

Finally, Chapter One ends with the sound of a cricket match being played in the background. In one sense there is an emphatic divergence from prototype here. Cricket was rarely in the background of the public-school novel. Indeed, it was typically and famously foregrounded. In some of the most influential exemplars, it was centrally connected to the heroizing agendas key to these stories – in *The Fifth Form at Saint Dominic's*, the 'heroes of the sixth' 'stalk' 'majestically to their quarters' at the start of a new term; the arrival of younger boys constitutes 'a phalanx of small heroes'; the fifth are 'a wonderful lot of heroes' – and it applied especially to heroics on the cricket field. Oliver Greenfield's bowling at a cricket match between the fifth and the sixth makes him 'the hero of St Dominic's', for instance, although other 'manly' activities work in precisely the same way. Greenfields's younger brother's battle with a senior gives him a 'hero's nose' and so on.[21] In some versions the cricket field became positioned at the narrative heart of these stories, constituting the narrative climax of things. The penultimate chapter of *Tom Brown's Schooldays*, entitled 'Tom Brown's Match' moves into the present tense to convey the excitement of an end of year match, a game which has become an 'institution', 'the birthright of British boys old and young, as *habeas corpus* and trial by jury are for British men'.[22] Here in *A Portrait*, however, it figures only as a summer background noise to heroics being played out elsewhere – not on the field, but in the rector's office, where Stephen complains about the behaviour of Father Dolan.

In reality, Clongowes especially would have been obsessed with cricket in Joyce's day – Joyce was a promising batsman himself and retained an interest in the game throughout his life. Bradley points out that his period at Clongowes coincided with the emergence of a first-class cricket team, which included Paddy Rath and Jimmy Magee, both of whom became celebrated players as adults. He suggests that the mention of these figures in *A Portrait* evokes 'a whole golden era not only in the history of Clongowes cricket but of the game in Ireland'.[23] In fact, the names of these players are not connected to cricket in Joyce's novel at all, nor are their cricketing exploits at Clongowes alluded to, let alone celebrated, in any way. It is not the presence of cricket that characterizes Joyce's representation of Clongowes but, on the contrary, its virtual erasure; a decolonizing gesture perhaps, although the colonial associations of the game did not prevent its appropriation by other cultures, notably colonial cultures, and Ireland was no exception. Cricket was popular in Ireland even among nationalists where it was reconciled to nationalist agendas and Irish identities at least up to the 1900s, at which time the Gaelic League placed an embargo on what it called 'playing foreign'. The *Nation* newspaper, the organ of Daniel O'Connell's Repeal Association and future mouthpiece of Young Ireland, at one stage regretted that the 'manly game of cricket was making insufficient progress in Ireland'. Land Leaguers continued to play the game well in the 1880s and John Lawrence's *Handbook of Cricket in Ireland*, the Irish equivalent to *Wisden*, spoke routinely of 'our noble game'. As historian Sean Reid points out, there was no necessary contradiction between Irish nationalism and being a cricket fan or player for most of the nineteenth century. The more likely explanation for the erasure of cricket for *A Portrait*, is an obvious one – this book is a portrait of the artist as a young man, not a sportsman, and it is in the figure of the artist that the heroizing dimensions of the sportsman are displaced. Clearly that central element, however compromised, is *not* missing from *A Portrait*. It carries over from the title of Joyce's first draft of *A Portrait* and becomes the dominant motif in *A Portrait*, where Stephen is imagined at the end of the first chapter being hoisted onto the shoulders of his fellows in recognition of his achievement. His victory may be short-lived, but the ambition for heroic distinction remains. As a would-be priest, his days begin with 'an heroic offering of its every moment of thought or action for the intentions of the sovereign pontiff and with an early mass' (*P*, 124). The same instinct comes into play in his refusal to kowtow before Heron, his much more serious refusal to serve church and state and, in countless further details in the novel, not least, in his elevated determination to 'forge in the smithy of my soul the uncreated conscience of my race' (*P*, 213).

The second chapter *of A Portrait* marks a break in Stephen's schooling as his family's fortunes decline and the status that attendance at a good public school confers becomes less and less connected to the materiality of Stephen's real life. Still, the public-school narrative retains its powerful presence. The break-up with the father, a focal point of the beginning of the second chapter of *A Portrait*, was again a convention, one taken to comic extremes in Anstey's *Vice Versa*, in which exotic magic creates the conditions allowing the son to switch power relations by swapping bodies with the father. More conventionally, the Tom Brown narrative is substantially built around a transfer of allegiance from Tom's real father, the outdated Tory squire, to the new liberalism of a figure representing Thomas Arnold, the headmaster of Rugby School worshipped by Tom. In order to develop, Tom has to move on from the benign but ineffectual paternalism of the rural squirearchy represented by his father, just as Stephen has to move on from his father's vague, romantic and hypocritical notions of what it is to be 'a gentleman' and a 'bloody good honest [Irishman] too', with the difference that here the model Stephen turns to is not a single person but a role and is provisional (*P*, 77). This makes Stephen's sense of identity more compelling and unstable as it shifts from romantic lover, through the boy-priest phase to rebellious artist. Quite small narrative details featuring in the public-school novel figure in this section of *A Portrait*. Simon Dedalus's search for his initials carved in the desks of the anatomy theatre of Queen's College echoes other texts in the genre. In *Eric: Or, Little by Little*, Eric finds himself in the boarders' room looking at names 'rudely cut' into 'oak panels' and wondering about the fate of each boy – 'what *noble* histories would the records unfold of honour and success, of baffled temptations and hard-won triumphs; what *awful* histories of hopes blighted and habits learned, of wasted talents and ruined lives'.[24] Likewise, this occurs in *Tom Brown's Schooldays*, which imagines future 'fourth-formers' who will read the names of current boys 'rudely cut out on the old hall tables' and wonder 'what manner of boys they were'.[25] Closer to Joyce's reversal, perhaps, is the scene in *Vice Versa* where Mr Bultitude realizes with horror that his son has carved his name on the head teacher's writing table and that he himself will be blamed for it.[26]

Theatre scenes, like the one in which Stephen, now at Belvedere College, plays the part of 'a farcical pedagogue', again, were commonplace across these novels. At the beginning of the public-school novel tradition, theatre performance in Maria Edgeworth's *The Barring Out* (1796) figures as a dubious entertainment encouraging boys towards the frivolous and sometimes to disorder. Later traditions considered performance to be an essential skill for men in the public eye. Canning advised Gladstone, preparing for a political career at Eton in 1824, to 'give plenty of time to your verses' on the grounds that 'every good copy you do will set in memory some poetical thought or well-turned form of speech which you will find useful when you speak in public'.[27] In *Stalky and Co*, performance has a more *fin de siècle* feel, allowing Dickson Quartus, the boy who plays Aladdin, 'who had passed his Army Preliminary and hoped to enter Sandhurst next spring', to experiment with wearing 'pink cotton tights', a shift closer in spirit to *A Portrait*, in which young Bertie Tallon dances 'the sunbonnet dance by himself' (*P*, 62).[28] In the same chapter, the scenes where Heron torments Stephen as a 'heretic' and yet 'a model youth' revisit the bullying issues so much the subject of the public-school novel and the fraught question of the traditional rights of senior boys. When Father Dolan sends a junior boy to bring Stephen to the stage for his curtain call, Heron protests that conventions have been broken. 'That's no way', he insists, 'to send for one of the senior boys'. Stephen is himself confused by the contradictions between his rebellious streak and his predisposition to obey authority. Above all, he is shocked by his 'equivocal position in Belvedere, a free boy, a leader afraid of his own authority, proud and sensitive and suspicious, battling against the squalor of his life, against the riot of his mind' (*P*, 70, 76).

Stephen's turn to 'sin', an offence to God and ideologies of manliness, is, again, a version of the essential public-school plot which sees the schoolboy hero either rising to authority over the everyday life and institutional culture of the school world by virtue of his strength, courage and moral sensibility or suffering the slow drift into degeneracy, the rise and fall pattern that went on to characterize the shape of the public-school novel as its central characters struggled to become properly manly.[29] Tom Brown, after a period of what the novel constructs as dissipation, is eventually led on to higher things, including piety, when his headmaster gives him the responsibility for looking after a new, vulnerable boy. Eric in Farrar's novel, in the end feeling himself sunk in 'degradation' and unable to bear 'public expulsion or even another birching' escapes from Roslyn School but dies after a terrifying experience at sea. Religious conversion was commonplace in these novels, a kind of end point towards which narrative reached in the earlier part of the tradition. By the turn of the century, however, it was linked specifically to the invention of adolescence as a psychological condition, a 'necessary rebirth' when 'life pivots over from an autocentric to an heterocentric basis' – so much so that literary culture in the 1880s could imagine comic versions of the phenomenon, paving the way for Stephen's temporary conversion in Chapter Four of *A Portrait*.[30] Mr Blinkhorn, one of the teachers in Anstey's *Vice Versa*, makes the assumption that the strange behaviour of the boy he believes to be Dick Bultitude is a product of new-found grace. Blinkhorn is:

> an ardent believer in the Good Boy of a certain order of school tales – the boy who is seized by a sudden conviction of the intrinsic baseness of boyhood, and does all in his power to get rid of the harmful taint; the boy who renounces his old comrades and his natural tastes . . . to don a panoply of priggishness which is too often kick-proof'.[31]

In novels following in the traditions of *Tom Brown* and *Eric: Or, Little by Little* narrative events are heightened by elevated emotions and accompanied by both formal sermons and a generally sermonizing discourse felt everywhere in the storytelling. A *Portrait* emphatically eschews moralizing narrative, but it is centrally structured around the rise and fall rhythm usually associated with the flight and fall of Icarus and connected to the imagined state of the soul. It takes up real sermons – notably Giovanni Pietro Pinamonti's *Hell Opened to Christians, to Caution them from Entering into It* (1688) – and reproduces them with harrowing effects on Stephen Dedalus in the retreat scene of A *Portrait*. This representation of Church indoctrination will seem the most Irish of markers, especially in a school novel. As Joyceans have shown, it can be related to the spread of devotionalism that characterized the history of Catholicism in Ireland in the second half of the nineteenth century.[32] But it also evokes traditions of English evangelism which were once at the centre of public-school reform. For Thomas Arnold, who published no fewer than six volumes of sermons in his lifetime, most of them preached in the chapel at Rugby school, reformed education for social elites meant a shift away from the classical notion of disputatious learning towards romanticism and the education of the emotions. A combination of evangelism and Wordsworth's Preface to *Lyrical Ballads* produces the preaching style appropriated in texts like *Tom Brown* and *Eric: Or, Little by Little*.[33] Here is an example of this kind of overblown sermonizing narrative intervention. It is addressed to 'good spirits' protecting a boy who has 'a sense of sin' weighing on his mind:

> Guard that young boy; and give him grace in this his hour of trial! Open his eyes that he may see the fiery horses and the fiery chariots of the angels who would defend him, and the dark array of spiritual foes who throng around his bed. Point a prying finger to the yawing abyss of shame, ruin, and despair that even now perhaps is being cleft under his feet. Show him the garlands of the present and the past, withering at the touch of the Erinnys in the future. In pity, in pity, show him the canker which he is introducing into the sap of the tree of life, which shall cause its root to be hereafter as bitterness, and its blossom to go up as dust.[34]

Elsewhere the rhetoric is directed at Eric himself by a narrator imagining himself in direct communication with the characters in his narrative. This extract occurs after Eric has heard indecent words in the dormitory spoken from 'a degraded and corrupting mind':

> Now Eric, now or never! Life and death, ruin and salvation, corruption and purity, are perhaps in balance together and the scale of your destiny may hang on a single word of yours. Speak out, boy! Tell these fellows that these unseemly words wound your conscience; tell them that they are ruinous, sinful, damnable; speak out and save yourself and the rest. Virtue is strong and beautiful, Eric, and vice is downcast in her awful presence. Lose your purity of heart, Eric, and you have lost a jewel which the whole world, if it were 'one entire and perfect chrysolite', cannot replace.[35]

Rhetoric manipulated in the later chapters of *A Portrait* derives from the Victorian sensibilities evident in the school novel, sometime transferred to inappropriate contexts, as when Stephen is moved and inspired by the girl wading on the beach:

> Her image had passed into his soul for ever and no word had broken the holy silence of his ecstasy. . . . A wild angel had appeared to him, the angel of mortal youth and beauty, an envoy from the fair courts of life, to throw open before him in an instant of ecstasy the gates of all the ways of error and glory. On and on and on and on!
>
> (*P*, 145)

More conventionally, in Chapter Three Stephen is assailed by shame rising from 'a smitten heart'. The 'image of Emma appeared before him and, under her eyes, the flood of shame rushed forth anew. If she knew to what his mind had subjected her or how his brutelike lust had torn and trampled on her innocence! Was that boyish love? Was that chivalry?' (*P*, 97).

In style, then, as well as structure and countless motifs, Joyce's novel inhabits the model it outdoes, completely and without comic distancing. Narrative events are lifted from the conventions of a genre novel and incorporated into the perimeters of what is a self-consciously formulated art novel. *A Portrait* is genuinely entangled with the once popular school novel to become something of a paradox – a text which both is and yet cannot be a 'true' public-school novel. Its separation, the distinction that distinguishes it from its prototype, has been established by generations of critical tradition. It is partly a product of the open handling of territory where the likes of Edgeworth, Hughes, Farrar, Talbot Baines Reed and all the other countless contributors to the public-school story simply would never have ventured. The shame and fear generated by the 'smugging' incident; Stephen's visit to the prostitute when he is still a schoolboy; the references to masturbation alarmingly caught up with the creative process – these were deep offences to conventional 'boyology'. Reviewing the book in 1917, *The Irish Book Lover* saw *A Portrait* as fascinating and 'unsparing' in its 'realism' but, nevertheless, 'no clean minded person could possibly allow it to remain within reach of his wife, his sons or daughters'.[36] But whatever distinctions one makes, whatever Joyce's transgressions, his novel is framed by familiarity, by sheer everydayness, and one of the things that makes it so is the investment in the formulas of the school novel. In this way *A Portrait* becomes both exemplary and at the same time a studied undoing, an outperformance soaked in the traditions of the public-school story.

An Irish Tom Brown?

Historian Brendan Walsh's 2016 essay, '"Injurious to the best interests of education": Teaching and learning under the intermediate education system 1878–1922', is an historical account of intermediate education in Ireland, but it begins with an intriguing literary reference, making the observation that 'neither Dr Arnold nor Tom Brown has any equivalent in Irish literature'. It is difficult to say from the context whether Walsh regards this as a sign of strength or deficiency – one suspects the latter.[37] Whatever the case, Walsh's statement seems to cry out for reference to Joyce's *A Portrait*. If there is any text that conflates the lines between the high ambition of the classic *bildungsroman* and the cheap formulas of the school novel, this must be it. Historically, there has been no difficulty in reconciling *Stephen Hero* and *A Portrait* to the *bildungsroman* tradition, one as an early incomplete fragment of a great artist, the other a fully fledged modernist exemplification. Indeed, the latter is rarely written about *without* reference to the tradition. By contrast, there has been something close to silence about its relation to the public-school or college novel – the forms are very much distinct now but were not so in the earlier period.[38] Both Joyceans and experts in the popular genre – the latter making only the coyest of references to Joyce's narrative – appear to have conspired to protect Joyce's text from a contamination that it expressly invites.[39] This is why the point has had to be so emphasized here. In quite a fundamental sense, it appears to go against the grain.

On some levels, this oddity is easily explained. It confirms obvious and familiar hierarchical systems of cultural value, and its basis is historical. In the early days of Joyce criticism, when Joyce scholars had to battle for Joyce's place in the canon against considerable resistance, it was imperative to identify his work with prestigious traditions, an identification that Joyce made sure his work collaborated with. Some 40 years on from the high point of a postmodernism that reinvented Joyce studies, however, it is surprising that the critical project has retained this silence over *A Portrait*. After all, there has been no difficulty in assimilating 'popular culture' and kitsch to the later Joyce text. Indeed, both its aesthetic and political status in recent years has rested precisely on the extent to which the Joyce text is said to 'interrogate', 'parody' and 'appropriate' the authority of popular genres and specific texts once taken seriously, especially by the English – although, to be clear, *A Portrait* has none of the usual features that would designate it as parody. Against this background, the invitation to render up

A Portrait as an Irish version of *Tom Brown* would seem impossible to resist, and yet, for the most part, it has been.

How should this refusal be registered? From some perspectives, it creates a space for *A Portrait* to be joined up with a small but significant tradition of Irish versions of the form. Although the genre overwhelmingly was a product of English writers and uniquely associated with English culture, it is quite feasible to construct a history of Irish writing in the genre. Its defining characteristic, however, is its dependency on an English counterpart with which it is either problematically mixed up or entirely complicit.[40] Maria Edgeworth's *The Barring Out* goes further still, becoming a classic model of the English type. It first appeared in *The Parent's Assistant*, a collection of moral tales for parents and their children published in 1796. In it, the civilized regime of Dr Middleton's reforming school is disrupted by the arrival of an aristocratic Archer, fresh from 'a great public school, at which he has acquired a sufficient quantity of Latin and Greek, and a superabundant quantity of party spirit'.[41] The purpose of the narrative is to educate Archer out of an ill-informed and disruptive passion for 'faction' and bring him over to a modern regime characterized by reason and cooperation without crushing his spirit. Far from being postcolonial in any sense, this was an early example of the turn that formulated 'manly piety' as a response to aristocratic dissipation, leading eventually to the classic formulation represented by *Tom Brown* where an 'Arnoldian brotherhood' introduced nothing less than 'a new deity into our mythology and a new ideal into our aspirations'. The transformation of the Headmaster into 'the god and the Public Schoolboy . . . the ideal, of this new creed' was due in no small part to Edgeworth and her school narratives.[42]

Likewise, later Irish school novels, Helen Elrington's *Schoolboy Outlaws* (1904) and Shan Bullock's *The Cubs* (1906) were set in Protestant schools in Ireland and remained firmly in the English tradition. Early Catholic versions of the public-school novel – William Patrick Kelly's *Schoolboys Three* (1895), for example and Canon P.A. Sheehan's *The Triumph of Failure* (1899) were sensitive to the need to imagine the Irish schoolboy as a distinct subject but were written 'through' English models in an imitative way. The earliest of them, Fitzgerald's *School days at Saxonhurst*, was a conventional boyology in almost all respects and, as with Edgeworth, contributed to the development of the form. It represented a strategically enlivened, 'realistic' version of the school narrative, itself imitated later in the century across countless stories published in boys' papers and comics – *The Fifth Form at St Dominic's*, serialized by Talbot Raines Reed in *The Boy's Own Paper* (1879), would be the obvious example. Outside of that, the sole distinction of Fitzgerald's book was the assimilation of the broad principles of convention to the education of Catholic elites.

William O'Brien's *When We Boys* (1890), which Leopold Bloom has on his book shelves in *Ulysses*, was more interesting in this respect, more interruption to the standard school novel than imitation or confirmation, but from some angles an indecisive intervention. Dedicated to fellow nationalist John Dillon 'in memory of anxious years and glorious hopes', it begins conventionally with the hero leaving home for school, but soon mutates into a romance novel and then a Fenian adventure story set around the land wars.[43] To the extent that it 'gives up' on the premises of the school novel, it could be read in postcolonial terms as a response to the challenges of writing a 'robust' school novel in the relative absence of a genuinely empowered Catholic elite.[44]

A Portrait, however, is neither an incapacitated postcolonial school novel, nor, for all the obvious influence, is it beholden to the English tradition. It might *inhabit* the English public-school novel, but it separates itself out, too, distinguishing itself from it at every turn, partly through its uncompromising realism, but primarily by being a much better novel than anything produced in the standard form. In this respect, the refusal of the critical tradition to read the novel as a public-school narrative is not just a strategy of reception but a response to a demand made by the book itself, a book that crashes through borders and checkpoints containing the genre novel in formula to burst into the ranks of the 'genuine' *bildungsroman*.

Whatever we call texts like Goethe's *Wilhelm Meister's Apprenticeship* (1795–6), Stendhal's *The Red and the Black* (1830), Flaubert's *Sentimental Education* (1869) or Musil's modernist novel *The Confusions of Young Torless* (1906) and so on, they are not 'public-school' novels. *A Portrait* writes itself out of the public-school novel into genuinely distinguished company and from this perspective becomes more connected to the textuality of the later Joyce texts than is usually imagined. Reinserting the search for distinction into an aesthetic order of things, *A Portrait* marks a significant move in the nature of Joyce's engagement with education – from the discursive, in which Stephen pronounces on the failures of systemization, into the aesthetic in which the text takes over from the subject as the embodiment of the drive towards meaningful status. Here rank is insidiously achieved through a pervasive and sustained occupation. Just as *Ulysses* takes aesthetic position within the idea of a classical epic of modern Western culture, so *A Portrait* takes aesthetic position within the model of the public-school novel. From this point, the critique of 'education' in *A Portrait* goes well beyond criticism of tedious and repetitive pedagogic styles and archaic curriculum, identified by some Joyce readers as being 'English'. *A Portrait* immeasurably raises the stakes for the school novel. It operates as a challenge to the English genre novel and at the same time undoes the central connections that tied modern schooling together with the idea of civilization and progress. Here a radical fiction joins up seamlessly with the kind of radical education represented by Nietzsche. With its understanding that formal education, then as now, was founded on profoundly ideologically informed versions of the world, *A Portrait* points the way towards the later texts, where the full effect of unstable epistemologies and ontologies and false claims to distinction will be put outrageously on show.

Notes

1 Finn Fordham, 'Biography', in John McCourt (ed.), *James Joyce in Context* (Cambridge: Cambridge University Press, 2009), 17–26 [19].

2 Fordham, 'Biography', 22.
3 See Ciaran O'Neill, 'The Irish Schoolboy Novel', *Eire-Ireland*, 44, 1/2, 2009, 147–68 [151].
4 Isabel Quigly, *The Heirs of Tom Brown: The English School Story* (Oxford: Oxford University Press, 1984), 1.
5 These fictions were exclusively about public schools, but since all schooling at intermediate levels in the nineteenth and early twentieth centuries had to be paid for, some cultural historians have felt that the confusing term 'public school' can be dispensed with. The subtitle to Isabel Quigly, *The Heirs of Tom Brown* is simply 'The English School Story'. Writing in 2008 Jenny Holt entitles her study *Public School Literature, Civic Education and the Politics of Male Adolescence.*
6 *The Heirs of Tom Brown*, 1.
7 *The Heirs of Tom Brown*, 109–25.
8 Kipling, *Stalky and Co.*, 35.
9 Farrar, *Eric: Or, Little by Little*, 192–93, 241.
10 John Neubauer, *The Fin de Siècle Culture of Adolescence* (New Haven and London: Yale University Press, 1993), 10.
11 Quigly, *The Heirs of Tom Brown*, 45.
12 See Bradley, *James Joyce's Schooldays*, 5.
13 Thomas Hughes, *Tom Brown's Schooldays* (1857; London: Thames, 1951), vi.
14 See Jenny Holt, *Public School Literature, Civic Education and the Politics of Male Adolescence* (Farnham: Ashgate, 2008), 51–2. In Joyce's third year at Clongowes, a 16-year-old boy, Peter Stanislaus Little, died of rheumatic fever in the College infirmary and was buried at Clongowes. See Bradley, *James Joyce's Schooldays*, 64.
15 Holt, *Public School Literature*, 35.
16 Fitzgerald, *School Days at Saxonhurst*, 82, 75.
17 *School Days at Saxonhurst*, 146.
18 *School Days at Saxonhurst*, 52, 150, 154.
19 *School Days at Saxonhurst*, 5.
20 G.A. Hutchison, Preface to Talbot Baines Reed, *The Fifth Form at Saint Dominic's: A School Story*, online Gutenberg version at www.gutenberg.org/files/24632/24632-h/24632-h.htm, no bibliographical details, np.
21 Talbot Baines Reed, *The Fifth Form at Saint Dominic's: A School Story* (London: Religious Tract Society, 1887), 43, 61.
22 Hughes, *Tom Brown's Schooldays*, 264.
23 Bradley, *James Joyce's Schooldays*, 29.
24 Farrar, *Eric: Or, Little by Little*, 80–1.
25 Hughes, *Tom Brown's Schooldays*, 112.
26 See F. Anstey, *Vice Versa, or a Lesson to Fathers* (1882; Horses Mouth, 2017), np., chapter XV.
27 Quoted in Holt, *Public School Literature*, 30–1.
28 Kipling, *Stalky and Co.*, 54. Joyce acted in a version of the Aladdin pantomime at Clongowes as part of a group generically identified as 'courtiers, attendants imps etc.' In the photograph published in Bradley's account of Joyce's schooldays, at least 60 per cent of the cast appear to be in drag. See Bradley, *James Joyce's Schooldays*, 54–6.
29 In *Vice Versa*, Mr Bultitude, trapped in the body of his son and packed off to school, fears for his life in the school environment: '"I shall be killed soon if I stay here", he moaned: "I know I shall. These young brigands would murder me cheerfully, if they were not afraid of being caned for it. I'm a miserable man, and I wish I was dead"' (np., chapter x).
30 John Neubauer, *The Fin de Siècle Culture of Adolescence* (New Haven and London: Yale University Press, 1992), 177. G. Stanley Hall's, *Adolescence: Its Psychology and Its Relations to Physiology, Anthropology, Sociology, Sex, Crime, Religion and Education* (London:

Appleton, 1904) was seminal here. It contained a chapter in Volume Two entitled 'The Adolescent Psychology of Conversion', in which conversion was seen as a kind of rebirth, 'natural, normal, universal and necessary'.

31 See Anstey, *Vice Versa*, np., chapter vii.

32 See Gibson, *The Strong Spirit*, 154–82.

33 Arnold owed a particular debt to Wordsworth's text. See Holt, *Public School Literature*, 44.

34 Farrar, *Eric: Or, Little by Little*, 99.

35 *Eric: Or, Little by Little*, 99.

36 Quoted in Morris Beja (ed.), *James Joyce's 'Dubliners' and 'A Portrait of the Artist as a Young Man': A Selection of Critical Essays* (1973; London and Basingstoke: Macmillan, 1982), 21.

37 Walsh, '"Injurious to the Best Interests of Education"', 129.

38 School and university novels now are very distinct. They cater to different age groups, different markets and are written in very different styles. In the nineteenth and early twentieth centuries they were not. The heroism of the 'fourth' and 'fifth' shaded off easily into tales of young manhood, producing one continuous story driven by a single telos of growth and development. Here, the last chapter of the school often pointed to future fantasies of upper-class lives lived out in universities, seminaries and military academies. *Stalky and Co*, for instance, works precisely in this way. For Thomas Hughes, the treatment of College required the writing of a sequel to *Tom Brown's Schooldays*, *Tom Brown at Oxford* (1861), but the principle remained of one continuous narrative stretching out across school and college.

39 O'Neill's, 'The Irish Schoolboy Novel' is a partial exception. It sees *A Portrait* as central but focuses on lesser known examples in the tradition.

40 O'Neill, 'The Irish Schoolboy Novel', 153–9.

41 'Eton Montem' in the same collection is sometimes taken as a school story. Despite the Eton setting, it is not strictly of the genre but, rather, a curious hybrid of newspaper report and play.

42 *Blackwood's*, 1876, quoted in Quigly, *The Heirs of Tom Brown*, 18.

43 William O'Brien, *When We Were Boys* (London: Longman, 1890), dedication page.

44 For an account of this traditional view of the nineteenth-century Irish novel, and criticism of it, see James H. Murphy, *Irish Novelists and the Victorian Age* (Oxford, New York: Oxford University Press, 2011). See also Murphy's essay on O'Brien's novel 'William O'Brien's, *When We Were Boys*: A New Voice from Old Conventions', *Irish University Review*, 22/2, 1992, 298–304.

Chapter 6

Education and the social worlds of *Ulysses*

> – This race and this country and this life produced me, he said. I shall express myself as I am.
>
> James Joyce, *A Portrait of the Artist as a Young Man* (1914)

Whatever its continuities with earlier Joyce texts, *Ulysses* is a new departure. A standard way of viewing that shift might be summarized as follows.

The *Ulysses* reader, even now, submits to a culture where the rules of novel writing appear to be in the process of being rewritten. This does not mean that *Ulysses* feels provisional or unfinished, but it does alter reader expectations about the kind of thing the novel is. 'Character' remains a focal point, but what character might mean is complicated by new ways of representing human beings and their psychologies. At the same time, any centredness in the primacy of the individual subject must compete with a barrage of techniques that insist on the madeness of the novel and on its relations with other writing forms and traditions. 'Plot' becomes arrested in the sense that it is potentially overpowered by 'technic' – the styles which comprise the 'episodes' of this book and which make increasingly challenging departures from standard narrative as the text moves on.[1]

Schooling in *Ulysses* loses the direct representational purchase it has in *A Portrait* and *Stephen Hero*. This is partly dictated by what happens in the book and the kind of book *Ulysses* is. Whatever else, it is not a school novel or a college novel. Its ambitions have shifted. It takes place to a significant extent on the street and, in moving from Stephen to Leopold Bloom, establishes a shift from childhood and adolescence to something closer to maturity, middle age and adult.

This does not mean, however, that education vanishes from the novel. On the contrary, Stephen's continued presence in the book and his association with teaching and student life in Dublin means that the social logic of education and its relation to both subject and state formation remains central to the fictional configuration of reality. As if to register the continuing importance of education as a domain in which *Ulysses* operates, its second episode, 'Nestor', revisits the schooling process in familiar representational ways confirming the critique of formal schooling in the early texts and repositioning it in terms of the *Ulysses* agenda. The former student has become teacher, and, interestingly, the Catholic school is displaced by a Protestant one. A slightly older and perhaps wiser Stephen Dedalus is specifically 'not a hero' now (*U*1, 62). He has lost much of his radical energy, a standard dynamic in the representation of adolescence and especially characteristic of this period where adolescence has sometimes been seen as a social construction, 'a middle-class social formation in industrial societies generated by the expansion of secondary education'.[2] In his account of the representation of adolescence at the *fin de siècle*, John Neubauer notes how the 'canonised view' of adolescents as rebels and revolutionaries almost always involved a psychological and social 'hollowing out' of the 'heroic and emancipatory posture', characterized by the emergence of 'fits of self-doubt' and 'the sudden sprouting of organisations (whether founded by adults or initiated by youth itself) that forced the individual back into bonds'.[3]

The first is evidently true of Stephen Dedalus in *Ulysses* and the second an immanence always threatened. The representation of social elites remains an important focus played out in episodes like 'Aeolus', 'Scylla and Charybdis' and 'Oxen of the Sun' and connected to issues of social, cultural and political status. The fractious but contingent relation between Buck Mulligan and Stephen Dedalus embodies those issues in especially sharp ways. It may not be immediately obvious how the opening chapter of *Ulysses*, with its strange atmosphere of betrayal and usurpation, ties into the world of elite education in Dublin at the turn of the twentieth century, but it surely does. One way of seeing how is to consider its curious relation with a book written some 15 years after the full publication of Joyce's great novel by the model for the 'Usurper' of 'Telemachus', Oliver St John Gogarty (*U*1, 74). That textual relation is one that illustrates how the Stephen/Mulligan dynamic, so central in *Ulysses*, is, whatever else, fundamentally 'social' and intimately connected to schooled cultures.

'Telemachus' and *As I Was Going Down Sackville Street* (1937)

Just over halfway through Chapter One of *When I Was Going Down Sackville Street*, there is a moment when the narrator – Gogarty himself – is accused by his friend, the poet Austin Clarke, of being irreverent. The same accusation is made several times in *Ulysses*. Gogarty pulls up short and retaliates with the assertion that Clarke himself is too pious and insists that his own 'amplitude' is entirely consistent with how the Catholic Church is in the real world. People of the Republic, 'who never went to Rome' and yet talk of 'irreverence in Ireland', infuriate Gogarty – Gogarty had been in 1925, as a Free State representative no less, and had met the Pope. These insular bumpkins, he says, cannot live their religion without 'excommunicating' a clergy of whom they have wildly unrealistic expectations. 'They are all suffering', according to Gogarty, 'from a feeling of inferiority to Protestantism yet'. By 'yet' he means not just any period of long duration but 'in spite of' all the relatively immediate upheaval of the battle for national independence – rebellion, civil war and the creation of the new South. 'They deny themselves joy in religion, and they conduct themselves as if their clergy were a lot of old maids or parsons' wives. They forget that the Devil is the Spirit who denies'.[4]

The moment is classic Gogarty, and classic Buck Mulligan too. The grab for modernity, the Nietzschean gesture, the allusion to high literature – Goethe's *Dr Faustus* in this illustration – the cosmopolitan superiority which so separates Gogarty out, distinguishing him not least from what he sees as plebeian Gaelicism, the 'epidemic of the disinterred' that he mocked as a 'Celtic chloroform' capable of 'freezing 'the Sapphic current of his soul' – this is all very close to Buck Mulligan in *Ulysses* and his ambition to 'Hellenise' Ireland.[5] The postcolonial framing is clear. Writing from the new nation-state that he is now representing as an Irish senator, Gogarty sets out to position himself outside the characteristic psychodrama still being worked through by the miserably colonized, the 'gratefully oppressed' of Joyce's early short story 'After the Race' (*D*, 44). This set of morbid insecurities Gogarty will have none of. In real life he registers himself, and was so registered in memoir after memoir, as a supremely confident 'Renaissance man', itself a socially inscribed construct that turns human inquisitiveness into a special order of superior intelligence. Recognized as a poet – Yeats thought him 'one of the best lyric poets of the age' – as well as a dramatist, champion athlete and swimmer, aviator, surgeon, political figure, social reformer, well-known man about town and *bon viveur*, Gogarty places himself within a specific cultural tradition that had a special connection with the aristocratic imaginary and the medical profession and its nineteenth-century history in Ireland.[6] In himself he sees a continuation of a Trinity medical elite that bought modern science and scholarly humanism to Dublin in the wake of the post-Union departure of the political class much earlier in the nineteenth century. He has the authority to speak both for and with this culture, or so he believes. In all these respects Gogarty is a classic example of the fantasies of elite schooling in its early-twentieth-century Catholic formation in Ireland, which is why is he is so important to Joyce and so close to him.

There are complexities and contradictions to Gogarty's compulsive urge to dazzle. For all the distance he puts between himself and stereotypes of the Irish, the brilliant, witty sophisticated Irish buck is itself a stereotype. It is a postcolonial performance that cannot help but be complicit with a string of colonial discourses. At the same time Gogarty's absurd notion of a return to a 'Corinthian' age of sparkle, wit and glamour is quite at odds with the country in which he takes such a leading role in the 1920s and 1930s. However modern he claims to be, and reformist, what he advocates for is nothing short of a restoration, albeit one in which what was a once traditional landed Anglo-Irish elite is replaced, or at least partnered, with a new Catholic one. The very title of his book is an announcement of this cultural, and social, agenda. It not only preserves Sackville Street in its colonial form – the street was originally named after the Earl of Dorset, who once owned it – but also represents a challenge to the authority of the Free State which renamed it O'Connell Street, after the Liberator, a full 13 years before Gogarty's book was published. This is an outrageous, even dangerous, gesture. It is also a reactionary one from many, perhaps most, Irish perspectives, one which could explain what Stephen/Joyce means when he insists on describing Gogarty/Mulligan as a 'gay betrayer' (see *U*1, 405). For all the similarities in their background – both Catholic, both ex-Clongowes, both one-time University College students – in Joyce's book, Gogarty/Mulligan is imagined as complicit with the State in ways that Joyce/Stephen is not.

Gogarty's book shares with *Ulysses* the appetite for style and erudition, a performance imagined by Gogarty himself as a warm, generous tribute to classical humanism. The sentiment is considerably spiced up by the author's awareness of his own mediated performance as 'Buck Mulligan' in a book that had already established a serious following among European and American intelligentsias. His own book might seek largeness of spirit, but Gogarty's text is compelled to reply and compete. It situates itself in the precarious position of offering a riposte, a proper corrective, to Joyce and *his* outrageously ambitious novel. The first chapter especially illustrates the point by redrawing the Dublin territory of *Ulysses*. It follows the route of 'Endymion', also known as James Boyle Tisdell Burke Stewart Fitzsimons Farrell, the real-life eccentric who also features in *Ulysses*, to the National Library. Here librarian Thomas William Lyster holds forth, just as he does at the beginning of the 'Scylla and Charybdis' episode in *Ulysses*, only more so and in a rendition much more sympathetic than Joyce's. Repositioning himself in a postcolonial text 'mirroring' another postcolonial text, Gogarty sets out to remap the territory that Joyce had already made his own. There are references to revivalist writers George Moore and John Eglinton, to Church heresies and to the cattle trade and its licensing, all of which curiously place and date the text – not to the Republic but much closer to the belle époque convened in *Ulysses* and which is now forever Dublin by virtue of Joyce's extraordinary intervention. It is not coincidental that Gogarty's book begins with an epigram from Homer's *The Odyssey*, given in Greek. In its vain attempt to put Joyce's Romanized mock epic in its upstart place, the opening chapter makes such demands that Francis Hackett in his introduction to the book signals initial alarm. He wonders if this piece of writing is really going to be 'another *Ulysses*. I rather trembled'.[7] Reviewing for *The New York Times*, Horace Reynolds saw it as 'an extraordinary book' written by 'an extraordinary Irishman' and predicted that it would take its 'rightful place in the distinguished company of Moore's trilogy, Yeats's Autobiographies' and, in a telling phrase, 'James Joyce's Odyssey of an Irish intellect'.[8] Reynolds was wrong, of course, on a number of counts.

There can be little doubt that *As I Was Walking Down Sackville Street* writes back to *Ulysses* but, strangely enough, there are senses in which Joyce's book writes forward to Gogarty's too. The competitive, disputatious nature of the relationship between these two texts strikes the same keynote evident in *Ulysses*, in which Stephen and Mulligan, two members of a new and highly educated Catholic elite, jostle for position. They are wary of each other – Stephen thinks that Mulligan 'fears the lancet of my art as I fear that of his' (*U*1, 152–3). They compete for authority over Ireland, signified in part by the dispute over who holds the key to the round tower, but also by the old milkwoman, who defers to Mulligan's status as a medical man – 'her bonesetter' – while, as Stephen pointedly observes, 'me she slights' (*U*1, 419). Mulligan is cajoling, praising Stephen for the 'spirit' he possesses and at the same time mocking his name and his appearance which he offers to improve by making condescending offers of second-hand clothes (see *U*1, 151). Stephen is, for Mulligan, a laughably unfitting bard, but one to be watched and seemingly supported, up to a point. It is not often remarked how much Stephen replies in kind, knowing Mulligan to be untrustworthy and yet keeping him close, lending him money, doing his bidding. They are, for all the mutual suspicion, a duo, a double act, routinely striving to outdo each other in all sorts of ways but especially in intellectual, cultural terms. Here, Mulligan, shows Stephen his own face in a mirror, producing an exchange of Wilde quotes, the first from the preface to *The Picture of Dorian Gray* (1890), the second a more interesting working of a lesser-known phrase from 'The Decay of Lying' (1891). Stephen not only recognizes Mulligan's allusion, he bests it:

> Laughing again, he brought the mirror away from Stephen's peering eyes.
> —The rage of Caliban at not seeing his face in a mirror, he said. If Wilde were only alive to see you!
> Drawing back and pointing, Stephen said with bitterness:
> —It is a symbol of Irish art. The cracked looking glass of a servant.
> Buck Mulligan suddenly linked his arm in Stephen's and walked with him round the tower. . . .
> —It's not fair to tease you like that, Kinch, is it? he said kindly. God knows you have more spirit than any of them.
>
> (*U*1, 141–51)

In the following extract, the two men put on a more unified demonstration, not precisely in competition with each other but for the benefit of the Englishman, Haines, who they are trying to impress and shock – this in a cultural climate where revivalism and mysticism both have particular currency:

> —Can you recall, brother, is mother Grogan's tea and water pot spoken of in the Mabinogion, or is it in the Upanishads?
> —I doubt it, said Stephen gravely.
> —Do you now? Buck Mulligan said in the same tone. Your reasons, pray?
> —I fancy, Stephen said as he ate, it did not exist in or out of the Mabinogion. Mother Grogan was, one imagines, a kinswoman of Mary Ann.
> Buck Mulligan's face smiled with delight.
> —Charming! he said in a finical sweet voice, showing his white teeth and blinking his eyes pleasantly. Do you think she was? Quite charming!
>
> (*U*1, 370–79)

The same pattern is repeated in 'Oxen of the Sun', with a particular focus on Dublin's Theosophy crowd:

> Warily, Malachi whispered, preserve a druid silence. His soul is far away. It is as painful perhaps to be awakened from a vision as to be born. Any object, intensely regarded, maybe a gate of access to the incorruptible eon of the gods. Do you not think it, Stephen? Theosophos told me so, Stephen answered, whom in a previous existence Egyptian priests initiated into the mysteries of karmic law. The lords of the moon, Theosophos told me, an orangefiery shipload from planet Alpha of the lunar chain would not assume the etheric doubles and these were therefore incarcerated by the rubycoloured egos from the second constellation.
>
> (*U*14, 1165–73)

Here, as in Gogarty's *As I Walking Down Sackville Street*, social interaction is a complex and ornate performance laid on by a polished, sophisticated Irish elite, fundamentally shaped by schooled knowledge and school cultures of precise historical dimensions. The world of *Ulysses* is a post-Parnell, pre-Republic world in which Irish cultural elites are 'becoming important, it seems' (*U*9, 312–13). The essential distinction to be made, however, is that the performance that appears in Gogarty as a signifier of real intelligence and cultural authority in Joyce has a very different registration as social formation, itself the product of colonial histories that Gogarty thinks himself somehow above and beyond. From this position, *Ulysses* develops the critique of elite education started in the early fiction, incorporating it into an increasingly complex aesthetic. *Ulysses* becomes a forensic analysis of the outcomes of elite education, not so much a 'thick description' as a thick enactment which both Stephen and Mulligan are positioned firmly within rather than outside of. It is also a decisive unravelling of the Hellenizing renaissance Mulligan/Gogarty imagines for Ireland and only half-jokingly takes himself to somehow embody. In these respects, *Ulysses* is a continuation of *Dubliners*, *Stephen Hero* and *A Portrait* and shaped by elite education. Here schooling comes alive in the representation of Stephen's interior monologues and the group scenes in such episodes as 'Aeolus', 'Scylla and Charybdis' and 'Oxen of the Sun', in which Stephen is positioned as attempting to work though encounters with other members of both Catholic and Protestant elites. They help define him as an intellectual and as an artist. They also configure the sense in which *Ulysses* becomes an embodiment of, as Marilyn French put it back in the early 1970s, 'the book as world'.[9]

'On his wise shoulders' – Deasy and the doctors

'Nestor', the second chapter of *Ulysses*, is a realistic portrayal of a lesson followed by an interview between headmaster and teacher. Like *A Portrait* and *Stephen Hero*, it draws directly on personal experience from the past. In March or early April 1904, Joyce took the part-time post of usher, or assistant master, in a private preparatory school in Dalkey. It was called Clifton House, and the owner and headmaster was Francis Irwin, a Protestant and graduate of Trinity College. Clifton was one of many schools operating largely outside of formal state regulation. Teachers working in such institutions would have had no structured salary scales, no contracts of employment or pension rights and no facilities for training. There is little in the archive about this man and his particular school – all we know for sure is that the house had once been the home of poet and translator Denis Florence McCarthy, a figure alluded to both in *Ulysses* – Bloom has one of his books of poetry in his library – and *Finnegans Wake*, where he figures as 'Dinny Fineen, me canty' (FW, 231.6). But it is likely that the prototype of Deasy's school would have been one of those many establishments – 'academic, commercial and classical schools' – that were operated by lay people as private businesses. In this unsupervised context, teaching would have been 'an amateur and unattractive occupation' for 'clerics, ex-clerics or layman from various backgrounds. No regulations existed requiring teaching qualifications, no formal training was available or demanded of teachers, no inspection system operated'.[10]

For all the unregulated nature of these schools, they nevertheless would have had to fashion themselves in acknowledgment of contemporary market conditions if they wanted to survive, which would have meant being 'geared to the examinations which proliferated in the second half of the nineteenth century'.[11] This explains why in 'Nestor', alongside the immediate exchanges of the classroom, the structures of education in late-nineteenth- and early-twentieth-century Ireland are again on show – the systematic correlation between education, gender and class, for example. The boys Stephen Dedalus teaches are socially homogeneous – the sons of 'Welloff people, proud that their eldest son was in the navy. Vico road, Dalkey' (*U*2, 24–5). The denominational basis of Irish education is implied in the names of his students – Armstrong, Comyn, Talbot and Sargent. The curriculum pays excessive attention to classical culture. The chapter begins with Stephen asking pointless questions about Pyrrhus and the Pyrrhic War. It is also Anglicized. For no apparent reason, Stephen's lesson switches midway from classical history to literature, and students are asked to read from Milton's 'Lycidas', a one-time standard of school poetry compilations. As the scene with the headmaster makes clear, the transaction between Stephen and the school is materialistic above all, a cash exchange in which Stephen receives three sovereigns, two crowns and two shillings in payment for his services and is treated to such proverbial wise words as ' – the proudest word you will ever hear from an Englishman's mouth' is '*I paid my way*' (*U*2, 242–3; 251). 'Nestor' is emphatic in this respect. It insists that teaching and learning is first and foremost an economic relationship. The first order of business between Stephen and Deasy is 'our little financial settlement'. Coins, 'a tray of Stuart coins, base treasure of a bog' and other forms of wealth and currency – 12 silver spoons in a case, 'the twelve apostles having preached to all the gentiles', and a collection of shells, a currency in some cultures and thus 'dead treasure' – decorate the headmaster's study. It is not difficult to see why for some readers these 'symbols too of beauty and power. . . . soiled by greed and misery', tie the representation of education in 'Nestor' into critical theory and a much wider argument with the modern world (*U*2, 207; 203–5; 215; 227–8).[12] Certainly, the representational image of education is unremittingly depressing, apart from one half-redeeming moment where a vulnerable student, Sargent, reports to Stephen after class, as he has been told to do by Deasy, to show him some 'sums' copied down off the board, presumably as some sort of punishment. Stephen asks the boy if he can now do the calculations himself. He cannot. Stephen shows him the working out, and Sargent follows his routine. The scene is framed in terms of a weak boy who is nonetheless loved by his mother, which reminds Stephen of his own mother who has recently died – 'Was that then real? The only true thing in life' (*U*2, 143). As the critical tradition on this exchange insists, something, however small, seems to have been achieved. Outside of that, Stephen is a cog in a wheel and his lesson a waste of time. A fragmented mess in terms of content, in style it is characterized by meaningless tests of memory, a poor joke which his pupils fail to get and an incomprehensible riddle. As Dedalus knows too well, this is a class on the edge of chaos: 'In a moment they will laugh more loudly, aware of my lack of rule and of the fees their papas pay' (*U*2, 28–9). It seems right for Deasy to intuit that Dedalus will 'not remain here very long at this work', although his explanation – 'You were not born to be a teacher, I think' – is no more than cliché (*U*2, 401–2). It gets nowhere in relation to the true problematics of education as Stephen faces them in this novel.

Deasy is key to this representation of institutional schooling in action. He has literary dimensions in that he is partly drawn in relation to the myth correspondences that run throughout *Ulysses*. In Homeric terms, 'Dominie' Deasy, the Ulsterman headmaster of this school, is Nestor – the first person Telemachus visits in his attempt to trace his father Odysseus.[13] A one-time warrior, in his rousing response to the 'abduction' of Helen of Troy, Deasy's prototype had once 'preached a jehad', summoning up 'each Greek hero . . . to take up arms and join in avenging the national disgrace' – a view of the world Deasy takes up when, as well as blaming Helen for the Trojan Wars, he brings to account Eve for bringing sin to the world, MacMurrough's wife for the first invasion of Ireland and Kitty O'Shea for Parnell's fall (see *U*2, 389–95).[14] Nestor was the wise advisor to the Achaeans, long-winded but worth listening to and known specifically for his intelligence. Like Deasy again, who persuades Stephen to place in the press a letter he has written about a cure for foot-and-mouth disease, Nestor was also a friend to cattle. In the *Iliad* he tells stories about how he once rescued cattle stolen by the Epeians and led them back to their rightful owners in Pylos.[15] By the time Telemachus gets to him, however, Nestor is old, long-winded and living on past glories. Deasy, likewise, assumes the right of wisdom and experience, but is now pompous, rambling and repetitive.

There are other models behind Joyce's formulation of Deasy, however, these much closer in time and culture to *Ulysses* and specifically related to the education world in which Deasy is positioned – the headmaster as represented in school magazines, reminiscences, school celebrations of anniversaries and, again, public-school novels of the day. At various times, headmasters have figured in literature as comic figures struggling to maintain order in their schools. But the standard registration in the late nineteenth and early twentieth centuries would have been very different. In Owen Dudley Edward's account 'Belvedere in history', republished in *Portraits – Belvedere College, 1932–1982*, the reforming rector of Belvedere, Rev. T.J. Finlay S.J., was elevated as 'one of the most extraordinary men of a truly extraordinary Irish Renaissance – yet today he is in danger of oblivion. As educator, writer, administrator, economist, politician, agriculturist and Heaven knows how much more, he was pre-eminently the Renaissance man of the Irish Renaissance'. Here Finlay is located within a potentially radical social mission. Deeply aware of the 'priorities' facing 'the New Ireland', he 'intended to train its ruling class' and was 'concerned with turning out people for jobs that would have to be eased away from the grasp of the Protestant elite which once monopolised preferential positions'.[16] Similarly heroizing accounts can be found for such figures as Rev. John Conmee S.J. (1847–1910), who was prefect of studies and then rector of Clongowes between 1881 and 1891, and prefect of studies at University College, Dublin, afterwards dean. However Stephen remembers him, *Ulysses* laughs at this figure in the 'Wandering Rocks' episode, in which Conmee figures as the sycophantic writer of a nostalgic elegy to the aristocracy entitled *Old Times in the Barony*.[17] Likewise for Rev. William Delaney S.J. (1835–1924), the modernizer of Tullabeg who established the Catholic Headmasters' Association (1878) and was President of University College, Dublin, from 1883 to 1888 when Thomas Arnold, the younger, was on the staff.

It was Thomas's father, of course, who was the most celebrated Victorian pedagogue, perhaps the single most influential model for the headmaster role as it emerged in nineteenth-century Britain. His idealized image figures at the heart of *Tom Brown's Schooldays* as the doctor/headmaster of Rugby school, 'the only little corner of the British Empire which is thoroughly, wisely, and strongly ruled just now. I'm more and more thankful every day of my life that I came here to be under him'.[18] There were others who made significant impacts in England – John Percival at Clifton College, Bristol, for example; Frances Mary Buss at Cheltenham and, later in the nineteenth century when headmasters were having to manage increasing government intervention, Arthur Gilkes at Dulwich. George Cotton was the reformer at Marlborough, Edward Thring at Uppingham, Charles Vaughan at Harrow, later forced to leave after a sexual abuse scandal. But it was Arnold, attributed with creating the professional status of the headmaster role virtually single-handed, who towered in this field of representation. In real life his status has been contested, both in terms of the nature and extent of his genuine influence on the public-school system and in relation to his relationship with traditions of Victorian gender identity, Kingsley's 'muscular Christianity'.[19] In fiction, however, his place was certain and unambiguous. He figures in *Tom Brown Schooldays* (1857) as nearly omniscient. His knowledge of his school and calm supervision of it extends to every corner. He is beyond self-interest and unstinting in the care he bestows on his charges, whom he educates in an ethical, moral and, above all, Christian code. All these qualities were transferred to other headmasters in fictional versions of the public school, who likewise became not just personifications of the gentlemanly ideal and rational intervention but also figures of near superhuman powers of wisdom. Dr Rowland in Farrar's *Eric: Or, Little by Little* is 'a kindly-looking gentlemanly man and when he turned to address Eric, after a few minutes' conversation with his father, the boy felt instantly reassured by the pleasant sincerity and frank courtesy of his manner'. For the boys, 'the Doctor was to all their imaginations as a regular *Deus ex machina*'.[20] As the century wore on and the fashion for more conventionally masculinist identities grew, headmasters were also invested with great courage. The headmaster in Kipling's *Stalky and Co* sucks infection through a tube from a choking boy suffering from diphtheria and 'about to croak'. According to Stalky and his pals, this puts him among the heroes of boys' own adventures. The Head 'ought to get a V.C.', he declares. '"I've read o' somethin' like that in a book," said Beetle. "Gummy, what a chap! Just think of it!"'[21]

Only the reference to Milton relates the 'Nestor' episode specifically to anything approaching these traditions – Milton has a strong connection with education. Between 1639 and 1648, before the headmaster role formally existed, he was a schoolmaster and education consultant who set up his own small schools in London, one at Aldersgate which later moved to the Barbican. He wrote about education, most famously in the 'Tractate on Education' (1644) which begins in an orthodox way by claiming the first purpose of education to be 'learning to repair the ruins of our first parents by regaining to know God aright', but goes on to attack the Cambridge curriculum – based on the seven liberal arts and their divisions in the trivium and quadrivium – and methods of language teaching characterized by an overreliance on memory and repetition at the expense of praxis. In 1649, he was appointed Latin Secretary of State in the Cromwell government and went on to write a number of textbooks and histories – *Accedence Commenced Grammar* (1669), *Art of Logic* (1672), *History of Britain* (1670) and *A Brief History of Muscovy* (1682). But notwithstanding the relative absence of specific reference, it is against the later genre orthodoxy that the force of Joyce's intervention, indeed the sense in which it *is* an intervention, becomes clear.[22] Deasy's ignorance about the narratives current in his own school here take on new dimensions. He has to find out from Stephen why the boys are making a fuss – because the two best players of hockey, Cochrane and Halliday, have been placed in the same side (*U*2, 190). Any claims to Arnold-like omniscience are ousted by his ignorance on further counts. Indeed, his defining characteristic is his almost total fallibility. Stephen half-reminds him that Iago's words in *Othello* are not Shakespeare's. He wrongly attributes the phrase about the sun never setting on the British Empire to 'a French Celt'(*U*2, 249) and is also wrong about his ancestor Sir John Blackwood voting 'for the union' (*U*2, 279). He is technically correct that the orange lodges did in the very early days agitate for 'repeal of the union' (*U*2, 270), but the implication that this somehow produces an alignment between Irish nationalism and unionism in the early twentieth century is absurd, and he is, again, just wrong in his assertion that Stephen is a Fenian (see *U*2,272). It was Devorghil, the wife of Tiernan O' Rourke, 'prince of Breffini' who in 1152 deserted her husband for Dermot MacMurrough, King of Leinster, not MacMurrough's wife, who deserted him for her leman O'Rourke, as Deasy maintains (see *U*2, 390–4). His belief that 'all human history moves towards one great goal, the manifestation of God' (*U*2, 380–1) might align him with Arnold, but his obsession with his own status in the world and irritation with the pupils who get in his way runs counter to it. His status as right-wing ideologue mired in anti-Semitism and anti-feminism likewise puts him at a long distance from the traditional associations made between rational liberalism and fair play and the educational leaders of the traditional public-school novel. For Joyce critic Trevor Williams, Deasy is 'steeped in ideology and bears a professional responsibility for reproducing it'.[23] He is also a comic Ulsterman, mocked and completely outshone by Stephen.

If there is any episode in *Ulysses* that could be said to be neglected by criticism, 'Nestor' would be it. It has none of the stylistic fireworks of later chapters, and it also seems relatively underpowered in relation to the chapters closest to it – 'Telemachus', which has attracted considerable critical attention as the book's beginning, and 'Proteus', an almost completely unmediated display of the interior monologue that once helped to stamp this book as something radically new. For the purpose of this account, however, 'Nestor' takes on a particular significance. It positions education centrally in relation to Stephen's flight, not because he is tempted by the 'riches' offered by Deasy and the teaching profession, as some have claimed – on the contrary – but because this chapter reaffirms how much education is implicated in the 'nets' of family, state and church that he is determined to escape.[24] It is part of a conservative modern, a religious and secular authority that Stephen resists and protests against, which is he why he constructs formal education in such politicized ways. At the same time, it has played into the formation of his own social consciousness. It has shaped his disposition towards hierarchical order and distinction and apparently condemned him to an endless performance of his intellectual credentials, which is also evident in this chapter and well beyond into the furthest reaches of *Ulysses*.

'Is it French you are talking, sir?' – *Ulysses* and schooled discourse

Joyceans have realized for a long time that there is a connection between schooling and the social worlds constructed in Joyce's fiction. One focus has been on the formation of social consciousness in Stephen Dedalus, another on the reproduction of failures of knowledge in the Joyce text, where characters devoted to the social order maintained by modern schooling consistently fail to retrieve meaningful information from the worlds around them. The scramble to articulate accurate versions of late-nineteenth-century Church history rendered up by the Dublin burghers in the short story 'Grace' is symptomatic in this respect. In a 2011 essay entitled 'Error and Education in *Ulysses*', Matthew Creasy notes the satirical element in the story and tries to frame both the ignorance and pretension of characters like Mr Cunningham, Mr Power, Mr Kernan and McCoy in the slow rate of educational development in colonial Ireland which is attributed to English educational policy. One difficulty is that there is no such gravitas in the Joyce text which, however contextualized, makes no concession to that history and no attempt to stop itself from laughing at the gaffes of an aspiring bourgeoisie. Another is that rates of growth in education provision across social classes were slow in England itself and throughout Europe.

The further difficulty with such a reading is that it skews the social criticism of Joyce's writing in relation to education. Joyce's version of education as social practice is not contained by the social borders circumscribing the undereducated, bourgeois Dubliner. On the contrary, the main focus of *Ulysses* in this respect extends deep into the circles of what from most perspectives would be taken to be well-educated elites, where Joyce himself was positioned at one time – modern elites, as opposed to traditional elects, socially framed, historically determined and characterized by multiplicity. In Joyce, elites of law, education, religion, medicine, journalism and the arts predominate, a reflection of the colonial world in which *Ulysses* operates. There are few genuine political elites represented in any version of Joyce's Dublin, nor any industrial elites or traditional ones based on land ownership. Here the schooled mind in all its dimensions – its wit and its ambition but also its pretension, divisiveness, and ambiguous and contradictory relations to State and Church – becomes an important domain. It is registered not by the comic detail of Leopold Bloom failing to remember whether black refracts or reflects heat or misremembering lines of poetry, but, more fundamentally, through the highly schooled discourses of social elites which become performances embodying the competitive world of elite education and the frustration of its will to exercise genuine authority. The representation of this social world is a *tour de force* in *Ulysses*, a significant element in the ornate performance that this book is required to enact. 'Are you condemned to do this?', Stephen asks himself in the middle of the 'Shakespeare theory' he delivers in the 'Scylla and Charybdis' episode of *Ulysses*, and the same could be asked of the book he is in (*U*9, 849).

As we have seen, the opening chapter of *Ulysses* sets the keynote with the powerful sense of competition that dominates every aspect of Stephen's relationship to Buck Mulligan. Gogarty, the model for this figure, at one time had been quite close to Joyce. Their schooling, while far from identical – Gogarty's family was much wealthier than Joyce's at this stage – was comparable. Gogarty went to Stonyhurst in England, which he hated, but then to Clongowes, where he thrived, excelling at sports and becoming extremely popular – the most popular boy in the school, according to his biographer. He started his medical degree at the Medical School of University College Joyce's college, a rising school at the end of the nineteenth century and growing in reputation, but after failing eight out of ten examination papers, Gogarty transferred to Trinity. He also spent some time at Oxford, where 'the rumour of the entertaining Irishman quickly spread'.[25] Joyce stayed the course at University College and similarly spent a short time overseas in pursuit of further education; in his case in Paris, where the intention at least was to take a medical training. For just over a year, Joyce and Gogarty were friends, with Joyce tagging on to a pre-existing group of medical students, forming an association of young men with similarly privileged education histories. Bright futures would have been expected of them, the brightest possible for Irish young men at the turn of the nineteenth century. Ulick O'Connor, Gogarty's biographer, establishes how much the coherence of the group was dependent on language codes and forms of knowledge they all shared and through which they competed. Gogarty, naturally, is positioned at the centre of the group. His friends, O'Connor writes,

> had alert minds and an abundance of wit. An allusion or pun among them was caught at once, and rewarded with a swift glance of acknowledgement before another capped it. Their language, laced with medical or classical argot, was often incomprehensible to outsiders, and their double entendres and allusions were too swift for less rapid minds to follow. Vincent Cosgrave, John Elwood and Simon Broderick, with James Joyce tacked on as a 'medical student's pal', were his chief companions about this time.[26]

'Joyce and education' is configured not least though the reproduction of this social world in *Ulysses*. Over and over in Joyce's book, the insiderly exchanges that O'Connor admires so much implicate the education system that produced them, one reason why almost every chapter in which Stephen has a significant presence returns to Clongowes, the original training ground. In 'Scylla and Charybdis' he sees himself again as a child 'saved from pandies' by the College rector (*U*9, 211) and returns to the routines of language learning and the schoolboy play that renders schooled language education in terms of the naughty vulgar. Stephen's '*Mingo, minxi, mictum, mingere*' in this episode (*U*9,762) is a cod conjugation involving a Latin verb meaning 'to urinate' and a noun denoting heavy menstrual bleeding. In 'Oxen of the Sun', Frank Costello reminds Stephen of the time they shared at Clongowes, and fellow students are elevated by textual intervention to prominent figures in classical Athenian culture, as if Dublin really had fulfilled Mulligan's fantasy and become 'Hellenised': 'He asked about Glaucon, Alcibiades, Pisistratus. Where were they now? Neither knew' (*U*14, 1111–12). And so on. The 'schoolmen' of classical philosophy, as Stephen points outs in 'Scylla and Charybdis', really were 'schoolboys first' (*U*9, 56). *Ulysses* insists on that. Echoes of privileged schooling are everywhere, not least in the classical framing that, Joyce maintains, supports *Ulysses*. Its pedagogic cultures are inscribed in cod Latin and the countless allusions to an education in the classics. This is true of relatively early chapters, like 'Scylla and Charybdis', which begins with George Russell dismissing the kind of biographical criticism that Stephen seems to be promoting as 'the speculation of schoolboys for schoolboys' and

Eglinton imagining Aristotle as Plato's 'model schoolboy with his diploma under his arm' (*U*9, 55–8), and of the later ones too.

'Oxen of the Sun' is built around the carousing of a group of medical students in a maternity hospital, where a woman is attempting to give birth amidst a good deal of noisy disruption. The 'subject matter' of 'Oxen' is determined largely by the conversation it is made up of, what Hugh Kenner called 'student talk'.[27] In fact, 'Oxen' is the most elaborate performance of schooled identities in all of *Ulysses*. Although the episode is physically located in a maternity hospital, it operates mostly in a social domain of schooled cultures, which is why it includes so many allusions to texts which we know Joyce studied at school. These reappear as a kind of baroque ornamentation decorating loud and often crude, masculinist comic banter. Ovid's *Metamorphosis*, for example, selections from which Joyce studied for the Middle Grade at Belvedere, is drawn upon by 'an outlandish delegate' (*U*14, 991) to support the view that certain human deformities are the result of women copulating with animals and Lenehan's story about a sexual encounter and a close shave with Father Conmee is dressed up with several allusions to Horace's *Odes*, a selection of which Joyce studied at the Senior Grade and admired enough to translate.[28] Horace also figures much later in the episode when the group depart the hospital for the pub. The call for more drinking, 'Per deam Partulam et Pertundam nunc est bibendum!' ('By the goddess Partula and Pertunda, now we must drink!'), includes the opening words of Horace's Ode xxxvii, which begins 'now we must drink' (*U*14,1439).

The signs of a classical education are everywhere in the episode. Its expression, again, contributes both to the notorious difficulty of 'Oxen' and the self-conscious awareness that only an elite will be able to read certain elements of it, a reality that Mulligan jokingly, but with a telling social edge, pretends to mitigate. When he defends his schoolboy fantasy for 'a national fertilising farm to be named *Omphalos*' and expresses his willingness to 'offer his dutiful yeoman services for the fecundation of any female of what grade of life soever', he offers first, for Stephen and the medicos, a 'tasteful support of his contention' in Ciceronian style and cod Latin: '*Talis ac tanta depravatio hujus seculi, O quirites, ut matresfamiliarum nostrae lascivas cujuslibet semiviri libici titillationnes testibus ponderosis atque excelsis erectionibus centurionum Romanorum magnopere anteponunt*' (*U*14, 684–6; 707–10) – which translates as 'such and so great is the depravity of our age, O citizens, that our women greatly prefer the lascivious titillations of half men to the ponderous testes and the grand erection of the Roman centurion'. Weldon Thornton suggests that there is an allusion here to the idea that Christ was fathered by a Roman centurion.[29] For 'those of ruder wit', like Bloom, Mulligan draws on the traditional distinction between the intellectual mind and the corporeal body driving 'home his point by analogies of the animal kingdom more suitable to their stomach, the buck and doe of the forest glade, the farmyard drake and duck' (*U*14, 710–12). To the extent that this group is held together at all, the binding is a shared culture of schooling in which a particular kind of language and behaviour ritual establishes a common ground that is highly performative, brilliant, comic, sometimes ugly and vulgar, especially in this episode, and often divisive and contested. News of the birth of another Purefoy produces a rowdy 'display of that discursiveness which seemed the only bond of union among tempers so divergent' (*U*14, 954–5). All of which seems a long way from the 'convivial atmosphere of Socratic discussion' that the narrator of this episode at one point visualizes as the respectable signifier of a high-class education (1215–16). For Bloom in his traditional reasonable, conservative role, the group are brilliant but ultimately childish: 'The young sparks, it is true, were as full of extravagancies as overgrown children: the words of their tumultuary discussions were with difficulty understood and not very nice' (848–50). He wonders how 'the mere acquisition of academic titles should suffice to transform in a pinch of time these votaries of levity into exemplary practitioners of an art which most men anywise eminent have esteemed the noblest' (899–902), never realizing that their intelligent playfulness is indispensable, the most obvious sign of their elevated social literacy.

What is often experienced as the 'difficulty' of *Ulysses*, then, is often precisely the difficulty of infiltrating the codes of cliques schooled in particular ways. This is not to say that there is only one kind of difficulty in Joyce's text, but simply to point to a familiar problematic which is characteristically signified by schoolboy Latin, classical terms of reference and the powerful imperative to compete which frames so much of *Ulysses*. It figures often in quite incidental ways. In the extract that follows from *U*9, a discussion around why Shakespeare left Ann Hathaway only his second-best bed in his will, the 'Stagyrite school urchin and bald heathen sage' is an entirely typical reference to Aristotle; Herpyllis was Aristotle's mistress and in contrast to Shakespeare's treatment of Ann Hathaway, he made sure she was well provided for in his will:

> —It is clear that there were two beds, a best and a secondbest, Mr Secondbest Best said finely.
> —*Separatio a mensa et a thalamo*, bettered Buck Mulligan and was smiled on.
> —Antiquity mentions famous beds, Second Eglinton puckered, bedsmiling. Let me think.
> —Antiquity mentions that Stagyrite schoolurchin and bald heathen sage, Stephen said, who when dying in exile frees and endows his slaves, pays tribute to his elders, wills to be laid in earth near the bones of his dead wife and bids his friends be kind to an old mistress (don't forget Nell Gwynn Herpyllis) and let her live in his villa.
>
> (*U*9, 714–24)

'Translating' this material can be a complex matter, even in the age of digitized information systems. Sometimes it involves literal language translation, typically from what was once the most prestigious of languages. Mulligan's use of the besting phrase '*separatio a mensa et a thalamo*' alludes to a legal term used to signify separation before 1857, when divorce became legal for those who could afford it.

The actual phrase used was *separatio a mensa et thoro*, meaning 'separation from board and bed', but Mulligan has made no error here. The substitution '*thalamo*' for '*thoro*' is a poeticization meaning 'bedchamber' or 'bower', a bardic intervention from a budding poet then, a challenge to Stephen, and a nod to Shakespeare the poet at the same time. At this point, the representation of the educated mind performing for an elite circle, becomes challenging and subtle, what it leaves unsaid being a substantial part of its intricacy. In this illustration, following the allusion and the variation does not help with the question of whether it is the added complexity that produces the knowing smiles of recognition in Mulligan's audience or just the use of a nicely-timed Latin phrase. The narrator, taking on a metatextual identity of his own by this stage of things, is of no help, which means that, as in reality, we can never be quite sure just how clever people in this company really are and how far they are posing. What we can be clear about is that schooling has produced distinctive elites, just as it was designed to do. They have stylized ways of interacting and powerfully competitive instincts. The impulse to do better and to best, a drive possessing Stephen and Buck Mulligan with particular force, is reproduced in the narrative voice in this extract, which delivers running commentary on how the characters are performing – a version of class ranking.

Here the erudition paraded in Gogarty's book, *As I Was Going Down Sackville Street*, as a gift of nature becomes instantiated as a particular discourse framed by the historical conditions of Ireland at the turn of the century and rendered up by Joyce as the social. The discourse itself is often unstable and compromised. It is sometimes used in an over-stylized, grandiose, Anglicized manner as with Lyster who opens 'Scylla' with a reference to Goethe: ' – And we have, have we not, these priceless pages of *Wilhelm Meister*. A great poet on a great brother poet' (*U*9, 2–3). It is often opportunistically, and strategically, mangled, as when Mulligan himself renders *Proverbs* 19:17 – 'He that hath pity upon the poor lendeth to the Lord' – as 'He who stealeth from the poor lendeth to the Lord' (*U*1, 728) or urges Stephen to return from his school job with some money using an unorthodox version of the kind of knowing about empire heroics that every schoolboy would have had at his fingertips: 'Ireland expects that every man this day will do his duty' (*U*1,467–8).[30] It is sometimes anachronistic, for example, when in interior monologue Stephen tries to explain colour using Aristotle at the beginning of 'Proteus', and full of slippages. In the same chapter, what might appear to be a pyrotechnic display of learning and memory is typically punctuated by 'real' mistakes. Los in Blake is not strictly speaking the creator of the material world as Stephen claims but, rather, shares that function with Urizen (see *U*3, 18). The word 'buss', which Stephen uses as an example of thieves cant, is actually archaic English (see *U*3, 378). There are misspellings of Irish words, mistranslations and misunderstandings of French phrases – *gros lots* does not mean public lotteries, as Stephen thinks, but rather first prizes or jackpots – and so on (see *U*3, 166). At the beginning of 'Scylla', George Russell conflates lines from Milton's *Paradise Lost* with Dante's *Inferno*. The Dante line he remembers is itself a misquote. The original refers not to Satan but to another demon, Barbaricca, who is one of the Malabranche (see *U*9, 32). Some of these 'mistakes' may be unintended. It cannot be known whether the schoolboy Talbot in 'Nestor' misreads the line from 'Lycidas' as ' – *Weep, no more, woful shepherds, weep no more*' (*U*2, 64) (the noun is actually singular), correctly articulates an editorial error in the text he is reading or is the victim of a misremembrance on the part of Joyce. But the profligacy of such cases means that they cannot all be true errors. This aspect of the *Ulysses* text is part of Joyce's design. It can be brilliant, crude and unfathomable but, above all, it is staged and performative.

The uncertainties generated by the sheer weight of allusiveness to schooled knowledge complicate any easy equation between schooling and a meaningful order of intelligence and have a profound effect on how we read *Ulysses*. The point becomes evident in relation to the allusion literature that has built up around the book. The range and sheer weight of allusiveness in *Ulysses* is part of its extraordinariness, but the precise identification of an allusion is characteristically problematic and awkward. There are reasons to think that the phrase that describes Mulligan as 'a prelate, patron of the art in the middle ages' (*U*1, 32) might be a reference to Pope Alexander IV, the father of Cesare and Lucrezia Borgia, but we cannot make the reference stick unequivocally. Similarly, there is a case for thinking that Mulligan's phrase 'I remember only ideas and sensation' (*U*1, 192–3) is signposted to Locke, but we cannot be sure. In this way *Ulysses*, even in its very early stages, insists on implicating the reader in cultures of schooled knowledge and does so with considerable risk. We are not just watching the Stephen/Mulligan relationship unfold in *Ulysses* in a neutral way. We are being involved by the intricacies of the novel's aesthetic, invited not only to identify what clearly is there, but prompted by what might be there and tempted by what is almost certainly not – often without knowing unequivocally whether we are right or wrong or what the value of such a judgment might bring to our understanding of *Ulysses*.

The fact that our own insertion into modern systems of education and our commitments to high-status forms of knowledge are being brought into the play of reading only makes the engagement between reader and text more problematic. Just as the representation of everyday language in 'Eumaeus' or popular science in 'Ithaca' is famously flawed, to the point of virtual unreadability, so with the reproduction of what were, and still are, prestigious, aristocratic forms of knowledge. This is how, in *Ulysses*, elite schooling moves away from the representational domain of fiction to become textual in itself; a constructed language world that is worked on across *Ulysses*, from the over-schooled schema that Joyce sent to his friends, through the splattering of 'Aeolus' with rhetorical devices, through to the later stages of the book and episodes such as 'Oxen of the Sun', a radical remaking of the literature manual used for teaching literature; 'Eumaeus', a bizarre exercise in grammar pedagogy, and the extraordinary assimilation of high-status school learning to encyclopaedism that is enacted in 'Ithaca'.

Notes

1 The term 'technic' is used by Joyce in the schema of *Ulysses* he sent to various friends.
2 Neubauer, *The Fin de Siècle Culture of Adolescence*, 6.
3 *The Fin de Siècle Culture of Adolescence*, 11.
4 Oliver St. John Gogarty, *As I Was Going Down Sackville Street* (New York: Harvest Brace, 1937), 19.
5 Gogarty, quoted in Ulick O'Connor, *Oliver St John Gogarty: A Poet and His Times* (London: Jonathan Cape, 1964), 65.
6 W.B. Yeats, Preface to *The Oxford Book of Modern Verse 1892–1935* (Oxford: Clarendon Press, 1936), xv.
7 Francis Hackett, 'Introduction', *As I Was Going Down Sackville Street*, vii.
8 Horace Reynolds, 'The Odyssey of an Irishman', *New York Times*, April 4, 1937, 97.
9 See Marilyn French, *The Book as World: James Joyce's 'Ulysses'* (Cambridge, MA: Harvard University Press, 1976).
10 Coolahan, *Irish Education: Its History and Its Structure*, 54. For Joyce and Clifton School, see Ellmann, *James Joyce*, 158–9 and Costello, *James Joyce: The Years of Growth*, 223.
11 Coolahan, *Irish Education: Its History and Its Structure*, 54.
12 See Trevor L. Williams, '"As It Was in the Beginning": The Struggle for History in the "Nestor" Episode of *Ulysses*', *Canadian Review of Irish Studies*, 1990, 16/2, 36–46 [39–41]. Williams goes on to make the strained argument that Stephen's 'fragmented' classroom and his alienation from his pupils is a refusal to complete embodied everywhere in *Ulysses*. He politicizes that as a refusal of consumption.
13 'Dominie' is attached to Deasy's name by Stephen Dedalus at *U*3,19–20. It means 'schoolmaster' or 'pedagogue'.
14 Anon, 'More Reflections of a Schoolmaster: Waverley and *The Illiad*', *Blackwood's Edinburgh Magazine*, 160/971, September 1896, 374–85 [375]. There are some incidental parallels between this schoolmaster and Deasy in 'Nestor'. He too blames women for war, for instance, noting that 'the sin of Mother Eve when she ate "the apple of Discord" in the Garden of Eden was the ultimate cause not only of the Crusades, but of every war that has been waged since the world began'.
15 See Book Eleven of *The Iliad*.
16 Owen Dudley Edwards, 'Belvedere in History', in John Bowman and Ronan O'Donoghue (eds.), *Portraits: Belvedere College, Dublin 1832–1982* (Dublin: Gill & Macmillan, 1982), 13–32 (13).
17 For an account of how this works in 'Wandering Rocks', see Len Platt, *Joyce and the Anglo-Irish: A Study of Joyce and the Literary Revival* (Amsterdam: Rodopi, 1998), 86–96.
18 Hughes, *Tom Brown's Schooldays*, 265.
19 See Heather Ellis, 'Thomas Arnold, Christian Manliness and the Problem of Boyhood', *Journal of Victorian Culture*, 19/4, 2014, 425–41. See also Niko Gärtner, 'The Victorian Headmaster: Biographical Research into an Emerging Profession', *Reflecting Education*, 6/1, 2010, 49–62.
20 Farrar, *Eric: Or, Little by Little*, 20, 25.
21 Kipling, *The Complete Stalky and Co*, 192.
22 See Jon Lee A. Jacobus, '"Lycidas' in the "Nestor" Episode', *James Joyce Quarterly*, 19/2, 1982, 189–94.
23 Williams, "As It Was in the Beginning" 39.
24 See *P*, 171.
25 O'Connor, *Oliver St John Gogarty*, 69.
26 *Oliver St John Gogarty*, 53.
27 Hugh Kenner, *Joyce's Voices* (London: Faber, 1978), 91.

28 See Ellmann, *JJ*, 52. *Metamorphosis* contains the story of Pasiphaë and the Minotaur.

29 Weldon Thornton, *Allusions in Ulysses* (1961; New York: Simon & Schuster, 1973), 338–9.

30 O'Connor notes that Gogarty often broke into Biblical parody. He cites a letter in which Gogarty replies to Joyce: 'This epistle pleased me. Thy remarks concerning chastity pained me. . . . Most marvellous foul sin in chiding sin, when thou thyself has been a libertine'. See *Oliver St John Gogarty*, 71.

Chapter 7

Ulysses and the age of informatics

> What coloured cloth absorbs, but does not conduct heat?
>
> Black cloth absorbs but does not conduct heat.
>
> *1000 Answers to 1000 Questions* (1884)

At the same time as there are continuities between *Ulysses* and the earlier fiction, the social idea of knowledge – its technologies, transmission and social meanings – gets an entirely new treatment in the later work. This is a text obsessively concerned with versions of knowledge, in its socialized forms as status but now in its more obviously commodified forms as 'information' specifically understood in relation to the condition of modernity and the Enlightenment project.

The movement from schooling to information does not mean the two can be understood as separate and distinct systems. The maintenance of an absolute border between information – contingent, ephemeral and practical – and schooled knowledge – internalized, high-status and transferable – is a central part of the logic that normalizes epistemological value systems and the social hierarchies associated with them. The mature Joyce text, as clever as it is and whatever it knows or does not know, wrecks that certainty, not because it seeks to give both equal worth but because it seeks to undermine the basis on which both rest. A considerable part of its impact involves the illustration of how commercial and school systems for constructing and dispersing knowledge are related to each other, as are the cultural values behind them. To put that another way, the impact of *Ulysses* in particular is produced by its mastery of the performance of both schooled knowledge and information culture, or 'informatics'. Education in late Joyce, then, cannot be properly read just in relation to schooling and formal pedagogy. The argument of this chapter is that the radicalism of the later Joyce texts derives precisely from the positioning which puts the high-status education of elites on a parallel course with the late nineteenth century surge in the currency of what is sometimes understood as 'encyclopaedism'. It is this move that extends the viability of education in relation to Joyce's version of modernity. It becomes not just the privileged domain of an elite, but an everyday marketplace which shapes us all as social beings and in which we all operate.

Following Raymond Williams and the 50-year anniversary of his *Keywords*, in 2018 the journal *Victorian Literature and Culture* dedicated an issue to terms important to our understanding of the Victorian era. One of the more surprising inclusions was the word 'information', a term more often used to describe the late twentieth and early twenty-first centuries, where contemporaneity takes shape as an 'information society' or an 'age of information'. The author of the entry was Richard Menke, who published a book in 2008 with the striking title *Telegraphic Realism: Victorian Fiction and Other Information Systems*. He begins his entry with an examination of the usage of the term 'information' in Jane Austen's writing in the early nineteenth century, as in Emma Wodehouse's comment to Harriet Smith when she assumes Robert Martin will not be 'a man of information beyond the line of his own business'. She is asserting that a practical man, like Martin, a farmer, is unlikely to be a man of 'culture' – a product of cultivated reading and understanding. She imagines Frank Churchill very differently, as a broadly educated gentleman who

> can adapt his conversation to the taste of every body, and has the power as well as the wish of being universally agreeable. To you, he will talk of farming; to me, of drawing or music; and so on to every body, having that general information on all subjects which will enable him to follow the lead, or take the lead, just as propriety may require, and to speak extremely well on each.[1]

By the end of the nineteenth century, the word has taken on quite different associations and the social dimensions in which information becomes an important signifier have shifted. Menke illustrates his point with reference to Gissing's satirical novel on professional writing culture and modern times, *New Grub Street* (1891). Here a would-be writer/journalist, Whelpdale, has a plan to turn a failing periodical called *Chat* into something more modern – *Chit-Chat*. He visualizes this publication as a 'frothy assemblage of excerpted information – bits of stories, bits of description, bits of scandal, bit of jokes, bits of statistics' where 'no article in the paper is to measure more than two inches in length, and every inch must be broken into two paragraphs'. It is intended for 'the great new generation being turned out by the Board schools, the young men and women who can just read, but are incapable of sustained attention'.[2] Specifically linked to the growth of the formal education of the 'masses', *Chit-Chat*, with the help of new injections of capital, is designed as an interactive knowledge digest, and becomes not just a great commercial success but a signifier of what Gissing anatomizes as a degenerative age.[3]

Menke's short account may well have been shaped by such theoretical work as *The Structural Transformation of the Public Sphere* (Jürgen Habermas, 1962); *The Consequences of Modernity* (Anthony Giddens, 1990); *The Information Age: Economy, Society and Culture* (Manuel Castells, 1996–8) and *Theories of the Information Society* (Frank Webster, 1995). These texts have figured significantly in a narrative that has identified the contemporary condition in terms of its relation with information.[4] At the same time, Menke's entry joins ranks with applied research in the fields of media and library science, or 'information science', which has been retrieving a history of information from the idea that the world is newly made in this respect. From this perspective, information culture goes back as far as human existence itself and is shaped by technology in all eras, with some obvious peaks of change – the Reformation and the spread of printing presses in Europe would be an obvious illustration, but there are many others, much closer in time to Joyce.

Indeed, the late modern period plays a particular part in that history. Texts with such titles as *The Analogue Revolution: Communication Technology 1901–1914* (Simon Webb, 2018); *Information Beyond Borders: intellectual and cultural exchange in the Belle Époque* (W. B. Rayward [ed.], 2014); *The Victorians and Information: a social and cultural history* (Toni Weller, 2009) and *The Early Information Society: information management in Britain before the computer age* (Alistair Black *et al*, 2007) have constructed the late nineteenth and early twentieth centuries as a 'nascent information age' where for the first time there was a move 'from pre-modern to modern understandings of what constituted information, the ways in which it could be manifested through cultural mediums and the cultural value it manifested'.[5]

There were technological dimensions to this shift, characterized by a great acceleration in the application of existing technologies, refinements to mechanical printing for example and further aspects of book production. Steam-powered printing, machine-made paper and machined book binding together helped make print available on an hitherto unimaginable scale.[6] The information domain became configured anew, linked through such technologies to the concerns that political reform generated about stability, social cohesion and social order. Its instruments, the means by which it was promoted, became increasingly evident across a wide range of social levels and extended into some of the most characteristic institutions of the modern age – libraries, museums, art galleries, publishing houses and newspapers as well as schools and universities. Further innovation associated with this shift, such as the telegraph and the telephone, not only sped up the process of conveying information but also changed the nature of how knowledge and information could be imagined. The former in particular had the effect of breaking the reliance of communication and information transmission on physical transportation and even human agency. Now information could 'move independently of and faster than physical entities', a fact that shaped the development of capitalism, not least through its profound effect on such institutions as the stock exchange and the futures market.[7] As James Y. Carey points out in an essay entitled 'Time, Space and the Telegraph', before the telegraph, dealers traded on the difference of commodity prices in different places which involved the physical movement of goods, taking them from one market to another where higher prices could be obtained. The telegraph removed the necessity for physical transportation and made speculating between present prices and estimated future ones a reality. Trade which had once been geographical and material was now temporal and, if not digital, electrical.[8]

The transformation is illustrative of why, for many working in this field, the key feature of information in this period is that it becomes separated out from its traditional function as rhetorical device to become context-free, 'not tied to any function it might serve', and the phenomenon extended well beyond the stock market.[9] According to Toni Weller, 'Victorians were explicitly recognising the value of information as a thing in its own right, and as a commodity'.[10] They were also inhabiting a world where the 'informed public sphere' was being displaced by a global market which controlled the content and dispersal of social information. It made fundamental changes to the form of information, appearing now as spectacle, advertisement and directory as opposed to a rhetorical performance of argument or persuasion. This is the domain of *Ulysses*, in which an encyclopaedist version of epistemology defines modernity and, in the later stages of the book, takes on an entirely self-referential nature quite removed from the traditional business of the novel or, more precisely, against which its conventionalities struggle to make meaningful purchase.

Thom's and *Tit-Bits*

'Informatics', information as technical and cultural system, became a commodified dimension of the modern world at the level of business and trade, but this was only one aspect of the information revolution in the late nineteenth century. The period saw the growth of new forms of information, presented now on an everyday basis as statistics, directories, railways timetables and popular encyclopaedias like *Chambers* (1859), a product branded as 'information for the people'. By the end of the century, periodicals such as *Answers* and *Tit-Bits*, 'tipbids and answers' in *Finnegans Wake* (*FW*, 101.5), were reproducing encyclopaedia cultures in new pocket-sized weekly editions, popularizing new forms and substantially outselling the now old-fashioned newspaper weeklies. The former, for example, gave information on whether a landowner could prosecute someone for taking mushrooms from his fields ('all you can do is prosecute for damage, if any, caused by trespass') and tips on how to maintain health and strength – 'never hurry; eat plenty of fruit; take plenty of rest; practice deep breathing; sleep with your window open; take meals at the same time every day; take a day in the country whenever possible; take a cold bath every morning, unless your doctor forbids it'.[11]

Such publications had, in effect, become early versions of the internet search engine, indispensable not just to what people knew but also to who they imagined they were in a consumerist age where, for the first time in human history, ordinary people had surplus incomes. The publications reflected a world in which information itself was increasingly becoming a cultural commodity. As historian Alan Rauch has shown, information in the Victorian period took on 'a new kind of social and cultural currency', its acquisition representing the climbing of 'important rungs in the social-climbing ladder'.[12] Although hierarchies of knowledge remained firmly in place, Victorians now had to define their status in relation to an information world that was no longer the exclusive domain of an elite but the familiar territory of the modern world. Knowledge was increasingly being understood as a product, produced for a new market of imagined autodidacts. According to Aileen Fyfe, who writes of a nineteenth century 'information revolution', the consumer market that produced *Chambers* in the later 1850s was still very much on the rise at the end of the century. It captured the public imagination, shaping the production of 'general knowledge' but also, as Fyfe points out, the 'practical' and 'useful' knowledges of a 'how to' and 'guide' culture.[13] These had impacts across traditional class and gender lines at the same time as they helped define them and marked a shift from traditional versions of knowledge which delineated idealized behaviour as opposed to functionality.

Many texts important to *Ulysses* – often taken to be symptomatic of it, in fact – belong to this world of informatics. *Thom's Directory* has long been recognised as a source book for the people and streets of Dublin. Writing in the late 1990's, Morton P. Levitt was neither the first nor last to imagine Joyce constructing the geographics of his novel with 'Thom's Post Office Directory at his elbow'.[14] But *Thom's* is not just a source of information for names and addresses of people living in Dublin in 1904. It is also an example of the kind of informatics described here. Its compilers possessed the general aim of making 'their work indispensable to all classes of the community as a library or office companion' through the making of 'a précis of authentic information, combined with a Peerage, Parliamentary Directory etc, thus proving in one volume, a reading book for reference on almost all subjects of public interest'.[15] It is not simply a source of information for Joyce to plunder, but, rather, an information system to be reproduced, one which, in ambition at least, makes a play for totality and complete authority. Alongside the 220 pages of 'The Post Office Dublin City and County Directory', *Thom's* also contains another 1,800 pages or so of other information, including chronological cycles for 1904 which give the year's equivalent in Jewish and Islamic traditions, its 'golden number 5', its epact configuration, its position in the solar cycle, its relation to 'Roman indiction' and how it would appear in terms of the Julian period – exactly the kind of thing Joyce remakes in the 'Ithaca' episode of *Ulysses*, where an inhuman narrator tells us that Bloom weighed himself a few weeks prior to the now time of the novel, on 'the twelfth day of May of the bissextile year one thousand nine hundred and four of the christian era (jewish era five thousand six hundred and sixtyfour, mohammadan era one thousand three hundred and seventy two), golden number 5, epact 13, solar cycle 9, dominical letters C.B., Roman indiction 2, Julian period 6617, MCMIV' (*U*17, 94–9).[16] Likewise *Thom's* lists 'memorable' feasts of the year, the formal dates of the seasons, and the dates of Irish court sittings including the Quarter sessions. It gives the dates of college terms for Dublin University and Belfast, Cork, and Galway Colleges. Alongside this Irish schedule, *Thom's* includes the date when English Courts sit and the term dates for Oxford and Cambridge. It gives the dates of eclipses for 1904, tide tables, a racing calendar and a salmon fishing calendar. There are tables for the calculation of simple interest, for weights and measures conversion and for both statute and Irish land measures. It gives stamp duties and the names of foreign sovereigns, princes and presidents and includes a colonial directory and a very long record of state honours and duties that goes on for some 300 pages, as well as a navy directory and an army directory. A little over 100 pages are devoted to statistical information regarding Ireland, including census material for 1901.

Tit-Bits, or, to give it its full title, *Tit-Bits of information from all the most interesting books, periodical and contributions in the world*, is likewise entirely typical of this knowledge culture. It was founded in 1881 by George Newnes, who also owned and edited the publication. Until 1910, when Newnes sold it, its average weekly circulation varied from 400,000 to 600,000 copies a week. Historian Kate Jackson describes it as a 'paper of the miscellany variety that became popular in the late-nineteenth century: a sixteen-page patchwork of advice, humorous anecdote, romantic fiction, statistical information, historical explanation, advertisement and reader correspondence'. She identifies its readers in social terms as 'lower middle class' and 'upper working class', described in relation to formal education as 'the backbone of university extension courses and vocational evening classes', although in reality it had its fans among a very different bourgeoisie too.[17] John Joyce was so regular an entrant to a *Tit-Bits* competition involving a buried bag of gold sovereigns that his son once identified this activity as his father's full-time occupation.[18] At the same time, Jackson sees Newnes, 'a well-meaning philanthropist', as the creator of a new readership offering 'mutual support, a wide range of social services, and a sense of citizenship and community'.[19] Jackson also emphasizes the interactive element of the publication, its appeal to readers through advice pages, publication of readers' stories and so on, an idea taken up by Joyceans who have indicated parallels with *Ulysses* and the modernist aesthetic generally where, according to R.B. Kershner, for example, 'readers are invited, in some ways required, to take an active part in the book's composition – to write parts of the book that have been left blank by the original author'.[20]

These ideas of a heterogeneous item made up of random bits and pieces are not exactly false, but they are misleading. *Tit-Bits* did include puzzles, pictures, letters and stories and competitions – one of the latter promised to pay £100 to the nearest relative of anyone who died on a train with the latest copy of *Tit-Bits* in their pocket, another 'a fortnight's free holiday in Switzerland'.[21] Increasingly, as the twentieth century wore on, the visual elements took up more space, here as in other cultural forms such as newspapers – and it did invite reader participation. At the same time, the emphasis on informatics in periodicals like *Tit-Bits* was clear and gave such publications their essential character and identity. The New Year's edition published in 1900, for instance, includes odd and comic facts, one about a retired French postman who calculated on retirement that he had walked over 720,000 miles over the course of his career, or 'the equivalent of a return trip to the moon'.[22] It framed and answered random questions such as: 'In which country have farmers obtained the benefits of the telephone system?', 'Can a bee carry its own weight in honey?' and 'Where is the most perfect example of Norman architecture in Scotland?'[23] It also contained an inquiry column to which readers could pose their own questions and receive responses, some of which were written by Newnes himself but which also involved experts. As in modern media 'magazine' shows, Newnes employed the services of a lawyer to answer legal questions on such topics as income tax, life insurance, employment laws and laws governing marriage. He engaged a doctor to answer medical questions, who did so in a discourse standing for social responsibility and temperance against urban degeneration – one much reminiscent, as is so much of this culture, of Leopold Bloom.[24] *Tit-Bits*, like Bloom, was devoted to personal hygiene, health and well-being, offering healthy eating advice and criticizing 'the hurried meals partaken of by a large number of clerks and warehousemen' which 'cannot but produce indigestion' and which violate 'all the laws of healthy digestion'.[25] Similarly *Answers*, very like *Tit-Bits* in form and content, contained a health education page. Entitled 'Helping Hands to Health and Strength', it partnered a column attributed to the famous strongman Eugen Sandow, also prominent in *Ulysses*, which was itself called 'Health and Strength'.

Another page in *Tit-Bits* gave more detailed answers to correspondents' general questions about the world and how it worked and offered corrections to errors: 'Harry E – we are afraid you have a very wrong conception of the size of Transvaal which you describe as "a country no bigger than Wales"'. The same page also complimented readers deemed to make useful contributions, although sometimes it is not clear how sincere the response really is: 'E.P. says that all lions are left-handed – that whenever one wishes to strike a killing blow it always does so with its left paw. This is useful information'. Another page offered 'Tit-Bits of General Information', again in quite random and decontextualized ways, highly suggestive of the disembodied information offered everywhere in *Ulysses*. 'The height of the atmosphere is supposed to be about fifty miles'; 'Eleven cubic feet of water, when frozen, makes about twelve cubic feet of ice'; 'Twenty-five women have been hanged in England during Queen Victoria's reign'; 'A Suffolk gentleman has sent to the Suffolk hospital £100 saved in twelve years by travelling third instead of first class' and so on.[26] Personal advice pages took on the shape of a more intimate and sometimes playful informatics:

> Economy is a capital thing, particularly when practised by those whose matrimonial plunge is within the verge of practical politics, so to speak. At the same time, there are many reasons why you should not carry it to the extent of asking your fiancée to accept an engagement ring which your former young lady wore under a similar contract. Girls are very sensitive on these matters.[27]

Informatics extended to advertisements too, especially those related to health and personal hygiene, where the knowing rational subject became specifically constructed in relation to the commercialism of modern consumption. Eno's fruit salts, for example, cured everything from boils to 'functional derangement of the liver'; 'Cigares de joy' relieved 'asthma, wheezing and chronic bronchitis'; 'Lait Lorda' made the skin soft and so on.[28] Virtually every aspect of the periodical was in some way shaped by an epistemological framework, so much so that Newness published several editions of *Answers to Questions posed by readers of Tit-Bits* in book form in 1884, 1888, 1890 and 1895, each one containing a thousand questions, questions which in various ways evoke the world of *Ulysses*, not just the specifics of its contents but in relation to the particular version of 'epic' it configures as a dominion over the world of facts: 'What is the greatest depth of water known?'; 'Of what extent were the hanging gardens of Babylon?'; 'When and by whom was the Manx House of Keyes established?'; 'What was the origin of the saying "Appeal from Philip drunk to Philip sober"?';[29] 'What became of the original harp of Brian Boru?'[30] and 'What is meant by squaring the circle?'[31] The following 'science'-based questions all come from the same source but could just as easily have figured in *Ulysses*:

> What proportion of rainfall finds it way directly to the streams and river?[32]
> What is the weight of water in the largest ocean in the world?[33]
> How can the candle power of a light be ascertained?
> Why do cats' eyes shine in the dark?
> How are the areas of a circle, and the solidity of the globe respectively ascertained?
> What is the velocity of the solar system?[34]
> What is the average duration of human life?[35]
> Does water evaporate at all temperatures?
> How are ocean currents caused?[36]

Magazines like *Tit-Bits* and the culture they represent are sometimes used in quite incidental ways in *Ulysses*. In 'Sirens', for example, Bloom hears Ben Dollard, a 'Decent soul', singing in a bar and remembers for no apparent reason that the singer once entered a competition set in *Answers*: 'poets' picture puzzle. We hand you a crisp five pound note. Bird sitting hatching in a nest. Lay of the last minstrel he thought it was' (*U*11,1023–25). Bloom has a copy of *Thom's* on his bookshelf at home and, as Joyceans have noted, there is also an extended direct reference to *Tit-Bits* in *Ulysses*, which begins with Bloom's early-morning visit to the lavatory. He takes a copy of the magazine with him and reads from a short story called '*Matcham's Masterstroke*'. Bloom works out that at a rate of one guinea a column, its author 'Mr Philip Beaufoy' would have received 'Three pounds, thirteen and six' in payment (*U*4, 502–5). Bloom 'envied kindly' Beaufoy and wonders if his success can be emulated, a thought which returns throughout the day. Admiring but far from overawed, he tears away 'half the prize story sharply' and wipes himself with it (*U*4, 537). Much later, in the hallucinatory world of the 'Circe' episode, Bloom is placed in the dock, accused of plagiarism, among many other crimes, and confronted by an outraged Beaufoy determined to get justice. The 'real' author is armed with 'damning evidence, the *corpus delicti*, my lord, a specimen of my mature work disfigured by the hallmark of the beast' (*U*15,

843–5). In this kind of reading, *Tit-Bits* becomes part of a particular version of a classic modern masterpiece that comically encompasses everything, including the trivial and ephemeral popular culture of the day. In fact, the kind of informatics culture represented by *Tit-Bits* is much more central to *Ulysses* and extends way beyond this comic narrative thread. The point is made clear in this comparison between the compilations of questions and their answers sold by Newnes thorough the 1880s and 1890s under the *Tit-Bits* label and an extract taken from the penultimate chapter of *Ulysses*, 'Ithaca'. The first is by Joyce and describes the relation between the ages of Stephen and Bloom. It begins with that very question explicitly framed:

> What relation existed between their ages?
>
> 16 years before in 1888 when Bloom was of Stephen's present age Stephen was 6.16 years after in 1920 when Stephen would be of Bloom's present age Bloom would be 54. In 1936 when Bloom would be 70 and Stephen 54 their ages initially in the ratio of 16 to 0 would be as 17 1/2 to 13 1/2, the proportion increasing and the disparity diminishing according as arbitrary future years were added, for if the proportion existing in 1883 had continued immutable, conceiving that to be possible, till then 1904 when Stephen was 22 Bloom would be 374 and in 1920 when Stephen would be 38, as Bloom then was, Bloom would be 646 while in 1952 when Stephen would have attained the maximum postdiluvian age of 70 Bloom, being 1190 years alive having been born in the year 714, would have surpassed by 221 years the maximum antediluvian age, that of Methuselah, 969 years, while, if Stephen would continue to live until he would attain that age in the year 3072 A.D., Bloom would have been obliged to have been alive 83,300 years, having been obliged to have been born in the year 81,396 B.C.
>
> (*U*17, 446–461)

The second is taken from *Tit-Bits – 1,000 Answers and 1,000 Questions*, (1884):

> What is the average duration of human life?
>
> If the death rates for the last few years keep constant they will show that the average duration of human life is increasing. Whilst under Dr Farr's life tables the mean duration of life, or the mean after lifetime of males at birth, was put at 39.91 years, the recent death rates warrant an increase to 41.92, an increase of more than two years or 5 per cent. Similarly with females there is an increase from 41.85 to 45.25, or 3.40 years. Taking the two sexes together (the sex proportions being fixed by that of the births of live-born children) the mean duration of a generation has been raised from 40.80 to 43.56, or 2.76 years. In other words one fifteenth has been added to the expectation of life of every infant born. It is to be remarked that in order to arrive at a fair estimate of the average duration of life it is not enough to take the ages of death of those dying within a limited period of, say, five years. For whereas

> the average duration of life for a generation is shown by the death rate to be stated above, *viz*. 43.56 years, the mean age at death of all the persons dying in the five years 1876–1880 was only thirty two. The reason for this is that the deaths of infants and children are so numerous, and that the first year of life yields the greatest number of victims.[37]

There are important distinctions to be made between these passages. Although both take straightforward questions and subject them to an elaborative calculative process in which statistics and scientism are given full rein, Joyce's version overextends and drifts further into the excessive reaches of the unnecessary and the absurd. In this it exemplifies fictional versions of encyclopedic culture in modernist fiction culture, where the tensions between totalization and completeness become 'transposed into a radical uncertainty built into the very project of encompassing knowledge'.[38] But in order to effect this acceleration and distortion, the fictional account must become entangled, as it surely is here. The forms, the rhythms, the styles of the real thing are captured with great subtlety by Joyce, down to the smallest of details. Precisely what this means in relation to formal schooling is developed later in this chapter. For now, it is sufficient to register just how far modernity for Joyce is made manifest in social systems of knowledge.

'A raw onion the last thing at night would benefit your complexion' – informatics, Bloom, technics

Joyce's use of this material in *Ulysses* is not limited to 'Ithaca'. It is the most powerful and emblematic signifier of the modern world in Joyce and has a particular locus in the character Leopold Bloom, the main circulatory system through which information culture spreads in *Ulysses*. Bloom's curiosity, his interest in everything from schemes for social reform to astronomy is a human configuration of the encyclopaedist world popularized in magazines like *Tit-Bits*. His status as a rational subject is not a universal condition but a product of a particular historical position in a specific epistemological culture, a social regime of knowing. His orientation towards science, for example, has little or nothing to with the professional scientific world and everything to do with the popular culture that once framed scientific knowledge as a domain of the everyday. As Toni Weller points out, science information was regularly and increasingly disseminated through the periodical and newspaper press during the nineteenth century.[39] When Bloom wonders what he looks like to his cat ('Height of a tower?') and whether his cat's whiskers shine in the dark, or 'why is it that saltwater fish are not salty?', how the heart pumps or how X-rays work, he reproduces the informatics culture which characteristically poses the same kinds of questions (*U*4, 29; *U*8, 86). Sometimes such questions cross texts more or less precisely. The science issues that most recur throughout Bloom's day, about colour and heat absorption for instance – 'Black conducts, reflects, (refracts is it?), the heat' (*U*4, 79–80) – are also *Tit-Bits* questions ('What coloured cloth absorbs but does not conduct heat?').[40] Likewise, Bloom's thoughts on the law of falling bodies – 'They all fall to the ground. The earth. It's the force of gravity of the earth is the weight' (*U*5, 45–6) – are framed in the *Tit-Bits* question that asks 'If two balls of equal size, one of lead, the other of wood, be dropped from a tower, say 200 feet high, will they reach the ground at the same time?'[41]

None of this inquiry makes Bloom a standard representative of his world. On the contrary, the particular investment he makes in knowing marks him out as an oddity, a curious example of the exemplary taken to extremes. The seriousness with which he approaches understanding and makes such a performance of sharing knowledge produces an oddball figure positioned just this side of the outlandish. If Lenehan famously elevates Bloom as 'a cultured allroundman' with a 'touch of the artist' about him, most of his contemporaries do not (*U*10, 581–2). Even Molly, generally defending of her husband and his possession of 'a few brains' (*U*18, 321), complains that he often gets things badly wrong – he 'knows a lot of mixed up things' (*U*18, 179–80). His appropriation of the encyclopaedist's claim to know everything under the sun, including 'a great lot about a woman's dress and cooking' 'gets on your nerves' (*U*18, 518–20). Information is often mangled by Bloom, just as school learning is, got wrong or misremembered, or not remembered at all. He notes that you 'couldn't sink' in the Dead Sea, 'if you tried: so thick with salt. Because the weight of the water, no, the weight of the body in the water is equal to the weight of the what? Or is it the volume that is equal to the weight. It's a law something like that' (*U*5, 39–42). He is not just occasionally but characteristically pretentious and pompous. Even in the privacy of his own home, Bloom, completely unable to 'explain a thing simply the way a body can understand', is always coming out with 'jawbreakers' (*U*18, 566–7).

In fairness to Bloom, if such an idea can be meaningful, he is not simply a would-be know-it-all. In fact, his configuration in relation to knowledge as a social world is astonishingly complex. Through it, Bloom reproduces a system which, in its desire to render up everything in terms of verifiable certainty, must forever stumble against its own limits. The more complex the domains it seeks to control, the more the absence of relative value, perspective and qualitative context becomes exposed. Bloom's confusions and errors, then, are presented not just as personal failures but also as signifiers of the failures of a knowledge system that claims to bring everything within the reach of the 'common man'. Thus, it is the knowledge society itself that is so fragile in Joyce. Its instability is manifest in Bloom's posing of so many questions; misfiring so badly in understanding; conflating modern knowledge with superstition and commercial guile and so on. In the 'Nausicaa' episode, for example, as part of his bid to grasp the world around him, he wonders 'why don't all women menstruate at the same time with the same moon, I mean?' and in the same vein thinks about the effect menstruating women might have on the material world around them: 'Turns milk, makes fiddlestrings snap. Something about withering plants' (*U*13, 783–4; 826). In the same short section of some 300 lines, he questions whether there can be a real magnetic influence between people and asks what it is that acts as a conductor to smell, how smell travels. He thinks that the human body might somehow feel atmosphere and tries to remember what the colours of the rainbows are. He wonders whether birds can smell and what bats are flying for and, in his mind, advises Gerty McDowell not to sit on 'that stone. Brings on white fluxions' (see *U*13, 987–1082). Whole narrative sequences are built up in these ways, creating an idiosyncratic figure, but one designed to fully exemplify the culture he represents. The errors are comic, but also indicative of a much wider critique of an epistemological world, a critique which Bloom himself has no access to. It can be no surprise that Bloom fantasizes about becoming a professional dispenser of expert knowledge – 'Uncle Toby's page for tiny tots. Country bumpkin's queries. Dear Mr Editor, what is a good cure for flatulence? I'd like that part, learn a lot teaching others' (*U*7, 94–7).

Bloom's desire to impress, his engagement in the public sphere and his sense of what it is to be a good citizen – all are decisively shaped by the culture of informatics. In 'Circe', a fantasist Bloom participates in a community of readership and social action. He claims to have procured the 'public boon' of a signpost for cyclists 'planted by the Touring Club at Stepaside' by contributing a letter 'to the columns of the *Irish Cyclist*' (*U*15, 231–3). The same episode represents how far Bloom's investment in a knowledge society penetrates his psychological insecurities over social acceptance and frames his desire to be loved. In an extended 'hallucination', Bloom's power fantasies are imaged in terms of the paternalist dispensation of useful knowledge. The citizens of Emperor Bloom's 'Bloomusalem' are presented with such gifts as '*Maundy money*', '*bottles of Jeyes Fluid*' and '*cheap reprints of the World's Twelve Worst Books*', including '*Care of the Baby (infantilic), 50 meals for 7/6 (culinic) . . . Expel That Pain (medic), Infant's Compendium of the Universe (cosmic)*' and '*Pennywise's Way to Wealth (parsimonic)*' (*U*15, 1569–84). Later in the same fantasy sequence, Bloom's power is exemplified precisely by his mastery over knowledge in a public forum that dramatizes the question and answer form drawn on so centrally in *Tit-Bits*. Here he responds to a random series of questions from across a range of fields of expertise – including law, insurance, citizenship, medical science and astronomy – all of which he is confident in:

PADDY LEONARD

What am I to do about my rates and taxes?

BLOOM

Pay them, my friend.

PADDY LEONARD

Thank you.

NOSEY FLYNN

Can I raise a mortgage on my fire insurance?

BLOOM

(*obdurately*) Sirs, take notice that by the law of torts you are bound over in your own recognisances for six months in the sum of five pounds.

J J. O.MOLLOY

A Daniel did I say? Nay! A Peter O'Brien!

NOSEY FLYNN

Where do I draw the five pounds?

PISSER BURKE

For bladder trouble?

BLOOM

Acid. nit. hydrochlor. dil., 20 minims
Tinct. nux vom., 5 minims
Extra. taraxel, liq., 30 minims
Aq. dis. ter in die.

CHRIS CALLINAN

What is the parallax of the subsolar ecliptic of Aldebaran?

BLOOM

Pleased to hear for you, Chris. K.11.

(*U*15, 1633–58)

As this representation of Bloom's unconscious mind indicates, Bloom's sense of self is intimately tied up with what he thinks he knows about the world and the social value which he believes rightly devolves on the well-informed man. In the real world, Bloom the rational subject struggles to make an impact in a society constructed in much more complex ways. In 'Cyclops', for instance, where his outsiderly status is at its greatest and his self-respect at most risk, he attempts to stand his ground, not least by performing sensibly and knowledgably. He refuses the offer of 'liquid refreshment' by pointing out that he is only present in the pub to carry out an act of charity:

—Thank you, no, says Bloom. As a matter of fact I just wanted to meet Martin Cunningham, don't you see, about this insurance of poor Dignam's.

> Martin asked me to go to the house. You see, he, Dignam, I mean, didn't serve any notice of the assignment on the company at the time and nominally under the act the mortgagee can't recover on the policy.
>
> (*U*12, 760–64)

As so often happens, his lack of control over a complex knowledge field lets him down. The intervention misfires in what is a masculinist, highly ritualized social environment that has little or no sympathy with Bloom's version of rationality and citizenship:

> Then he starts all confused mucking it up about mortgagor under the act like the lord chancellor giving it out on the bench and for the benefit of the wife and that a trust is created but on the other hand that Dignam owed Bridgeman the money and if now the wife or the widow contested the mortgagee's right till he near had the head of me addled with his mortgagor under the act.
>
> (*U*12, 770–75)

In the same episode, a potentially controversial discussion about 'Irish sports and shoneen games the like of lawn tennis' has Bloom attempting to find a moderating way into the company with an 'interesting' fact of a generalist kind that appears to entirely miss the point being made by the drinkers in Kernan's bar: 'And of course Bloom had to have his say too about if a fellow had rower's heart violent exercise was bad' (*U*12, 889; 891–2).

Examples like these can be found all over the pages of *Ulysses*. Bloom himself has little or no sense that he is so much a product of his times in this respect or that the basis of his formal knowledge system is so fundamentally unstable. For him, the world is made of demonstrable facts, and there is no real distinction to be made between formal education, the education he received first at the dame's school and later the high school and the informatics culture he so embodies. In the following extract from the 'Nausicaa' episode, the one shades easily into the other. Bloom is thinking about twilight, which leads him to remember one of his old teachers: 'Best time to spray plants too in the shade after the sun. Some light still. Red rays are longest. Roygbiv. Vance taught us: red, orange, yellow, green, blue, indigo, violet. A star I see. Venus?'(*U*13,1075–6). In this respect, Bloom, often idealized in Joyce criticism, is not so much a self-determined hero as a much-flawed product of his world. Ironically, it is precisely the cultural equipment which he thinks prepares him to operate in this world that renders him so much at sea.

It used to be thought in Joyce criticism that the earlier chapters of *Ulysses*, especially the Bloom chapters, belonged to traditions of 'realistic' representation undermined by the later ones, and that Bloom was especially related to those earlier chapters and that mode of representation. This was in some ways consistent with the construction of the book which involved the later episodes becoming so radical in style or 'technic' that the early ones had to be revised to make for greater consistency. The result, for some critics, was a marginalization of Bloom. As early as 1972, Joycean William M. Schutte, for example, was complaining about how in critical discussions Bloom had 'all too often been shoved firmly, if politely into the background while discussions have raged about structural patterning and the manifold techniques of the novel'.[42] In this way, Bloom-centred readings of *Ulysses*, assuming such a thing possible in contemporary critical cultures, would mean returning *Ulysses* to the 'representational mode' from which it escapes in such celebrated ways.

The handling of informatics in this novel shows how fundamental Joyce's integration of representation and technical innovation really is and how far both operate on a modern world conceived to be defined by cultures of schooling and knowledge. Informatics are not just reproduced in *Ulysses* by reference to cultural products or in terms of qualities and attitudes possessed by characters. They are built into the styles and techniques of the text. So pervasive are they that they figure in episodes where the dominant 'technic' is substantively positioned elsewhere. The prettified style of 'Nausicaa', for example, is often taken to parody the romance literature of novels like Maria S. Cummins's *The Lamplighter* (1854) or the short stories published in *The Princess's Novelette* (1886–1904) or *The Lady's Pictorial* (1880-?), all three mentioned in the 'Nausicaa' text. At the same time, they implicate the informatics culture represented by *Tit-Bits* – coincidentally, Newnes reprised the second of these titles as *Newnes Princess Novelettes* in 1919. The modernity of the central figure in *U*13, Gerty McDowell, is precisely a product of fashionable and highly gendered systems of knowledge – knowing how to behave, how to cook, how to attract a man, how to make the best of things. Thus Gerty, inseparable from the narrative style of the episode, leans heavily on 'Madame Vera Verity, directress of the Woman Beautiful page of the Princess Novelette', to learn about 'eyebrowline which gave that haunting expression to the eyes, so becoming in leaders of fashion, and she never regretted it'. From the same source, she has learned and been defined by knowledge about 'blushing scientifically cured and how to be tall increase your height' and what to do if 'you have a beautiful face but your nose?' (*U*13, 109–14). She buys a 'neat blouse of electric blue selftinted by dolly dyes. . . (because it was expected in the *Lady's Pictorial* that electric blue would be worn)' (150–1). The same culture will inform how she makes a 'Queen Ann's pudding of delightful creaminess' (225) and why she goes for 'chintz covers for the chairs' (233–4) and buys 'Lazenby's salad dressing' (314). Here identity is processed out of highly commercialized systems of knowledge formation.

Similarly, in 'Cyclops' where the dominant style is formed out of interpolations, many of them parodying the texts produced by revivalist literature in the late nineteenth and early twentieth centuries. At the same time, chunks of expertise from other sources are parachuted into the text, dispersed in units just as it is in *Tit-Bits*. This episode, too, is the product of an encyclopedic culture that implicates, for example, scientific knowledge in the interpolation where 'The distinguished scientist Herr Professor Luitpold Blumenduft' explains how the hanging of a man produces 'the instantaneous fracture of the cervical vertebrae and consequent scission of the spinal cord' which results in an erection through 'a violent ganglionic stimulus of the nerve centres of the genital apparatus' (*U*12, 468–73). Another interpolation in the same episode concerns the kind of story that might very well appear in publications like *Tit-Bits*. Its subject is of the astounding fact variety – the forerunner of 'fake news' but much harder to mistake for 'real' news. Here, the writer reports on a dog that not only makes human sounds but recites verse which bears 'a *striking* resemblance (the italics are ours) to the ranns of ancient Celtic bards' (*U*12, 722–3). The interpolation is addressed to a specific readership: 'All those who are interested in the spread of human culture among the lower animals (and their name is legion)' (*U*12, 712–13).

There may well be further influences of informatics on *Ulysses*. The splitting up of 'Wandering Rocks' into manageable blocks – Whelpdale's 'bits of stories, bits of description, bits of scandal, bit of jokes' referred to previously – is suggestive of the magazine style. Above all, however, it is in the penultimate chapter of *Ulysses*, 'Ithaca', that the culture of informatics is let loose 'in technic' and the limitations of its will to knowledge performed to such devastating effect.

'Ithaca', informatics, schooling

In June 1924, Joyce wrote a letter to his benefactress and publisher Harriet Shaw Weaver in which he described *Ulysses* as a book written from 'eighteen different points of view and in as many styles, all apparently unknown or undiscovered by my fellow tradesmen'.[43] As many Joyceans have pointed out, there are not 18 distinct points of view in *Ulysses*, or 18 styles. 'Telemachus' and 'Nestor' could easily be constructed in terms of equivalence in both respects, as could 'Calypso', 'Lotus-Eaters', 'Hades' and 'Lestrygonians'. 'Aeolus' is a relatively straight-forward narrative event apart from the fact that it is broken up by newspaper headlines and showered with rhetorical devices, both added after the episode was originally formulated as continuous prose. 'Cyclops' does have a distinct point of view, that of the unnamed narrator, but this is fragmented by interpolations written not in one but several styles. Nor, contrary to what Joyce implies, do 'styles' always represent points of view. The musical treatment of 'Sirens' has been read in terms of a narrative personality, David Hayman's playful 'self-reflexive arranger', but others would not see it in this way at all.[44] Writing an episode which includes imitating an overture in its beginning, falling into musical time, and reproducing in words the sound of a long-held note does not necessarily establish a 'point of view', but, rather, implies the technical application of musical 'devices'. Other episodes, however, go well beyond representing 'points of view'. They are world building, formulations built on deep social formations ('Eumaeus'), privileged modern forms of knowledge, like psychoanalysis ('Circe') and other epistemic foundations.

'Ithaca' exemplifies the latter. Its narrator is steeped in positivism, rationalism and progress historiography, related world views that energize what appears to be a supremely confident first ending to Joyce's novel. The problem is that this narrative style, far from controlling and resolving, has such a flattening effect that it actually robs us of meaning. We get facts in piles, but no meaningful value system in which to place them. The information that, as part of the process of making two cups of cocoa, water flows from the tap in Bloom's kitchen from a reservoir in Wicklow 'with a cubic capacity of 2400 million gallons, percolating through a subterranean aqueduct of filter mains of single and double pipeage constructed at an initial plant cost of £5 per linear yard', is illustrative (*U*17,164–67). Who needs this information? This is the chapter that is supposed to tell us everything we want to know about Stephen and Bloom and the book they are in – or, at least, that is the expectation set up by a form which consists entirely of questions and answers. The narrator appears to be a superlative exemplar of the informatics culture designed to bridge the gap between 'the people' and 'the learned', parading the kind of knowledge once expected to 'elevate the faculties above low pursuits', 'refine' and 'purify' and 'help our reason to assuage' the 'violence of human passion' as well as offering 'some positive advantage' in the achievement of 'worldly wealth and comfort'.[45] In Joyce's version, however, that identity belongs to a faceless, flattened world. All information has equivalent status, which in the end means that it has is no status at all. The world represented is a cold, scientific one, objective, but also denuded of any emotion. Where different kinds of responses register at all, they are buried, ambiguous, ambivalent and sometimes not much more than disguised cliché. The much-commented-on description of the spectacle of the heavens in 'Ithaca' as 'the heaventree of stars hung with humid nightblue fruit' (*U*17, 1039), and the series of questions and answers that follow it, might appear to represent a crack in the surface of the detached world of 'Ithaca', but what it expresses is the commonplace dressed up. The same kind of thing is echoed in *Tit-Bits*, where the answer to the question 'What is the velocity of the solar system?' includes the following response:

> No person who, even in our own climate, has viewed the vault of the stars in the stillness of night, can be insensible of the impression which the contemplation imparts. It is, in its vastness and splendour, a glance at the infinite universe, and the highest example of the sublime. It penetrates the soul with indescribable emotions of reverence for the Eternal Creator, and reminds man of his littleness, and his ephemeral character.[46]

Under such conditions, the delivery of responses to questions becomes routinized and literalized. The certainties of the world it represents are thoroughly compromised by errors, mistakes, limitations, endless qualifiers and so on; this in part wickedly worked up by Joyce but on the basis of characteristics already embedded in the cultures behind 'Ithaca' – cultures rendered unstable by the claim to finally, irresistibly, know everything. Here, for example, is another example taken from the 1884 edition of Newnes's compendium *1,000 Tit-Bits of*

Curious Information, although it could, with some adjustment, easily be slotted into 'Ithaca':

> How many miles does the earth travel in a year?
>
> As the mean distance of the earth from the sun is nearly 95,000,000 of miles, the earth describes a yearly path of upwards of 596,000,000 of miles, or about 19 million miles a second, which is the mean velocity for the year; but in January the earth travels at a rate of 69,600 miles an hour, exceeding by more than 3,000 miles an hour its rate of motion in July, when it is only 66,400 miles an hour. If the mean distance of the earth from the sun be taken at 91,718,000 (according to recent measurements), the earth travels at 569, 680,703 miles a year.[47]

Put that question now into a contemporary search engine and the phrase in parentheses becomes powerfully activated. Not one of the speeds or distances between objects remains the same – which means, of course, that the result comes out differently at 'about' 584,000,000 miles travelled – a small difference perhaps set against the scale of things, but one with big implications.

It has always been known that the 'Ithaca' technic, referred to variously by Joyce as 'catechism impersonal' or the 'mathematico-astronomico-physico-mechanico-geomerico-chemico sublimation of Bloom and Stephen', is somehow caught up with schooling – school textbooks, schooled knowledge, assessment regimes and discourses of pedagogy.[48] Parallels have been found between the episode and specific textbooks and pedagogic procedures. Here, the question/answer format of 'Ithaca' becomes suggestive of the religious catechism to which Joyce would have been exposed as a schoolboy, and the secularization of catechism that produced such textbooks as Mangnall's *Historical and Miscellaneous Questions for the use of Young People*. Remembering school books of the past, 'a very old boy' in 1900 noted how, in his elite school, 'besides spelling and reading, and desperate struggles at writing, much time was spent in learning answers to almost absolutely useless questions contained in little catechisms or bigger question books, such as Mangnall's "Miscellaneous Questions"'.[49] Alongside many other things, this text asked students to 'Name the English lines of kings' and 'the three most remarkable events in the reign of Edward III' as well as the plant that Druids held in high esteem and the inanimate object the priestly order once worshipped.[50] The same culture influenced more homely publications; the 'Peter Parley's Tales' series, for instance. *Tales about the Mythology of the Greeks and Romans* (1839) was genially addressed to members of 'the rising generation' from 'their old friend', but nevertheless had questions at the end of each page, like footnotes – off-putting, invasive even. At the end of the first page on *The Odyssey*, students are asked ' 'What does the Odyssey relate?' and 'How long had Odysseus remained at the isle of Calypso?'[51]

Likewise, parallels have been made between 'Ithaca' and examination questions. Traditionalist pedagogy has been positioned in relation to Stephen's educational history in Catholic elite schools. From this starting point, Robert Hampson, writing in the late 1990s, argues that 'Ithaca' constructs schooled knowledge as a religious and colonial form of oppression, although there is little in 'Ithaca' itself to substantiate a postcolonial reading in any of these terms, perhaps unsurprisingly. Such a reading sits uneasily both against the Catholic Church's infamous opposition to science and modern rationalism and the slipping away of Britain's right to be exclusively identified with modernity in the early twentieth century. It also produces a Stephen perspective that obscures the part Bloom and what Bloom represents has in the episode, a tendency the episode itself refuses to support.[52]

This is not to say, however, that illustrations used to establish links between the Ithacan technic and schooled knowledge are anything but convincing. Hampson shows that there are questions in 'Ithaca' which 'use the register of the school examination fairly straightforwardly'. In relation to the question 'what, reduced to their simplest reciprocal form, were Bloom's thoughts about Stephen's thoughts about Bloom and about Stephen's thoughts about Bloom's thoughts about Stephen', Hampson points out that, 'the answer – "He thought that he thought that he was a jew whereas he knew that he knew that he knew that he was not"' – invites the use of algebra 'to clarify its pronominal references' (*U*17, 526–31). Hampson also points out that there are precise similarities between the questions posed in 'Ithaca' and the intermediate examinations that Joyce would have sat as a student in Ireland. The Middle Grade arithmetic paper for 1879, for example, 'includes an exercise in compound addition (Question 6) which resembles the 'budget for June 16 1904' set out in 'Ithaca' (see *U*17, 1455–78) and an exercise in simple interest (Question 13) resembles the calculation by which Bloom could pay for his 'country residence' (see *U*17, 1657–71).[53] Hampson finds further echoes of particular textbooks in 'Ithaca', the episode that tells us everything whether we want to know it or not. Mangnall's *Historical Miscellaneous Questions*, for example, often gives answers in the form of lists. The response to the invitation to 'name the discoveries, inventions and improvements, in Elizabeth's reign' includes 'stops were introduced in reading and writing; microscopes invented; coaches and watches first common in England; the study of botany was revived; Holland declared a republic; and criminals first sentenced to transportation'. For Hampson, these catalogues undoubtedly lie behind the account of Bloom's interest in 'inventions now common but once revolutionary . . . the spiral corkscrew, the safety pin, the mineral water siphon, the canal lock with winch and sluice, the suction pump' (*U*17, 565–8).[54] It might be added that the random quality of 'Ithaca', its rapid shift from one domain of knowledge to another, also owes something to Mangnall. Alongside the historical material, her once popular textbook contains information on words and terms seldom 'Englished' – such as *ad hominem*, *nem com* and *vidlicet* – 'elements' of astronomy, which defines parallax as 'the differences between the true and apparent place of a planet', has information on 'heathen' mythology, and tells the reader/student where cocoanuts are to be found.[55]

Indeed, it is difficult to overplay the importance of schooling to 'Ithaca', an episode that orientates itself to education at almost every point. The two characters talk about education and reminisce about their schooldays. Stephen remembers an occasion when Brother Michael in the Clongowes infirmary lit a fire for him and Bloom recalls how his 'abnormally developed abdominal muscles' once enabled him to excel as a schoolboy at the 'half lever movement on the parallel bars' (*U*17, 522–4). At one point, the narrative uses childish merges of name, quite out of character with the high formality of the episode, to process what would happen if the education histories of Stephen and Bloom were swapped:

> Did they find their educational careers similar?
>
> Substituting Stephen for Bloom Stoom would have been passed successively through a dame's school and the high school. Substituting Bloom for Stephen Blephen would have passed successively through the preparatory junior, middle and senior grades of the intermediate and through the matriculation, first arts, second arts and arts degree course of the university.
>
> (*U*17, 548–54)

Bloom also thinks that Stephen's essays and other writings could be collected as 'model pedagogical themes . . . for the use of preparatory and junior grade students' (*U*17, 647–9), and that Molly would benefit from 'courses of evening instruction' on the grounds that she has 'deficient mental development' (U17, 672–4). Stimulated by the 'financial success achieved by Ephraim A. Mark and Charles A. James', Bloom also thinks about progressive educational toys for use in what was perhaps the most eye-catching of education forms in the late nineteenth and early twentieth centuries – the kindergarten. They are listed as, 'astronomical kaleidoscopes exhibiting the twelve constellations of the zodiac from Aries to Pisces, miniature mechanical orreries, arithmetical gelatine lozenges, geometrical to correspond with zoological biscuits, globemap playing balls, historically costumed dolls' (*U*17,570–5).[56]

The language of schooling and schooled learning is likewise extremely visible in 'Ithaca', built into the narrative in seemingly random ways. At the beginning of 'Ithaca', Bloom and Stephen cross the 'circus before George's church diametrically, the chord in any circle being less than the arc which it subtends' (*U*17, 9–10). In the middle, they take their leave of each other: 'the lines of their valedictory arms, meeting at any point and forming any angle less than the sum of two right angles' (*U*17, 1222–3). As Bloom undresses for bed, he follows a line of body hair from his pubis to its termination 'on the summits of the mammary prominences' around 'two equidistant points' (*U*17,1442–3). There are many further references to schooled geometry and mathematics, as with the identification of Bloom's house as the '4th of the equidistant uneven numbers' (*U*17, 71). The casual and meaningless repetition of rule and formula is typical of the episode and circumscribes the epistemological world it inhabits. Other school subjects are implicated too – elementary chemistry and physics, for example. Lighting a match to boil a kettle releases energy by allowing 'carbon and hydrogen elements to enter free union with the oxygen in the air' (*U*17, 132). In the famous description of the qualities Bloom admires in water – 'Its universality: its democratic equality and constancy to its nature in seeking its own level' – we are told about the 'simplicity of its composition, two constituent parts of hydrogen with one constituent part of oxygen' (*U*17, 211–12). Rules of English grammar appear, again randomly, in a question about the contraction of schemes for acquiring 'vast wealth' by means of 'industrial channels': 'Positing what protasis would the contraction for such several schemes become a natural and necessary apodosis?' (*U*17, 1698; 1744–5). The unpicking required to fathom this is something Stephen might conceivably have at his fingertips, Bloom almost certainly not. In traditionalist grammar a complete conditional sentence consists of two clauses. The clause containing the condition (what if) is called the 'protasis', the clause containing the consequence is called the 'apodosis'. As the answer to the question makes reasonably clear, one eventuality that would render the development of Bloom's schemes unnecessary would be the deed of gift or bequest of 'eminent financiers' (*U*17, 1748).

The epistemological world behind 'Ithaca', then, usually conceptualized in terms of science or rationalism, is heavily schooled, but not exclusively so. As we have seen, there are other, equally compelling models behind the episode and its style and format, notably the informatics culture that is also everywhere in this chapter, in its broad form and its details. A question like 'What advantages attended shaving by night?' belongs to the *Tit-Bits* world (U17, 277). Likewise, the responses that explains Stephen's earlier collapse in in Nighttown as a combination of 'gastric inanition and certain chemical compounds of varying degrees of adulteration and alcoholic strength' (*U*17, 37–8). The same culture is contained in the episode as part of its implied physical reality. *Thom's Directory* is a volume on Bloom's bookshelf, just as information contained in that volume – the population of Ireland according to the 1901 census, for instance – also appears inside the Ithacan narrative. The connection between informatics and commodity culture is everywhere implied in the account of the contents of Bloom's kitchen dresser, a collection of commodities which help determine who Bloom is, or who he thinks he is, as it is in the description of the dream home Bloom would like to purchase 'by private treaty in fee simple' (*U*17,1504). This is reproduced in great detail as, a thatched bungalowshaped 2 storey dwellinghouse of southerly aspect' consisting of '1 drawingroom with baywindow . . ., 1 sittingroom, 4 bedrooms, 2 servants' rooms, tiled kitchen with close range and scullery, lounge hall with fitted linen presses, fumed oak sectional bookcase containing the Encyclopaedia Britannica and New Century Dictionary' (*U*17, 1504–5; 1520–24). The point here is not just the reference to two classic volumes of information culture but that the consumer world is ordered as taxonomy, like the taxonomy of the scientific world. The discourses of magazines like *Tit-Bits* – its disposition towards community, citizenship and social order, and its construction of its own audience – all are likewise fully inscribed in 'Ithaca' where the narrator notes Bloom's expression of 'the importance of dietary and civic selfhelp', 'the counsels of hygiene' that he keeps to himself and the advice 'concerning the respective percentage of protein and calorific energy in bacon, salt ling and butter' which he chooses to keep quiet about (*U*17, 28–9, 241, 249–50). The exposure of water wastage and its effects on 'self-supporting taxpayers, solvent, sound' addresses a *Tit-Bits* constituency in a *Tit-Bits* way as does Bloom's idea of a 'syllabus of intellectual pursuits' to be implemented when he is ensconced in his dream home (*U*17, 182, 1588). Incidentally, there are echoes in Bloom's suburban fantasy of a famous *Tit-Bits* short story–writing competition held in late 1883 which had for its prize a dream suburban home having 'eight rooms plus bathroom, scullery and cellars', including a room adjoining the dining room which 'a vulgar person might call a back sitting room' but *Tit-Bits* preferred to call a 'bijou drawing room'.[57]

These discourses – schooled and informatic – do not inhabit distinct narrative domains at any level of the narrative technic of 'Ithaca'. As the exchange of Stephen's education history for Bloom's suggests, they intermingle, converge and conflate, confounding any idea of the distinct tracing and positioning of cultural reference. The one, typically seen as commercial, ephemeral and practical, is barely distinguishable from the other – usually understood as internalized, high status and transferable. With this a central part of the logic that normalizes epistemological value systems and the social distinctions associated with them likewise collapses. This effect is in part a reflection of the culture itself, albeit one much exaggerated in the extreme cold and indifference of 'Ithaca'. The design of a child's textbook, Mangnall's *Historical Questions* for instance, is different but not that different from the 'inquiry column' of a popular periodical such as *Tit-Bits*, or the 'general information' column featured in the same publication. Both give answers to random questions like 'Why are "Martello Towers" so called?' or 'At what rate do bodies fall through the air?' (*Tit-Bits*) and 'What great events mark the opening of the nineteenth century?' or 'What is Gum Arabic'? (Mangnall).[58] The model for the 'Ithaca' episode of *Ulysses* might be examination papers or school textbooks, but equally it might just as well be something like a popular periodical, *Tit-Bits* or its competitor *Answers*. Some of the elements taken to refer specifically to text-book culture and pedagogies, like the listing, for example, are just as evident in a magazine like *Tit-Bits*. The question 'how are ocean currents caused?', produces in the latter the response:

> the sun's heat; the trade winds; the rotation of the earth on its axis; the rise and fall of tides all over the globe; the variations of density of the water according to its temperature, and the evaporating powers of its atmospherics; its depth, and degree of saltiness; and finally, the variations of barometric pressure.[59]

Informatics are not simply *equally* the common currency of the episode as schooling. They are intermingled and exchanged to such an extent that together they constitute one single epistemological universe that figures not as Stephen's domain or Bloom's, but as the commonality they both inhabit. The challenge of 'Ithaca', then, is that it represents an entanglement of high-status forms of knowledge and the prestigious institutions that produced them with the commercial world of something like *Tit-Bits*, so much so that the distinction between the two, the very distinction that systemized, modern schooling was designed to maintain at all costs, is conflated and confused.

It is worth emphasizing how transgressive this really is. In theory the formal education of elites, based so much on classicism, and the information culture that so characterized the modern world, were distinct regimes, designed to be kept well apart and, indeed, seemingly entirely contradictory in nature. The first tried to establish superior knowledge as the preserve of an educated elite. The second imagined itself as participating in the *encyclopédie* tradition and the European enlightenment, seeking connections with ideas about the public character of knowledge and the desirability of its free exchange. The goal of the makers of the 1911 edition of the *Encyclopaedia Britannica*, used so much in the making of *Finnegans Wake*, was to 'maintain direct relations with the whole of the English speaking world' and to bring 'all extant knowledge within the reach of every class of reader'.[60] 'Ithaca' has formal schooling and information culture spilling over into each other in all sorts of ways. The contradictions they jointly represent illustrate how far they inhabit the same world and, indeed, the extent to which they constitute it.

This, the unravelling of schooling as exceptionalism, constitutes the challenge of 'Ithaca' in education terms. However much elite schooling was shaped by material cultures of the modern world, it could only preserve its status if its claims of distinction and superiority could be properly maintained. The assimilative dynamic of 'Ithaca' robs school knowledge of that claim. It takes the undereducated bourgeois Bloom and the hypereducated Stephen and positions them in a contiguous and contingent cultural domain, joining *Ulysses* up with the radicalism of Stephen Dedalus in *Stephen Hero* and *A Portrait* which disdains modern schooling and speaking once more to the influence of Nietzsche's parallel dismantling of modern education in the late nineteenth century. From this perspective, the merging of 'Bloom's scientific penchant and Stephen's scholastic obsessions' is not as 'preposterous' as it has seemed.[61] It points to a convergence which, for Joyce, is the fate of Western rationalism in the modern world, again a comic formulation but a disturbing one. Behind its extraordinary articulation lies a vision of broken social promises on the one hand and cultural degeneration on the other where the reality of ambitions for the public dispersal of information are rendered up as ridiculous farce.

Notes

1 Jane Austen, *Emma* (1815; Leipzig: Tauchnitz, 1877), 27, 142.
2 George Gissing, *New Grub Street*, vol. 3 (London: Smith & Elder, 1891), 231–2.
3 See Richard Menke, 'Information', *Victorian, Literature and Culture*, 46/3–4, 2018, 739–42.
4 For a brief account of the theoretical background to historical work on Victorian information cultures, see Toni Weller (ed.), *Information History in the Modern World: Histories of the Information Age* (Basingstoke: Palgrave Macmillan, 2010), 14–16.
5 Toni Weller, *The Victorians and Information: A Social and Cultural History* (Saabrücken: VDM Verlag, 2009), 15.
6 See Alistair Black, Dave Muddiman and Helen Plant, *The Early Information Society: Information Management in Britain before the Computer* (London: Routledge, 2007).

7 James W. Carey, 'Time, Space and the Telegraph', in David Crowley and Paul Heyer (eds.), *Communication in History: Technology, Culture, Society* (Boston: Allyn & Bacon, 2003), 125–31 [126].
8 Carey, 'Time, Space and the Telegraph', 126.
9 Weller, *The Victorians and Information*, 11.
10 Toni Weller, 'The Puffery and Practicality of Etiquette Book: A New Take on Victorian Information Culture', *Library Trends*, 62/3, 2014, 663–80 [666].
11 *Answers*, June 4, 1904, 77, 82.
12 Alan Rauch, *Useful Knowledge: The Victorians, Morality and the March of the Intellect* (Durham, NC, London: Duke University Press, 2001), 2.
13 See Aileen Fyfe, 'The Information Revolution', in David McKitterick (ed.), *The Cambridge History of the Book in Britain 1830–1914*, vol. 6 (Cambridge: Cambridge University Press, 2009), 567–94.
14 Morton P. Levitt, 'Beyond Dublin, Joyce and Modernism', *Journal of Modern Literature*, 22/2, 1998/9, 385–94 [385].
15 *Thom's Directory of the United Kingdom of Great Britain and Ireland* (Dublin: Thom's, 1904), 1399.
16 *Thom's Directory*, 2. Weldon Thornton thinks Thom's is 'most likely' the source for this part of 'Ithaca'. In fact, there can no doubt. The material is used almost without change. See *Allusions to Ulysses*, 462.
17 Kate Jackson, 'George Newnes and the "Loyal Tit-Bitites": Educational Identity and Textual Interaction in *Tit-Bits*', in Laurel Brake, Bill Bell and David Finkelstein (eds.), *Nineteenth-Century Media and the Construction of Identities* (Basingstoke: Palgrave, 2000), 11–26, [13–14].
18 See Robert Scholes and Richard M. Kain (eds.), *The Workshop of Daedalus: James Joyce and the Raw Materials for 'A Portrait of the Artist as a Young Man'* (Evanston, IL: Northwestern University Press, 1965), 175.
19 Jackson, 'George Newnes and the "Loyal Tit-Bitites"', 17.
20 R.B. Kershner, *The Culture of Joyce's 'Ulysses'* (New York: Palgrave Macmillan, 2010), 144.
21 *Tit-Bits*, January 6, 1900, 342; *Tit-Bits*, June 6, 1904, 250.
22 *Tit-Bits*, January 6, 1900, 339.
23 *Tit-Bits*, January 6, 1900, 342.
24 See Jackson, 'George Newnes and the "Loyal Tit-Bitites"', 18–19.
25 Quoted in 'George Newnes and the "Loyal Tit-Bitites"', 19.
26 *Tit-Bits*, January 6, 1900, 351–2.
27 *Tit-Bits*, January 6, 1900, 351.
28 *Tit-Bits*, January 6, 1900, 355.
29 *1000 Answers to 1000 Questions: Being a Reprint of the First 1,000 Questions in the 'Tit-Bits' Inquiry Column with the Replies Thereto* (London: Tit-Bits, 1884), questions 258, 290, 854, 993.
30 *1000 Answers and 1000 Questions: Being a Reprint of the Second 1,000 Questions in the 'Tit-Bits' Inquiry Column with the Replies Thereto* (London: Tit-Bits, 1888), question 1018.
31 *1000 Answers and 1000 Questions: Being a Reprint of the Fourth 1,000 Questions in the 'Tit-Bits' Inquiry Column with the Replies Thereto* (London: Tit-Bits, 1895), question, 3484.
32 *1000 Answers to 1000 Questions: Being a Reprint of the Third 1,000 Questions in the 'Tit-Bits' Inquiry Column with the Replies Thereto* (London: Tit-Bits, 1890), question 2874.
33 *Notable Answers to 1000 Questions* (London: Tit-Bits, 1896), question 69.
34 *1000 Answers to 1000 Questions* (1884), questions 356, 350, 252.
35 *1000 Answers to 1000 Questions* (1888), question 1695.
36 *1000 Answers to 1000 Questions* (1895), questions 3276, 3302.
37 *1000 Answers to 1000 Questions* (1888), question 1695.

38 Hilary Clark, *The Fictional Encyclopaedia: Joyce, Pound, Sollers* (New York: Garland, 1990), 17.
39 See Weller, 'The Puffery and Practicality of Etiquette Books', 670.
40 *1000 Answers to 1000 Questions* (1884), question 264.
41 *1000 Answers to 1000 Questions* (1888), question 1674.
42 William M. Schutte, 'Leopold Bloom: A Touch of the Artist', *James Joyce Quarterly*, 10/1, 1972, 118–31 (118).
43 See Stuart Gilbert (ed.), *Letters of James Joyce* (London: Faber & Faber, 1957), 167.
44 For the 'arranger', see David Hayman, *'Ulysses': The Mechanics of Meaning*, rev. and exp. (1970; Madison: University of Wisconsin Press, 1988), especially 88–104. Hugh Kenner became a keen advocate of the idea in *'Ulysses'* (Baltimore: Johns Hopkins University Press, 1987), especially 61–71, as was Marilyn French in *The Book as World: James Joyce's 'Ulysses'* and Karen Lawrence in *The Odyssey of Style in 'Ulysses'* (Princeton: Princeton University Press, 1981). See also John Somer, 'The Self Reflexive Arranger in the Initial Style of Joyce's *Ulysses*', *James Joyce Quarterly*, 31/2, 1994, 65–79.
45 James Wylde (ed.), *Circles of the Sciences* (London: The London Printing & Publishing Co., 1862.), iii–iv.
46 *1000 Answers to 1000 Questions* (1884), question 252.
47 *1000 Answers to 1000 Questions* (1884), question 850.
48 The phrase 'catechism impersonal' is used to describe the style of 'Ithaca' in one of the schemas of *Ulysses*. See Peake, *James Joyce: The Citizen and the Artist*, 120–1. For the longer descriptor see Gilbert (ed.), *Letters of James Joyce*, 164.
49 'School Books of the Past, by a Very Old Boy', *The Publishers Circular and Bookseller's Record*, January 13, 1900, 41.
50 Richmal Mangnall, *Historical and Miscellaneous Questions for the Use of Young People*, 6th edn. (London: Longman, Hurst, Rees & Orme, 1808), 78, 79.
51 'Peter Parley', *Peter Parley's Tales about the Mythology of the Greeks and Romans* (London: 1839), iv, 329. 'Peter Parley' was Samuel Griswold Goodwich, a bookseller and publisher who amassed a fortune publishing children's books, most of which he did not author. These included *Tales about Ireland and the Irish* (1848?) dedicated to 'the neglected people of Ireland' by 'their friend Peter Parley'. The repeated claim of this part-'history', part-'tour' was that the Irish were responsible for their own downfall – 'the Irish as usual, had turned their arms against themselves' (329).
52 See Robert Hampson, '"Allowing for Possible Error": Education and Catechism in "Ithaca"', in Andrew Gibson (ed.), *Joyce's 'Ithaca'* (Amsterdam – Atlanta, GA: Rodopi, 1996), 229–67.
53 Hampson, '"Allowing for Possible Error"', 252–3, 242, 244.
54 '"Allowing for Possible Error"', 242.
55 Mangnall, *Historical and Miscellaneous Questions*, 330, 350.
56 Fröbel's progressivist version of pre-schooling had attracted considerable interest in Ireland, but not been implemented with much seriousness. For an account of kindergarten in late nineteenth and early twentieth century Ireland, see Margaret Fitzgerald, 'The Influence of Froebel's Kindergarten on the Belmore-Commission, 1897–1898', *The Maynooth Review*, 19, 1983, 3–30.
57 Quoted in Sharon O'Connor, 'The *Tit-Bits* Villa', *The Dulwich Society*, Winter 1916, www.dulwichsociety.com/journal-archive/113-winter-2016/1439-tit-bits-villa
58 *1000 Answers and 1000 Questions* (1884), question 949; *1000 Answers and 1000 Questions* (1890), question 2768; Mangnall, *Historical and Miscellaneous Questions*, 112, 364.
59 *1000 Answers to 1000 Questions* (1895), question 3302.
60 *Encyclopedia Britannica*, 11th edn., vol. 1, vii–x.
61 Fritz Senn, '"Ithaca": Portrait of the Chapter as a Long List', in Gibson (ed.), *Joyce's 'Ithaca'*, 31–76 [39].

Chapter 8

Joyce and the textbook – 'Oxen of the Sun' and 'Eumaeus'

– Very good. Where?
The boy's blank face asked a blank window. . . .
– I forget the place, sir. 279 B.C.
– Asculum, Stephen said, glancing at the name and place in the gorescarred book.

James Joyce, *Ulysses* (1921)

This question of the books

In February 1874, the controversial English historian and novelist J.A. Froude published an account of 'lesson books' written for the use of students and teachers in Christian Brothers' schools in Ireland. In it, Froude constructs the education of the youth of Ireland in terms of an attempt by the Catholic Church to regain 'her lost dominion over the intellect of the world'. Having lost 'the force of arms', he imagines a Church seeking to use the 'agency of popular education' to 'wield the force of public opinion'. It faces insurmountable difficulties in this campaign, nothing less than an undoing of three of 'the most creative' centuries in all history, which have seen the rise of science, rationalism and democracy and the corresponding falling away of Papal authority. From this charged position, Froude begins his analysis of the Christian Brothers' textbooks, 'a complete school literature' designed to counter the influence of materials used by the National School Board of Ireland.[1] There is nothing particularly objectionable in the 'more rudimentary lesson books', although they are 'thoroughly Roman Catholic in tone, and therefore unfitted for a Protestant education'.[2] The *Historical Class Book*, however, and the *Treatise on Modern Geography*, both published by the Christian Brothers and used across their schools, are a different matter. Constructed according to a 'thoroughly sectarian design', they 'set forth the social and intellectual development of all countries in a way to exalt Romanism and disparage Protestantism'. The *Geography* is 'as remarkable for its omissions as for its direct misrepresentations', perhaps no part of it 'more audaciously false and Jesuitical than that which attempts to vindicate the Church of Rome in the case of Galileo'. In terms of political bias, both seem 'specially constructed to train up a nation of Irish repealers'.[3] A fourth volume, *The Literary Class Book; or Fourth Series of Select Reading Lessons* is even worse in this respect: 'Master Brooke, a Member of the Royal Commission on Primary Education pronounced it to be the best preparation for Fenianism that can be imagined'.[4]

More than 50 years later, Professor Timothy Corcoran S.J. wrote an article for *The Irish Monthly* entitled 'Official Text Books and Irish Schools'. In it, he draws attention to the fact that, seven years previously, radical changes 'initiated under Irish authority' had been implemented and that these had 'great and durable effects' on the Irish education system. He is referring to the National Programme Conference on Primary Instruction (1921–1922) and the Dail Commission on Secondary Education (1921–1922), both of which he was advisor to. According to an article written in the 1980s and highly critical of Corcoran, many of the recommendations 'emerging from these deliberations bore the unmistakeable stamp of Timothy Corcoran'.[5] One of them is framed by Corcoran as establishing 'the fullest freedom' for Irish schools in 'settling all the details of their course of study', including their textbooks, with the addition that 'the same liberty to direct their own school studies in accordance with their own religious systems is, of course, the right of every religious body possessing schools'.[6] Here freedom from the state is measured by the authority of the church to exercise absolute control over the books used in National schools.

Despite the new agency of Irish Catholicism in Ireland, however, Corcoran is far from complaisant about the future safety of textbook 'freedom'. Indeed, the main purpose of his article is not to draw attention to the achievements of the Republic in this respect but, on the contrary, to emphasize the need, even as late as 1928, to maintain vigilance over school 'independence'. He reports back on public debates on the Education Estimates, held in Dublin in the summer of that year, in which traditional social deference towards Anglicization is perceived to be creeping back into Irish life. Corcoran describes a call made for the return of 'an official series of National School books, both in English and Irish'. Some nostalgia for the old-school textbooks produced by the Stationery Office is expressed. Their absence is held by some to be 'a great loss', not just from their own point of view – a British point of view – but from 'any point of view'. It is this tendency to be drawn to the thraldom of the past that Corcoran wants to warn against. As part of that campaign, he reminds his readers of the long history of resistance to 'official' textbooks, the effects of which were 'manifold and pervasive' – this was resistance led, as Corcoran points out, by Cardinal Cullen in the 1860s and 1870s and thereafter taken up 'by his most illustrious successor, the Most Rev. Dr Walsh'. The latter is the same William Walsh excoriated as an anti-Parnellite by Simon Dedalus who refers to him as 'Billy with the lip' in *A Portrait* (*P*, 27). In real life, Walsh was to see 'the official series of textbooks' dismantled in 1900, but apparently not forever.[7]

As we have seen, Joyce's use of school textbooks, in both early and later fictions, has sometimes been associated with Anglicized school systems and the historical controversy that raged over them throughout the nineteenth century, outlasting the formation of the Republic. Elite public schools like the ones Joyce attended were not subject to the same kind of direct interference as National schools and Christian Brothers schools, but it is the case that they would have used Anglicized textbooks. Alongside the *Prosida*, for example, the Latin primer written by Emanuel Alvarez S.J. in the sixteenth century, Joyce has Stephen Dedalus in *A Portrait* working from James Cornwell's *Spelling for Beginners*. This was part of a well-known series. The implied pedagogical technique that shapes the series design was ostensibly liberal and interactive, but the examples through which it operated were stuffed with aristocratic, racialized and colonial ideologies at every point. In the spelling book, schoolchildren were taught spelling through such sentences as 'the archers in our army at Crecy wore some armour', 'the deer was shot in the haunch' and 'the war-like Indians are now in a state of warfare with white men'.[8] In a grammar book in the same series, they are invited to write out and underscore the possessive in such sentences as 'Wellington's victory cannot be forgotten' and to copy the following sentences, turning them from active to passive: 'We love our country'; 'England has produced many great poets' and 'The British youth are distinguishable by their sense of honour'.[9] There is nothing innocent here of course. Basic training in grammar is being used as a vehicle for what now reads as the crassest propaganda. Further examples used in different exercises work in the same way, such as 'To possess an empire on which the sun never sets, as England does, can be said of no other country, either ancient or modern' and 'England only performs her duty in aiming at the improvement of the world'.[10] The text is Anglocentric in all senses, including the geographical. In the following sequence, students are required to underscore nouns and write the capital P over proper nouns: 'Where is Samuel. He is living in Tonbridge'; 'Is your brother in London? No, he is at Liverpool'. Ireland is quite literally erased from this landscape. A lesson on singular nominatives includes the sentence 'England, Scotland, and Wales form Great Britain'.[11] The process of creating an Anglocentric map of the world is taken to new levels in Cornwell's *Geography for Beginners* where height in both man-made buildings and nature is exemplified by St Paul's Cathedral and Ben Nevis, length by the Thames and the Severn and population size by reference to London, England and Wales and Scotland. The visibility or rising and setting of constellations are given in relation to Britain's capital city. Examples of islands include the Isle of Wight and the Isle of Man, the isthmus is exemplified by Chesil Bank, the peninsula by 'Portland Peninsula in England', a cape by Land's End, a coast by the 'South Coast, England', a valley by the 'vale of York', a mountain range by the Pennines, a plain by 'the eastern plain of England' and so on.[12]

What really stands out about Joyce's usage of this kind of material in the earlier fiction is not how much it is emphasized but how much it is underplayed. The single direct incorporation in *A Portrait*, the spelling aid that Stephen recites from 'Dr Cornwell's Spelling Book' in the early pages, is not neutral – 'Wolsey died in Leicester abbey/Where the abbots buried him. Canker is a disease of plants, Cancer one of animal' – but neither is it especially ideologically charged.[13]

There is a relative silence about this issue in early Joyce, a detachment from what was in reality a highly controversial topic. The writer *of A Portrait*, like the prototype artist in it, seems largely indifferent to the ideological battle surrounding textbooks or, in the early chapters at any rate, throws the controversy outside the perimeters of what a young boy would be aware of. Either way, textbooks would seem to be largely off the agenda of an early fiction that makes its impact, political and otherwise, elsewhere.

The late fiction, however, is a different matter. In *Ulysses*, textbooks are more frequently referenced in relation to narrative logic and as part of the landscape of the everyday social world. Dilly Dedalus seeks her brother's opinion on a French language primer picked up from a second-hand bookstall (*U*10, 867–8). Gerty McDowell, who feels her lack of education letting her down, refers to Walker's *Pronouncing Dictionary*, a standard textbook that contained 'hints for softening Irish brogue' (*U*13, 342).[14] Bloom's bookshelves include a copy of a very old text book *Short but yet Plain Elements of Geometry* (1734) written in French by F. Ignatius Pardies and 'rendered into English' by John Harris, an old schoolbook or perhaps a more recent investment made to assist him in the winning of prize money offered for the solution of how to square the circle (see *U*17, 1398). More substantially, textbooks appear to be 'structural' in both *Ulysses* and *Finnegan Wake*, implicated, as we have seen, in 'Ithaca' but also in the styles, or 'technics', of other late episodes. Indeed, no fewer than three of them – 'Ithaca', 'Oxen of the Sun' and 'Eumaeus', all three considered to be amongst the most challenging in the entire book – are articulations that draw on discourses variously connected to institutionalized learning and signified substantially by the textbook. In *Finnegans Wake*, Book Two, Chapter Two (2.2) is designed to replicate the appearance of a textbook. It may have started off differently, but by 1935, when it had taken on its current form, it had become set out to reproduce 'a schoolboy's (and schoolgirl's) old classbook, complete with marginalia by the twins, who change sides at half time, footnotes by a girl (who doesn't), a Euclid diagram, funny drawings etc.'.[15] At its heart is not just *a* textbook but arguably *the* textbook – *Euclid's Elements*, perhaps the oldest, the most reproduced, quite simply the most *used* textbook of all time and centrally connected to elitist forms of education. Running into more than 1,000 editions since its first printing in 1482, for centuries Euclid's book remained the primary deductive treatment of mathematics, contingent on mathematical proofs of propositions rather than routinized applications of process by which calculation could be operated in abstract ways without understanding of anything observable in the real world. Thus, the *Elements* had a very particular status. It represented nothing less than a universal standard in applied logic and reasoning. For centuries, it was taught to all university students as part of the quadrivium and, by the eighteenth century, entered the wider social domain as a knowledge form indispensable to everyone aspiring to appear educated.

Elements is the most extensively used textbook in *FW*, 2.2, but not the only one. Other classic classroom textbooks and their authors are alluded to throughout, dozens of them. Lindley Murray (1754–1826), the grammarian discussed later on, appears at 269.29, albeit as a retailer – 'Lindley's and Murray's'. Isaac Todhunter, a well-known nineteenth-century mathematician who revised Robert Simpson's translation of *Euclid's Elements* in 1862, figures, for example, as 'doddhunter' at 283.25–6, as do H.S. Hall and S.R. Knight, also authors of textbooks in the nineteenth century. All three names combine in a sentence that explores Shaun's difficulties in grasping aspects of mathematics. He can 'reckan' (do arithmetic) but he always got 'dullmarks for his nucleuds and alegobrew. . . . O them doddhunters and allanights, aabs and baas for agonmes, yees and zees for incognits, bate him up jerrybly' (*FW*, 283. 23–8). Vere Foster (1819–1900), the once revered Irish philanthropist who wrote handwriting books for children, figures at 280.17 as 'Poppa Vere Foster'. George Brown (1650–1730), the inventor of a 'simple' way of teaching children arithmetic appears at 286.1 as 'neuralgiabrown'; John Casey (1820–1891), the author of *A Sequel to Euclid* who taught mathematics at University College, Dublin (UCD) and became famous for his demonstrations in relation to the circle, is referred to at 286.9. Girolamo Cardan (1501–1576) infamous mathematics plagiarist is mentioned at 286.9, and John Alexander Ellis (1814–1890), the philologist and mathematician who wrote *Algebra Identified with Geometry* and was G.B. Shaw's model for Henry Higgins is alluded to at 294.8. Robert Scott (1811–1887), the English divine and lexicographer and Master of Balliol who collaborated with Henry George Liddell on a widely used Greek-English Dictionary appears at 301.9–10; Michael Stiffel (1487–1567), the sixteenth-century German mathematician who invented the signs for 'plus' and 'square root' is alluded to at 301.18, and so on.[16] There are many further references to pedagogues and their textbooks in 2.2, especially to figures important in schooled mathematics, including to John Pell (1601–1685), the English mathematician and to the Dublin mathematician Sir William Rowan Hamilton (1805–65). John Casey who taught mathematics at UCD and authored *A Sequel to Euclid* likewise features, as does John Napier (1550–1617), the Scottish mathematician who devised logarithms. Edward Cocker (1631–1675), the London engraver who also taught arithmetic, produced *Aritimetick*, a textbook so popular that it led to the proverbial expression 'according to Cocker' – which is repeated, amongst other places in the *Wake*, in the right margin note of page 303.

The extraordinary investment in textbook culture makes the late Joyce text contingent on schooled learning in quite emphatic ways. In the sense that they are products of schooled learning, all modern books exist in this same domain of course – they are all results of the schooling that, at some level, enables them – and there are particular conjunctions that could be taken to align text-books with the modernist text in some ways. The historical period that produced Joyce's fiction saw an astonishing rise in the production of textbooks. No fewer than 790 new books in education were published in Britain in 1899, and 200 new editions, forming the second largest category of book sales outside of 'Novels, Tales and Juvenile Works'.[17] This wave, like exhibition culture and press coverage, was exemplary of the authority of education in the modern world and its association with commodification, massification and a surplus of things. From

1842, the British trade journal *The Publishers Circular and Booksellers Record* had produced special education editions twice a year, in which publishers advertised their education wares, a fast-growing market throughout the nineteenth century and beyond. Its January 1900 edition had Blackwood advertising new titles in classical texts, English, French and German, mathematics, Greek and Latin. Longman promoted textbooks in classical history, and Latin primers and French dictionaries. It also produced a new teachers' *Handbook of Psychology*. Crosby and Lockwood sold books in French and commercial education and its list included a 'handbook of English literature' and 'Civil Service handbooks'. The school publications division of Frederick Warne and Co. stocked histories, dictionaries, pronouncing dictionaries, spelling books and 'Table Book Atlases' – and the lists went on, from publishers such as Cassell, J.M. Dent, Macmillan, John Murray, Methuen, W.B. Clive, George Phillip, Asher and Co, Clarendon Press, Oliver Boyd, and the Oxford and Cambridge Local Examination Boards which published syllabuses and past examination papers as well as textbooks and teachers' guides.[18] Some of the most prestigious public schools established specific links with publishers – Eton with John Murray, for instance, and Uppingham with Macmillan.[19]

For all this resonance with the conditions of modernity, usually the relationship between writing and textbook worlds is hidden, naturalized and nonfunctional – even in modernist literary culture. In late Joyce, however, it is writ large, exaggerated and entirely mediative of any notion of the real. Chapters like 'Oxen of the Sun', 'Eumaeus', 'Ithaca' and *FW* 2.2 continually reference a narrative reality that is ostensibly 'unfolding'. But there is no direct accessing of that reality outside of the narrative technics which make them. Here, schooled textbooks become constitutive of the social world in unusually direct, albeit strained and often outlandish, ways. In fact, it is arguable whether any novelist has ever taken such pains to imagine the education text in relation to the formation of social reality as does Joyce in his later work. How this operates in 'Oxen of the Sun' and 'Eumaeus' is the subject of what follows.

Textbooks and the making of 'Oxen of the Sun'

'Oxen of the Sun' is related to schooling in two distinct but connected ways. In the first, as we have seen, 'Oxen' becomes an extraordinary display of schooled learning, evident in the 'student talk' that characterizes the episode. The second relates to the design of the episode, a design that Joyce was famously explicit about in some ways but not all. In a well-known letter to his friend Frank Budgen, Joyce provides what appears to be a detailed account of the chapter's design. Behind it is the idea of 'the crime committed against fecundity by sterilizing the act of coition', an obscure reference even if you know the allusion to *The Odyssey* and the slaughter of cattle owned by the sun god Helios – this being the crime that leads to the destruction of Odysseus's ship and all his men and his subsequent wanderings. Exactly what parallel crime is committed in Joyce's version, however, and who is punished for it is not identified in the letter and remains the subject of critical debate. The relationship between letter and final text becomes much clearer, however, in what follows. Joyce explains, step by step, the plan from which he has operated. The scene is 'the lying-in hospital'. In terms of 'technique', this is to be a 'nineparted episode without divisions' representing the history of literature from a 'Sallustian-Tacitean prelude' through to 'Defoe-Swift and Steele-Addison-Sterne and Landor-Pater-Newman' until

> it ends in a frightful jumble of pidgin English, nigger English, Cockney, Irish, Bowery slang and broken doggerel. This procession is also linked back at each part subtly with some foregoing episode of the day and, besides this, with the natural stages of development in the embryo and the periods of faunal evolution in general. The double-thudding Anglo-Saxon motif recurs from time to time . . . to give the sense of the hoofs of oxen. Bloom is the spermatozoon, the hospital the womb, the nurse the ovum, Stephen the embryo.
>
> How's that for high?[20]

For all this detailed specification, however, Joyce's letter neglects to mention a crucial fact about the episode, central now to our understanding of how it was written and, indeed, how it works. The 'parodies' of historical literature and the associations the chapter makes between literary history and natural evolution, central elements in what makes the design so 'high', are both characteristic of a very particular and quite everyday kind of pedagogic instrument – literature manuals that were used in schools and colleges across Britain, Germany, Spain, Italy, Russia and many other countries, more or less at the same time across the turn of the nineteenth century. Later, the same kind of compilations were reproduced in postcolonial versions – in South America for example, and, indeed, Ireland – and continued to be in standard use well into the later twentieth century, when they began to be displaced by anthologies of criticism.[21] This model, critical for 'Oxen', is simply unreferenced in a Joyce letter otherwise full and revealing. We only know now how much Joyce lent on the source material as a result of the work of genetic critics, tracing backwards from Joyce's notesheets for 'Oxen' to the origins. This enables an exact identification of where the notes were taken from and shows us how Joyce used them.

One such source was *The Treasury of English Literature* (1908), which Joyce had in his Trieste library. Its introduction indicates how and in what sense the book is connected to teaching and learning. Originally, it was compiled by Kate M. Warren, a lecturer at Westfield College, an early women's college set up as part of the University of London in 1882. Quite incidentally, book, author and institution all operate as a direct challenge to the masculinist world set up in 'Oxen', ironically enough, against the background of a maternity hospital – a fact that could not have been lost on Joyce.

Warren points out in her preface that the volume was put together as a companion piece to Stopford A. Brook's *Primer of English Literature* 'with the intention of illustrating, by prose and verse selections, the literary history and criticism to be found in that well-known book', 'a classic among manuals of the kind' used by 'teachers and pupils who have adopted it in schools and colleges'.[22] She goes on to explain that the selections she has chosen have been tested out on her own undergraduate students. Invited to write the introduction to the *Treasury*, Brook himself commends the volume in a somewhat patronizing way as likely to prove 'of great use in the teaching of English literature', as well as being of 'much help to students in the early years of their study of English writing'.[23] He also spells out what the chronology of styles illustrates and what is invested in the book's making. Its purpose is to provide a 'miniature image of English Literature' demonstrating what Brook takes to be its essential characteristics – its 'great age', meaning its antiquity, 'its continuity, its changing history, its growth, its innate elements, the outside influence which it assimilates and its general excellence'. The central ideas here, both deriving from readings of evolutionary science, are the claims that literature 'grows', as Mina Purefoy's embryo grows in 'Oxen', and has a progressive destiny bound up with a national identity that survives whatever influences the culture assimilates. However strongly affected by other cultures, English literature will always remain 'original', Brook insists, because 'the original cells of its thought and passion' are so defining, so irreducible. A bio-culture, an imagined bloodline highly characteristic of intellectual cultures in Europe in the nineteenth and early twentieth centuries up to 1945, ensures that literary history will always bear the imprint of its 'organic' and deeply racialized origins. From this position, English literature will 'always be English'. Even beyond the fall of empires, it will retain its 'voice'. 'If England, like other empires, should fall, the English tongue will not pass way with England, nor her literature'.[24]

Likewise W. Peacock's *English Prose from Mandeville to Ruskin* (1912), also in the Trieste library and used in the construction of 'Oxen', was a 'volume of selections' designed to 'illustrate the development of English prose' intended 'mainly for the use of students'.[25] So was A.F. Murison's *Selections from the Best English Authors – Beowulf to the Present Time* (1907), an anthology used in intermediate schools and universities as a sampler and again a volume in Joyce's library. Other sources used in the composition of 'Oxen' might not have been conceived of or used as teaching manuals in quite the same way, but all were related to the same education culture and the progressivist developmentalism that characterized it. George Saintsbury's *A History of English Prose Rhythm*, for example, one of the most commonly cited sources for 'Oxen' – some 75 usages of it have been identified in the episode – was not a true anthology, but it used examples from literary history organized on a chronological basis to illustrate its argument and positioned itself within contemporary education debates. A scholarly work, responsible for the idea that the characteristic rhythm of English prose is 'the double-thudding' of 'Anglo-Saxon' that Joyce adopts as his own in the Budgen letter, Saintsbury's book was devoted to a subject likely to struggle in what the author sees as a depressing education future – the familiar decline deemed by many to be the fate of modern mass education.[26] 'That it is possible to use prose rhythm', he writes with obvious irritation, 'without knowing or thinking anything about it, is established by one of the great and greatly quoted things which it is now considered unlawful to mention, because everyone is supposed to know them; and which in the near future of what is now called *education*, nobody at all will know'.[27]

Just as we now understand that 'Oxen' is not comprised of imitations of individual writers but, rather, of groups of writers, so the forms of its models are not entirely singular either. Nevertheless, Joyce's extraordinary reworking of the material and its organization into a familiar chronology is clear, establishing without any doubt that 'Oxen' was conceived in relation to the traditional sampler or 'manual'. It is an attempt to encompass an entire historical literature only in the much-qualified sense that it imitates a certain kind of pedagogic instrument, a distinction sometimes blurred in criticism of this episode, but an important one. It means that whatever transformation 'Oxen' effects on its model, it is an engagement with a highly mediated version of literature, one entirely implicated with the learning of elites.

It also means that the idea of 'Oxen' as being comprised of Kenner's 'student's talk' applies not only to the social world imagined in the chapter and the characters made to act it out, but also to the literary mechanics that constitute it and the highly schooled process that preceded its transformation into writing – taking notes from textbooks. The chapter has often been regarded as an overdone Joyce text, where style overwhelms substance and content becomes insufficient to bear the weight of the technic. But in some senses, there is an obvious consistency here. If the narrative substance is deemed to be underpowered in some way, so is the method that produced it and its portentous structural design. The 'Oxen' narrative is a performance of schooled identities; its style reproduces what was once a commonplace kind of textbook and is a version of the classic pedagogic instruction to model, to 'write in the style of'. In this way, the text often taken to be exemplary of the impossibly hard-to-read Joyce – as irresistible to the 'serious' Joyce reader as it is objectionable to others – is self-consciously engaged in its entirety as a product of 'schooling'.

How are we to visualize the relationship between the 'student talk' that constitutes the content of 'Oxen' and the writing practice that constitutes its style? There are significant comparisons to be made between the two. These are broad and general, but telling nevertheless. Both are remarkable, both brilliant, both designed to impress. Both thrive on mastery, and in both, competition, the instinct to outdo, is a powerful motivating force. In both, control is caught up with a certain form, an aesthetic, where ornate 'allusion' is central. This is often indirect, and combinative, or contaminative, often blending material from across cultural forms. It is also characterized by stylized transgression, a comic form of dissent which insulates elevated 'student talk' from the charge of orthodoxy at the same time as it embeds it as a superior social discourse. Stephen and Mulligan's characteristic mutilation of the Mass and many other religious texts is symptomatic here. The point is not just that the allusion is made but that it is cleverly manipulated, and therein lies it complexity. The principle might approximate quotation, but it is, in fact, organized cultural interference functioning as social code.

The connections between student talk and the method Joyce adapts in his parodies of historical literary styles in this latter respect are clear. These, too, are precise but also approximate and subject to a very specific form of intervention which impacts at the level of the tiniest detail of execution. For literary history as it is reproduced in 'Oxen', far from falling into line with historical progressivism, is subject to a huge degree of disruption. Although its broad divisions confirm the presence of particular groups of writers positioned more or less correctly in traditional chronology, there are also many passages in which traditional order is broken up and substantially rearranged. Much of the diction Joyce sourced from Swift, for example, appears not in the 'bovine fantasia' section of the episode, which is written in the general manner of the discourse of bulls from *A Tale of the Tub* but, as genetic critic Sarah Davison shows, dispersed across the whole episode. The same passage itself, across lines 564–650, contains precise echoes of multiple others taken from across literary periods and crosses a period of some 180 years. These include the Dublin writer Richard Steele (1672–1729), Sir Walter Raleigh (1552–1618), the English bishop John Earle (1601–1655), John Bunyan (1628–1688), Daniel Defoe (1660–1731), Shakespeare (c.1564–1616), Edmund Spenser (c.1552–1599) and the poet and essayist Sir Thomas Overbury (1581–1613). 'Oxen' might appear structured in confirmation of traditional literary historiography, indeed, that was Joyce's claim, but it also undermines that very same history.[28] An even shorter section of just 16 lines, starting at 854 ('But the word of Mr Costello was an unwelcome language for him') ranges across an even wider historical period of almost 320 years, using materials taken from the work of historians, politicians, philosophers and naturalists – Robert South (1634–1716), Philip Dormer Stanhope (1694–1773), Samuel Johnson (1709–1784), David Hume (1711–1776), Gilbert White (1720–1793), Charles Lamb (1775–1834), Sir Thomas More (1478–1535) and, again, Edmund Burke (1729–1797). The same pattern repeats over and over across the chapter, as astonishing display of erudition but one closely related to the historically specific forms of 'banter' that also characterize the episode, not least in its capacity for outdoing cleverness.

The result has been read as a 'colourful miscellany', a carnivalesque liberation which operates freely outside of what is referenced in terms of 'the nightmare of history' from which Stephen Dedalus is famously trying to awake (*U*2, 77).[29] But in some senses the episode is not free at all. On the contrary, for all its mastery, exuberance and inventiveness, 'Oxen' is circumscribed by the schooling that frames it. This is not to deny the distance 'Oxen' travels into disruption, the reason why the chapter has become so much an exemplar of deconstructive 'textuality'. It laughs at the foundational idea of literature as 'a living organism with a living soul' whose history was grandiosely imagined by Stopford Brook 'as a vital and enlinked evolution' in which 'each period of its growth not only brings up to all the excellence outward circumstances will permit to its special forms, but produces underneath these special forms, the germs which in the next period will grow into the excellences of that period'.[30] This kind of thinking is unravelled in 'Oxen', where the perceived irreducibility of national literary culture is wrecked by the simple fact of its mechanical reproduction. Here the destination imagined for literature – the growth Brook imagines taking 'root in the Old English work of Cadmon and Cyrewolf' and whose progress 'has been continuous, climbing steadily' – is completely undermined.[31] For 'Oxen' ends in that cultural mess beyond the refinements of form as they are normally understood, a mess that includes what Joyce calls 'nigger English'. In terms which are now highly objectionable, Joyce in 'Oxen' moves from ridicule of the historiography he was taught as a schoolboy and college student to a disruption of the wide-ranging epistemology behind it that would have been entirely recognizable to degeneration theorists of his day. However 'high' this may all be, the implication is that Joyce's writing at the end of 'Oxen' not only 'reflects' that mess but, from some perspectives, becomes a version of that mess itself. In this sense, 'Oxen', for all the work ethic that goes into it, is not so much a prize-winning essay as a badly blotted illustration of learning gone to the dogs.

'Eumaeus' and Lindley Murray's *Grammar*

From this perspective, the 'traditionalism' of 'Oxen', suggested not least in its method of composition, becomes both an exemplar of schooled knowledge and a genuinely radical force. Its contingency on schooled learning writes back to Nietzsche's critique of the modern school curriculum and the civilization it produced, and it also looks forward to anti-philosophies of the 1960s and 1970s in quite specific ways. Indeed, the whole chapter resonates deeply with a lecture given by Roland Barthes almost 50 years after the publication of *Ulysses* which also has a pedagogic frame of reference. The conference at which it was delivered, organized by Tzvetan Todorov and Serge Doubrovsky and featuring other influential theorists including Gérard Genette and A.J. Greimas, was called the 'The Teaching of Literature'. Barthes's contribution, 'Reflections on a Manual', makes no reference to Joyce but takes as its starting point French versions of the literary anthologies that were still apparently being used in the teaching of literature in France in the 1960s. The substance of Barthes's talk is directed against how schooled knowledge had produced epistemologies of literature heavily framed by idealizing and reactionary fantasies.[32] These were underpinned by the status of canonical literature – a cultural authoritarianism captured in the idiomatic expression that appears near the start of Barthes's lecture: 'Literature is what gets taught. Period'. The dislocation between 'real' literary practice and the teaching of high-status literature – resonating against Joyce's 'crime committed against fecundity by sterilizing the act of coition' – is important because it is 'connected to what may be today's most pressing problem, the problem of the transmission of knowledge'. 'Undoubtedly', Barthes continues, 'the problem is at present fundamentally one of alienation, for if the grand structures of economic alienation have been more or less revealed, the structures of the alienation of knowledge have not been'.[33] For Barthes, literature manuals are signifiers of nothing less than those 'grand structures'.

However one reads the parodies/pastiches of 'Oxen', they are entirely consistent with such a view. Whatever else, 'Oxen' is activated by a deeply ironic version of literary historiography which insists that its style must be ever changing and 'evolving'. 'Eumaeus' is locked in a modern language world which is endlessly circumlocutory. Like the strange characters in the episode – the keeper of the cabman's shelter, for instance, who might or might not be a political assassin – the sentences comprising this narrative are often structurally oblique which renders meaning uncertain and often ambiguous. Its characteristic mode is repetition and redundancy. If the language world of 'Oxen' can be characterized by the remoteness of archaic diction and syntax, 'Eumaeus', however strange and clumsy its grammatical forms, is typically familiar, an episode, as many Joyceans have demonstrated, largely comprised of idiom, repetition and cliché, but also characterized by obscurity and even outright language failure. In the extract that follows, syntax starts off in an orderly fashion, but soon unravels to the point where meaning collapses. Bloom is ostensibly attempting to protect and offer support to Stephen, an 'educated, *distingué*' young man whose company 'he certainly relished' (*U*16.1476–7). He has just shown Stephen a photograph of his wife in which Molly's 'fleshy charms' are 'on evidence in an open fashion as she was in the full bloom of womanhood in evening dress cut ostentatiously low for the occasion' (*U*16, 1428–9). As Bloom's thoughts move closer towards the darker side of sexual desire and the pain of Molly's infidelity, 'technic' becomes entangled with interior monologue, stumbles and, not for the first or last time, effectively folds. It is at this point that the narrative voice refers us to the authority of education orthodoxy by making its apology to the grammarian Lindley Murray, the compiler of one of the most well-known textbooks of the nineteenth century, *English Grammar* (1795), as well as samplers and many other textbooks:

> [Bloom] sat tight just viewing the slightly soiled photo creased by opulent curves, none the worse for wear however, and looked away thoughtfully with the intention of not further increasing the other's possible embarrassment while gauging her symmetry of heaving *embonpoint*. In fact the slight soiling was only an added charm like the case of linen slightly soiled, good as new, much better in fact with the starch out. Suppose she was gone when he? I looked for the lamp which she told me came into his mind but merely as a passing fancy of his because he then recollected the morning littered bed etcetera and the book about the Ruby with met him pike hoses (*sic*) in it which must have fell down sufficiently appropriately beside the domestic chamberpot with apologies to Lindley Murray.
>
> (*U*17, 1464–75)

For Joyceans, this reference to Murray and his famous *Grammar* is particularly significant. The *Grammar* has been seen as an important reference point for the episode's linguistic transgressions, just as the literature samplers are for 'Oxen'.[34] In the case of 'Oxen', however, the influence of manuals can be traced back in the form of what genetic critics call 'units', specific phrases lifted from the textbooks Joyce worked with and incorporated more or less directly into the pages of 'Oxen'. This is probably not the case, however, with 'Eumaeus' and Murray's *Grammar*. From the late eighteenth century onwards, the formulation of a comprehensive English grammar became something of a national, even world, obsession. Murray was important to this tradition, but, as things stand, there is little or no evidence of precise usages of his specific text in 'Eumaeus'.[35] It is true that 'Eumaeus' invests great energy in both the deployment and the transgression of rules that Murray formulates, but so does every episode in *Ulysses* and, perhaps, every text in existence, so unstable is the knowledge base on which Murray's work rests.

At the same time, whilst Joyce's engagement with the literary manual is highly original, linking him, as it turns out, to critical theory of the future, there would have been nothing new or original about laughing at Lindley Murray in the early twentieth century. On the contrary, if Murray was the 'father of English grammar', his *Grammar* translated into French, German, Dutch, Swedish, Spanish, Russian and Japanese, he also became, in a relatively short space of time, its standing joke. As Ingrid Tieken-Boon van Ostade points out in her edited volume *Two Hundred Years of Lindley Murray* (1996), Murray's grammar rules became old-fashioned even in his own lifetime – and he died in 1826.[36] Already by 1840, an anonymous *Comic English Grammar – a new and facetious introduction to the English tongue*, attributed to Perceval Leigh, was mocking traditional grammars and the conventional procedures of linguistic analysis embodied in parsing. It used the structure of Murray's book to do so, reproducing comic versions of his chapters on 'Orthography', 'Pronunciation', 'Etymology' and so on. Some years later, in 1869, the writer, poet and critic George Washington Moon was undermining Murray's position both as a linguist and a pedagogue. In *Bad English Exposed: a series of criticisms on the errors and inconsistencies of Lindley Murray and Other Grammarians*, Moon articulates his desire to 'render some little service to those who are desirous of acquiring a critical knowledge of the English language but who are in danger of being misled in their studies by the bad English of one who has been considered our principle grammarian'.[37] This was Murray of course, like all the other bad grammarians featured in this account, an American by birth and for that reason disenfranchised from his own project before he started.[38] He also was held responsible for the worst experiences of generations of privileged schoolboys:

> Of all the tasks of our schooldays, perhaps none was more repugnant to any of us than the study of good grammar; and when, after many a good caning, we had at last, in some fashion, mastered its rules, our estimate of the value was not very different from the charity boy's estimate of the value of the

alphabet which he had just learned; – we questioned whether it was worthwhile going through so much to learn so little.[39]

Formalist methods of teaching English Language at intermediate and higher levels continued to be used throughout the nineteenth century and beyond, but Murray was far from being the approved exemplar. The remainder of Moon's account is a demonstration of how he, and other grammarians, offend against their own rules, particularly devastating because Murray's textbook contains its own examples of rule-breaking for every rule it insists on and *still* goes on to serially offend. There is a kind of epistemological nightmare at work here, from which there appears to be no escape into genuine clarity, let alone eloquence. The more insistent the grammarian is on the importance of 'propriety' and 'perspicuity' – the latter being 'the fundamental quality so essential to every kind of writing, that for the want of it nothing can atone' – the more obscure his own writing becomes, not least because the material it works on is so resistant to the application of rule.[40] In this extract, for example, Murray instructs on the complexities of the diphthong:

> As the diphthong derives its name and nature from its sound, and not from its letters, and properly denotes a double vowel sound, no union of two vowels, where one is silent, can, in strictness, be entitled to that appellation; the single letters i and u, when pronounced long must, in this view, be considered as diphthongs. The triphthongs, having at most but two sounds, are mainly ocular, and are, therefore, by some grammarians, classed with the diphthongs.[41]

Here he tries to explain the mysteries of the passive:

> Even the Greek and Latin passive verbs require an auxiliary to conjugate some of their tenses, namely, the former, in the preterit of the optative and subjunctive moods; and the latter, in the perfect and pluperfect of the indicative, the perfect, pluperfect, and future, of the subjunctive mood, and the perfect of the infinitive.[42]

In both illustrations, Murray makes a bold bid for precision and clarity, and fails beyond all expectation. The same condition of failure, or something very like it, is the operative mode of 'Eumaeus', likewise motivated by the determination to produce good writing at all costs and equally crippled by endless qualifiers, repetitions and parentheses. The point, however, is that critiques of Murray were already standard by the 1900s, so why does Joyce bother to continue with it so far on into the twentieth century in what was to become a classic of modernist literature?

It is worth emphasizing at this point that, just as 'Oxen' does not seek to replace conventional literary historiography with a better one, 'Eumaeus' does not seek to rectify grammar either. In this sense neither, however much control is exercised over the school learning they dismantle, can be unequivocally insiderly. The target of 'Oxen' in this respect is more fundamental. The same is true of 'Eumaeus'. Both are thrown outside the boundaries of anything like reform and it is from this position that 'Eumaeus' becomes more centrally engaged with Lindley and his work.

The standard condition of grammars at this time was that they imagined grammatical failure, deviations from the rules of grammar, not just as offences to correctness but as affronts dangerous to the social and cultural order of modern society. Lindley was not just typical here, he was evangelical. His work made a powerfully strong insistence on constructing poor grammar in relation to disorderly worlds. His primary aim was to secure 'youth' from risk and threat, from the 'hazards' of 'misunderstanding others' and being 'misunderstood ourselves'. Examples used by Lindley 'for the instruction of youth' and 'the ease and advancement of young persons' were 'led by the cause of virtue as well as learning'. They were chosen precisely to avoid the perils of 'an improper effect on the minds of youth'.[43] As he spells out in his introduction, Murray uses illustrative sentences which have a moral and religious tendency, such as 'Virtue ennobles us', 'Goodness will be rewarded', 'Strive to improve' and 'Gratitude is a delightful emotion'.[44] The message, repeated over and over, is that correct grammar leads to the living of correct and successful lives, a coding which implies the inherent rightness of authority and the danger of transgression and dissipation.

Significantly, many of Lindley's examples relate specifically to social order and the threat of subversion. Rule two in Lindley's account asserts that 'Two or more nouns, &c, in the singular number, joined together by a copulative conjunction, expressed or understood, must have verbs, nouns and pronouns agreeing with them in plural number'. The rule is illustrated by such examples as: 'Patriots, morality, every public consideration, demand our submission to just and lawful government' and 'The king, with the lords and commons, form an excellent frame of government'.[45] The idiosyncrasy that '*it is*, and *it was*, are often, after the manner of the French, used in a plural construction, and by some of our best writers', is exemplified by the following: 'It is either a few great men who decide for the whole, or it is the rabble that follow a seditious ring leader', also an illustration that deviations and even innovations, especially when agreed on an authoritative basis, have to be respected too – 'with respect to anomalies and variations of language, thus established, it is the grammarian's business to submit, not to remonstrate'.[46] A virtuous circle is set up where 'good' language stands in for the organization of an entire social, moral and political order. The obvious corollary is that improper language is encoded with signifiers of serious social danger:

> To preserve propriety, therefore, in our words and phrases, we must avoid low expressions; supply words that are wanting; be careful not to use the same word in different senses; avoid the injudicious use of technical phrases, equivocal or ambiguous words, unintelligible expressions, and all such words and phrases as are not adapted to our meaning.[47]

The hierarchical dimensions of true social order and its link to good grammar are made explicit. There is, says Lindley, 'scarcely any thing which more distinguishes a person of poor education, from a person of a good one, than the pronunciation of the unaccented vowels'.[48] Grammar, it turns out, is precisely related to the well-being of society and a historiography linked to biological recapitulation in which, as in literature teaching, the development of the single human parallels notions of racial improvement:

> Ignorant people, and children, generally speak in short and separate sentences. The same thing is true of barbarous nations, and hence uncultivated languages are not well-supplied with connecting particals. The Greeks were the greatest reasoners that ever appeared in the world; and their language accordingly, abounds more than any other.[49]

'Eumaeus' is a comic version of the world under siege imagined in Murray's *Grammar*. Significantly, it begins with a quest for 'the propriety of the cabman's shelter' as being the only place where Stephen's 'desire for some beveridge to drink' can be met 'in view of the hour' (*U*14, 5–8). The word 'propriety' is important. It echoes throughout Murray where it is used for both fit and proper social behaviour and grammatical correctness. As in Murray's *Grammar*, addressed to youthful 'scholars', educated youth in 'Eumaeus' is in need of protection. '*En route*' to the shelter, the narrator, like Bloom, counsels against acting without caution, advises against 'squandermania' and warns about over-indulgence and 'fast women of the *demimonde*' (*U*16, 60, 87). From the outset, the city as he formulates it is not a safe place:

> it was not by any means unknown for desperadoes who had next to nothing to live on . . . abroad waylaying and generally terrorising peaceable pedestrians by placing a pistol at their head in some secluded spot outside the city proper, famished loiterers of the Thames embankment category they might be hanging about there or simply marauders ready to decamp with whatever boodle they could in one fell swoop at a moment's notice, your money or your life, leaving you there to point a moral, gagged and garrotted.
>
> (*U*17, 120–27)

In this extract, the narrator is so unseated by the threats he relates that towards the end of his statement subjects are left out and whole clauses vanished away. Again, syntax breaks down and phrases trip over each other. This is exemplary of Murray, where grammatical order is undone by the dangers reality presents. Even where the imagined threats diminish and grammar more or less holds up, still the narrative struggles with contradiction and ambiguity. When Stephen is greeted by someone from the shadows, his companion does his best to retain decorum but cannot help fearing the worst. 'Mr Bloom actuated by motives of inherent delicacy inasmuch as he always believed in minding his own business moved off but nevertheless remained on the *qui vive* with just a shade of anxiety though not funkyish in the least' (*U*16, 116–19). The balancing act between maintaining a good front and giving in to something close to hysteria is typical both of Bloom's mood and the characteristic syntax of the episode.

Inside the cabman's shelter, a 'decidedly miscellaneous collection of waifs and strays and other nondescript specimens of the genus *homo*' are both ordinary and familiar and yet strange and worrying (*U*16, 327–28). They confirm the connection Murray makes between poor grammar and the maintenance of social order, partly by the routine breaking of basic grammatical rules in their speech but also by embodying the obtuseness that Murray so despises in bad grammar. Just as their sentences involve obscure relations between subjects and verbs, or omit subjects altogether, so they themselves have obscure identities. The stories they tell repeat the instabilities of bad grammar. They also have doubtful relations to reality. Sometimes the tellers themselves behave in intimidating ways, exemplifying the dangers that disorderly grammar brings to the social in Murray's account. The story D.B. Murphy tells about a man he once saw stabbed involves all these elements. It is doubtful in relation to truthfulness, punctuated by technical error in its telling and ends in a 'harrowing denouement sufficient to appal the stoutest'. Murphy draws a knife: '– And I seen a man killed in Trieste by an Italian chap. Knife in the back. Knife like that' (*U*16, 586; 576–7).

One irony of this entanglement is that this sense of danger and vulnerability is completely lost on Stephen, as is so much of what goes on in the episode – Bloom's attempts to appeal to what he assumes will be Stephen's student instincts for the political left, for instance, or his fantasies about how a future relationship with Stephen might lead to social advantage and 'pecuniary emolument' (*U*14, 1840). The wider irony, however, runs much deeper and draws 'Eumaeus' closer to 'Oxen'. Just as the latter disrupts progressivist histories of literature, so the former does the same with language, producing a discourse which, for all its pretence and superiority, fails in its objectives to stabilize meaning, to eradicate ambiguity and thus in its ambition to establish a linguistic order of superiority. As with 'Oxen', none of this makes 'Eumaeus' any less of an impressive performance, a form of writing that revels in its own mastery. The fumbles, confusions and outright errors can only be operated from a position of absolute authority over rules of correctness, as Murray insists. 'Proprieties' of language are nothing more than the reverse side of to its 'improprieties' – a fact upon which the very design of Murray's book was based, one that only confirms the degree to which both chapters of *Ulysses*, leaning so heavily on schooled forms of knowledge that were taught alongside Latin and the classics, upturn those forms of knowledge. They are undoubtedly comic, but that does not make them innocent. As the products of elite schooling, these chapters are in some ways beyond exemplary. At the same time, they remain the highly disruptive interventions of a public-school boy in the modern world gone very wayward indeed.

Textbooks, then, are for Joyce much more than reminders of his old school days, although it is true that they often connected to a *passé* world. Indeed, the textbooks utilized most extensively in Joyce – Mangnall, Cornwell, Murray,

Saintsbury's *A History of English Prose Rhythm*, Isaac Todhunter's edition of *Euclid's Elements* and so on – tend to be exemplars already old-fashioned by 1900 or on the conservative, if not reactionary, side of contemporary education cultures. They were even more so by the 1920s and 1930s. In this respect, Joyce's writing of the quintessential texts of literary modernism look backwards to education culture in the nineteenth century, and, even further, back into the eighteenth century and the days of pre-state schooling. But if this is a reminder of the traditionalist Joyce, formal and tied into scholasticism in some ways, it should also, ironically enough, help configure the modernity of the Joyce text, inasmuch as the contemporary character of elite schooling depended precisely on the links it made between itself and cultures of hierarchy dominated by a traditionalist aristocracy. This is how old-fashioned textbooks become so serviceable to the later *Ulysses* chapters, focusing through a radical aesthetic both the powerful connections made everywhere in Joyce between identity formation and what has been called the 'cult' of the 'gentleman' and a cultural politics related to the dispersal of power as modern epistemology.

Notes

1 J.A. Froude, 'The Christian Brothers and Their Lesson Books', *Fraser's Magazine*, 9/50, 1874, 186–99 [186–88]. By 1851, there were some 51 titles in this National School Board series, many of them selling well in England and overseas in British colonies; Canada, for instance. For a modern account of their content, see Patrick Walsh, 'Education and the "Universalist" Idiom of Empire: Irish National School Books in Ireland and Ontario', *History of Education*, 37/5, 2008, 645–60.
2 Froude, 'The Christian Brothers and Their Lesson Books', 187.
3 'The Christian Brothers and Their Lesson Books', 195, 193.
4 'The Christian Brothers and Their Lesson Books', 196.
5 E. Brian Titley, 'Rejecting the Modern World: The Educational Ideas of Timothy Corcoran', *Oxford Review of Education*, 9/2, 1983, 137–45 [138].
6 T. Corcoran, S.J., 'Official Text Books and Irish Schools', *The Irish Monthly*, 56/662, August 1928, 398–402 [398].
7 Corcoran, 'Official Text Books and Irish Schools', 399, 401. According to a modern reading of the National School textbooks, they had 'been marked by religious moralising and earnest moral tales, and useful knowledge, including political economy; the endless struggles for political correctness in the sectarian conflicts which begat Irish elementary provision produced texts of surpassing dullness'. See Christopher Stray and Gillian Sutherland, 'Mass Markets: Education', in McKitterick (ed.), *The Cambridge History of the Book in Britain*, 4, 359–81 [376].
8 James Cornwell, *Spelling for Beginners: A Method for Teaching* (London: Simpkin & Marshall, 1870), 53, 27, 55.
9 James Cornwell, *A Grammar for Beginners* (1869; London: Simpkin & Marshall, 1904), 15, 55, 78. James Cornwell (1812–1902) established something close to an industry in education textbooks, publishing beginners' guides to geography, English composition, spelling and arithmetic, as well as atlases and collections of poetry.
10 Cornwell, *A Grammar for Beginners*, 125, 150.
11 *A Grammar for Beginners*, 13, 244.
12 James Cornwell, *Geography for Beginners*, 72nd edn. (London: Simpkin, Marshall Hamilton & Kent, 1913), 8–14.

13 See Cornwell, *Spelling for Beginners*, 49.
14 John Walker, *Pronouncing Dictionary* (1791; London: Frederick Warne, ca 1875), 12.
15 Gilbert, *Letters of James Joyce*, 406.
16 Most of these are identified in Roland McHugh, *Annotations to Finnegans Wake* (London and Henley: Routledge & Kegan Paul, 1980), 260–308.
17 *The Publishers' Circular and Booksellers' Record*, 1749, January 13, 1900, 5.
18 *The Publishers' Circular*, 22–36.
19 See Stray and Sutherland, 'Mass Markets and Education', in McKitterick (ed.), *The Cambridge History of the Book in Britain*, 372.
20 Gilbert, *Letters of James Joyce*, 139.
21 See Mildred Adams, 'Literary Criticism in Spanish America', *Comparative Literature Studies*, 1/3, 1964, 217–29 [219].
22 Kate M. Warren, *A Treasury of English Literature (From the Beginning to the Eighteenth Century)* (1906; New York: Dodge, 1908), v.
23 Stopford A. Brook, 'Introduction', in Warren, *A Treasury of English Literature*, ix.
24 Brook, 'Introduction', in Warren, *A Treasury of English Literature*, xv, xix.
25 W. Peacock (ed.), *English Prose from Mandeville to Ruskin* (Oxford: Oxford University Press, 1912), iii.
26 Gilbert (ed.), *Letters of James Joyce*, 138–9. Saintsbury asserts that the 'general trochaic rhythm' of Anglo-Saxon 'has beyond all doubt persisted in English prose more fully than it has in English poetry'. See George Saintsbury, *A History of Prose Rhythm* (London: Macmillan, 1912), 21.
27 Saintsbury, *A History of Prose Rhythm*, i.
28 See Sarah Davison, 'Joyce's Incorporation of Literary Sources in "Oxen of the Sun"', *Genetic Joyce Studies*, 9 (2009), np., www.geneticjoycestudies.org/GJS9/GJS9_Sarah DavisonOxen.htm
29 Davison, 'Joyce's Incorporation of Literary Sources in "Oxen of the Sun"', np.
30 Brook, 'Introduction', in Warren, *A Treasury of English Literature*, xi, xix.
31 Brook, 'Introduction', x.
32 Sandy Petrey's introduction to Barthes's piece, for example, takes the former line but acknowledges the latter when she concludes with the idea that his 'rejection of history affirms a different kind of history'. See Roland Barthes and Sandy Petrey, 'Reflections on a Manual', *PMLA*, 112/1, 1997, 69–75 [71, 72].
33 Barthes and Petry, 'Reflections on a Manual', 72.
34 See Derek Attridge, *Peculiar Language: Literature as Difference from the Renaissance to James Joyce* (London: Methuen, 1988), 172–83; Katie Wales, '"With Apologies to Lindley Murray": The Narrative Method of the "Eumaeus" Episode in *Ulysses*', in Ingrid Tieken-Boon van Ostade (ed.), *Two Hundred Years of Lindley Murray* (Münster: Nodus, 1996), 207–16.
35 Some of the notebook and drafting materials for 'Eumaeus' are privately owned and not available to scholars.
36 See van Ostade (ed.), 'Introduction', *Two Hundred Years of Lindley Murray*, 4–26, [9–10].
37 G. Washington Moon, *The Bad English of Lindley Murray and Other Writers on the English Language: A Series of Criticisms* (London: Hatchards, 1869), 3.
38 The 'father' of English grammar was born into a Quaker family who were also loyalists. In his unpublished autobiography, he claims that he came to England for health reasons, although his departure from America could be read as a necessity inflicted on a mercantile business family that had attempted to avoid non-importation agreements in the early 1770s. The entry for Murray in the DNB writes of his journey to England as being 'by way of banishment'.
39 Moon, *The Bad English of Lindley*, 1.
40 Lindley Murray, *English Grammar* (1795; New York: n.pub., 1811?), 250.
41 Murray, *English Grammar*, 20.

42 *English Grammar*, 100.
43 *English Grammar*, 3–6.
44 *English Grammar*, 195–7.
45 *English Grammar*, 130–3.
46 *English Grammar*, 138, 144.
47 *English Grammar*, 251.
48 *English Grammar*, 29.
49 *English Grammar*, 118.

Chapter 9

'I'm not so ignorant' – women and education

> The only knowledge of the world available to nuns is derived from reading bishops' pastorals, which describe the 'immoral literature', the 'dens of seductive vice' . . . 'the drunkenness and delirium tremens', and all the other horrors of life in the outside world. The result of a convent education is that many of the more emotional and sensitive of our Catholic girls become nuns themselves from sheer fright, as the easiest way of solving the horrible problem of life thus presented to them.
>
> Michael J.F. McCarthy, *Priests and People in Ireland* (1903)

> I'll let him know if that's what he wanted that his wife is fucked yes and damn well fucked too up to my neck nearly not by him 5 or 6 times handrunning theres the mark of his spunk on the clean sheet
>
> Molly Bloom, *Ulysses* (1921)

The idea that 'Joyce and education' is informed by the circumstances of Joyce's own life is central to this book. Joyce is not an education theorist or historian or practitioner, but a writer writing obsessively out of his own experience at a time when the schooling of middle-class boys became the central instrument in the regulation of the social hierarchy. From this perspective, Joyce's writing reproduces, and speaks to, educated masculinity and the expectations of bourgeois elites, because this was the position he himself inhabited. It counters the English stereotype of the 'thick' Irishman with monstrously overdone versions of hyper-education. Simultaneously, it mounts a dazzling dismantling of the central principles underlying the systemization characteristic of modern education systems, a controversial and inevitably contradictory position, not least because the author of these interventions was himself a product of that system.

Some of this formulation overlaps with familiar versions of nationalist politics and modern education historiographies that write back to such agendas. Writing in the 1990s, for example, Mary E. Daly decisively challenges the notion that Ireland in the early twentieth century was an education backwater for women. She develops an account in some ways consistent with the representational world of texts like *Dubliners*, *Stephen Hero* and *A Portrait*. Here, the education of women in Ireland is relatively 'advanced', as it is for the likes of Kathleen Kearney in 'A Mother', Julia Morkan and the 'hypereducated' Molly Ivors in 'The Dead' and Emma Cleary in *Stephen Hero* and *A Portrait*. Daly points out that by 1914, 'only in England, Wales and Norway did women constitute a higher percentage of secondary school pupils, and only Finland and the Netherlands had a higher proportion of women in primary education training'. Similarly, only 'Finland and the Netherlands appears to have had a higher proportion of girls in primary education'. Most significantly in relation to Joyce, Daly shows how an educated elite amongst Irish women was formed at the higher levels of formal institutionalized learning. The obstacles faced by women in gaining access to university entrance would have been great, as Daly shows, but, again, only Finland 'appears to have had a higher percentage of women university students'.[1]

For a modern Irish historian like Daly, this kind of analysis is significant because it frames Irish independence in the 1920s in the context of a progressive and progressivist modernity. If the later legislative interventions of a republic transformed under De Valera represents an ideological return of women to the kitchen and the hearth, the Irish state has more egalitarian beginnings, at least, and even in the 1930s is to be distinguished from the pronatalism of such regimes as fascist Italy and Germany. In the latter, the ideological fantasy of racial purity in the familial state was a reality manifested in the demand for a higher Aryan birth rate. In Ireland, the overriding context, however objectionable, was something rather more familiar in modern times, according to Daly. Thirty per cent of clerks, both in the civil service and in private businesses, Daly points out, were women in 1916. However, 'the supply of educated candidates seeking white-collared employment' in Ireland was far in excess of the number of jobs available. There might have been a 'superficial resemblance' between the social objectives of Irish governments in the 1930s and 'right wing European states such as Italy and Germany' but there was also an important difference 'in emphasis'. In Ireland, it was not the higher birthrate that was the 'primary concern' but, rather, the imperative to establish the priority of jobs for men over jobs for women.[2]

In these kinds of areas, the Joyce text separates out from both the feminist agendas of the early twentieth century and the designs of late-twentieth-century historiography. The logic of the arguments developed in this book would suggest that Joyce's critique of modern education, far from celebrating progressive change, would have applied equally to middle-class women. If the modernization of educational reform was a sham for men, its extension to women must have been a sham also. There is not too much difficulty in showing how this works in the earlier texts. Molly Ivors constitutes a more ambivalent case, but the irony of a modern young woman like Kathleen Kearney being educated in emulation of traditional aristocracy in 'a high-class convent where she had learned French and music' (*D*, 153), is clear and consistent with the 'systematic compensation' that Stephen Dedalus identifies in relation to the education of middle-class young men. Thus, Stephen's analysis of why Emma Cleary refuses to have sex with him is assimilated into the broad terms of his social and political critique. It is illustrative of her 'burgher cowardice' (*SH*, 187). For all her sophisticated education, she is an oppressed young woman who allows her body to become 'a corporate asset of the State' (*SH*, 180). The difficulties come with the later writing. In *Ulysses*, conventional representational aesthetics, however under pressure, are broadly maintained, but there is little or no space reserved for the performance of educated women, repressed or otherwise, in this text. Here the question becomes not *how* does Joyce represent educated women but, rather, *where* is Joyce's representation of educated woman? However much she may be implied in the readership of *Ulysses*, she is significantly absent from inside its pages. What does this absence signify? This is the central question raised in this chapter.

Aristocrats Masterpiece

Three late episodes of *Ulysses* – 'Oxen', 'Eumaeus' and 'Ithaca' – are all connected with schooling. In various ways, all imagine masculinist worlds and the erosion of their epistemological foundations. This gendered dynamic is not, as some critics have implied, a product of the fads and fashions of critical theory and the currency of late-twentieth and early-twenty-first century insecurities about the 'Enlightenment project'.[3] The gendering is insisted upon by the design of *Ulysses* and the position of its penultimate episode, at the near finish of a book that imagines a terminal endgame for Western systems of knowledge formation and yet does not, because 'Ithaca' is not the true end of *Ulysses*. The real termination of the novel comes only after 'Penelope', ostensibly Molly's chapter, makes stopping possible. In this respect, as many critics have observed, 'Penelope' is set up in relation to 'Ithaca'.

In sharp contrast to the hyper-schooling enacted in these late chapters and elsewhere in *Ulysses*, this last episode is conceived in terms of non-discourse, or anti-discourse. It operates under the conceit of being both completely unwritten and very much unschooled – one reason, perhaps the main one, for the absence of punctuation. To the schooled mind, what Joyce reproduces as aesthetic design in the last chapter of his book is the giveaway signification of the unschooling that is its antithesis – failure of sentence recognition, absence of comma and apostrophe and so on, the standard errors rectified by teacher intervention everywhere. What has historically been imagined as the female 'flow' of 'Penelope' – new writing composed out of Heléné Cixous's 'white ink' – consequently becomes a comedy of errors, related to in some ways, but nevertheless quite distinct from, the slippages characteristic of schooled discourses in such episodes as 'Scylla and Charybdis'.[4] Here, in contrast, there can be no doubt where 'mistakes' are being scripted. Molly's misnaming of *Aristotle's Masterpiece* as 'Aristocrats Masterpiece' is significantly overplayed in 'Penelope', not least because the correct title of this once well-known example of popular medicine/early erotica appears not in some extra-textual reality but elsewhere in *Ulysses* (*U*18, 1238). Banned in Britain until the 1960s, *Aristotle's Masterpiece* is, as it were, under our noses in *Ulysses*, correctly titled and properly placed in cultural terms not just in one place but in two. In 'Wandering Rocks', it turns up on the street stall of a decidedly seedy booksellers, where Bloom spots it and flicks through its plates: 'infants cuddled in a ball in bloodred wombs like liver of slaughted cows' (*U*10, 585). In 'Oxen of the Sun' it figures in the 'student talk' about birth deformities. The men of two worlds – *petit-bourgeois* commercial and *haute bourgeois* professional – get its title right, which means that Molly's mistake, for all the privacy in which it is made, finds itself exposed in harsh and highly gendered light.

The relative ease of recognition of this 'error' is symptomatic. Unlike the insiderly and testing subtleties of misquotation and obscure allusion typical of Stephen Dedalus playing off Mulligan, Molly's 'mistakes' can be easily spotted. In marked contrast to a chapter such as 'Oxen', so much an examination of our ability to 'keep up', 'Penelope' is a chapter that invokes the pleasures of correction, and it does so over and over. We all know that the fish 'plaice' is not spelled 'place' and it is not difficult to assume superiority over the imagined mind that frames such errors. We are, after all, voyeurs not just of Molly's sex life but of something potentially just as shaming in the modern world: her ignorance and her comic over-reaching for schooled respectability. She posits 'flirtyfying' as the continuous verb form of 'to flirt', turns 'flagellate' into a noun that can be 'given' to someone, struggles to recall what the word is for the 'thing' a doctor writes out for his patient, determines that the ropes that turn the rudder on a rowing boat ('lines') are called 'reins' and complains about 'the old alarm next door next door' going off at 'cockshout clattering the brains out of itself' (*U*18, 939; 1290; 963; 1173; 958; 1544).

Molly herself is very much aware, or has been made aware, of her issues in this respect – some of them at least – and is sensitive to them. She is annoyed at herself for always making the mistake of spelling 'sympathy' with two aitches ('symphathy') and 'nephews' as 'newphews', a surplus of what is textualized as 'double yous'. Like the sexual 'deficiency' which, she thinks, characterizes her as a sexual subject ('whats the idea making us like that with a big hole in the middle of us'), Molly's ignorance in schooling terms could likewise easily be imagined in terms of absence or 'lack', a potential reading supported by the emphasis the episode puts on casting this narrative in the most simple form of everyday storytelling (*U*18, 730–31;151).

All kinds of markers distinguish 'Penelope' from chapters like 'Ithaca' and 'Oxen'. Outside of the accentuated genderizing, however, the most emphatic sign of this distinction is the movement from discourses of 'explication' to the anecdotal. A chapter like 'Ithaca' gives us information in abundance; 'Penelope' does too, but these are data of a particular kind, much disguised and much humanized. The information reaches us through the telling of stories. Alongside the accounts concerning Mrs Riordan and the Blooms' maid, there is another about the time when Molly left her gloves on the lavatory at the D B C on Dame street and one about how Bloom in the early days of their relationship asked Molly for 'a tiny bit cut off my drawers . . . of course hes mad on the subject of drawers' – the idea of 'drawers' being a subject made comic, of course, precisely by association with the idea of the formal curriculum (*U*18, 284–5; 289). We hear about how Lenehan flirted with Molly after the Glencree dinner and about Molly's life in Gibraltar; about Mulvey, 'the first man kissed me under the Moorish wall' (*U*18, 769–70); about Gardner, another young love, this one a soldier who was posted to South Africa 'where those Boers killed him' (*U*18, 867–8). And so on through the whole episode, from the first time Molly saw 'the Spanish cavalry at La Roque' (*U*18, 398), through to the departure of her friend Hestor Stanhope from Gibraltar, the birth and death of her only son in Dublin, until the end of the book which re-imagines the first time she made love to Bloom 'lying among the rhododendrons on Howth Head' (*U*18, 1572–3). In this narrative, anecdote is *the* central form, which is not to say that Molly herself is conscious that she is telling stories. She is, of course, 'speaking' to herself. If the masculinist textbook worlds of 'Oxen' and 'Eumaeus' lead to the mechanical formalities of scientism in 'Ithaca', 'Penelope' is designed to be human and to be human – a female human at the end of *Ulysses* – is to tell ourselves stories about ourselves.

Lying behind the 'Penelope' discourse is the traditional separation between high-status abstraction and generalization and a particular form of concretization, the latter again representing a kind inferiority or failure. The ability to 'tell an anecdote' is not much rated on the scale of high-level learning outcomes in traditional education culture. Indeed, it specifically precedes the development of higher-placed 'critical skills' as a lower order of thinking. As feminist writers on this chapter have decisively shown, the 'Penelope' discourse, even now almost 100 years after publication, is a remarkably liberating thing – 'fluid and feminine, deracinated and polymorphic, uncontaminated by the limits of logocentric authority', even if its 'contours' are 'frequently phallomorphic, determined by the pervasive presence of a male register of desire'.[5] Writing in 1988, the author of these words, Suzette A. Henke, was fully prepared to manage the nuanced celebration of a highly sexualized Molly. How now do we process the idea of Molly as a figure that remains still so much unloved in contemporary intellectual cultures, no longer the much sexualized stereotype/archetype and 'crude' anti-self so offensive to Joyce's earlier readers but something just as controversial and problematic – the 'not very bright'?

A 'decidedly sophisticated political consciousness'

The great subversion of 'Penelope', one that frames the wider controversies around it, is that for all the inferior status inscribed in the smallest details of its form, the episode refuses to substantiate any notion of intellectual inferiority in its subject. It is important to be clear how the text works in this respect. As with Molly's sexuality, there are all kinds of ways in which Molly's 'vulgarity' *could* be contextualized and apologized for but all are ruled out of play, not just by the terms of Joyce's radical version of interior monologue but also because *Ulysses* and the cultural history of *Ulysses* refuses to countenance shame on the basis of sexuality. The relationship between *Ulysses* and education can rarely have been thought about in any analogous way. Nevertheless, this is broadly how education works in 'Penelope', a chapter in tune with the rest of *Ulysses* and, indeed, the whole Joyce oeuvre in that it refuses to equate intelligence with schooling. For all its self-referential nature, its 'mistakes' and the apparent simplicity of its ostensible narrative form, 'Penelope' retains its capacity for registering wisdom, insight and intelligent dissent, a paradox which is given a particular context in 'Penelope' *around* notions of schooling and education. Molly is impressed with education to the extent that she holds it as an aspiration for her daughter, although she is under no illusions that Milly's real future will be shaped substantially by the zest and good looks she inherits from her mother and grandmother. She also welcomes Stephen's presence in the house as an opportunity to fulfil her desire for 'a long talk with an intelligent person'. But the appreciation is contingent on him being neither 'the stuckup university sort' nor, for all his 'education', a crude 'ignoramus' like her lover, Boylan, who 'doesn't know poetry from a cabbage' (*U*18, 1484; 1329; 1370). Molly's response to education, then, is not unconditional. On the contrary, it is bound up with her realism and understanding of what drives the world and of how schooling and its validation really operates.

For all its formal 'errors', this is a text that realizes how the status conferred by formal education is no real guarantee of intelligence and how status and its validation is entangled with conservative social attitudes, conformist moral values, gender privilege and the reproduction of social class. This is part of the rationale behind Molly's criticism of figures like Kathleen Kearney and her friends, educated young women dismissed as a

> lot of squealers Miss This Miss That Miss Theother lot of sparrowfarts skitting around talking about politics they know as much about as my backside anything in the world to make themselves someway interesting Irish homemade beauties soldiers daughter am I ay . . . theyd die down dead off their feet if ever they got a chance of walking down the Alameda on an officers arm like me on the bandnight my eyes flash my bust that they haven't passion God help their poor head I knew more about men and life when I was 15 than they'll all know at 50
>
> (*U*18, 878–87)

However much this may respond to professional pique (Miss Kearney has replaced Molly at one of the music venues where she performs), or register narcissism and insecurity, it is also critical in social ways. These daughters of 'bootmakers and publicans' are what Simon Dedalus would call 'counterjumpers', young women who, in Molly's mind and for all their education, remain the bloodless products of a system still orchestrated by 'the old Bishop that spoke of the altar his long preach [sermon] about womens higher functions about girls now riding the bicycle and wearing peak caps and the new woman bloomers God send him sense and me more money' (837–40). New 'Irish homemade beauties' in Molly's account, for all their 'modernity', remain wedded to Church and state. They are in this respect the direct descendants of a prototypical Mrs Riordan, an 'educated woman' as Molly admits, but one who has

> too much old chat in her about politics and earthquakes and the end of the world let us have a bit of fun first God help the world if all the woman were her sort down on bathingsuits and lownecks of course nobody wanted her to wear them I suppose she was pious because no man would look at her twice
>
> (*U*18, 7–11)

Despite her lack of schooling, and perhaps because of it, this kind of perspective produces an unorthodox kind of radicalism in the 'Penelope' text, characterized by a sympathy for and attraction to ordinary working men. Her liking for 'the man with the curly hair in the Lucan dairy thats so polite' is a subtle interference with the conventions of a schooled hierarchy that attempts to define the status of the true gentleman. Likewise, her appreciation of 'two gentlemen in the 3rd class carriage' and 'the exceptional man that common workman who left us alone in the carriage that day going to Howth' (*U*18, 271, 362, 370–1). In Molly's world, social hierarchies are turned on their head and her appreciation and sympathy extends to others who have not sparked or facilitated her desire in any way – like railway workers, 'the poor men that have to be out all the night from their wives and families in those roasting engines' (598–600).

The undermining of professional men, the products of elite education, is likewise typical of Molly, a characteristic that brings her into alignment with Stephen Dedalus's version of radical education in some ways. Menton, 'not long married', is caught by Molly 'flirting with a young girl at Pooles Myriorama – 'of all the big stupoes I ever met and thats called a solicitor'. Val Dillon, Dublin's Lord Mayor, is a 'big heathen'. The medical student who fails to recognize signals intended to register Molly's sexual interest becomes symptomatic – 'arent they thick . . . he didnt recognise me either when I half frowned at him outside Westland row chapel where does their great intelligence come in Id like to know grey matter they have it all in their tail if you ask me' (*U*18, 43–4; 429; 706–10). Dr Collins, 'for womens diseases', is not coded as stupid, but he is a 'dry old stick' and a showy materialist, in it for the money and surrounding himself with symbols of power of authority and mystifying language – 'your vagina he called it I suppose thats how he got all the gilt mirrors and carpets getting round those rich ones off Stephens green running up to him for every little fiddlefaddle her vagina and her cochinchina theyve money of course so theyre all right' (*U*18, 1153–57). In relation to the education order around her, Molly is clear. She might be sensitive to her own educational limitations, but she is in no doubt as to the pretence behind modern education in its systematic dimensions, nor about its relatedness to patriarchy and paternalism. In this respect, schooling is Other for Molly and is determinedly male: 'I wouldnt give a snap of my two fingers for all their learning why dont they go and create something' (*U*18, 1564–5).

In this kind of reading, Molly's 'modern, emancipated and sensual self' is driven not just by powerful sexual desires, but by what a recent account calls 'anti-institutional logic'. What may look like very limited political knowledge on her part actually manifests a 'decidedly sophisticated political way of looking at the world'. Her signature perspective implies a 'deeper democratization than paternalistic liberalism can afford'. Here, Molly's status becomes a product of a considered opposition to social marginalization, including regulated standards of the feminine.[6] The impact is clear. In 'Penelope', the schooled woman is not simply absent but, rather, is decisively dispatched. This does not mean, however, that the intelligent woman suffers the same fate.

Rancière's work on education, referred to at the very beginning of this study, throws a particular light on how this new version of 'usurpation' can be read in ways that help with the processing of the controversial movement from 'Ithaca' to 'Penelope' – the dynamic change of gear which Joyce deploys to finally close this novel down. In *The Ignorant Schoolmaster* and a subsequent essay entitled 'On Ignorant Schoolmasters', Rancière identifies the traits of what he calls 'normal pedagogical logic', a logic that makes a 'radical distinction' between two types of intelligence – one 'empirical', the other 'systematic'. 'For children and common minds', Rancière writes, 'there are stories, for rational beings there are reasons': a division he insists is a product of the regulatory function of modern systems of schooling. 'Instruction's first accomplishment', Rancière continues, 'is to split the intellect in two, to consign to the everyday life of students the procedures which their minds have heretofore learned everything they know'.[7] From this position, education begins with an assumption of inequality and proceeds in the same fashion. Pedagogy is always in practice 'explicatory', and explication is always confirmation of inequality. 'To explain is to arrange the elements of knowledge to be transmitted in accordance with the supposed limited capacities of those under instruction', a process not only slow but interminable because 'its primary function is to infinitize the very distance it proposes to reduce. The practice of explanation is something completely different from a practical means of teaching some end. It is an end in itself, the infinite verification of a fundamental axiom: the axiom of inequality'.[8] Schooling can never address inequality, because it must always be complicit with inequality; in Rancière's terms, identical to it. 'Inequality asserts itself through equality. The equality of equality and inequality has a name. It is called progress'. From this perspective, 'scholarly progression', a microcosm of universal progression, becomes 'the art of limiting the transmission of knowledge, of organising delay, or deferring equality'. The 'ignorant schoolmaster' of Rancière's account, then, is 'the teacher who escapes from the game, by separating the sheer act of intellectual emancipation from the societal machine, and from progressive institutions'.[9]

There are many distinctions to be made between Joyce and Rancière in relation to education, some of them indicated at the beginning of this book which frames Rancière in a post-1960s context that Joyce could not have had to access to. Nevertheless, the commonalties around the understanding of schooling as social logic, linked in both cases to Nietzsche, are suggestive, as is the location of schooling in the ideologies of progressivism. Likewise, the strategic positioning of 'explication' – also 'stultification' in Rancière – against storytelling. This is why Rancière risked making 'philosophy' through telling the story of Jacotot, a potential conflation of codes and orders, but one worth taking because 'the very act of story-telling, an act that presumes in its interlocutor an equality of intelligence rather than an inequality of knowledge, posits equality, just as the act of explication posits inequality'.[10] This is one way of reading the shift from 'Ithaca' to 'Penelope', a movement from explication to the anecdotal which, however 'unreadable' as 'literature' it is considered, insists that the idea of human emancipation is achieved every minute of every day by everybody, however much emancipation operates in the 'domain of the unsayable'.[11] From this perspective, the central critical subversion of Rancière is identical to the central idea of 'Penelope' – the challenge at the heart of both is the radical idea that we are all, outside of schooling, fully capable beings. Here the telling of stories, endless stories, becomes not just one of the ways we process ourselves in the world but the central signifier of how we make sense of the world and engage with it – a key marker of the human presence and its agency in all kinds of ways, both profound and trivial.

FW 3.2 – 'You are an ignoratis!' – Shaun and 'the twenty-nine hedgedaughters'

One of Joyce's oldest friends, Hanna Sheehy Skeffington, was a distinguished product of the modern educational system. In 1943, 21 years after the creation of the Irish Free State, she stood as an independent candidate for election to the Irish Dáil. A feminist, a republican and an educationalist, Sheehy Skeffington was one of many Irish women responding to what she saw as the betrayal of Irish women in Ireland under Cosgrave and De Valera – the latter she described as being better than the former but, still, 'really essentially conservative and Church bound, anti-feminist, bourgeois and the like'.[12] In her election campaign literature, she excoriated the 1937 constitution and its infamous Article 44 as an attack on a 1922 Free State that had formally established equal constitutional rights for men and women. It was also an attempt to erase the contribution of Irish women to the creation of an independent Ireland. The result of a seemingly unbreakable alliance between Catholic Church and Irish government, the new constitution proclaimed 'that by her life within the home, woman gives to the State a support without which the common good cannot be achieved'. The State 'shall therefore endeavour to ensure that mothers shall not be obliged by economic necessity to engage in labour to the neglect of their duties in the home'.[13] The new constitution, Sheehy Skeffington wrote, was based on 'a Fascist Model, in which women would be relegated to permanent inferiority, their avocations and choice of callings limited because of an implied invalidism as the weaker sex' – not a popular view in Ireland in the 1930s, or even much later in the 1990s, but Sheehy Skeffington had a point.[14]

Many European countries, including England, had passed anti-feminist legislation in the 1920s and 1930s as part of the post-1918 restoration of the masculine order, but it was in Italy, Germany and France under occupation that 'familism' and radical pronatalism had the most profound, and devastating, impact. Hitler declared in 1933, 'in my State the mother is the most important citizen', a view endorsed by Goebbels, who spoke of 'a women's primary, rightful, and appropriate place' as being 'in the family, and the most wonderful task that she can perform [being] to present her country and people with children'.[15] A whole series of paternalist and patriarchal laws forced women out of work in Germany, especially prestigious work in the professions, and into the family where there was overwhelming social pressure to breed, as well as economic incentive.[16] Divorce laws were amended 'in the interests of terminating unproductive marriages'. Alongside adultery, 'the Marriage Law of 1938 in Germany included refusal to conceive, abortion, and irretrievable marital breakdown reflected in three-year separation as grounds for divorce'.[17]

Divorce remained illegal in republican Ireland until 1955, but this kind of legislation was otherwise echoed in the 1937 Irish constitution, with the central distinction that in Ireland it was the Catholic Church, underwritten by the State, that took direct responsibility for rescuing 'Irish maidenhood from the grip of the pagan world'. The Church established for itself authority over all domains of behaviour, defining the codification of standards that were precise and uncompromising. Dresses were 'not to be cut less than four inches below the knee' and should not be 'suggestive in style'. Sleeves should always be two inches below the elbow, although 'one inch for evening wear was considered acceptable'. Shades of stockings suggesting 'the nude' should never be worn. Young women were 'to refrain from smoking and from talking or laughing loudly in public. Immodest dances, cinema shows and plays were to be avoided at all cost'. The primary agencies though which such cultures were made reality were the pulpit and the education system. These rules were formalized in an Annual of the Mary Immaculate College Crusade, an organization set up in a teacher's training college for women which asserted that 'the Irishwoman who is ashamed to be a truechild of Mary is a sham Irishwoman'.[18] Countless memoires of Irish women educated in the 1930s, 1940s and beyond, testify to how this indoctrination operated. Nuala O'Faolain, for example, has written about the punishment inflicted on children in schools by nuns charged with enforcing discipline and full compliance. 'In my first nuns' school', she writes:

> I was the angel Gabriel in a Christmas tableau, but I spoiled everything by waving my wings. The nuns beat me very hard afterwards with the leg of a chair. In my second nuns' school, they wore leather straps as part of their habit. They had a double strap in a cupboard, and I was often beaten with that.[19]

Others have talked about more insidious means to achieve the same ends. Writing in the 1980s about her experiences in the 1940s and 1950s, educationalist

Grainne O'Flynn explains how 'our institutionalisation into what it meant to be Catholic women', began in school. Her account vividly recalls the school 'retreat'. At home, she writes, references to sex:

> were usually limited to vague talk about seeds and mysterious implantations. Because of all this vague home atmosphere, the school 'retreat' . . . became a focal point for questions about sex. In our school, the two senior classes were given what was called a 'special' session and written anonymous questions to the retreat director were allowed. What we all wanted to know was, was it a sin to kiss?
>
> The replies had a pattern. First, we were warned about our sex. The warnings were couched in obscure language and delivered in dramatic tones which thrilled but did not enlighten us. References were made to the arousal of passion, provocative female dress, perfume and 'challenging talk'. Since neither biology or any science was taught to us, and since our reading was extremely limited, we were quite vague about what arousal meant. We did realise, however, that our normal dress – tightly tied navy gymslips, lisle stockings and gabardine coats – were highly unlikely to be provocative. Perfume as a stimulus to wild male response seemed interesting, though unviable at a distance, and what was 'challenging talk'? However, at the end of 'special' sessions, one thing was very clear to us: we were potentially dangerous.[20]

What does this material have to do with 'Joyce and education'? It is true that within the terms of its own extraordinary aesthetic, and in contrast to *Ulysses*, the world of girls in schooling is invoked over and over in Joyce's last great work, *Finnegans Wake*. Part One Book Three (1.3) refers to 'Sylvia Silence', the schoolgirl detective who once featured in a comic published in the 1920s. Part One Book Four (1.4) includes a flight of schoolgirls who 'gushed away, the penny fares, a whole school for scamper, with their sashes flying sish behind them, all the little pirlypettes'. Later in the same chapter, 'every schoolfilly of sevenscore moons or more who knows her intimologies' is also in the know about one of the central events chronicled in the *Wake* – the shooting of the Russian general while he defecates in a field. It was 'Buckleyself (we need no blooding newspaper to tell it neither) who struck and the Russian generals, da! da!, instead of Buckley who was caddishly struck by him when be herselves' (*FW*, 61.1; 80.34–35; 101.16–22).The girls playing the Floras in the mime of Mick, Nick and the Maggies are 'Girl Scouts from St Bride's Finishing Establishment' (220.3–4). In 1.7, Shem is imagined by 'Petty constable Sisterson' surrounded by 'accomplished women, indeed fully educanded' (189.14–15); in 3.2, Father Francis Finn's 1894 collection of short stories, *Mostly Boys*, becomes displaced by an alternative publication, '*Chiefly Girls*' (440.21). In these ways, the *Wake* registers what was the most controversial and arguably most emblematic extension of educational opportunity in the twentieth-century West. But, in these examples at least, it does so in more or less neutral ways, without much reference to the ideological frames outlined here.

Although Hanna Sheehy Skeffington, now an icon of Irish feminism, visited the Joyces in the 1920s and the 1930s – long after her husband had been killed by the British – it is in her role as the wife of Francis Skeffington, Joyce's fellow student at University College, that Hanna invariably figures, rather than as a feminist. Or, at least, that has been the case in Joyce criticism. At the same time, Joyce's response to feminism has often been thought of as being ambiguous at best and frequently assimilated to the Stephen Dedalus persona, who mistrusts all 'enthusiasms' other than his own. It is also entangled with the archetyping/stereotyping dimensions seemingly embedded in the 'Penelope' set up. The idea of 'Joyce and education', including the one worked through in this account, struggles to reconcile the egoism of the Joyce text with any version of education as social justice. Pretty well all of that formulation and what it implies, however, is compromised by the particular place 3.2 has in the cycles of *Finnegans Wake* and the extraordinary vision of schooling it imagines.

The chapter begins with the central figure in Book Three of the *Wake* in a new incarnation. Shaun is in a barrel travelling a river on his way to death and resurrection as his own father, HCE. He is Christ and God at the same time, coded over and over as Irish hero – St Patrick, Cuchulain, the post-office hero of the rebellion who has 'the vote of the Irish' (407.13–14) – specifically De Valera, who shades off into Shaun as the man adored by 'true' Irish womanhood everywhere. He encounters 'the twenty-nine hedge daughters', students at 'Benent Saint Berched's national nightschool' (430.1–2). The girls are outside in the open air, 'learning their antemeridian lesson of life', the central lesson of orthodoxies everywhere about how the world divides into distinct and opposed forces, the great dualisms of East and West – good and evil, right and wrong, black and white, male and female (430.4). The name of the institution – combining a hedge school with a national school and a night school – traverses the history of Irish education, a history tagged here by association with Catholicism, punishment and brutality. Shaun – as 'Jaunty Jaun' – is greeted wildly. '[R]ushing sowarmly for the post', making a tremendous 'girlfuss over him pellmale', the girls muss 'his frizzy hair', 'feeling his full fat pouch for him so tactily and jingaling his jellybags' (430. 20–31). He greets his sister, Issy, who is amongst them and representative of them all – 'our pet pupil of the whole rhythmetic class and the mainsay of our erigenal house, the time we younkers twain were fairly tossing ourselves (O Phoebus! O Pollux!) in bed, having been laid up with Castor's oil' (431.34–432.1). He recalls that she used to write 'exceeding nice letters . . . telling us anun . . . thy oldworld tales of homespinning and derring do and dieobscure and daddyho' (431.29–32). After this strange and distinctly dodgy reunion, Shaun begins his lecture. He rises to speak to the 'fair assemblage' from his barrel, having taken advice on offering 'directions to henservants' from 'Father Mike, P.P., my orational dominican and confessor doctor' (432.4–7) and the 'most eminent bishop titular of Dubloonik' (432.20). He warns the girls that they must 'ever never miss you lostsomewhere mass'(433.10) and begins to recite his commandments. 'First thou shalt not smile. Twice thou shalt not love. Lust, thou shalt not commix idolatry' (433.22–23). 'Especially' they must 'beware please of being at a party to any demoralizing home life. That saps a chap'(433.36–434.1). He warns them of the 'yella perals' that 'all too often beset green girls' – that is, girls both inexperienced and Irish – 'once they gethobbyhorsical', tempted by the stage to play 'breeches parts for Betsy Sudlow in flesh coloured pantos instead of earthing down in the coalhole trying to boil the big gun's dinner' (434.6–10). They must spurn revealing and lacy clothes – 'foulardy pneumonia shertwaists, irriconcilible with true fiminin risirvition and ribbons of lace, limenick's disgrace' (434.19–21). The more he gets into the stride of his lecture, the more outraged, and stimulated, he becomes. Under the pretence of warning against unladylike behaviour, Shaun's own sexual desires begin to rise to the surface, becoming both increasingly uncontrollable and violent. The girls are told in great detail how to behave with boys. They may lay their 'lilylike long his shoulder' if they like, but 'if you've got some brainy notion to raise cancan and rouse commotion I'll be apt to flail that tail for you til its borning' (436.33–437.1). They are encouraged to be 'a sportive' and reminded how their housewifely duties are biologically determined. 'Deal with Nature the great greengrocer and pay regularly the monthlies' (437.16–17). While Shaun is away, he will be thinking of them. He prescribes their reading, which includes 'The Arsidiken's *An Traitey on Miracula or Viewed to Death by a Priest*' and '*Through Hell with the Papes*' (440.2–440.6), and tells them how to entertain themselves while he is away: 'Trip over sacramental tea into the long lives of our saints and saucerdotes, with vignettes, cut short into instructual primers by those in authority for the bittermint of your soughts' (440.21–24). But if they 'get into trouble with a party', especially an outsider beyond the tribe, an 'enemy of our country' (441.30; 442.2), he will get to hear about it and take action: 'we'll dumb well soon show him what the Shaun way is like how we'll go a long way towards breaking his outsider's face for him' (442.21–3). And the girls will suffer too. At this point the violence becomes really ugly, visceral:

> I'll be over you myselx horizontally. . . . I'll smack your fruitflavoured jujube lips well for you, so I will well for you. . . . I'll tear up your limpshades and lock all your trotters in the closet, I will and cut your silkskin into a garters. You'll give up your ask unbrodhel ways when I make you reely smart. . . . For your own good, you understand, for the man who lifts his pud to a woman is saving the way for kindness. . . . For I'll just draw my prancer and give you one splitpuck in the crupper, you understand, that will bring the poppy blush of shame to your peony hindmost till you yelp papapardon.
>
> (444.18–445.17)

Finally, at the prospect of 'Lights out now' (445.22), Shaun seems to calm down. His message has been clear, although whether it has been heard or not is uncertain. One of the girls, at least, seems to have taken little notice of this violent outburst. She cannot, or will not, give over control of her own image. '[D]o you hear me, now, lickspoon, and stop looking at your bussycat bow in the slate' (445.18–21). He sets his charges, 'vocational scholars', their homework – an essay on 'mortinatality in the life of jewries' (447.7–9), or birth and death in the life of Jews. When they go out to do their research, he warns again of how they must take care over their clothes and about the imperatives of decency and decorum. This is third or fourth time Shaun has warned them about dress. Each time there is far too much delight taken in the articulation of his proscriptions. They are to be sure to wear, he insists, 'the midlimb and vestee endorsed by the hierarchy fitted with ecclastics' (447.33–4). There will come a time, 'post purification' (446.28), when he will return, and he hopes to be united with them, the 'little lay mothers' (457.8): 'the mingling of our meeting waters, wish to wisher, like massive mountains to part no more' (446. 14–15). In a reconciliation that reconciles the seemingly irreconcilable – Church, radical socialism and hierarchical order – they 'shall all be hooked and happy, communionistically, among the fieldnights eliceam, *élite* of the elect' (453.31–33).

It is tempting to imagine how Joyce's friend, Hanna Sheehy Skeffington, would have responded to this darkest of comedies of schooling in a new and dangerous modernity. It is not at all difficult to see her laughing at this representation of the patriarchy that so attempted to define her. She would probably have been shocked, too, by the uncompromising associations Joyce makes between education, sexual violence and authoritarian power. She may have implied such associations herself, but Joyce's version is starker and, at the same time, a more much ornate affair, distanced because it is so much a self-consciously worked version of things. We can guess that she would have been even more shocked, and perhaps annoyed, by the unorthodox version of 'feminism' 3.2 appears to construct. Issy's response to her brother's seedy and vicious authoritarianism is not to educate, organize and demonstrate, as did Sheehy Skeffington herself. It is to lisp and dance, 'to fluster sweet nunsongs in' her brother's 'quickturned ear', to infuriate and tempt and stimulate her brother with stories of her lover, stories which unravel his sense of ownership and attack him where it hurts most, in his virility (457.28–30). 'He fell for my lips, for my lisp, for my lewd speaker. I felt for his strength, his manhood, his do you mind? There can be no candle to hold to it, can there?' (459.28–30) She tells him how she will meet with her lover in Shaun's absence. She manipulates his forbidden incestuous desire. 'I'll strip straight after devotions before his fond stare . . . and your name of Shane will come forth between my shamefaced whesen with other lipth I nakest open my thight when just woken by his toccatottletoo my first morning' (461.21–8). This is not, by any means, a formal version of feminism. However much it wrecks Shaun's sense of his own authority, it also plays into stereotypes, just as 'Penelope' does. In the end we cannot know, of course, what Hanna Sheehy Skeffington would have made of all this, or even if she saw it. With her in mind, however, we move closer to an understanding of how the complex and controversial matter of 'Joyce's politics' is embedded in the social world he inhabited and that formed him. In Joyce at the end, as in Joyce at the beginning, schooling, however rhetorically disposed to the development of the individual, is a system, maintained as state enterprise – a powerful conformity operating through and maintained by family, church and state and a central orthodoxy against which his 'revolution of the word' operates.

Notes

1 See Mary E. Daly, 'Women in the Irish Free State, 1922–1939: The Interaction between Economics and Ideology', *Journal of Women's History*, 6/6; 7/1, 1995, 99–116 [106–7].
2 Daly, 'Women in the Irish Free State, 1922–1939', 108–10.
3 See Senn, '"Ithaca": Portrait of the Chapter as a Long List', 39.
4 In her seminal essay 'The Laugh of Medusa' (1975), Helénè Cixous issued a call for women to write against 'a history of writing' that had been 'confounded with the history of reason, of which it is at once the effect, the support and one of the privileged alibis. It has been one with the phallocentric traditions'. In this account, Joyce's 'Penelope' was imagined as a product of 'white ink', the 'good mother's milk' that 'carried off *écriture feminine*, 'beyond any book' into the future of 'the new writing'. See Helénè Cixous, *The Laugh of Medusa*, translated by Keith Cohen and Paula Cohen, *Signs*, 1/4, 1976, 875–93 (884; 881).
5 Suzette A. Henke, 'Speculum of the Other Molly: A Feminist/Psychoanalytic Inquiry into James Joyce's Politics of Desire', *Mosaic: A Journal for the Interdisciplinary Study of Literature*, 21, 2/3, 1988, 149–64.
6 Irina Rasmussen Goloubeva, 'Molly Bloom: A Re-Immersion in the Concrete', *James Joyce Quarterly*, 47/3, 2010, 395–415 [402; 404–5; 407; 410].
7 Rancière, 'On Ignorant Schoolmasters', in Bingham and Biesta, *Jacques Rancière: Education, Truth, Emancipation*, 4.
8 Rancière, 'On Ignorant Schoolmasters', 3.
9 Rancière, 'On Ignorant Schoolmasters', 8–9.
10 Kristin Ross, 'Translator's Introduction' in Jacques Rancière, *The Ignorant Schoolmaster*, xii.
11 See Laura Teague's essay, 'The Curriculum as a Site of Counter Politics: Theorising the Domain of the Sayable', *British Journal of Sociology of Education*, 39/1, 2018, 92–106. This draws on Judith Butler's concept of 'the domain of the sayable' as it is used in *Excitable Speech: A Politics of the Performative* (London: Routledge, 1997).
12 Draft letter (n.d.), Hanna Sheehy Skeffington papers, MS 24, 134, National Library of Ireland, quoted in Catriona Beaumont, 'Women, Citizenship and Catholicism in the Irish Free State, 1922–1948', *Women's History Review*, 6/4, 1997, 563–85.
13 The 1937 Constitution of the Irish Republic, quoted in Thomas Mohr, 'The Rights of Women Under the Constitution of the Irish Free State', *Irish Jurist*, new series, 41, 2006, 20–59 [20].
14 *Irish Independent*, May 11, 1937.
15 Hitler's speech to the N-S Frauenschaft on 8 September 1934 cited in Max Domarus (ed.), *Hitler. Reden und Proklamationen 1932–1945*, vol. 1 (Munich: Neustadt, 1965), 449–52. The Goebbels quote is cited in Renate Wiggershaus, *Frauen unterm Nationalsozialismus* (Wuppertal: P. Hammer, 1984, 15).
16 See the Law for the Reduction of Unemployment, June 1, 1933, which taxed single persons in order to offer interest-free loans to families, contingent on the wife giving up work.
17 Michael Burleigh and Wolfgang Wippermann, *The Racial State: Germany 1933–45* (Cambridge: Cambridge University Press, 1991), 253.
18 See Beaumont, 'Women, Citizenship and Catholicism in the Irish Free State', 567.
19 Nuala O'Faolain, 'My Memories of Nuns' (1992), first published in *Religious Life Review* (1992), reprinted in Angela Bourke *et al.* (eds.), *The Field Day Anthology of Irish Writing; Irish Women's Writing and Traditions*, vol. 4 (New York: New York University Press, 2002), 594–6 [595].
20 Grainne O'Flynn, 'Our Age of Innocence', first published in 1987, reprinted in Bourke *et al.* (eds.), *The Field Day Anthology of Irish Writing*, 591–4 [593].

Chapter 10

'Come si compita cunctitititilatus?' – education and *Finnegans Wake*

Reading the *Wake*, writing the *Wake*

The subject of 'Joyce and education' in this book is primarily about an engagement with the social and psychological aspects of schooling, a mechanism designed by the state to maintain a modern elite. There can be little doubt that the Joyce text is an interrogation of the impact of formal education and its systemization on the schooled subject. Joyce's early work is by no means unusual in this respect. The list of fiction writers who critically engage with their own formal education on structural grounds such as these is long indeed. Perspectives on schooling taken by the Joyce text were focused in particularly sharp and contemporary ways by the work of Nietzsche, but the broad history of the Enlightenment turning in on itself via one of its own most characteristic and cherished institutions includes almost everything in the romantic tradition and a good deal outside it – including literary modernism itself which has been formulated in critical approaches of the past as a species of romanticism.[1] The great leap of the Joyce text, most evident in the mature versions, is the move that places both the writing of literature and reading itself in relation to schooling and other modern systems of knowledge formation. Here the textbook or the encyclopaedia, both particularly significant to the writing of *Ulysses*, become epistemological forms remade and undone in the textuality of episodes like 'Oxen of the Sun', 'Eumaeus' and 'Ithaca'. In the late Joyce text, however exemplary it may appear in terms of the reproduction of schooled knowledge, the anti-schooling tradition takes a new turn, partly through the contaminative association it makes between high-status and highly privileged school knowledge and highly commodified informatic cultures of the everyday, represented in *Finnegans Wake* by such products as 'Hirish tutores Cornish made easy' (*FW*, 126.25). It is here that the destabilizing implications of the identification Joyce makes between modernity and education become most manifest.

Where does *Finnegans Wake* sit in relation to all this? This is a text famously imagined in critical cultures as forever shifting, 'unencompassable' and 'endlessly redefinable'.[2] It has been variously described as a machine, a test, a dream where subject identities change and merge and narrative units are repeated over and over, not only with no resolution but subject to every variation imaginable.

Under these circumstances what can be said about education in relation to *Finnegans Wake*?

In her 2016 account, Elizabeth Switaj argues for a discursive line that can be taken through this extraordinary text and she does so by thinking about it in pedagogic terms. However much pedagogy is laughed at and, indeed, ridiculed in the *Wake*, the promotion of a particular kind of pedagogy – as Switaj claims, 'radical' pedagogy – remains at the heart of the book. This is because reading the *Wake* is akin to learning a language, where learning is constructed in modern contextual, 'conversational' ways which Joyce would have picked up when he worked as a tutor at the Berlitz school, rather than through traditional formalism.

But even the author of *this* reading must accept that any learning the *Wake* promotes, however radical it might appear as implied technique, is essentially pointless. Through it, Joyce apparently creates a 'lect' – a term that 'refers to a language variety without specifying it as a dialect, an independent language, an idiolect, or otherwise'. It has the defining characteristic that it 'does not and cannot have speakers outside the pages of the book'; in this case, just one particular book.[3]

If that is the case, then it appears that the *Wake*, whatever else it sets out to achieve, takes position at the endpoint of a careering anti-progressivist dynamic. Here Joyce's radical critique of modern education, representing an exemplary 'advance from savagery to barbarism', leads to an aesthetic formulation that makes a huge investment in schooled knowledge only to insist that modern education is an impossiblist culture of meaningless routines (*FW*, 114.13).

This must seem counterintuitive in relation to a text framed so typically in terms of its inaccessibility, where 'difficulty' stands in precisely for what we do not know, what we have failed to learn. Everyone who reads the *Wake* will feel both hugely impressed by it but horribly exposed in this respect, the reason why reading the *Wake* can seem so much a matter of feeling under qualified, unnervingly deficient in just about every department. It is difficult to conceive of any *Wake* reader who does not at times feel returned to the classroom, traditional or not, sometimes at specific invitation. In 1.6, for example, a chapter comprised of 12 questions on the text of which it is part, the response to question 10 not only speaks back to the question and the questioner but also reaches out towards the imagined reader:

> As my explanations here are probably above your understandings, lattlebrattons, though as augmentatively uncomparisoned as Cadwan, Cadwallon and Cadwalloner, I shall revert to a more expletive method which I frequently use when I have to sermo with muddlecrass pupils. . . . As none of you knows javanese I will give all my easyfree translation of the old fabulist's parable. Allaboy Minor, take your head out of your satchel! *Audi*, Joe Peters! *Exaudi* facts!
>
> (152. 4–14)

In the same chapter, the first question asks: 'What secondtonone myther rector and maximost bridgesmaker was the first to rise taller through his beanstale than the bluegum buaboababbaun or the giganteous Wellingtonia Sequoia', an opening gambit that takes 12 pages to reach a question mark. The answer, a two-word response roared out with great certitude and enthusiasm, is 'Finn MacCool!'– a classroom celebration of certainty where, for once, everyone knows the answer and with which the reader, again, is complicit (126.10–12; 139.14). More often than not, however, this frustrating writing simply goes beyond us, a position which privileges the challenge of the *Wake* at the same time as it rationalizes our retreat and is itself related to education systems so much invested in selection and hierarchy and the social reproduction of intelligence. The first page of *Finnegans Wake* is symptomatic. To 'read' just this one page, we apparently require English, Latin, Greek, Italian, French, Japanese, Chinese, Hindustani, Swedish, Danish, Portuguese, Basque and Old Rumanian. To be more precise, we would need to be soaked in these languages, if – in some bizarre parallel universe – we planned to unpick the precise allusions invoked on this page without the assistance of the annotative literature.[4] Joyce himself was fluent in only three of them and thus would be unable to read his own book had he not written it. Likewise with, say, Vico and *The New Science* (1725) or the stories of Tristan and Isolde. Or Irish history; American and Irish geography; song lyrics; the works of Jonathan Swift, in particular, *Journal to Stella* (1766); pubs in Dublin and its suburbs; the Bible and the life cycle of the salmon. A knowledge of all these subject fields and more is implied as a prerequisite for reading just page one, again, a very detailed and specific knowledge. Indeed, the aesthetic viability of the *Wake* seems precisely contingent on the subtlety of how these 'references' work – the point being that the demands on knowledge made by the *Wake* are not just great. They are impossible. That is, they are rendered impossible by design. The book remains, without doubt, the most incredible example of the orders underlying epistemological systems in the West and, at the same time, the most extraordinary illustration of their precise and exact undoing.

In this way the *Wake*, from its first word onwards, embodies knowledge systems as we have seen them reproduced elsewhere in the Joyce text, although never with this degree of interference. This is the real reason why 'education' is everywhere implicated in the *Wake*, not because the text posits some social or pedagogical correction but because it embodies the contradictions of the schooled identity in a radical new form. This book, as Beckett famously maintained, 'is not *about* something; *it is that something itself*' and what it is, at a most fundamental level, is a huge interference in the Western intellectual tradition.[5] This is also why not only reading the *Wake* but also scholarly study of the *Wake* has such affinity with schooling. It becomes very much a matter of tracing back, taking notes, returning with annotations, plot summaries and so on – old-fashioned 'scholarship', as opposed to 'research', as it is more commonly called in contemporary cultures today – always with the understanding that in doing so we are not adding to the stock of human knowledge but, rather, returning the *Wake* to the order it has so carefully taken apart. From this perspective, many of the most characteristic and prestigious cultures in the *Wake* critical tradition, however impressive and designed to help, can only be a form of the reactionary.

Ironically enough, writing the *Wake* drew on the same traditions. It was significantly constructed from a practice that every schoolboy and schoolgirl learns at an early stage of schooling. The Ellmann biography records Joyce's friends and collaborators on the *Wake*, Stuart Gilbert and Helen Fleischman, reading articles from the *Encyclopaedia Britannica*, taken from a list of 30 cities provided by Joyce, 'among them New York, Budapest, Rio de Janeiro, Amsterdam, and Copenhagen. . . . At the names of streets, buildings, parks, and city-founders they paused to give Joyce time to think whether they could be brought by pun into his work. So Amsterdam became Amtsadam . . . and Slottsgarten in Oslo became Slutsgarten'.[6] The same note-taking practice was observed in *Reflections on James Joyce: Stuart Gilbert's Paris Journal* – the idea of transformation into 'pun' does not adequately describe it, and in most cases, transcription was direct and not distorted at all, as Geert Lernout has definitively shown.[7] Gilbert records Joyce working with several volumes of the *Encyclopaedia* spread out on his sofa, assisted by Fleischman, Padraic Colum, Paul Léon and himself, recording words and phrases in his notebooks.[8] Such a description deflates some of the more pious and ideologically informed conceptions of the range and depth of Joyce's 'knowledge'. It absolutely confirms that the *Wake* is closely related to the ubiquitous command of the pedagogue to 'take notes', an instruction that Joyce, 'that odious and still today insufficiently malestimated note snatcher' in the Shem incarnation, followed throughout his writing life but adopted most religiously in the notebooks used in the making of this book (125.21).

The *Wake* represents, in the most pervasive form, an extraordinary process of a kind of assimilative disarticulation, an incorporating which is at the same time an undoing. Here the composition history of the *Wake* is as emblematic as it is illustrative. From the first draft of the 'Roderick O'Connor' sketch, written in the early 1920s, to the publication of the complete text in the late 1930s, *Finnegans Wake* took some 16 years to write. The working-up of the text from 48 notebooks and no less than 25,000 pages of textual record famously involved the creation, as Switaj says, of a 'new' language, one essentially English in its structure and many of its word forms, but radical enough to be unique to Joyce and to warrant naming as a separate entity. Establishing full facility in 'Wakese', or 'Wake-speak', involved a great deal of labour. This means that the writing of the *Wake* was literally a specifically learned skill, evidenced not least by the endless revision of sections written at earlier stages of development so that, as far as possible, the consistency of the full *Wake* text that we now have could be established, and it *is* quite uniform in style by comparison to the parade of technics that comprise *Ulysses*. Thus, the earliest written sections of the *Wake* were originally much 'easier' than they later became. Even then, it is often claimed that the last structural section of the text to have been formulated, now known as Book Two, remains the most 'difficult' part. This is not because Book Two deals with more complex ideas, but because, as genetic criticism has shown in one of the central narratives about *Wake* composition, it was written when Joyce's mastery of this form of writing was at its most developed and thus at its most fluid.[9] Built out of

60-odd languages and many other fragments taken from novels, poems, plays, religious literature, academic books, textbooks, biographies and autobiographies, comics, newspaper articles and so on, the language of the *Wake* is why Joyce's last book remains his most challenging by a very long way. Its great strangeness formulates a unique challenge, even for the most 'abcedminded' (18.17). That is, even for the most schooled of readers, the qualified but forgetful intelligence imagined variously in its pages as struggling mathematician, academician, grammarian, archaeologist, historian, anthropologist, linguist, graphologist and the four old masters who form 'mamalujo' – all figures implied as much in the writing of the *Wake* as the reading of it and emblematic not of a golden age of learning but of something quite different, a 'leaden age of letters' (61.29).

'Pencylmania' – schooling in the *Wake*

There are many new elements in the handling of schooling in the *Wake*, none of which can be separated out from the astonishing originality of the *Wake*-world they are placed in. At the same time, the *Wake* also refocuses some of the dominant interpretative frames that Joyce insists on placing on schooled learning in earlier writing. The connections between school and the formation of social identity are, again, prominent, both in incidentals where Professor Lowry-Brueller writes a book entitled '*Why am I not born like a Gentileman*' and in the more fundamental – the Shem/Shaun dynamic, for example, in which rival brothers fight it out for supremacy (150.26).

In 1.5, Shaun explains his brother's dissipation as a corruption of *bildung*: 'Neither of those clean little cherubum, Nero or Nobookisonester himself, ever nursed such a spoiled opinion of his monstrous marvellosity as did this mental and moral defective', and his egoism is framed in social terms. Shem, according to Shaun, is a 'bumpersprinkler', an 'arestocrank', who 'used to boast aloud to himself with a haccent on it . . . (trying to copy the stage Englesemen he broughts their house down on, shouting: Bravure, surr Chorles!)' (177.14–16; 424.10; 180.34–181.2). Learning becomes a kind of over-schooling, here and elsewhere in the *Wake* associated with fake aristocracy as it is in *Stephen Hero*, *A Portrait* and *Ulysses*, and also with hubris and fall. In 1.5, ALP takes the blame herself for her son, a 'windblasted tree of the knowledge andevil'. In 2.2 Shem as Glugg, 'divorced into disgrace court' because 'he knew to mutch', has the 'duvlin suph' (devil's sulphur) in him and is 'lost-to-lurning' (194.14–15; 220.1–2; 222.25).

The same conflict in reverse returns in 2.2 and is, again, framed by the hierarchies of schooling that so characterize education systems in Joyce. When Shaun, as Dolph, for all his facility in basic arithmetic, fails to grasp the first and simplest of Euclid's propositions, he is mocked by his brother and what begins as an intellectual issue is soon interrogated for its social implications. Shem – a 'gentlemine born, milady bread' – laughs at Shaun, an underbred 'sadfellow', 'like a purate out of pensionee with a gouvernament job'. He is, according to Shem, a dullard condemned to a bourgeois life of obedience, routine and misery: 'All moanday, tearsday, wailsday, thumpsday, frightday, shatterday till the fear of the Law' (301.11–22). As a consequence of his intellectual failings, Shem asks him if he 'ever thought about Guinness's', that is, about a job as a clerk in the brewery, an occupation more than once recommended to Joyce by his father (299.30). The rivalry between them may be familial and gender-based, but it is framed in social terms and in this sense connected to the competitive hierarchy that lies at the heart of Joyce's version of modern education.

The fact that Shem and Shaun are so interchangeable returns the Joyce text yet again to the contradictions of the public schoolboy identity, a figure who is not just *both* a conformist and a rebel but a conformist whose rebellion is a *product* of the social fantasies that lie behind elite schooling. This contradiction is evident in the margin notes of 2.2 which embody the two sides of a single identity and thus are interchangeable – indeed, halfway through, Shem and Shaun change sides. The notes at 264 are typically Shaun-sounding – conservative, serious and deferential. Their summaries of sections of narrative text on this page are, however bizarre, sedulous in their observance of proper schooling procedures. They characteristically take classical Greek and Latinate forms – 'ARCHAIC ZELOTYPIA AND THE ODIUM TELEOLOGICUM' and 'THE LOCALISATION OF LEGEND TO THE LEGALISATION OF LATIFUNDISM' – echoing the Latinization repeated over and over in the *Wake* as an emblem of the book at is its most pompous. This species of cod Latin, used to denote the educated mind, is not exclusively associated with Shaun – in 1.8, one of the old washerwomen speaks in unlikely terms of 'contemplation of the fluctuation and the undification of her [ALP's] filimentation' (209.2–3). But it frequently is, as in 4.3, when Shaun is asked by the four old men to suggest a middle way for the modern – 'the Mod needs a rebus' – a request invoking not just Latin language but the classical curriculum more generally. 'Est modus in rebus', a middle course in all things, comes from Horace and the first of his *Satires*. Shaun responds in kind with ' – Pro general continuation and in particular explication to your singular interrogation our asseveralation' (523.19–22). Shem is every bit as schooled as his brother, but much less compelled to play the particular games that orthodox schooled cultures demand. On the contrary, his instinct is to mock, to rebel, which makes his interventions very different – schooled but also disruptive and often rude. They include demotic versions of dancing and cricketing ('*Swing the banjo, bantams, bounce-the baller's blown to fook*' – 262) and the heretical temptation offered to a school friend from a generalized classical past at 266: '*Bet you fippence, anythesious, there's no purgatory, are yous game?*'

Indeed, the reach and range of schooling in the *Wake*, and the connections between schooling and both the reading and writing of this text are exceptionally strong, made especially in relation to processes of writing and reading. Signs of 'Joyce and education' figure in quite local ways everywhere, which may be why the book is so entangled with sites of the acquisition, preservation and performance of knowledge. The museum, the science lab, the library, the quiz show, the examination hall, the lecture theatre – these are special places in this 'novel'.

For all the radical nature of the new form to which 'Joyce and education' must now be assimilated, its signature is writ large and becomes part of the process of learning how to read the *Wake*; part of its language, as it were; part of its grammar and its everyday vocabulary.

In this way, the educational institutions that Joyce attended are incorporated into the fabric of the *Wake*. Clongowes becomes implicated in 'Old Clo' who 'goes through the wood'; the competitive houses of Lancaster and Yorkshire from *A Portrait* are refigured as 'Rose Lankester and Blanche Yorke', and 'Dagobert', a seventh-century king of the Franks, is reimagined in 'Clane's clean hometown . . . prepping up his prepueratory' – Clongowes is in Clane, County Kildare (453.15; 485.12; 274.29–30). Likewise, Belvedere and the intermediate exams its students sat returns as 'The Belvedarean exhibitioners. In their cruisery caps and and oarsclub colours' (205.5–6). Whatever else the *Wake* is, like the earlier fiction it makes an investment in Joyce's educational biography, often, invariably in fact, in quite incidental ways so that the whole experience of schooling becomes a kind of source for the *Wake*. Examining a fragment of ALP's letter in the most minute detail in 1.5, the expert notes that 'the geegees too' are 'jesuistically formed at first but afterwards genuflected aggrily toewards the occident', which makes them part of Joyce's real history and his journey into exile too, as well as of the fictional life of the mysterious letter (120.21–2). Essays written by schoolboys at Belvedere were required to be framed by the abbreviation AMDG (*Ad Majorem Dei Gloriam* – 'for the greater glory of God'), placed at the beginning, and LDS (*Laus Deo Semper* – 'praise to God forever'), placed at the end. These same formulas appear, too, in *Finnegans Wake*, where, in 2.2, they are used to signal particular performances including the working through of a problem every public schoolboy in Joyce's day would have been expected to be able to solve: the first problem in Euclid's geometry – how to construct an equilateral triangle or 'Problem: To define an equilateral triangle on a finite line', which in the *Wake* becomes 'Problem ye ferst, construct ann aquilittoral dryankle Probe loom!' (286.19).[10] In 2.3, they have a more twentieth-century context, framing a radio/television sequence, a publically transmitted 'Welter focussed' (weather forecast) combined with a series of news items presented in a mix-up of Viconian cycles: 'Giant crash in Aden. Birdflights confirm abbroaching nubtials. Burial of Lifetenant-Groevenor Hatchett, R.I.D. Devine's Previdence' (324.24–325.2) or, age of giants, age of men, age of gods. Almost 100 pages later, during the first watch of Shaun (3.1), the two abbreviations are conflated in a prelude to a rendition of a song written by the Ondt, a 'melody' that, in contrast to the 'phoney', unreadable writings of the Gracehoper, 'mints the money': '*Ad majorem lsd.! Divi gloriam*' (418.4).

The pedagogic voice, a continuity in Joyce from 'An Encounter' onwards, is similarly never far away in the *Wake* and anyone who tries to teach in it – the genealogist in 1.2, the 'entomophilust' in 1.5, 'Professor Loewy-Brueller' in 1.6, the 'four collegians' in 2.4 and Shaun as Jaun in 3.2 – is laughed at and must fail (107.13; 150.15; 385.08). The 'beginning' of the book, a historical/mythical commentary ostensibly given by Kate Strong, echoes the 'Peter Parley' books for children, instructional 'histories' on some levels but also myths and fables of ancient times, sometimes, by the author's own admission, 'altogether destitute of the truth'.[11] Similarly, Kate's account in 1.1 is part authenticity, underwritten by the 'Four things therefore, saith our herodotary Mammon Lujius in his grand old historiorum, wrote near Boriorum', but, often, complete speculation: 'Somewhere, parently, in the ginnandgo gap between antediluvious and annadominant the copyist must have fled with his scroll' (13.20–1; 14.16–18). Likewise, the characteristic 'Peter Parley' narrative was conceptualized as 'part history', but also part 'tour'. The *Universal History on the Basis of Geography* (1837) was specifically designed to register historical sweep but in an immediate way, to deliver the personal experience of a 'clear, vivid continuous tale of the great human family', which is why it so often 'talks' directly to its reader, inviting him or her into its world.[12] It begins, by asking its young readers to imagine climbing into a balloon to see their country from above and to encounter difference, traveling to a 'different country' and coming across 'a building different from any we had seen'.[13] 'If we were to meet', the text asks, 'with some old man who had lived so long, should we not wish to sit down by his side and hear him tell how the edifice had been built?'[14] This conjures up the tone of 1.1, constructed as an educational tour of the contents of 'Wallingstone national museum' that crashes through the fourth wall when Kate visualizes the 'carl on the kopje. . . . What a quhare sort of a mahan. It is evident the michindaddy. Lets we overstep his fire defences and these kraals of slitsucked marrogbones' (8. 1–2; 15.29; 16.1–3). Similarly the reader checks in 'Parley', designed to reassure teachers and parents that the real purpose behind these 'stories' is educational, are replicated in 1.1 where Kate comments on the 'curios of signs' used in the 'allaphbed' of this 'claybook', asking whether her 'abcedminded' readers can understand it – 'Can you rede its . . . world?' (18.17–19). From the beginning, pedagogy is explicitly connected with the strangeness of the book and the bizarre difficulties of reading it.

Pedagogic voice is present elsewhere in the *Wake*, perhaps especially in Book One, where punctuation rules are part of narrative design and explicit injunctions visible as words on the page, as in 'Fillstup. So you need hardly spell me', and where verb tenses stand in for the names of characters. The 'free boardschool shirkers' in 1.2, for example are 'Will, Conn and Otto' (will, can and ought to) (20.13–14; 51.11). Likewise with maths rules which appear in 1.1 in the middle of one of many histories: 'One by one place one be three dittoh and one before' (19.20–21); 1.2, which concerns 'the genesis of Harold or Humphrey Chimpden's occupational agnomen', opens with the word 'Now', delivered as teacherly intervention signalling the request for silence and attention, followed by a parenthetical reminder of context – '(we are back in the presurnames prodromarith period of course just when enos chalked halltraps)' – and then by a theoretical positioning that is a 'discarding once for all those theories from older sources which would link him [HCE] back with such pivotal ancestors as the Glues, the Gravys, the Northeasts, the Ankers and the Earwickers of Sidlesham' (30. 1–8).

Explication in the *Wake*, however much frustrated, is substantially the domain of the pedagogue, a voicing that surfaces again in 1.5, where the fragment of ALP's letter, a 'proteiform graph . . . laden with the loot of learning' is also 'a polyhedron of scripture', subjected to scholarly scrutiny, revealing 'the learning betrayed at almost every line's end' (107.8; 108.7;120.24).

As in 'Ithaca', examination papers reappear as part of the 'narrative' of the *Wake* text:

> 4. What Irish capitol city (a dea o dea!) of two syllables and six letters, with a deltic origin and a nuinous end, (ah dust oh dust!) can boast of having a) the most extensive public park in the world, b) the most expensive brewing industry in the world, c) the most expansive peopling thoroughfare in the world, d) the most phillohippuc theobibous paùpulation in the world: and harmonise your abecedeed responses.
>
> (140. 8–14)

And so do examination responses. The answer to this question begins, as required with 'Answer: a) Delfas' and proceeds to 'd) Dalway' by way of b) and c), with a signal, in italics, to the examiner that all parts of the rubric have been observed – '*abcd*' (see 140.15–141.4).

Textbooks, likewise, are ubiquitous in the language and grammar of the *Wake* discourse and so are their routines and registers. The language of 2.2, like language everywhere in the *Wake*, is hugely modified, but at its heart is textbook language. Perhaps in a further reflection of the influence of Lindley Murray, Issy has learnt social protocols from her 'gramma's grammar', which tells her that 'if there is a third person, mascarine, phelinine or nuder, being spoken abad it moods prosodes from a person speaking to her second which is the direct object that has been spoken to, with and at' (268.17–22). 'Gramma', with no 'r', is Latin for a drawing of the alphabet, but it also evokes grandma, just as grandpa (and the Italian drink) is evoked in 'grappa' later on in this section and what starts out sounding so formal now begins to mutate, becoming inseparable from an informal discourse that appears to have something to do with sexuality and is connected to the notion of grandmotherly advice to a granddaughter. In that context, the word 'neuter', which in grammar signifies a verb condition or the gender of a noun, becomes 'nuder', suggesting 'more naked'. Later in the same chapter, the 'split in the infinitive from to have to have been to will be' is likewise grammar rule operating as narrative discourse (271.21–2).

All languages utilized in the *Wake* are subject to distortion, but Latin is especially subject to play based on language teaching strategies – such as declensions and mock declensions and mnemonic rhymes like the ones presented at the end of *Kennedy's Latin Primer*, a text book Joyce would have known. These are not strictly 'allusions' or 'quotations', although there are a great number of Latin quotations in the *Wake*, but, again, part of this text's fabric and put to its service. The principle is usage and assimilation, so that the Latin progression for 'sad', 'sadder', 'saddest' becomes in the *Wake* a name – 'Tristis Tristior Tristissimus' – used in one of many retellings of the story of Tristan and Isolde. Here in an astonishing performance, Latinization is both excessively deployed and decisively upturned, so that the Latin word 'meretrix', meaning prostitute, becomes 'translated' in reverse as a thoroughly Anglo-Saxonized 'merrytricks', for example. Latin is routinely mangled in such a way to upset associations with class and status. '*Ipse dixit*' ('he said') in the *Wake* becomes 'upsieduxit' (158.1; 60.6; 60.33), for example, closer to the idiomatic 'upsy daisy', and the 'Federals' Uniteds' Transports' Unions' for Exultations' of Triumphants' Ecstasies' is an acrostic that makes the word Latin word 'futuete', meaning 'fuck' (66.8–9). Throughout the *Wake*, as in *A Portrait* and *Ulysses*, a highly complex version of schoolboy 'dog' Latin, is everywhere in evidence. Cod Latin verb conjugation and progressions from comparatives to superlatives are worked into Wakese, as in 'Alo, alass, aladdin, amobus' (for 'amo', 'amas', 'amat', 'amamus' etc – 407.27). So are mnemonics from Latin textbooks. 'From *nemo* let me never see *neminis* or *nemine*' becomes mixed up with, again, advice to the Earwicker daughter, Issy, from her grandmother – this time on sexual conduct in the context of how to behave in order to capture a husband, 'from Nebob . . . see you never stray who'll nimm you nice and nehm the day'.[15] The same mnemonic is used by Shaun as Yaun in 3.2 in his lecture to the 29 schoolgirls: 'Fond namer, let me never see thee blame a kiss for shame a knee' (270.27–8; 468.18–19). At 256.24–25, in a passage that points towards the beginning of 'night lessons', a different mnemonic for Latin nouns of the third declension appears as 'Amnist anguished axes Collis' (*amnis*, *anguis*, *axis*, *collis* – meaning 'river', 'snake', 'axis', 'hill').

As in 'Ithaca', discourses of school mathematics are also built into the narrative fabric where Bygmester Finnegan would 'caligulate by multiplicables' and HCE, 'more mob than man', is 'Length Withought Breath' and, like a maths formula, 'constantly the same as and equal to himself' (4.32–3; 261.13–22; 32.20). Again, 2.2, the 'night lessons' episode of the *Wake*, takes this device to new extremes. Whole pages of the text are taken up with a narrative informed by approximate sounds and rhythms of mathematical routines, as here where the text is identifying the limited procedures that Shaun can control in order to find 'by practice the valuse of thine-to-mine articles with no reminder for an equality of relations' (283.10–12):

> To sum, borus pew notus pew eurus pew zipher. Ace, deuce, tricks, quarts, quims. Mumtiplay of course and carry to their whole number. While on the other hand, traduced by their comedy nominator to the loaferst terms to their aloquent parts, sexes, suppers, ogglers, novels and dice.
>
> (283.3–9)

In the same chapter, geometrical designs are incorporated into the text, as are the mathematical symbols for 'because' and 'therefore' and typographical equivalents found for the abstract signs used for 'more than' and 'less than' in mathematics, so that 'the power of empthood be either greater THaN or less THaN the unitate' (see 292.11–12; 298.13–14).

This account of the ways in which the *Wake* incorporates schooled learning as a condition of its own writing, as astonishing as it might appear, is far from inclusive. Forms of the school history text book structured as annals with the dates of important events highlighted are replicated in 1.1 at pages 13–14, a timing of 'the cycles of events grand and national' (13.31–2); a music lesson is tabulated at 272; alphabets, number sequences and equations are endlessly recited, sometimes these 'as simple as A.B.C', sometimes not – as in 'the NCR⁵ • presents to us . . . an ottomantic turquo-indaco of pictorial shine' (65.27–28; 284.26–28).[16] School novels are returned to, notably *Vice Versa* which is referred to many times, utilized for its overlaps with Bruno's 'coincidence of contraries', one of the central philosophical ideas associated with the *Wake* aesthetic (see, for example, 'viceversa' at 63.3, 'visanvrerssas' at 173.25, 'vice o'verse' at 288.1, 'pending its viceversion' at 349.7, 'Viceversounding' at 355.10, a Latinized 'vicemversem' at 384.27, a New York style 'voicyverysy' at 453.17 and a French one at 'vites inversion' at 523.17). The cricketing cultures that Joyce first learnt at Clongowes are implicated everywhere in the *Wake*, again as part of its unfamiliar vocabulary. Here, where 'Life . . . is a wake, livit or krikit', cricket stands in for life itself and the passing of time in 'later in the century'; it figures in the multiple names of HCE, who is 'Tight before Teatime', 'W.D's Grace' and the 'Cumberer of Lord's Holy Ground' (55.7,12; 71.17, 19, 34). HCE is also a figure who 'offers changes to Long on but stands up to Legge before' (127.7–8). And so on, and so on; not quite *ad infinitum*, but for sure set up precisely to look that way.

Education in *FW* 2.2 – 'black and white wencraft', Freud, Viconian cycles

The spread of schooling in the *Wake* is extremely diffuse. There are a great many incidental textual plays, games and strategies throughout the *Wake* where schooling and pedagogic practice are implicated. Indeed these are so endemic that through them we are returned to some of the most basic questions that can be asked about the *Wake* – questions about how it was written, why it was written and what it is like to read this extraordinary book. In its contradictory dimensions of error, fake and authority, the *Wake* is a thoroughly schooled object, just as its imagined author – part rebel, part conformist – is a thoroughly schooled subject. For all the innovation of Joyce's last great book, education in the *Wake* seems in many ways like a restatement, a revisiting that stretches across the pages of this text from its beginning to its end and is registered in the minute details of its writing.

At the same time as it dispersed across the pages the *Wake* and built into processes of reading and writing the text, the idea of education also appears in concentrated passages and episodes and with some new emphases. In 2.2, for example, the obvious example of concentration, schooled knowledge is spliced together with a large dose of the neo-Platonism that once appealed to W.B. Yeats and the Dublin Theosophy group. Based around mystical nonsense posing as scientific knowledge, this was an exclusivist and reactionary culture that used the procedures of modern rationalism against the modern world. Joyce had mocked it in *Ulysses*, notably in 'Scylla and Charybdis 'and 'Oxen of the Sun', through the voicings of Stephen and Mulligan. In the *Wake*, theosophy merges with schooling in more formal aesthetic ways. Significantly, if 2.2, the night lessons episode, is *the* chapter of schooling in the *Wake*, it is also *the* most theosophically informed section of the *Wake*, partly through its misappropriation of Yeats *A Vision* (1925), but not exclusively so.[17] Many of the references to theosophy in 2.2 are more closely related to standard theosophical texts, such as Helena Petrovna Blavatsky's *Isis Unveiled.* At 261.23, for example, there is a reference to HCE as 'Ainsoph, this upright one', with ALP 'that noughty besighed him zeroine'. Ain-Soph is the first principle in theosophy, not the ultimate originator, whose name is never revealed, but the first 'emanation' of the creative spirit. Thus there are many references to Ain-Soph in *Isis Unveiled*, although what Joyce has most in mind at this point is probably *Isis Unveiled*, Volume 1, in which Ain-Soph is zeroed as 'no-thing'.[18] The references to mercury, salt and sulphur in *FW* 261 establish an additional theosophical context at this point. All these substances are indexed in *Isis Unveiled.* Similarly at 263.20–27, where

> since primal made alter in garden of Idem. The tasks above are as the flasks below, saith the emerald canticle of Hermes and all's loth and pleasestir, are we told, on excellent inkbottle authority, solarsystemised, seriolcosmically, in a more and almightily expanding universe under one, there is rhymeless reason to believe, original sun.

This is perhaps the closest *Finnegans Wake* comes to an expression of the key theosophical narrative – 'primal' and 'alter', are suggestive of the Latin for 'first' and 'second' and related to the theosophist formulation of the monad producing the duad at the origin of creation. The reference to Hermes Trismegistos and *The Emerald Table* alludes to the central theosophical idea of correspondence between the heavens and the earth. Sun worship is also fundamental to theosophy, as is the idea of an expanding universe, the breath of God that exhales in creation and will inhale in a return to the original void.[19] Such examples could be greatly multiplied. The broad point to register here, however, is that classical schooling and theosophy are connected in 2.2, a cross contamination that makes both ridiculous in epistemological terms. In effect, schooling becomes a kind of witchcraft or magic.

A second characteristic of 2.2 works similarly to undermine the stabilities and pieties of formal schooling. This is the association made between education and Freud, perhaps not an idea entirely new to the Joyce oeuvre but one given a hugely overplayed treatment in this chapter, as Joyceans have known for a very long time. Way back in 1966, Fritz Senn produced a short but seminal article on *FW*, 2.2 for A **Wake** *Newslitter* entitled 'The Aliments of Jumeantry'. It begins in a characteristically self-deprecatory way, noting that in the episode the Earwicker twins, Shem and Shaun, are doing their homework and 'above all' trying to solve a geometrical problem. Nothing much has been said about Euclid and 2.2 – maybe, Senn suggests, because the source is so obvious, or perhaps Euclid so old-fashioned in relation to the modern maths curriculum that no one remembers much about him beyond the title of his book. Whatever, Senn admits to being no expert in this field and proceeds to confine himself to write about what he says are no more than 'a few gleanings'. He begins with some provocations, suggesting that Joyce paid 'his respects to Euclid' in the first paragraph of his first prose work, 'The Sisters', with his use of the word 'gnomon'. The word has a double meaning. It refers, Senn says, to someone who knows, but also to something that is missing: 'Thus at the first opportunity Joyce introduces one of his most important themes, the search for knowledge which can only be incomplete'. In this way Euclid is associated with 'Joyce himself'. There is also an association with Freud. 'Knowledge is, in the elementary sense, an outgrowth of the child's curiosity about his origins', Senn writes. He adds that 'knowledge is likely to be carnally tainted'.[20]

As early as 1925, Joyce was reading Volume Three of Freud's recently published *Collected Papers*. Writing much later than Senn, in 2007 Daniel Ferrer shows how the source appears in no fewer than four of Joyce's notebooks for the *Wake* and is used in a number of *Wake* episodes, most extensively in 3.4.[21] On page 153 of the Freud volume, Joyce would have read the sentence 'Thirst for knowledge seems to be inseparable from sexual curiosity', an idea embodied large in 2.2 where bad twin Shem helps good twin Shaun to conceptualize an equilateral triangle by inviting him to peak under his mother's skirts: 'I'll make you to see figuratleavely the whome of your eternal geomater', the 'first of all usquiluteral threeingles (and why wouldn't she sit cressloggedlike the lass that lured a tailor?)' (296.30–297.1; 297.27–29). The Oedipal frame in 2.2 combines Euclid and schooled knowledge not just with a theosophical view of the earth as sacred mother, but also with a more demotic, erotically charged version of things, most evident in the long footnote at page 279, where Issy addresses a favourite teacher and links the swallowing of knowledge with exchanges of a very different kind: 'If it's me chews to swallow all you saidn't you can eat my words for it as sure as there's a key in my kiss. . . . When we will conjugate together', she continues. '[W]hen I slip through my pettigo I'll get my degree and take seidens when I'm not ploughed first by some Rolando the lasso' (fn. 1, 279). The physical world, the world of the body, is always rudely interpolating into the notional cerebralness of *Finnegans Wake*, often with disastrous effects on any attempt at authority, dignity and, even, 'decency', but a specific connection between sexuality and education is the particular focus of 2.2.

2.2 will always be of special importance to the reading of Joyce and education, partly because of these new elements. No other chapter approaches this level of attention in relation to schooling, but others do form less extensive examples of the same phenomenon. In a letter to Harriet Shaw Weaver, written in October 1923, Joyce explained how a passage which later became incorporated into 2.4 was 'a picture of an epicene professor of history in an Irish university college seated in the hospice for the dying etc after "eating a crab in the red sea"'.[22] The frame continued into the final version where the four old men become 'all four collegians . . . raising hell while the sin was shining, with their slates and satchels, playing Florian's fables and communic suctions and vellicar fractions with mixum members, in the Queen's Ultonian colleges' (385.8–13). The antiquarian feel of the episode is partly generated by the many further references to higher education, especially to Trinity College, comprised of 'oceanfuls of collegians green and high classes and the poor scholars and all the old trinitarian senate and saints and sages' (388.35–389.1).

Shaun's address to the 'twentynine hedge daughters' (430.1) in 3.2, as we have seen, represents a further concentration of references to education. This chapter is usually described in terms of a sermon, but, as the allusion to Irish hedge schools implies, Shaun is the teacher in charge here, a 'dear professor' at 459.30, and it is part of his responsibility to maintain order: 'Remember, maid, thou dust art powder but Cinderella thou must return (what are you robbing her sleeve for, Ruby? And pull in your tongue, Polly!). Cog that put of your teen times, everyone!' Again the pedagogic frame is clear and it shapes the entirety of the episode, including the arrival of Dave the dancekerl, the partial replacement whose qualifications to stand-in for Shaun are in part educational ones: ''Twas the quadra sent him and Trinity too. And he can cantab as chipper as any oxon ever I mood with, a tiptoe singer!' (440.26–9; 467.30–2).

Finally, I want to ask what these concentrations mean in the *Wake*. It is one thing to assert the importance of schooled learning across the piece where it impacts on writing practice, reader response, author identity and so on, but what is the purpose of these moments of centrifuge where education seems to move so much to the fore?

These indicate how far schooling in the *Wake* is connected to structure, the elaborate Viconian design to which everything in the *Wake is* potentially subject, and yet is not. Although all elements of the *Wake* are circumscribed by Vico's circular sequence of epochs – the ages of gods, heroes and men reproduced in Books One, Two and Three – none fit precisely, exclusively or with any singularity. With that important qualification in mind, there is a sequence that runs from an end stop brought to the children playing in the street at the close of 2.1 to Shaun's haranguing of the 'twentynine hedge daughters' in 3.2, representing some 250 pages of the book or some 40 per cent of its total. It constitutes a schooling cycle crossing epochs from 'the age of empire' to 'the age of democracy', or, more precisely, to the part of that latter period, the 1930s, that produced the democratic antithesis in the darkest of forms. It also indicates that however much education is linked to identity formation and the processes of reading and writing in the *Wake*, it is also significantly caught up with the political consciousness that echoes throughout Joyce's work.

The cycle that ends with Shaun's haranguing of the schoolgirls in 3.2 is significantly framed at the other end by the closure of 2.1, in which children out in the streets at play are being herded back to their 'habitations', and not enjoying the prospect, 'teartoretorning' to 'tasbooks and goody, hominy bread, and bible bee, with jaggery-yo and juju-jaw, Fine's French phrases from the Grandmére des Grammaires . . . and what happened to our eleven in thirtytwo antepostdating the Valgur Eire' (256.17–23). Here the Earwicker children are expected now to get back to their studies, a return not only to textbooks ('tasbooks') and a curriculum that includes religion, geography, French, history, Latin, chemistry, physics and maths, but also to a home/school paradigm, the 'sacramental family' that was so much a product of nineteenth-century nationalism and decisively imagined in terms of the security of church, state and nation.[23] After the freedom of playtime on the streets, the children are restored to an ideologically constituted order enforced by strict policing, in this case by the Garda of the new Republic, represented by the twins, who are both the recipients of schooling and appointed as its guardians. Going home to study is formulated as a people's grateful thanks to the state as divinity:

> Now have thy children entered into their habitations. And nationglad, camp meeting over, to shin it, Gov be thanked! Thou has closed the portals of the habitations of thy children and thou hast set guards thereby, even Garda Didymus and Garda Domas, that thy children may read in the book of the opening of the mind to light and err not in the darkness which is the afterthought of thy no-matter.
>
> (258.27–33)

By the end of 2.2, after 'steady steady steady studiavimus' (306.10–11), Shem, Shaun and Issy, have reached some kind of graduation from a schooling which is elitist and classical, but also modern and practical, although Issy seems barely to have engaged with it. Literally a footnote, 'with her tootpettypout of jemenfichue', she 'will sit and knit on solfa sofa' while the boys 'will cudgel about some a rhythmatick' (268.7–14). For her, 'Improper frictions is maledictions and mens uration makes me mad' (269, note 3). As critics have noted, 2.2 is specifically linked to old forms of curriculum and institution, the quadrivium and trivium of a liberal arts education said to have its origins in Boethius and the sixth century. But it also draws a significant line linking classical education with nineteenth- and early-twentieth-century modernization. 'We have had our day at triv and quad and writ our bit as intermidgets' (intermediates) (306.12–13). The children have studied 'Art, literature, politics, economy, chemistry, humanity, &c' and, by the end of the episode, have been trained to respond to such contemporary-sounding schooled posers as 'What Morals, if any, can be drawn from Grania and Diarmuid?'; 'Do you Approve of our Existing Parliamentary System?' and 'Is the Co-Education of Animus and Animas Wholly Desirable?' They can explain the need for 'Proper and Regular Diet' and expatiate on their likely destiny: 'A

Successful Career in the Civil Service' (see 306.13–308.1). In this way, a single night of homework becomes overlaid with a life in elite schooling, from entry through to graduation, a cramming ironically positioned in Viconian terms in the age of heroic aristocracy – a context for Issy's relegation – involving 'many, many, many, many manducabimus' (306.11–12), 'manducabismus' being Latin for 'we shall chew' and one of many images in the *Wake* linking schooling to cramming and ingestion.[24]

There are many gestures of defiance through 2.2, transgressions against the rule of the textbook, marks in the margins, culminating in the ominous note written by the children which sends 'our best youlldied greedings to Pep and Memmy and the old folkers below' and includes as a foot note the cartoon which is Issy's drawing of a nose-thumbing.[25] For all that, the outline of a repressive history of education, 'from tomtittot to teetootomtotalitarian' (260.2), is inscribed across these pages, a clear signal that Joyce's views of education as a bureaucratizing, commodifying condition of state-structured modernity were closer to those of his avatars in *Stephen Hero* and *A Portrait* than is sometimes thought. In terms of presentation, the anti-schooling sentiment becomes refined and conditioned by new aesthetics in all sorts of ways across the Joyce oeuvre, but, fundamentally, they do not change. Indeed, by the time he came to write the *Wake*, as the movement from 2.1 to 3.2 shows, there is good evidence to suggest that such views had become not just confirmed but hardened, a product of living through a period of the most reactionary political extremism that modern Europe has seen to date.

Postscript

This book began by making a case for reading 'Joyce and education' historically, a case centrally informed by the idea that Joyce imagined his own education history as coinciding with and exemplifying the emergence of state schooling. From this position, schooling became as emblematic of modernity for Joyce as, say, Catholic emancipation, or the rise of the commercially produced book – both histories linked to the state institutionalization of schooling, as so many nineteenth-century histories must be. This study has shown how one of the central features of the Joyce text is its dedication to the performance of schooling and education as modernity. In concluding the account, I want to raise the notion that such an orientation also gives the Joyce text continued viability at the current time.

The sustained contemporaneity of the Joyce text in this respect, as in so many others, is much characterized by paradox and contradiction. For all the length of time separating 2020 from the period in which Joyce was active as a writer, certain central continuities remain in relation to how we perceive education and the state. Our sense of modern education as the standardization, bureaucratization and commodification of learning must be stronger now than ever. From some perspectives, perhaps most informed ones, 'neoliberalism'– the return of education to the free market by government mandate – has produced a regime of centralization and scrutiny so radically under state control that it renders the kind of nineteenth-century modernization exemplified by the Intermediate Education Act (Ireland)

(1878) quite tame by comparison. Likewise, idealistic versions of education – education as human right, equality and opportunity – still continue to be forcefully upheld. But despite that, schooling remains central to the maintenance of social order and the reproduction of social hierarchy. The connection between power and schooling may not be *as* evident now as it was across the 1900s to the 1930s, but it remains at a highly significant level in some cultures once very close to Joyce. The current prime minster of Great Britain, for example, Boris Johnson, went to Eton, as did every British prime minister since 1937, with the exception of Gordon Brown. A recent report by the Sutton Trust caused a brief stir by reporting that almost two-thirds of Johnson's first cabinet were privately educated. Forty-five per cent were Oxbridge graduates. A further 25 per cent graduated from Russell Group universities.[26] This astonishing illustration of the survival of elitism in a modern democracy against every counter-influence helps to explain why the elitism of the Joyce text, where the embodiment of hierarchy and the upturning of the values on which it is based become inextricable, retains as much status in contemporary terms as it does. It satisfies both our contempt for elitism and the perverse satisfactions we still seem compelled to take in it.

It is not difficult, then, to make the argument that continuities have converged to produce a world in which the Joyce text makes an infinitely more contemporary registration in relation to education and schooling than any number of Victorian and Edwardian school novels which now speak to different worlds. Even where the contemporary world seems to radically diverge from the late nineteenth and early twentieth centuries, however, the movement seems to have been propitious for the continued readability of the unreadable Joyce text in terms of 'Joyce and education'.

The obvious illustration would be in relation to the information society and *its* relations to formal education, a problematic that Joyce identified as undermining the strategic distinction once made between 'information' and 'schooling' before a computer had been seen or the world wide web even dreamt of. Here elite forms of knowledge are already thoroughly compromised by the seemingly infinitely democratizing epistemologies once thought to reside in such forms as the almanac, directory, encyclopaedia and train timetable. The more profound change in this respect, however, may turn out to be positioned in the contemporary diminution of confidence in the education project, a shift which, in my view, brings many of us closer to the Joyce text – whether we like it or not.

Schooling continues to exercise great significance in modern culture but confidence in the capacity of schooling to deliver on its promise is under threat like never before. Just when mass education at all levels seems to be within reach of political achievement, the values of what American culture calls 'liberal education', and what in Britain remains just 'education', seem under assault. Belief in the capacity of higher education in particular to deliver something meaningful across the piece has deteriorated, perhaps beyond repair.

You can see the signs of this twenty-first century zeitgeist in all sorts of seemingly unrelated phenomena, from the much-commented-on rise in home education to changes in school governance. It is evident too in cultural terms, in the disappearance of once familiar icons and the rise of new ones. The cultural disposition is writ especially large in the rise of the new campus novel, in which the *bildung* fantasy of nineteenth-century Europe, transplanted into new world cultures, becomes utterly unravelled and truly dispossessed. In novels by the likes of Bret Easton Ellis (*The Rules of Attraction*, 1987), Donna Tartt (*The Secret History*, 1992), Joyce Carol Oates (*I'll Take You There*, 2002), Chad Harbach (*The Art of Fielding*, 2011) and almost countless others, the university campus is much more likely to be imagined now as a site of mayhem and nihilistic despair than of human development, let alone redemption. And the phenomenon is not limited to book culture. Across the media, in film cultures too, the school/university that was once the spiritual home of modern progressivism and the fulfilment of the 'Enlightenment project' now takes form as a site of contemporary cultural disaster and personal chaos.

Never in a long history of association with fiction, has schooling been put under so much destructive cultural pressure by so many – albeit by writers and other creatives who are invariably, maybe exclusively in the age of mass higher education, products of the system at it most hierarchical, as was James Joyce. The point here is not that the rest of the world is now in the process of catching up with this great writer, but that a cultural disposition that was once at the periphery of literary modernism is now very much at the centre of the cultural mainstream. For this reason, what once might have appeared avant-gardism trickery or faddism – writing a 'mock' school novel or a chapter of a novel in the form of a literature textbook, for example; another in the mock style of an examination paper; or constructing a language that utterly undermines the Western intellectual tradition it is framed by and so on – now no longer appears in that light. On the contrary, it seems suggestive of much engaged aesthetic that continues to speak to a modern world where both the pervasiveness of 'education' and its fragility seems especially constitutive and emblematic of the contemporary condition.

Notes

1 This was Richard Ellmann's line. See Richard Ellmann and Charles Feidelson, Jr. (eds.), *The Modern Tradition: Backgrounds of Modern Literature* (New York: Oxford University Press, 1965).

2 Finn Fordham, *Lots of Fun at 'Finnegans Wake': Unravelling Universals* (Oxford: Oxford University Press, 2007), 1–2.

3 Switaj, *James Joyce's Teaching Life and Methods*, 116.

4 Roland McHugh is the author of the standard annotative volume, *Annotations to 'Finnegans Wake'* (1980), but no single person could have produced it. It was significantly a group effort, compiled on the back of an astonishing annotative critical culture that included articles from *A 'Wake' Newslitter*, which ran from 1962–1984, as well as ground-breaking full-length works – such as Atherton's work on literature in the *Wake* (1959); Glasheen's census of people in the *Wake* (1957, 1963, 1977); Hodgart's work on song (1959); Christiani's work on the Scandinavian elements of *Finnegans Wake* (1965); Bonheim 's lexicon of German in the *Wake* (1967); O'Hehir's work on Gaelic in the *Wake* (1968); O'Hehir and Dillon's *Classical Lexicon* (1977) and so on. The tradition included unpublished work too, to which McHugh had privileged access. As

he notes in his introduction to *Annotations*, part of the process of making the book involved McHugh writing to the most eminent Joyceans of the day – such as Clive Hart, Matthew Hodgart, Leo Knuth, Charles Peake and Fritz Senn – asking to borrow their copies of the *Wake*, which would have included their personal annotations. These too were incorporated into *Annotations to Finnegans Wake*.

5 Samuel Beckett, 'Dante . . . Bruno. Vico. Joyce' in Samuel Becket and Others, *Our Exagmination Round His Factification for Incamination of Work in Progress* (1929; London: Faber & Faber, 1972), 3–22 [14].

6 Ellmann, *James Joyce*, 628.

7 Geert Lernout, 'Introduction to VI.B.29', *James Joyce: The Finnegans Wake Notebooks at Buffalo, Notebook VI.B.29*, gen. edited by Vincent Deane, Daniel Ferrer and Lernout (Turnout, Belgium: Brepols Publishers, 2001), 5.

8 Stuart Gilbert, *Reflections on James Joyce: Stuart Gilbert's Paris Journal*, edited by Thomas F. Staley and Randolph Lewis (Austin: University of Texas Press, 1993), 20–1; 27. For a fuller account of this process and of the *Encyclopaedia Britannica* in the *Wake* more generally, see Len Platt, '"Unfallable encyclicing": *Finnegans Wake* and the *Encyclopedia Britannica*', *James Joyce Quarterly*, 47/1, 2009, 107–18.

9 For an account of this process, see Crispi and Slote (eds.), *How Joyce Wrote 'Finnegans Wake'*, especially the introduction by Luca Crispi, Sam Slote and Dirk van Hulle, 3–48.

10 The Clarendon Report 1864 was explicit here, including the ability of public-school leavers too 'stumble through an easy proposition of Euclid' as a standard and expected competency. *The Clarendon Report: An Inquiry into the Revenues and Management of Certain Colleges and Schools and the Studies Pursued and Instruction Given Therein* (London: H.M. Stationery Office, 1864), 31.

11 *Peter Parley's Tales about Greece and Rome* (1837; London: Routledge, 1909), 15.

12 *Peter Parley's Universal History on the Basis of Geography* (London: John W. Parker, West Strand, 1937), vi.

13 *Peter Parley's Universal History*, 1.

14 *Peter Parley's Universal History*, 3.

15 See John Barrow Allen, *An Elementary Latin Grammar*, 2nd edn. (1874; Oxford: Clarendon, 1891), 189.

16 I am told by my mathematician friend, Peter Winbourne, that NCR is a formula for determining 'how many ways to choose R objects from N objects, where order does not matter', although it is not clear to me what NCR to the power of five means.

17 Yeats claimed his book was produced by automatic hand writing. See W.B. Yeats, *A Vision* (1925; London: Macmillan, 1938), 8–9.

18 H.P. Blavatsky, *Isis Unveiled*, vol. 1 (1877; CA Pasadena: The Aryan Philosophical Press, 1998), 292.

19 For a full account of this aspect of theosophy in the *Wake*, see Len Platt, *Joyce, Race and 'Finnegans Wake'* (Cambridge: Cambridge University Press, 2007), 95–120.

20 Fritz Senn, 'The Aliments of Jumeantry', *A 'Wake' Newslitter*, New Series, III/3, June 1966, 51–4.

21 Luca Crispi and Sam Slote (eds.), *How Joyce Wrote 'Finnegans Wake': A Chapter-by-Chapter Guide* (Madison, WI: University of Wisconsin Press, 2007), 410–35, [414].

22 Gilbert (ed.), *Selected Letters*, 205.

23 The term was used by Jeffrey Weeks in *Sex, Politics and Society: The Regulation of Sexuality since 1800* (1981; London and New York: Longman, 1989), see especially chapter three.

24 Viconian cycles are repeated over and over and in many ways in the *Wake*, from the tiniest of details to large structures, the largest of which is the book itself. Book One corresponds to Vico's age of gods; Book Two to the age of heroes; Book Three to the age of men, or democracy and Book Four to the ricorso, or return.

25 Gilbert, *Letters of James Joyce*, 406.

26 See *The Guardian*, 25 July, 2019, www.theguardian.com/education/ 2019/jul/25/two-thirds-of-boris-johnsons-cabinet-went-to-private-schools.

Bibliography

1000 Answers to 1000 Questions: Being a Reprint of the First 1,000 Questions in the 'Tit-Bits' Inquiry Column with the Replies Thereto (London: Tit-Bits, 1884).

1000 Answers and 1000 Questions: Being a Reprint of the Second 1,000 Questions in the 'Tit-Bits' Inquiry Column with the Replies Thereto (London: Tit-Bits, 1888).

1000 Answers to 1000 Questions: Being a Reprint of the Third 1,000 Questions in the 'Tit-Bits' Inquiry Column with the Replies Thereto (London: Tit-Bits, 1890).

1000 Answers and 1000 Questions: Being a Reprint of the Fourth 1,000 Questions in the 'Tit-Bits' Inquiry Column with the Replies Thereto (London: Tit-Bits, 1895).

Adams, Mildred, 'Literary Criticism in Spanish America', *Comparative Literature Studies*, 1/3, 1964, 217–29.

Allen, John Barrow, *An Elementary Latin Grammar*, 2nd edition (1874; Oxford: Clarendon, 1891).

Anderson, R.D., 'The Idea of the Secondary School in Nineteenth-Century Europe', *Paedagogica Historica*, 40/1–2, 2004, 93–106.

Anon, *Boys and Their Ways: A Book for and about Boys, by One Who Knows Them* (London: John Hogg, 1880).

Ansgar, Allen, 'Awaiting Education: Friedrich Nietzsche on the Future of Our Educational Institutions', *Philosophical Enquiry in Education*, 24/3, 2017, 197–210.

Anstey, F., *Vice Versa, or, a Lesson to Fathers* (1882; Horses Mouth, 2017).

Answers (London: 1899–1955).

Atkinson, Norman, 'The Educational Ideas of Patrick Pearse, 1879–1916', *Comparative Education Review*, 11/1, 1967, 68–74.

Attridge, Derek, *Peculiar Language: Literature as Difference from the Renaissance to James Joyce* (London: Methuen, 1988).

Austen, Jane, *Emma* (1815; Leipzig: Tauchnitz, 1877).

Baden-Powell of Gilwell, Baron, Robert Stephenson Smyth, *Scouting for Boys: A Handbook for Instruction in Good Citizenship Through Woodcraft* (London: Horace Cox, 1908).

Baer, Benjamin Conisbee, *Indigenous Vanguards: Education, National Liberation, and the Limits of Modernism* (New York: Columbia University Press, 2019).

Bakunin, Mikhail, *God and the State* (1882; London: Freedom Press, 1910).

Barthes, Roland, and Sandy Petrey, 'Reflections on a Manual', *Publications of the Modern Languages Association*, 112/1, 1997, 69–75.

Baylis, Gail, 'Boy Culture and Ireland 1916', *Early Popular Visual Culture*, 13/3, 2015, 192–208.

Beatty, Aidan, *Masculinist Power in Irish Nationalism 1884–1928* (London: Palgrave, 2016).

Beaumont, Catriona, 'Women, Citizenship and Catholicism in the Irish Free State, 1922–1948', *Women's History Review*, 6/4, 1997, 563–85.

Beckett, Samuel, 'Dante . . . Bruno. Vico. Joyce', in Samuel Becket and Others (eds.), *Our Exagmination Round His Factification for Incamination of Work in Progress* (1929; London: Faber & Faber, 1972), 3–22.

Beja, Morris (ed.), *James Joyce's 'Dubliners' and 'A Portrait of the Artist as a Young Man': A Selection of Critical Essays* (1973; London and Basingstoke: Macmillan, 1982).

The Belvederian (Dublin: Belvedere College, 1906 to date).

Bhabha, Homi, *The Location of Culture* (London: Routledge, 1994).

Black, Alistair, David Muddiman and Helen Plant, *The Early Information System: Information Management in Britain before the Computer* (London: Routledge, 2007).

Blackwood's Edinburgh Magazine (Edinburgh: William Blackwood, 1817–1903).

Blavatsky, H.P., *Isis Unveiled*, vol. 1 (1877; Pasadena, CA:, The Aryan Philosophical Press, 1998).

Bourke, Angela *et al.* (eds.), *The Field Day Anthology of Irish Writing: Irish Women's Writing and Traditions*, vol. 4 (New York: New York University Press, 2002).

Bowman, John and Ronan O'Donoghue (eds.), *Portraits: Belvedere College, Dublin 1832–1982* (Dublin: Gill & Macmillan, 1982).

Brook, Stoppard A. 'Introduction', in Kate M. Warren (ed.), *A Treasury of English Literature (From the Beginning to the Eighteenth Century)* (1906; New York: Dodge, 1908).

Bruce Bradley, S.J., *James Joyce's Schooldays* (Dublin: Gill & Macmillan, 1982).

———, '"Allude to Me as Jesuit": James Joyce and His Educators', in María Luz Suárez Castiñeira, Asier Altuna, García de Salazar and Olga Fernández Vicente (eds.), *New Perspectives on James Joyce: Ignatius Loyola Make Haste to Help Me!* (Bilbao: Desuto University Press, 2009), 246–62.

Budgen, Frank, *James Joyce and the Making of 'Ulysses' and other Writings* (London: Oxford University Press, 1972).

Burleigh, Michael and Wolfgang Wippermann, *The Racial State: Germany 1933–45* (Cambridge: Cambridge University Press, 1991).

Butler, Judith, *Excitable Speech: A Politics of the Performative* (London: Routledge, 1997).

Carey, James W., 'Time, Space and the Telegraph', in David Crowley and Paul Heyer (eds.), *Communication in History: Technology, Culture, Society* (Boston: Allyn & Bacon, 2003), 125–31.

Cixous, Helénè, *The Laugh of Medusa*, translated by Keith Cohen and Paula Cohen, *Signs*, 1/4, 1976, 875–93.

The Clarendon Report: An Inquiry Into the Revenues and Management of Certain Colleges and Schools and the Studies Pursued and Instruction Given Therein (London: H.M. Stationery Office, 1864).

Clark, Hilary, *The Fictional Encyclopaedia: Joyce, Pound, Sollers* (New York: Garland, 1990).

The Clongownian (Dublin: Clongowes Wood College, 1895–to date).

Coleman, Martin '"It doesn't . . . Matter Where You Begin": Pound and Santayana on Education', *Journal of Aesthetic Education*, 44/4, 2010, 1–17.

Coolahan, J., *Irish Education: Its History and Its Structure* (Dublin: Institute of Public Administration, 1981).

Cooper, David E., *Authenticity and Learning: Nietzsche's Education Philosophy* (London: Routledge and Kegan Paul, 1983).

Corcoran S.J., Rev Timothy, *The Story of Clongowes Wood AD 1450–1900* (Dublin: The Catholic Truth Society, 1900).

———, 'Official Text Books and Irish Schools', *The Irish Monthly*, 56/662, August 1928, 398–402.

Cornwell, James, *Spelling for Beginners: A Method for Teaching* (London: Simpkin & Marshall, 1870).

———, *A Grammar for Beginners* (London: Simpkin & Marshall, 1904).

———, *Geography for Beginners*, 72nd edition (London: Simpkin, Marshall Hamilton & Kent, 1913).

Costello, Peter, *James Joyce: The Years of Growth 1882–1915* (Cork: Roberts Rinehart, 1992).

Creasy, Matthew, 'Error and Education in *Ulysses*', *European Joyce Studies*, 20, 2011, 52–72.

Crispi, Luca and Sam Slote (eds.), *How Joyce Wrote 'Finnegans Wake': A Chapter-By-Chapter Genetic Guide* (Madison, Wis.: University of Wisconsin Press, 2007).

Curran, C.P., *James Joyce Remembered* (London: Oxford University Press, 1968).

Daly, Mary E., 'Women in the Irish Free State, 1922–1939: The Interaction between Economics and Ideology', *Journal of Women's History*, 6/6; 7/1, 1995, 99–116.

Davison, Sarah, 'Joyce's Incorporation of Literary Sources in "Oxen of the Sun"', *Genetic Joyce Studies*, 9, 2009.

Dickson, David, Justyna Pyz and Christopher Shepard (eds.), *Irish Classrooms and British Empire: Imperial Contexts in the Origins of Modern Education* (Dublin: Four Courts, 2012).

Dillon, John, 'The Classics at the *Wake*: Some Aspects of Classical Influence in Joyce's *Finnegans Wake*', *Classics Ireland*, 5, January 1, 1998, 9–29.

Domarus, Max (ed.), *Hitler. Reden und Proklamationen 1932–1945*, vol. 1 (Munich: Neustadt, 1965).

Dudley Edwards, Owen, 'Belvedere in History', in Bowman and O'Donoghue (eds.), *Portraits: Belvedere College, Dublin 1832–1982*, 13–32.

Dudley Edwards, Ruth, *Patrick Pearse: The Triumph of Failure* (1977, Dublin: Irish Academic Press, 2006).

Elias, Christopher Michael, 'What Makes Them Dubliners? James Joyce's "An Encounter" and the Foundations of Masculinist Nationalism in Ireland', *Journal of Men's Studies*, 24/3, 2016, 229–40.

Eliot, T.S., 'Modern Education and the Classics: A Revision of an Address Delivered to the Classical Club of Harvard', in *Essays Ancient and Modern* (1931; London: Faber & Faber, 1936), 161–74.

Ellis, Heather, 'Thomas Arnold, Christian Manliness and the Problem of Boyhood', *Journal of Victorian Culture*, 19/4, 2014, 425–41.

Ellmann, Richard, *James Joyce* (New York: Oxford University Press, 1959).

——— and Charles Feidelson, Jr. (eds.), *The Modern Tradition: Backgrounds of Modern Literature* (New York: Oxford University Press, 1965).

——— (ed.), *Letters of James Joyce*, vol. 2 (London: Faber & Faber, 1966).

———, *The Consciousness of Joyce* (London: Faber & Faber, 1977).

Farrar, F.W., *Eric: Or, Little by Little* (1858; New York: Rudd & Carlton, 1859).

Ferrer, Daniel, 'Wondrous Devices in the Dark: Chapter 111.4', in Crispi and Slote (eds.), *How Joyce Wrote 'Finnegans Wake'* (Madison, Wis.: University of Wisconsin Press, 2007), 410–35.

Fitzgerald, Margaret, 'The Influence of Froebel's Kindergarten on the Belmore-Commission, 1897–1898', *The Maynooth Review*, 19, 1983, 3–30.

Fitzgerald, Percy Hetherington, *School Days at Saxonhurst, by 'One of the Boys'* (Edinburgh: A.C. Black, 1867).

Fordham, Finn, *Lots of Fun at 'Finnegans Wake': Unravelling Universals* (Oxford: Oxford University Press, 2007).

———, 'Biography', in John McCourt (ed.), *James Joyce in Context* (Cambridge: Cambridge University Press, 2009), 17–26.
French, Marilyn, *The Book as World: James Joyce's 'Ulysses'* (Cambridge, MA: Harvard University Press, 1976).
Fröebel, Friedrich, *The Education of Man* (1826; New York: Appleton & Co., 1887).
Froude, J.A., 'The Christian Brothers and Their Lesson Books', *Fraser's Magazine*, 9/50, 1874, 186–99.
Fyfe, Aileen, 'The Information Revolution', in David McKitterick (ed.), *The Cambridge History of the Book in Britain, 1830–1914*, vol. 6, (Cambridge: Cambridge University Press, 2009), 567–94.
Gärtner, Niko, 'The Victorian Headmaster: Biographical Research Into an Emerging Profession', *Reflecting Education*, 6/1, 2010, 49–62.
Gibson, Andrew, *The Strong Spirit: History, Politics and Aesthetics in the Writings of James Joyce*, 1898–1915 (Oxford: Oxford University Press, 2013).
Gilbert, Stuart, *James Joyce's 'Ulysses'* (New York: Knopf, 1931).
——— (ed.), *Letters of James Joyce* (London: Faber & Faber, 1957).
———, *Reflections on James Joyce: Stuart Gilbert's Paris Journal*, edited by Thomas F. Staley and Randolph Lewis (Austin: University of Texas Press, 1993).
Gilliard, Derek, A *History of Education in England*, www.educationengland. org.uk/documents/clarendon1864/clarendon1.html.
Gissing, George, *New Grub Street* (London: Smith & Elder, 1891).
Gogarty, Oliver St. John, *As I Was Going Down Sackville Street* (New York: Harvest Brace, 1937).
Goloubeva, Irina Rasmussen, 'Molly Bloom: A Re-Immersion in the Concrete', *James Joyce Quarterly*, 47/3, 2010, 395–415.
Gorman, Herbert, *James Joyce* (London: John Lane The Bodley Head, 1941).
Hall, G. Stanley, *Adolescence: Its Psychology and Its Relations to Physiology, Anthropology, Sociology, Sex, Crime, Religion and Education* (1904; London: Appleton, 1908).
Hampson, Robert, '"Allowing for Possible Error": Education and Catechism in "Ithaca"', in Andrew Gibson (ed.), *Joyce's 'Ithaca'* (Amsterdam and Atlanta, GA: Rodopi, 1996), 229–67.
Hart, Thomas E. (ed.), *Nietzsche, Culture and Education* (London: Routledge, 2017).
Hayman, David, *'Ulysses': The Mechanics of Meaning*, rev. and exp. (1970; Madison: University of Wisconsin Press, 1988).
Henke, Suzette A., 'Speculum of the Other Molly: A Feminist/Psychoanalytic Inquiry Into James Joyce's Politics of Desire', *Mosaic: A Journal for the Interdisciplinary Study of Literature*, 21, 2/3, 1988, 149–64.
Holt, Jenny, *Public School Literature, Civic Education and the Politics of Male Adolescence* (Farnham: Ashgate, 2008).
Hughes, Thomas, *Tom Brown's Schooldays* (1857; London: Thames, 1951).
Hume, Maurice C., *Efficiency of Irish Schools and Their Superiority to English Schools* (London: Simpkin & Marshall, 1889).
Jackson, Kate, 'George Newnes and the "Loyal Tit-Bitites": Educational Identity and Textual Interaction in Tit-Bits', in Laurel Brake, Bill Bell and David Finkelstein (eds.), *Nineteenth-Century Media and the Construction of Identities* (Basingstoke: Palgrave, 2000), 11–26.
Jacobus, Jon Lee A. '"Lycidas" in the "Nestor" Episode', *James Joyce Quarterly*, 19/2, 1982, 189–94.
Jacques, *Irish Education as It Is and as It Should Be* (Dublin: Gill, 1906).
Jolas, Eugene (ed.), *transition vanguard* (New York: Vanguard, 1949).

Jones, Colin (ed.), *The French Revolution: Voices from a Momentous Epoch 1789–95* (London: Guild, 1988).

Jones, Mark 'Overcoming Ressentiment: Nietzsche's Education for an Aesthetic Aristocracy', *History of Political Thought*, 34/4, 2013, 669–701.

Joyce, James, *The Occasional, Critical and Political Writing*, edited with an introduction and notes by Kevin Barry (Oxford: Oxford University Press, 2000).

Kenner, Hugh, *Dublin's Joyce* (London: Chatto and Windus, 1955).

———, *Joyce's Voices* (London: Faber & Faber, 1978).

———, *'Ulysses'* (Baltimore: Johns Hopkins University Press, 1987).

Keogh, Dáire, 'The Christian Brothers and the Second Reformation in Ireland', *Eiré-Ireland*, 40/1&2, 2005, 42–59.

———, 'Patrick Pearse: "Studies" and the Birth of Revisionism', *Irish Quarterly Review*, 100/40, 2011, 421–32.

Kershner, R.B., *The Culture of Joyce's 'Ulysses'* (New York: Palgrave Macmillan, 2010).

Kidd, Kenneth B., 'Boyology in the Twentieth Century', *Children's Literature*, 28, 2000, 44–72.

———, *Making American Boys: Boyology and the Feral Tale* (Minneapolis: University of Minnesota Press, 2004).

Kipling, Rudyard, *The Complete Stalky and Co*, edited with an introduction and notes by Isabel Quigly (1899; Oxford: Oxford University Press, 2009).

Lawrence, Karen, *The Odyssey of Style in 'Ulysses'* (Princeton: Princeton University Press, 1981).

Lernout, Geert (ed.), *James Joyce: The 'Finnegans Wake' Notebooks at Buffalo, Notebook VI.B.29* (Turnout, Belgium: Brepols Publishers, 2001).

———, *Help My Unbelief: James Joyce and Religion* (London: Continuum, 2010).

Levitt, Morton P., 'Beyond Dublin, Joyce and Modernism', *Journal of Modern Literature*, 22/2, 1998/9, 385–94.

Limond, David, '"The Schoolmaster of all Ireland": The Progressive Credentials of Patrick Henry Pearse 1979–1916', *History of Education Review*, 34/1, 2005, 63–73.

Mangnall, Richmal, *Historical and Miscellaneous Questions for the Use of Young People* (London: Longman, Hurst, Rees and Orme, 1808).

McGlazer, Ramsey, *Old Schools: Modernism, Education, and the Critique of Progress* (New York: Fordham University Press, 2020).

McHugh, Roland, *Annotations to 'Finnegans Wake'* (London and Henley: Routledge & Kegan Paul, 1980).

McMahon, Timothy G., 'Irish Jesuit Education and Imperial Ideals', in Dickson *et al.* (eds.), *Irish Classrooms and British Empire: Imperial Contexts in the Origins of Modern Education* (Dublin: Four Courts, 2012), 111–23.

Menke, Richard, 'Information', *Victorian, Literature and Culture*, 46/3–4, 2018, 739–42.

Mohr, Thomas, 'The Rights of Women under the Constitution of the Irish Free State', *Irish Jurist*, New Series, 41, 2006, 20–59.

Moon, G. Washington, *The Bad English of Lindley Murray and Other Writers on the English Language: A Series of Criticisms* (London: Hatchards, 1869).

Mosse, Gosse, *The Image of Man: The Creation of Modern Masculinity* (New York: Oxford University Press, 1996).

Müller, Detlef K., Fritz Ringer and Brian Simon (eds.), *The Rise of the Modern Educational System: Structural Change and Social Reproduction 1870–1920* (Cambridge: Cambridge University Press, 1987).

Mullin, Katherine, *James Joyce, Sexuality and Social Purity* (Cambridge: Cambridge University Press, 2003).
Murphy, James H., 'William O'Brien's, When We Were Boys: A New Voice from Old Conventions', *Irish University Review*, 22/2, 1992, 298–304.
———, *Irish Novelists and the Victorian Age* (Oxford and New York: Oxford University Press, 2011).
Murray, Lindley, *English Grammar* (1795; New York: N.P., 1811?).
Neubauer, John, *The Fin de Siècle Culture of Adolescence* (New Haven and London: Yale University Press, 1992).
Nietzsche, Fredrich, *Ecce Homo: How One Becomes What One Is*, translated with notes by R.J. Hollingdale with an introduction by Michael Tanner (1908; Harmondsworth: Penguin, 1979).
———, *The Birth of Tragedy*, translated by W.A. Haussmann (Edinburgh and London: T.N. Foulis, 1909).
———, *The Joyful Wisdom*, translated by Thomas Common (London: T.N. Foulis, 1910).
———, *The Case of Wagner, Nietzsche Contra Wagner, Selected Aphorisms*, translated by A.M. Ludovici (Edinburgh and London: T.N. Foulis, 1911).
———, *Anti-Education – On the Future of Our Educational Institutions*, translated by Damion Searls, edited with an introduction by Paul Reitter and Chad Wellmon (New York: The New York Review of Books, 2016).
Norris, Margot, 'A Walk on the Wild(e) Side: The Doubled Reading of "An Encounter"', in Joseph Valente (ed.), *Quare Joyce* (Ann Arbour: University of Michigan Press, 1998), 19–33.
Notable Answers to 1000 Questions (London: Tit-Bits, 1896).
Nugent, Joseph, 'The Sword and the Prayerbook: Ideals of Authentic Irish Masculinities', *Victorian Studies*, 50/4, 2008, 587–613.
O'Brien, William, *When We Were Boys* (London: Longman, 1890).
O'Connor, Ulick, *Oliver St John Gogarty: A Poet and His Times* (London: Jonathan Cape, 1964).
O'Flynn, Grainne, 'Our Age of Innocence', reprinted in Bourke *et al.* (eds.), *The Field Day Anthology of Irish Writing*, 591–4.
O'Neill, Ciaran, 'The Irish Schoolboy Novel', *Eire-Ireland*, 44, 1/2, 2009, 147–68.
———, 'Education, Imperial Careers and the Irish Catholic Elite in the Nineteenth Century', in Dickson *et al.* (eds.), *Irish Classrooms and British Empire*, 98–110.
———, *Catholics of Consequence: Transnational Education, Social Mobility and the Irish Catholic Elite, 1850–1900* (Oxford: Oxford University Press, 2014).
Park, Joe, *Bertrand Russell on Education* (London: Routledge, 2013), 17, 21.
Parrinder, Patrick, *Nation and Novel: The English Novel from Its Origins to the Present Day* (Oxford: Oxford University Press, 2006).
Peacock, W. (ed.), *English Prose from Mandeville to Ruskin* (Oxford: Oxford University Press, 1912).
Peake, C.H., *James Joyce: The Citizen and the Artist* (London: Edward Arnold, 1977).
Pearse, Patrick, 'About Literature', *An Claidheamh Solais*, 26 May, 1906.
———, 'The Irish-Speaking Child', *An Claidheamh Solais*, 5 January, 1907.
———, *The Collected Works of Padraic H. Pearse: Political Writings and Speeches* (Dublin: Phoenix, 1917).
———, *Short Stories*, with an introduction by Anne Markey (Dublin: University College Dublin Press, 2009).

'Peter Parley', *Tales about the Mythology of the Greeks and Romans* (London, 1839).
———, *Tales about Greece and Rome* (1837; London: Routledge, 1909).
———, *Universal History on the Basis of Geography* (London: John W. Parker, 1837).
Pereto, Vilfredo, *The Rise and Fall of Elites: An Application of Theoretical Sociology*, with an introduction by Hans L. Zetterberg (Totowa, NJ: Bedminster, 1968).
Periyan, Natasha, *The Politics of 1930s British Literature: Education, Class, Gender* (London: Bloomsbury, 2018).
Platt, Len, *Joyce and the Anglo-Irish: A Study of Joyce and the Literary Revival* (Amsterdam: Rodopi, 1998).
———, *Aristocracies of Fiction: The Idea of Aristocracy in Late-Nineteenth-Century and Early-Twentieth-Century Literary Culture* (Westport, CT: Greenwood, 2001).
———, *Joyce, Race and 'Finnegans Wake'* (Cambridge: Cambridge University Press, 2007).
———, '"Unfallable Encyclicing": *Finnegans Wake* and the Encyclopedia Britannica', *James Joyce Quarterly*, 47/1, 2009, 107–18.
The Publishers Circular and Booksellers' Record (London: John Long, 1837–1959).
Quigly, Isabel, *The Heirs of Tom Brown: The English School Story* (London: Chatto & Windus, 1984).
Rancière, Jacques, *The Ignorant Schoolmaster: Five Lessons in Intellectual Emancipation*, with an introduction by Kristin Ross (1987; Stanford, CA: Stanford University Press, 1991).
———, 'On Ignorant Schoolmasters', in Charles Bingham and Gert Biesta, *Jacques Rancière: Education, Truth, Emancipation* (London: Continuum, 2010), 1–24.
Rauch, Alan, *Useful Knowledge: The Victorians, Morality and the March of the Intellect* (Durham, NC and London: Duke University Press, 2001).
Reed, Talbot Baines, *The Fifth Form at Saint Dominic's: A School Story* (London: The Catholic Truth Society, 1887).
Reynolds, Horace, 'The Odyssey of an Irishman', *New York Times*, April 4, 1937.
Richards, Jeffrey, *Happiest Days: The Public Schools in English Fiction* (Manchester: Manchester University Press, 1988).
Russell, Bertrand, *Education and the Social Order* (London: Allen & Unwin, 1982).
———, *Principles of Social Reconstruction* (London: George Allen & Unwin, 1917).
Ryan, Desmond, *The Man Called Pearse* (Dublin: Maunsel, 1919).
Saintsbury, George, *A History of Prose Rhythm* (London: Macmillan, 1912).
Scholes, Robert, and Richard M. Kain (eds.), *The Workshop of Daedalus: James Joyce and the Raw Materials for 'A Portrait of the Artist as a Young Man'* (Evanston, IL: Northwestern University Press, 1965).
Schutte, William M., 'Leopold Bloom: A Touch of the Artist', *James Joyce Quarterly*, 10/1, 1972, 118–31.
Senn, Fritz, 'The Aliments of Jumeantry', *A 'Wake' Newslitter*, New Series, 3/3, June 1966, 51–4.
———, '"Ithaca": Portrait of the Chapter as a Long List', in Andrew Gibson (ed.), *Joyce's 'Ithaca'* (Amsterdam and Atlanta, CA: Rodopi, 1996), 31–76.
Shaw, George Bernard, 'Socialism and Superior Brains', Tract 146, (London: The Fabian Society, 1926).
Simon, Brian, 'Systemisation and Segmentation in Education: The Case of England', in Müller *et al.* (eds.), *The Rise of the Modern Education System: Structural Change and Social Reproduction 1870–1920* (Cambridge: Cambridge University Press, 1987), 88–108.

Sisson, Elaine, *Pearse's Patriots: St Enda's and the Cult of the Boyhood* (Cork: Cork University Press, 2004).

Somer, John, 'The Self Reflexive Arranger in the Initial Style of Joyce's *Ulysses*', *James Joyce Quarterly*, 31/2, 1994, 65–79.

Steedman, Hilary, 'Defining Institutions: The Endowed Secondary Grammar Schools and the Systemisation of English Secondary Schools', in Müller *et al.* (eds.), *The Rise of the Modern Educational System: Structural Change and Social Reproduction 1870–1920* (Cambridge: Cambridge University Press, 1987), 111–34.

Stone, Harry, '"Araby" and the Writings of James Joyce', *The Antioch Review*, 25/3, 1965.

Stray, Christopher and Gillian Sutherland, 'Mass Markets: Education', in McKetterick (ed.), *The Cambridge History of the Book in Britain* 359–81.

Sullivan, Kevin, *Joyce among the Jesuits* (New York: Columbia University Press, 1958).

Switaj, Elizabeth, *James Joyce's Teaching Life and Methods: Language and Pedagogy in 'A Portrait of the Artist as a Young Man', 'Ulysses', and 'Finnegans Wake'* (London: Palgrave Macmillan, 2016).

Teague, Laura, 'The Curriculum as a Site of Counter Politics: Theorising the "Domain of the Sayable"', *British Journal of Sociology of Education*, 39/1, 2018, 92–106.

Thom's Directory of the United Kingdom of Great Britain and Ireland (Dublin: Thom's, 1844–1960).

Thornton, Weldon, *Allusions in 'Ulysses'* (1961; New York: Simon & Schuster, 1973).

Tit-Bits (London: George Newness, 1881–1910).

Titley, E. Brian, 'Rejecting the Modern World: The Educational Ideas of Timothy Corcoran', *Oxford Review of Education*, 9/2, 1983, 137–45.

Tolstoy, Leo, *Essays and Letters*, translated by Alymer Maude (London: Henry Frowde, 1904).

———, 'On Popular Education', in Bob Blaisdell (ed.) and Christopher Edgar (trans.), *Tolstoy as Teacher: Leo Tolstoy's Writings on Education* (New York: Teachers & Writers Collaborative, 2000).

Valente, Joseph, 'Beyond Truth and Freedom', *James Joyce Quarterly*, 25/11, 1987, 87–103.

———, *The Myth of Manliness in Irish National Culture, 1880–1922* (Urbana, IL: University of Illinois Press, 2011).

van Mierlo, Chrissie, *James Joyce and Catholicism: The Apostate's Wake* (London: Bloomsbury, 2016).

Veblen, Thorstein, *The Theory of the Leisure Class*, with an introduction by C. Wright Mills (1899; Abingdon, Oxon and New York: Routledge, 2017).

Wales, Katie, '"With Apologies to Lindley Murray": The Narrative Method of the "Eumaeus" Episode in *Ulysses*', in Ingrid Tieken-Boon van Ostade (ed.), *Two Hundred Years of Lindley Murray* (Münster: Nodus, 1996), 207–16.

Walker, John, *Pronouncing Dictionary* (1791; London: Frederick Warne, ca 1875).

Walsh, Brendan, 'The Progressive Credentials of Patrick Henry Pearse: A Response to David Limond', *History of Education Review*, Bundoora, 35/2, 2006, 32–44.

———, '"Injurious to the Best Interests of Education": Teaching and Learning under the Intermediate Education System 1878–1922', in Brendan Walsh (ed.), *Essays in the History of Irish Education: Past, Present and Future Perspectives* (London: Palgrave Macmillan, 2016).

Walsh, Patrick, 'Education and the "Universalist" Idiom of Empire: Irish National School Books in Ireland and Ontario', *History of Education*, 37/5, 2008, 645–60.

Warren, Kate M. *A Treasury of English Literature (From the Beginning to the Eighteenth Century)* (1906; New York: Dodge, 1908).

Waters, Johanna, 'Elites', *British Journal of Sociology*, 39/3, 2018, 412–19.

Webb, Sidney, 'Questions for School Board Candidates', in Fabian Tract 25 (London: The Fabian Society, 1891).

———, 'The Education Muddle and the Way Out: A Constructive Criticism of English Education Machinery', in Fabian Tract 109 (London: The Fabian Society, 1901).

———, 'The Education Act 1902: How to Make the Best of It', in Fabian Tract 114 (London: The Fabian Society, 1903).

Weeks, Jeffrey, *Sex, Politics and Society: The Regulation of Sexuality since 1800* (1981; London and New York: Longman, 1989).

Weller, Toni, *The Victorians and Information: A Social and Cultural History* (Sarbrücken: VDM Verlag, 2009).

——— (ed.), *Information History in the Modern World: Histories of the Information Age* (Basingstoke: Palgrave Macmillan, 2010).

———, 'The Puffery and Practicality of Etiquette Books: A New Take on Victorian Information Culture', *Library Trends*, 62/3, 2014, 663–80.

Weymann, Ansgar, *States, Markets and Education: The Rise and Limits of the Education State* (Basingstoke: Palgrave Macmillan, 2014).

Wiggershaus, Renate, *Frauen unterm Nationalsozialismus* (Wuppertal: P. Hammer, 1984).

Williams, Trevor L., '"As It Was in the Beginning": The Struggle for History in the 'Nestor' Episode of *Ulysses*', *Canadian Review of Irish Studies*, 16/2, 1990, 36–46.

Woolf, Virginia, *The Diary of Virginia Woolf*, edited by Anne Oliver Bell and assisted by Andrew McNeillie, vol. 2 (1978; Harmondsworth: Penguin, 1981).

Wylde, James (ed.), *Circles of the Sciences* (London: The London Printing and Publishing Co., 1862–7).

Yao, Steven G. and Michael Coyle (eds.), *Ezra Pound an Education* (Orono: University of Maine & National Poetry Foundation, 2012).

Yeats, W. B. (ed.), *The Oxford Book of Modern Verse 1892–1935* (Oxford: Clarendon Press, 1936).

Index

Made in the USA
Las Vegas, NV
31 October 2024

0668e715-8e59-436b-9175-ead3c805a79eR01